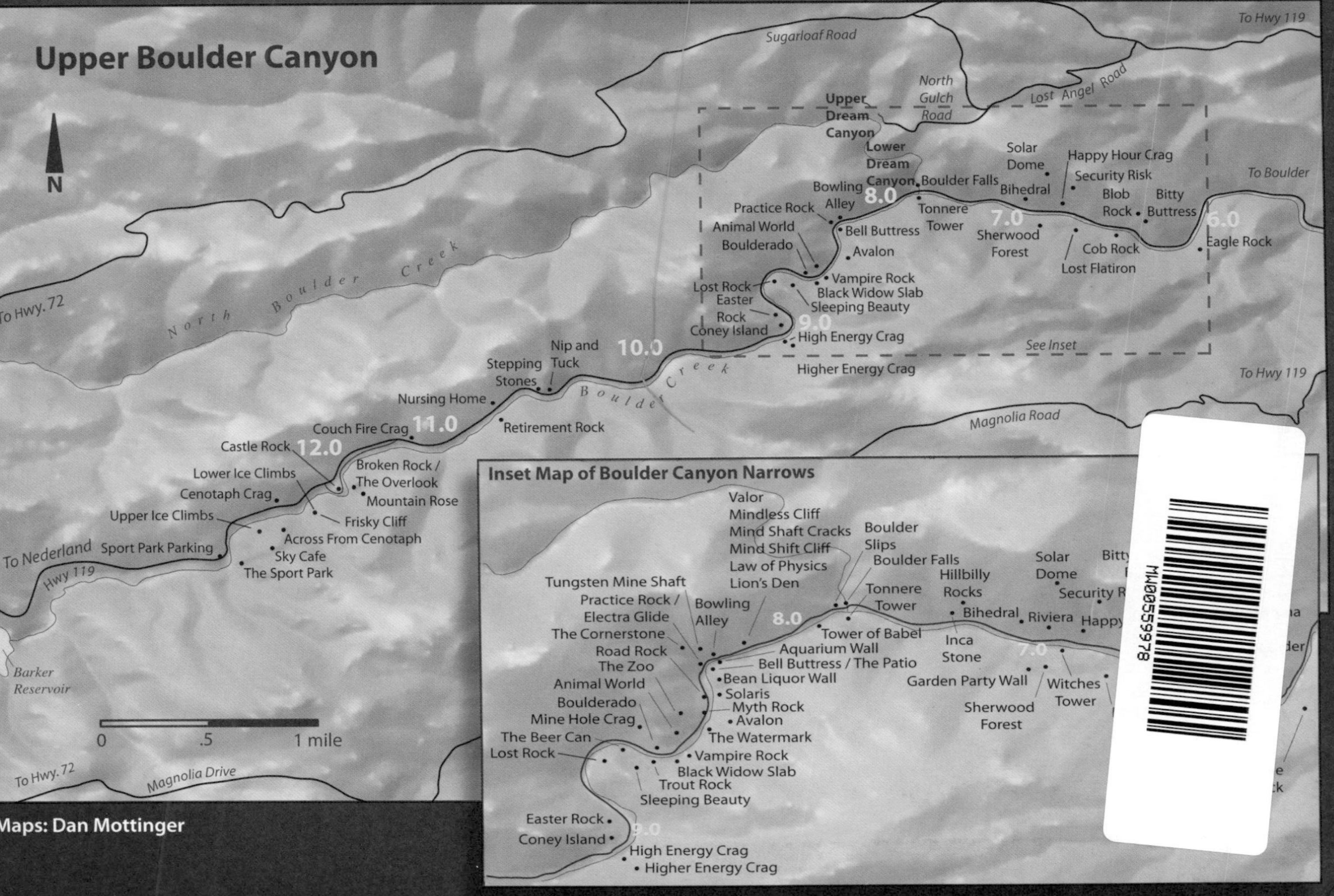
Upper Boulder Canyon
N
Sugarloaf Road
North Gulch Road
Lost Angel Road
To Hwy 119
To Boulder
To Hwy 119
To Hwy. 72
North Boulder Creek
Boulder Creek
Upper Dream Canyon
Lower Dream Canyon
Solar Dome
Happy Hour Crag
Security Risk
Bihedral
Boulder Falls
Blob Rock
Bitty Buttress
6.0
Eagle Rock
Cob Rock
Lost Flatiron
7.0
Sherwood Forest
Tonnere Tower
8.0
Bowling Alley
Practice Rock
Animal World
Boulderado
Bell Buttress
Avalon
Vampire Rock
Black Widow Slab
Sleeping Beauty
Lost Rock
Easter Rock
Coney Island
9.0
High Energy Crag
Higher Energy Crag
See Inset
10.0
Nip and Tuck
Stepping Stones
Nursing Home
Retirement Rock
Magnolia Road
11.0
Couch Fire Crag
12.0
Castle Rock
Broken Rock / The Overlook
Mountain Rose
Lower Ice Climbs
Cenotaph Crag
Frisky Cliff
Upper Ice Climbs
Across From Cenotaph
Sport Park Parking
Sky Cafe
The Sport Park
To Nederland
Hwy 119
Barker Reservoir
0 .5 1 mile
To Hwy. 72
Magnolia Drive
Inset Map of Boulder Canyon Narrows
Valor
Mindless Cliff
Mind Shaft Cracks
Mind Shift Cliff
Law of Physics
Lion's Den
Boulder Slips
Boulder Falls
Tonnere Tower
Hillbilly Rocks
Bihedral
Solar Dome
Security R
Riviera
Happy
Tungsten Mine Shaft
Practice Rock / Electra Glide
Bowling Alley
8.0
The Cornerstone
Road Rock
The Zoo
Tower of Babel
Aquarium Wall
Bell Buttress / The Patio
Bean Liquor Wall
Inca Stone
7.0
Garden Party Wall
Witches Tower
Sherwood Forest
Animal World
Solaris
Boulderado
Myth Rock
Avalon
Mine Hole Crag
The Watermark
The Beer Can
Vampire Rock
Lost Rock
Black Widow Slab
Trout Rock
Sleeping Beauty
Easter Rock
Coney Island
9.0
High Energy Crag
Higher Energy Crag
MW00559978
Maps: Dan Mottinger

Boulder Canyon
Rock Climbs

Bob D'Antonio

THIS BOOK BELONGS TO: ______________________________

____

ACKNOWLEDGEMENTS

***Bob D'Antonio*:** Many thanks go out to the following people. Greg Hand, Ron Olsen, Dan Levison, Dan Hare, Jim Erickson, John Gill, Pat Ament, Richard Rossiter, Alec Sharp, Bob Horan, Adam Brink, Stewart Green, Toper Donahue, Peter Beal, Vaino Kodas, Gary Neptune, Matt Samet, Chris Archer, and the countless others who somewhere along the line helped me.

To Dave Pegg: You are the best, thanks for making this book top-shelf.

This book is dedicated to my life partner, wife and best friend ... Laurel. Thanks for being there, you have been a constant source of kindness and love.

Dave Pegg: Bobby D for cranking out this book on fierce deadline — while suffering from an even fiercer toothache. Dan Mottinger for taking us on as a charity case with the maps. Andy Wellman who put in many hours on the layout, while hardly ever complaining about me playing all the techno ... and George Michael. Chris Archer for legal advice. Andy Mann for stepping up as a last minute super-sub. And last, but not least, my wife, Fiona, without whom nothing is possible.

Wolverine
PUBLISHING

BOULDER CANYON ROCK CLIMBS
2009 Edition

Author: Bob D'Antonio.
Maps: Dan Mottinger
Published and distributed by Wolverine Publishing, LLC.

Cover photo:
Dan Brockway on *Rama* 5.10c, Plotinus Wall, page 98. Photo: Bob D'Antonio.

Opening page photo:
Stevie Damboise works an unclimbed project left of *Dracula*, Black Widow Slab, page 178. Photo: Darek Krol.

International Standard Book Number:
ISBN-13: 978-0-9792644-8-1

Library of Congress Catalog in Publication Data:
Library of Congress Control Number: 9780979264481

Wolverine Publishing is continually expanding its range of guidebooks. If you have a manuscript or idea for a book, or would like to find out more about our company and publications, contact:

Dave Pegg
Wolverine Publishing
1491 County Road 237
Silt
CO 81652
970-876-0268
dave@wolverinepublishing.com
www.wolverinepublishing.com

Printed in South Korea.

TRAIN HARD
SEND HARDER
the Country's Premier
Bouldering Facility

WARNING

DO NOT USE THIS GUIDEBOOK UNLESS YOU READ AND AGREE TO THE FOLLOWING:

Rock climbing is dangerous sport that can result in death, paralysis or serious injury.

This book is intended as a reference tool for advanced/expert climbers. The activity and the terrain it describes can be or is extremely dangerous and requires a high degree of ability and experience to negotiate. This book is not intended for inexperienced or novice climbers, nor is it intended as an instructional manual. If you are unsure of your ability to handle any circumstances that may arise, employ the services of a professional instructor or guide.

This book relies upon information and opinions provided by others that may not be accurate. Opinions concerning the technical difficulties, ratings of climbs, and protection or lack thereof are subjective and may differ from yours and others opinions. Ratings may differ from area to area, holds may break, fixed protection may fail, fall out or be missing, and weather may deteriorate, these and other factors, such as rock fall, inadequate or faulty protection, etc., may all increase the danger of a climbing route and may contribute to the climb being other than as described in the book. Furthermore, errors may be made during the editing, designing, proofing, and printing of this book. Thus, the information in this book is unverified, and the authors and publisher cannot guarantee its accuracy. Numerous hazards exist that are not described in this book. Climbing on any terrain described in this book, regardless of its description or rating, may result in your death, paralysis or injury.

Do not use this book unless you are a skilled and experienced climber who understands and accepts the risks of rock climbing. If you choose to use any information in this book to plan, attempt, or climb a particular route, you do so at your own risk. Please take all precautions and use your own ability, evaluation, and judgment to assess the risks of your chosen climb, rather than relying on the information in this book.

THE AUTHORS AND PUBLISHER MAKE NO REPRESENTATIONS OR WARRANTIES, EXPRESSED OR IMPLIED, OF ANY KIND REGARDING THE CONTENTS OF THIS BOOK, AND EXPRESSLY DISCLAIM ANY AND ALL REPRESENTATIONS OR WARRANTIES REGARDING THE CONTENTS OF THIS BOOK, INCLUDING, WITHOUT LIMITATION, THE ACCURACY OR RELIABILITY OF INFORMATION CONTAINED HEREIN. WARRANTIES OF FITNESS FOR A PARTICULAR PURPOSE AND/OR MERCHANTABILITY ARE EXPRESSLY DISCLAIMED.

THE USER ASSUMES ALL RISKS ASSOCIATED WITH THE USE OF THIS BOOK INCLUDING, WITHOUT LIMITATION, ALL RISKS ASSOCIATED WITH ROCK CLIMBING.

FOREWORD

Lose The 'Tude

By Matt Samet

Live long enough, and life will beat the 'tude out of you — it doesn't matter who you are or how small a handhold you can grab or how calm you remain 20 feet above a microdot-sized RP. I'm 37, and I've learned this. Rock climbing has never made anyone special; it just lets us do something special in our free time.

The connection to Boulder Canyon is that, around 2000, Boulder erupted into an unfortunate bolt war centered largely on this oft-maligned but much-better-than-any-roadside-venue-has-a-right-to-be cragging hotspot. My involvement was tangential and mostly limited to drunken tirades on *climbingboulder.com* (now The Mountain Project); I suppose my stance was the crags were being rap-drilled "into submission," or something like that.

But really, I hadn't spent enough time in the canyon or put up enough routes there to be entitled to this opinion. I've since calmed down (life beat it out of me) and been fortunate to have spent untold happy, memorable days on the granite, clipping bolts, bouldering, slapping in pro, dipping my feet in the creek, and watching co-eds frolic in the swimming hole across from the Slips (good views from up there —try it sometime; the routes are killer, too). I harbor no more complaints, which is a good thing, because now I can enjoy the canyon's 1500 climbs, many of them bolted, without feeling like a hypocrite. *Booyah*: I've even rappelled in, drill in hand, to equip a few new ones myself. It's nice we still have a place in which you're free to climb (and establish first ascents) with only yourself, your buddies, and maybe a commenter or two on *mountainproject.com* to contend with. Climbers sometimes need that freedom and that immediate gratification — toprope a route, brush it, put drill to stone, and go.

But I digress. If you've bought Bob's book, you're one of the converted, or soon will be. One thing I come back to time and again is Boulder Canyon's sense of place, of exploration, aura, and possibility. The long snake of a ridge rising from Sleeping Beauty Slab into the forested highlands; the spill of North Boulder Creek, a white tumble of spume, boulders, and jammed logs low and distant from the ledge balcony at Berlin Wall; the sunny benches of Animal World; the airy, complex tiers and gullies at Avalon; the hidden, silent folds and buttresses at Solaris. ... This is damn-good climbing close to one of America's most livable cities and I, for one, am grateful for the route explosion. So keep it coming, keep it positive, and we'll see you out on the granite.

TABLE OF CONTENTS

39

51

53

144

184

191

215

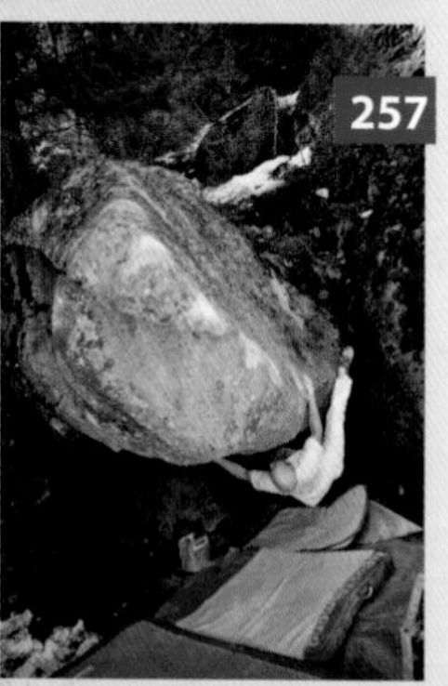
257

BOULDER CANYON WEST

UPPER DREAM CANYON . 232

ADVERTISER INDEX

BOULDERING.......... 256

ICE CLIMBING.......... 266

INDICES.......... 268

Essays

INTRODUCTION

By Bob D'Antonio

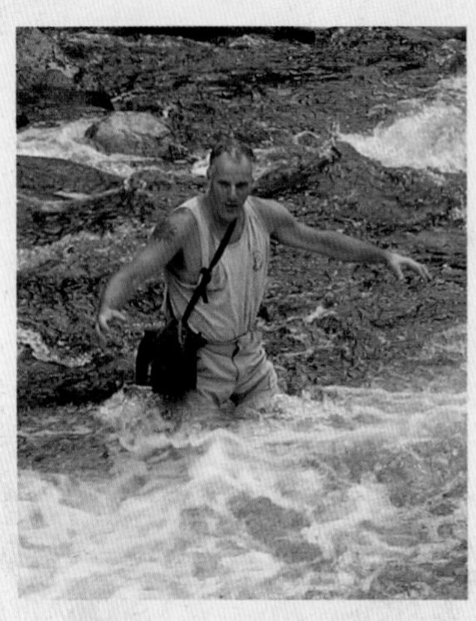

My first trip to Boulder Canyon was in the fall of 1975, my first year out of college and working in the real world. Armed with a tick list of then somewhat difficult climbs, the drive up from Santa Fe was filled with excitement and slight apprehension. We arrived late at night, pulled over and slept in the parking area near The Dome. The morning arrived quickly and after a short jaunt into town for chow and coffee we were back at The Dome ready for anything. We climbed *Cozyhang* for a warm-up and then ventured over to the left side of the rock to tackle *Gorilla's Delight*. I lead the route in one long pitch almost taking a big fall near the top of the upper corner/slab. The rock was slick and the crack flared, a far cry from the straight-in cracks and easy-to-set protection I was used to on the basalt rock near Santa Fe.

Castle Rock called the next day. First up was *Curving Crack* and good dose of reality check. A few falls and many choice words later we managed to reach the anchor of this slick and somewhat flared crack and move on to our main objective for the weekend: *Athlete's Feat*. After our performance on *Curving Crack* I felt our chances of getting up the route were nil to none. I was right, we got shot down on the first pitch and, after licking our wounds, went to the *South Face* instead. The first pitch went without a fight … it's amazing how your mood can change with a little success under your belt. Cockiness and slick granite don't mix well. I took off on the second pitch following a weird ramp and protection. I reached a pin and then did a series of moves that took me farther away from the crack and gear — sheer terror almost got the best of me and I barely managed to reach a good hold and then the belay ledge. 5.9 my ass! We finished the route and headed back to Santa Fe feeling fulfilled but also a little humbled. Running with the big dogs is not as easy as one may think.

Three years later with better skills and less cockiness I led both *Athlete's Feat* and *Country Club Crack*. Maybe, just maybe, I could someday learn to like this place…

Boulder Canyon offers a wonderful selection of routes on various granite formations featuring all styles of climbing. From low angle slabs, to steep continuous cracks, high angle face climbs and hundreds of easy accessible sport routes, the canyon has something for everyone.

METOLIUS
www.metoliusclimbing.com
Greater Holding Power

HOW TO USE THIS BOOK

CHAPTERS AND LAYOUT

The cliffs in this book are generally laid out from east to west, the order in which you approach them when driving up the canyon from Boulder. The cliffs in **Lower Dream Canyon**, traditionally approached from Boulder Falls, are grouped in a chapter, located at the 7.6-mile mark in the book. The cliffs in **Upper Dream Canyon**, approached from above, are grouped in a chapter at the end of the book.

Mileages: The mileages for the cliffs and parking areas in this book are measured from the bridge at the mouth of the canyon.

Chapter Colors / Warm Crags & Cool Crags:

Cliffs on the north side of the main canyon generally get lots of sunshine. These crags and are color-coded with red header bars in this book.

Cliffs on the south side of the main canyon generally get lots of shade. Approaching them involves crossing the creek. These crags and are color-coded with blue header bars in this book.

This chapter color denotes Lower Dream Canyon, where the cliffs face in multiple directions.

This chapter color denotes Upper Dream Canyon, where the cliffs face in multiple directions.

GEAR AND EQUIPMENT

Sport and Trad Routes:

Sport and traditional routes are differentiated by the color of the route number.

1 A red route number denotes a traditional route. These routes require a rack of natural protection devices, such as wires, nuts, and cams. Further, there is a reasonable chance of falling on natural protection and gear placements may be strenuous or unobvious on these routes.

1 A blue route number denotes a pure sport climb **or one that has the character of a sport climb.** A pure sport climb is entirely bolt or piton protected and can be climbed with a rack of quickdraws. Boulder Canyon has many mixed routes, so, in this book, **we also designated routes as "sport" if they are predominantly bolt protected, and any natural gear placements are easy, obvious and you are unlikely to fall on them if you are climbing the grade.** Where some natural protection is advised on a "sport" route we have tried to indicate the size of the piece(s) and location of the placement(s) in the equipment line.

QUALITY RATINGS

This book uses a four-star system to give an indication of route quality. We have tried to give consensus quality ratings wherever possible, however this is by nature highly subjective. One person's four-star classic may be another person's choss pile. At the very least we hope they encourage healthy debate. Quality ratings are intended to be global throughout the canyon, and are defined as follows.

★★★★	One of the very best climbs in Boulder Canyon. Utterly classic. Guaranteed to blow your mind.
★★★	A crag classic. A great climb, highly recommended.
★★	A good route, worth seeking out if you are in the area.
★	An OK route. Worth doing if you are in the area.
No Stars	Chossy, mossy, dirty, loose, mis-bolted … or maybe just a total mystery. Not necessarily a bad route — but probably not the first thing you should jump on when visiting an area.

Equipment Line

The last line of a route description **in gray** describes the protection for a climb. This may be the number of bolts or the size and number of natural protection devices. Please carry at least two more quickdraws than the indicated number of bolts to account for errors and clipping into anchors.

The abbreviation **SR** in the equipment line stands for **"standard rack"** (see below).

RECORDING YOUR ASCENTS

O-Box R-Box

No Wolverine guidebook would be complete without check boxes. Due to popular demand this guidebook contains two check boxes for each route. The left box, known as the "O-Box," is for recording an on-sight or flash (geeks like me can use different colored markers to differentiate between the two). The right box is the "R-Box" and is used to record a redpoint ascent.

SR. BOULDER CANYON STANDARD RACK:

A standard rack in Boulder Canyon consists of:

- A set of RPs, stoppers to one inch, cams to three inches, eight to ten quickdraws, and three to five long slings.

- Gear recommendations are just that. Use your own personal judgment and bring gear to suit your comfort level.

- Bolt counts are given for each route. Bring two extra quick draws for the anchors and maybe one or two more for piece of mind.

Photo: Topher Donahue

BOULDER BETA

Getting There: The city of Boulder is 25 miles northwest of Denver, Colorado. It can be easily accessed from major highways (I-70 and I-25) and Denver International Airport. Hourly shuttles and buses run from the airport to downtown Boulder.

Boulder Canyon is conveniently located just a few minutes drive from downtown. Canyon Blvd runs east-west through the center of Boulder (passing just south of the shopping district of Pearl Street). Follow Canyon Blvd (SR 119) west into Boulder Canyon. **Mileages for the cliffs and parking areas start from the bridge at the mouth of the canyon.**

When to visit: You can climb in Boulder Canyon year-round. The main canyon runs east-west and has a generally sunny (north) side and generally shady (south) side. (Crags on the south side of the main canyon have blue header bars in this book; crags on the north side have red header bars.) You can thus find sun or shade at any time of the year. Also, the higher you climb up the canyon, the cooler the temperatures. Upper Dream Canyon is particularly cool in the morning during the summer months.

In general, spring and fall offer the best conditions for the visiting climber, with fall being my favorite due to drier, more stable weather and the changing colors of the many aspens and cottonwoods in the canyon.

Where to stay: Boulder has many great hotels and a few good hostels: **Boulder International Hostel** (303) 442-0522 has bunk-style rooms for $27 a night. You can also pamper yourself after a hard day on the rocks by staying in one of many high-end hotels, like the Saint Julien or The Boulderado.

The best (free, National Forest) camping is located off Magnolia Rd just west of the town of Nederland, which is a mere five miles from Castle Rock in Boulder Canyon. West Magnolia Rd has the best sites and also has some of the best single-track mountain biking in the Boulder area. Nederland is a cool little mountain town located 8000 feet above sea level. Supplies, coffee shops, and restaurants can found here.

Climbing Stores: Boulder is an outdoor mecca and has many stores for every outdoor endeavor. **Neptune Mountaineering** (see back cover), **Boulder Mountaineering** (see ad page 13), and **REI** are the three major climbing shops in Boulder. If you are new to town and want to see museum-quality climbing artifacts, make Neptune's a must stop.
In Denver, check out **Wilderness Exchange Unlimited** (see ad page 6).

Climbing Gyms: Boulder has great climbing gyms. State-of-the-art indoor bouldering can be found at **The Spot** (see ad page 3) and **CATS** (the Colorado Athletic School). **The Boulder Rock Club**, features both lead climbing and bouldering.

Food and Libations: Boulder has an eclectic restaurant scene, serving foods from all parts of the world. Pearl Street is a good place to find lots of great restaurants within walking distance of each other.

BOB'S TOP 10 RESTAURANTS

Southern Sun 627 S Broadway
Pub food and beer. Popular with the hippie and climbing crowd.

Café Sole 637 S Broadway
Coffee and light fares. Free wi-fi and outdoor seating.

Mediterranean 1002 Walnut Street
Great tapas and happy hour.

Illegal Pete's 1447 Pearl St
Great burrito's and margs.

Sushi Tora 2014 10th St
One of the first sushi joints in Boulder and still among the best.

Snarf's 2128 Pearl St
High quality sandwiches at a reasonable price.

West End Tavern 926 Pearl St
Great food and beer selection.

Sunflower Restaurant 1701 Pearl St
High-end vegetarian.

Spruce Confections 767 Pearl St
Great coffee and desserts.

Gondolier on Pearl 1600 Pearl St # 1
This place has been around for ages. Good food at a reasonable price.

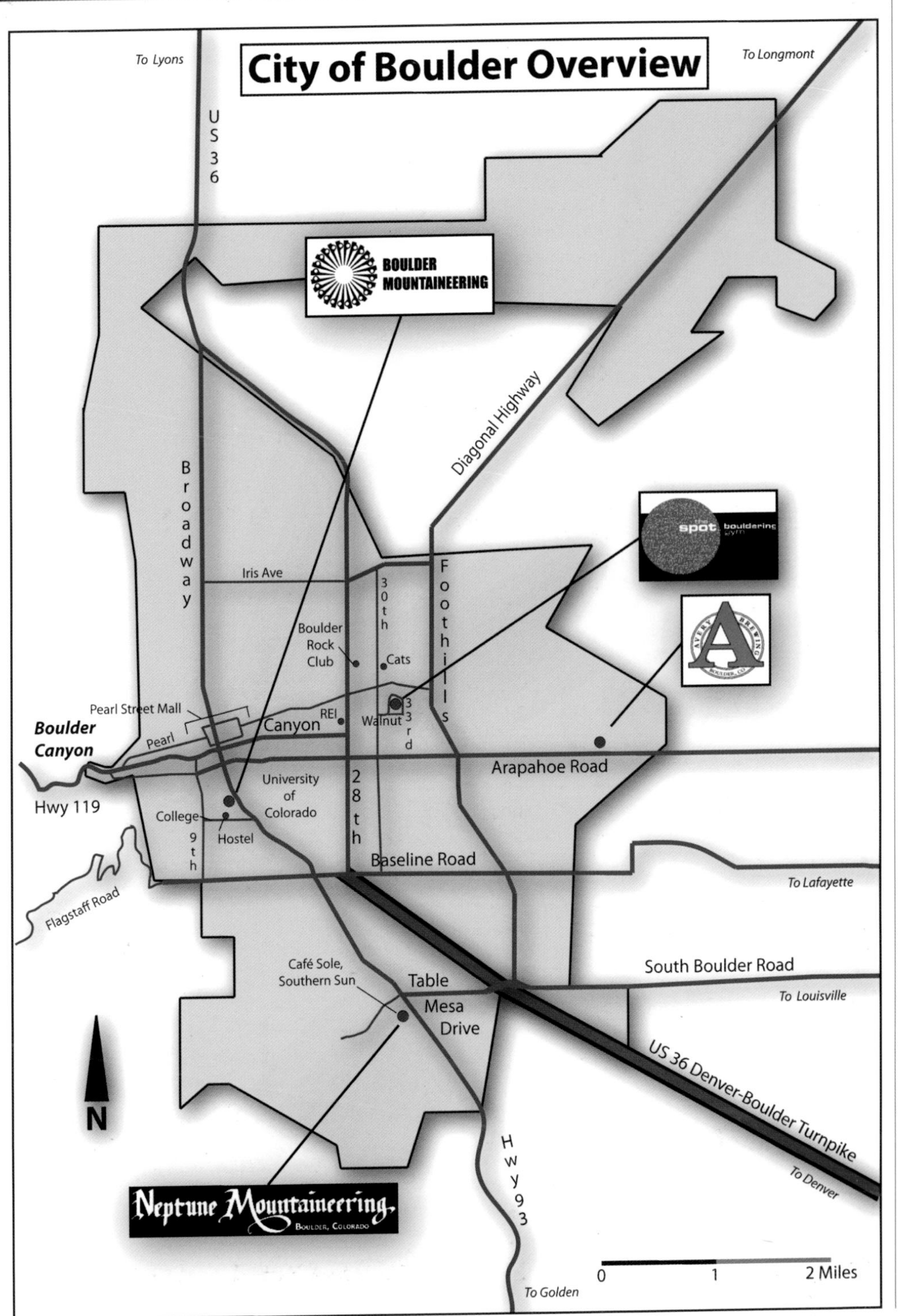
City of Boulder Overview
To Lyons
To Longmont
US 36
BOULDER MOUNTAINEERING
Diagonal Highway
Broadway
the spot bouldering gym
AVERY BREWING BOULDER, CO
Iris Ave
30th
Foothills
Boulder Rock Club
Cats
Pearl Street Mall
Boulder Canyon
Pearl
Canyon
REI
Walnut
33rd
Arapahoe Road
Hwy 119
University of Colorado
28th
College
9th
Hostel
Baseline Road
To Lafayette
Flagstaff Road
Café Sole, Southern Sun
Table Mesa Drive
South Boulder Road
To Louisville
US 36 Denver-Boulder Turnpike
To Denver
N
Hwy 93
Neptune Mountaineering
Boulder, Colorado
0
1
2 Miles
To Golden

CLIMBING OVERVIEW

The author crossing Boulder Creek during spring runoff. Photo: Greg Hand.

The beauty of Boulder Canyon and Dream Canyon lies in their accessibility and the diversity of the climbs at any given area. You can climb a well-protected sport route and then jump on a classic trad route — sometimes a mere 20 feet away from each other.

The rock is featured granite, providing varied climbing, from delicate slabs, to splitter cracks, to steep gymnastic faces.

This book describes the climbing in Boulder Canyon and Dream Canyon. Dream Canyon branches off to the north and west 7.6 miles into the main canyon at Boulder Falls. It is commonly divided into Lower Dream Canyon (traditionally approached from Boulder Falls) and Upper Dream Canyon (approached from a parking area above the canyon, off of Sugarloaf Road). Lower Dream Canyon has some access issues, for more on approach and access to Lower Dream Canyon see page 92. For approach information for Upper Dream Canyon see page 232.

LAND OWNERSHIP, AND BOLTING

The crags in Boulder Canyon are almost all on public lands, either City of Boulder Open Space or National Forest. There are also some plots of private land and old mining claims in the canyon. Unfortunately, boundaries between different land designations are sometimes unclear.

Boulder Canyon is an active new route area with no current restrictions on bolting on National Forest lands. Unfortunately, the City of Boulder Open Space does *not* allow bolting or the placement of any fixed gear on their lands. Please check land ownership status before placing bolts and fixed gear.

For questions contact:

City of Boulder Open Space:
P.O. Box 791 Boulder, CO 80306 (303) 441-3440.

Boulder Ranger District:
Roosevelt National Forest, 2140 Yarmouth Avenue, Boulder, CO 80301 (303) 541-2500.

RAPTOR CLOSURES

Some cliffs in Boulder Canyon are closed in the spring for raptor nesting. Annually, on February 1 the areas listed below are closed. Raptor closures end on or before August 1. For the current access status visit:
www.fs.fed.us/r2/arnf/recreation/rock-climbing/

- **Eagle Rock**
- **Wall of Voodoo**
- **Bitty and Peapod Buttresses**
- **Wall With Three Cracks**
- **Blob Rock**
- **Security Risk Crag**

HAZARDS

Be aware of the following hazards when climbing in Boulder Canyon.

Rock Fall: Popular cliffs can be extremely crowded, especially at the weekends. The canyon has some loose rock and cliffs are sometimes tiered one on top of another. Consider wearing a helmet, and be especially careful when climbing or scrambling above other climbers.

The Highway: Many parking areas described in this book are close to bends on a busy highway. Be careful when crossing the road and pulling out onto the highway. Some cliffs literally rise out of the road, be especially careful when belaying and lowering at these cliffs.

DOGS

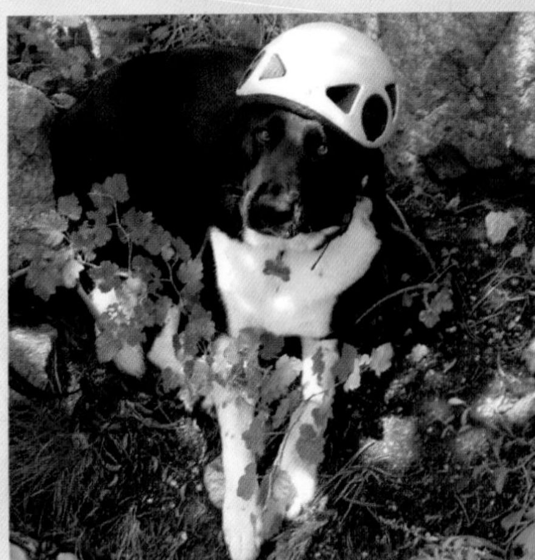

Carleton the Wonder Dog (RIP) enjoying a day at Lost Angel in Upper Dream Canyon. Photo: Ron Olsen.

Dogs must be leashed at Boulder Falls. Other than that there are no restrictions. However, the hazards described on this page — crowds, loose rock, the creek and the proximity of the highway — mean that many cliffs are unsuitable for dogs. Use good judgment, and if in doubt, leave your pooch at home.

Creek Crossings: Approaching the cliffs on the south side of the canyon involves crossing the creek — which can be dangerous during spring runoff. Several Tyrolean traverses are fixed as aids to crossing the creek; their locations are noted in the cliff approach descriptions.

RECOMMENDED CLIFFS

If your time in Boulder Canyon is limited, and you want to experience some of the best climbing, these crags (in order of appearance) are good destinations.

Traditional	Sport
The Dome (page 28)	**Eagle Rock** (page 43)
Cob Rock (page 48)	**The Bihedral** (page 82)
Blob Rock (page 59)	**Plotinus Wall - LDC** (page 98)
Happy Hour Crag (page 70)	**Tonnere Tower** (page 116)
Bell Buttress (page 146)	**Easter Rock** (page 188)
Castle Rock (page 206)	**The Sport Park** (page 222)

HISTORY

By Bob D'Antonio

Rock climbing in Boulder Canyon has a long and colorful history. This is a brief overview of some of the people and climbs that played a significant role in making Boulder Canyon the great climbing area it is today.

Climbers were first drawn to the canyon's most obvious cracks and chimneys in the early 1950s. These were the only lines that offered protection given the limited equipment of the day. The use of aid and other trickery were considered fair game on many early routes as the canyon's short granite cliffs were considered to be little more than training for the mountains. Dallas Jackson and George Lamb partnered during this period, producing several routes that are now considered classics for the grade, including *Jackson's Wall* (5.6) on Castle Rock and *Empor* (5.7+) on Cob Rock. Cary Huston's ascent of *Huston Crack* (5.9) on Cob Rock in 1955 was a huge jump in the free- climbing standard in the canyon, considering the width of the crack and the lack of gear to protect it.

The 1960s saw a change in attitude; climbing these small crags became an end in itself. Climbers grew more confident in their abilities and equipment and were willing to push beyond what seemed possible a mere five years before. Free climbing old aid routes came into vogue and the charge was led by a tall, lanky climber named Layton Kor. Castle Rock, a beautiful piece of gold and gray granite in a park-like setting bordered by Boulder Creek, presented an obvious challenge. In 1961 Kor managed to free an indistinct aid line on the south face. *South Face* (5.9+) opened the door to what was possible and expanding the realm of free climbing in the canyon.

Royal Robbins visited the canyon in 1964. Meeting Pat Ament through mutual friends, Royal found a protégé with the talent and vision to up the ante. On the right side of the south face of Castle Rock an almost-continuous series of cracks leads directly to the summit, the only problem: a blank slab at the base that provided a formidable obstacle to free climbing attempts. Honed on the smooth granite walls of Yosemite, Robbins made short work of the unprotected slab start (now sporting a couple of bolts and rated 5.11), gained the corners and cracks that led to the summit, and in a short afternoon of work established what was then the most continuously difficult free-climb in the world: *Athlete's Feat* (5.11a). Right of *Athlete's Feat* is a stunning left-leaning crack that runs the whole length of the upper south face. The climb had been aided in 1956 and named *Country Club Crack*. Once again a blank face at the start provided a seemingly insurmountable barrier to free attempts. Robbins aided the face, lowered, and freed it on toprope first try. In a brilliant display, he then almost led the upper crack free, resting on the rope just above the final roof. In 1967, Pat Ament finally freed both pitches of *Country Club Crack* (5.11c, 5.11a). (See Ament's essay on the following pages for more on this period.)

The Golden Age of free climbing that swept the country in the early 1970s largely bypassed Boulder Canyon. Liberated by the widespread use of wires and slung nuts, local climbers pushed standards in Rocky Mountain National Park, Eldorado and the Black Canyon. The standards set by Robbins and Ament, however, weren't surpassed in Boulder Canyon until the mid to late 1970s when Alex Sharp, an imported Englishman, burst upon the scene. With a newcomer's eye for potential lines and the talent to back his ambitions, Sharp quickly established a slew of testpieces in Boulder Canyon, including *Arms Bazaar* (5.12a R) and *The Grand Inquisitor* (5.12a R) on Bell Buttress, and *Englishman's Home* (5.11c/d) and *Never a Dull Moment* (5.12a/b) on Castle Rock — all rite-of-passage climbs that inspire climbers to this day.

Dan Hare, a quiet unassuming climber, impacted the local scene with little to no fanfare. With a huge appetite for unclimbed rock, Hare and few select friends went on a new-routing frenzy in the mid 1970s and early 1980s that would open the eyes of a new generation of Boulder Canyon climbers. Previously, attention had focused on the most prominent chunks of granite, like The Dome, Cob Rock, Bell Buttress, and Castle Rock. Looking beyond and between these cliffs, Hare and his small tribe of friends developed whole new areas and mined overlooked sections of forgotten rocks to unearth some of the most classic lines in the canyon.

Randy Leavitt, a talented big wall and free climber from California, made Boulder his home in the early 1980s. Extremely talented and somewhat fearless, he immediately established cutting edge climbs in a very bold fashion. On Blob Rock he led *Limits of Power* (5.12b) ground-up, using double ropes and RPs. This wild route requires a cool head under fire and may still be unrepeated. Other Leavitt routes to ponder are *Enemy of the People* (5.12b) and *Hot Flyer* (5.12a) — without the bolts — at Security Risk Crag.

Richard Rossiter and his wife Joyce were also very active in the Boulder area in the 1980s. Rossiter, with his keen eye for a good line, was not afraid to put in the time to clean and bolt improbable, challenging climbs. The immaculate *Radlands of Infinity* (5.13a) on the left side Blob Rock, climbed by Richard, Joyce and Bob Horan in 1988, is one of the finest slab routes in the Boulder area. Richard's contributions in Boulder Canyon are far reaching and continue to this day. He is responsible for hundreds of new routes and also does a large amount of trail work and maintenance in the canyon.

The way routes were established changed as the 1980s progressed. Most of the obvious clean cracks had been climbed; the lines that remained required extensive cleaning and/or would be hard to protect by traditional means. New climbs were rarely done ground-up on-sight. Climbers rappelled from the top looking for protection options and potential lines. Bolts were slowly accepted as protection devices.

Sport climbing ushered in a new way thinking about climbing. Difficulty was the name of the game and armed with power drills, sticky rubber (and lycra) anything seemed possible. For some it was. In 1987 Christian Griffith bolted and started to work on the beautiful and futuristic arête left of Cosmosis on Bell Buttress. He spent the better part of a week working the moves before succeeding on *Verve* (5.13c). One of the seminal sport routes in the Boulder area, it is rarely repeated and still has a fierce reputation.

Mark Rolofson started putting up routes in the canyon in the 1980s and continues to establish many new routes of high difficulty and quality to this day. *Comfortably Numb* (5.12a/b) on Security Risk Crag, *Tricks Are For Kids* (5.12a/b) on Canyon Block, *Coney Island Baby* (5.12a) on Coney Island, and *Vasodilotor* (5.13a) on Blob Rock are just a few of the great routes established by this talented climber. Mark has also done more than his fair share of anchor replacement and bolt maintenance in the canyon.

Roger Briggs and friend on *Athlete's Feat* 5.11a. Photo: Bob D'Antonio.

The infamous "Bolt Wars" marred the 1990s. The shutting down of new routes with fixed hardware in Eldorado and the Flatirons left Boulder Canyon as the only haven for unrestricted new route development. Sides were drawn, bolts were chopped, verbal battles raged. Freedom costs and the canyon paid the price.

Jessie Guthrie, using his store and home in Nederland as a base, developed and explored many unclimbed crags. Jessie took climbing at Coney Island on a personal level and established many classic climbs in the 5.12 to 5.13 range.

In 1996 the globetrotting British superstar Jerry Moffatt visited the canyon and quickly raised standards to world-class level with a couple of

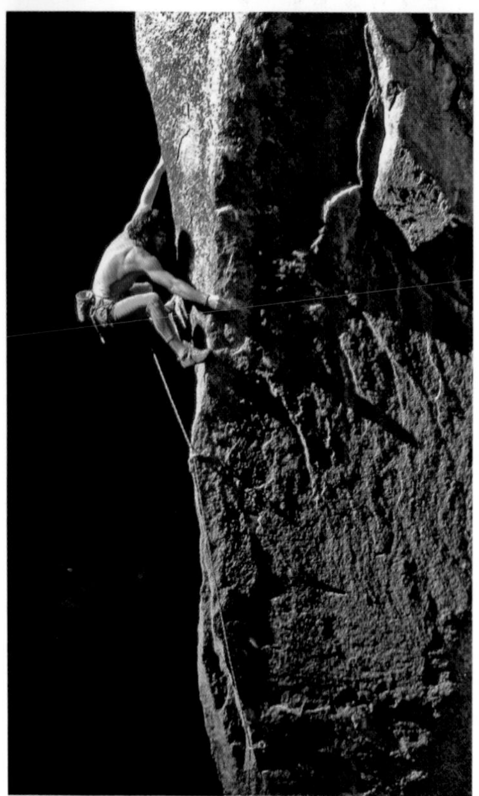

Chritian Griffith on *Verve* 5.13c. Photo: Dan Hare.

testpieces — *Gagger* (5.13d) a hideous steep slab and roof problem at Coney Island, and the "last great problem" of freeing the *Practice Aid Roof* at Castle Rock. The latter route *Deadline* (5.13d) was the source of controversy as both Moffatt and the local climber Rob Candelaria claimed the first ascent. Candelaria was belayed by his girlfriend and had no other witnesses. Moffatt publicly questioned Candelaria's ascent and had photographers and multiple witnesses to his own.

More controversy surrounded the development of The Sport Park, beginning in around 1998. Surprising Crag is cluster of short walls where Dan Hare and friends had established a number of hard and somewhat runout routes that had faded into obscurity. Using a new bag of tricks the Sport Crag Crew established over 60 routes at this previously neglected crag. Cracks were bolted, holds chipped, the bases of routes were landscaped to provide a comfortable staging areas. The Sport Park had the vibe of an outdoor rock gym. The sport crowd flocked to the cliffs and within a short period of time it became one of the most popular areas for Boulder climbers. Like a redheaded stepchild, it also became the brunt of many jokes and was even defamed in a national magazine as one of "The 10 Worst Crags in America." Nevertheless, The Sport Park offers some good natural climbs and a large concentration of sport routes. On any given summer weekend the crag is packed.

Dream Canyon is a collection of large granite domes and short cliffs along a fork of Boulder Creek. Strangely enough although Upper Dream Canyon, located just off Lost Angel Road, offers some of the longest routes in the area it was one of the last places to see intensive development. Bob Horan and Richard Rossiter along with several others attacked the place with a vengeance. New routes appeared on a weekly basis. With some of the best multi-pitch climbing in the area, Upper Dream Canyon quickly became popular. Bob Horan became fascinated with an old aid route on Lost Angel Wall, a stunning thin crack/corner that split the center of wall. Using traditional methods Bob, in a tour de force, climbed the corner to a fixed anchor and later returned to place bolts. The sport route *China Doll* (5.13c), became an instant classic. A 5.13+ second pitch was later added. In 2007, Mike Patz linked both pitches into one long pitch using only natural gear. This version of *China Doll* (5.14a R) is one of the hardest and finest traditional routes in the country (see page 245).

In the new Millenium climbers have continued to discover great new routes as well as whole new areas. Ron Olsen, a firmly established member of the gray-hair brigade at age 63, took it upon himself to unearth many new moderate routes on the forgotten Tonnere Tower. Vaino Kodas, a talented climber from California, arrived in Boulder and in a few short years established over a hundred new routes. A Vaino gem is the Plotinus Wall, which has become popular due to its well-thought-out routes and beautiful setting in Lower Dream Canyon. One of Vaino's best routes there is the classic arête *Lucid Dreaming* (5.12d).

Currently, the usual gray-haired suspects continue their assault: Bob D'Antonio, Greg Hand, Richard Rossiter, Mark Rolofson and Dan Hare, all well into their 40s and 50s, are still establishing many fine routes on old and new crags throughout the canyon.

Pat Ament

The Golden Age in Boulder Canyon

Dave Rearick. Photo: Pat Ament.

Early summer of 1964, on the southeast wall of Castle Rock, Dave Rearick and I did a route partly free that had been done previously all with aid. For expedience, we aided up the first twenty feet of *Country Club Crack* and traversed left, along a slab, to reach the bottom of what would be the second pitch of this free climb. Rearick used only a single piton for aid on this second pitch, a difficult overhanging crack. The third pitch was a short, fierce, right-leaning layback crack.

One of the Yosemite elite, Rearick had been Royal Robbins' partner on the Valley's first 5.10, *Rixon Pinnacle's East Chimney*, in 1960. They rated that climb 5.9, the upper level of the new California decimal system. Years later the *East Chimney* would be upgraded to 5.10. A few of us in Colorado had begun our own modest free climbing revolution, but Rearick brought with him the authenticity of Yosemite and its magical beginnings.

When Rearick moved to Boulder, we instantly became friends. He was not only a brilliant free climber but a fine gentleman. With distinctive calm, he began the strenuous layback up the third pitch of this route and, after 15 feet, held on with one hand while he hammered in a small bong-bong for protection. Most other climbers would now have needed to retreat to the ledge for a rest. Dave continued up the arm-draining layback to its top lip, where the good layback holds rounded and any jams found inside the crack were awkwardly wide. Dave decided to keep laybacking. Particles of sand and lichen, scraped loose by his shoes, fell toward me like flakes of snow.

He was far enough above the piton that, if he fell, he might hit the ledge. I slid my left hand far up the rope, ready to pull in slack fast if something happened. It seemed slow motion when his right foot slipped on that sandy stuff. His right leg swung under him and turned him upside down. As he flew toward me, I pulled in rope and did not let any out when his weight came onto the piton. I stopped him, his face an inch from hitting the ledge. He righted himself and stood beside me on the ledge, with his usual calm demeanor and smile. Most climbers would have rappelled at this point, happy to get away with their lives. Rearick thought for a minute, as we gazed out at the warm, gorgeous day of blue sky and pines. The river flowed serenely. Dave said, "If I don't go back up and try it right away, I'll develop a mental block." He returned to the crack, smeared his feet more attentively, and completed one of the hardest, most daring pitches in the country.

Also at Castle Rock in 1964, with me as his belayer, Rearick led a difficult short pitch, the *Coffin Crack*. This awkward, overhanging slot, though easy-looking, stopped cold quite a few good climbers. With the protection of a single, questionable, mid-size, horizontal piton driven straight up into a crack, Rearick maneuvered his body through the awkward, overhanging layback, leaning right, against smooth palm holds. He moved his body back into the crack, hoping his hands didn't pop off, and crossed the right hand over the left in order to make a huge reach high into the crack to a fingertip ledge on the left wall.

John Gill makes a casual solo repeat of *Final Exam* 5.11a. Photo: Pat Ament collection.

Rearick rated *Coffin Crack* 5.9. Later it would be rated sold 5.10. Most of our gradings during the mid-1960s were conservative. *Coffin Crack*, from a historical point of view, was one of the hardest free climbs in the country. Rearick had no sticky rubber shoes, no chalk, no "Friends" or other cams that now easily slide in for protection.

A year before, in 1963, I climbed with Royal Robbins, one of Yosemite's luminaries. This conquistador individual, with his brooding deportment, had heard about me from Kor and Rearick. In late summer 1964, I was one of the first people he contacted when he returned to Boulder. With the *Coffin Crack* and a free ascent of the third pitch of that five-pitch aid climb under my belt, I was hungry for more.

Royal heard the famous boulderer John Gill had done a few short climbs at Castle Rock. Royal and I looked for what those might have been as we walked along the road around the south side of the rock. There were no signs of Gill's chalk. Gill was the first to use chalk in climbing. I was probably the second. Both of us gymnasts, we had easily made the transfer of chalk from gymnastics to the rock. No one had yet invented chalk bags. I carried a small block in my right pants pocket.

A bulging, overhanging wall, split by a thin crack, caught Royal's eye. Gill must have climbed this. Royal was in a strong mood, determined to measure up to the powerful

Royal Robbins starts up *Country Club Crack*, August 1964. Photo: Pat Ament.

Gill – however futile such a desire would prove. We laced on our climbing shoes and tied into our swami belts – those several loops of flat webbing wrapped around our waist to ease the discomfort of a fall. Each of us tied an end of the climbing rope to our swami belt. Royal made a remarkable lead of this forearm-pumping wall. When a family drove by and stopped briefly to watch from their car, an elderly woman said through an open back window, "That must be the final exam."

We would learn Gill had not done this route, though he later would make its second ascent – as a free solo.

Royal and I then repeated *Coffin Crack*. He led it first try. We also did a new route Royal named *By Gully*, a squeeze chimney so steep it entirely overhung the base of the rock. He mumbled, "By golly it goes."

Royal and I returned to Castle Rock the next day, and I showed him the five pitches Rearick and I had played at, where Dave took the wild, head-first fall. With another pun, Royal named this route *Athlete's Feat*. The obvious start of the route, the direct line to the main crack system, had not yet been climbed, since Rearick and I, as well as the first ascent team, had done another pitch to the right. The direct start had no cracks and no protection of which to speak. It was a smooth, backward-leaning bulge ready to defy anyone who approached it. Starting off a spike of granite, itself a danger one might fall onto, Royal hammered a lone piton straight up under a thin flake. This would be his only protection.

He began a fingertip undercling of several moves upward left. His stiff Spider shoes smeared on the smooth granite. With his left hand he reached a finger-horn that formed the left end of the undercling flake. With the piton now far from him, he reached left, across his body with his right hand, to where he could make a hand switch on the horn, finger by finger replacing the left hand with the right. His shoes on a couple of small, downward sloping holds, he held himself in with the fingers of his right hand on the small horn. He raised his left hand above his head and found a fingertip edge on the outer, protruding rim of the bulge. He clung to this, let go of the horn with his right hand, stood up, and brought his right hand above to feel the smooth slab. There was nothing, but soon he found a small, downward-slant of rock near the limit of his reach. He pulled to the right, and slightly down, against this. By feel he lifted his left foot to a tiny, sloping foothold on the bulge and stepped up. At this point he shifted his right hand slightly higher into a better angle on the side-slant hold. Where his left fingertips had been, on the thin edge, he quickly set his left palm – his fingers pointed left. On this, he pushed. He threw his right foot high up, onto a saltine cracker edge. Had he fallen, I was ready to draw in rope. It was doubtful the piton would have helped much, below his feet when he was at the crux. Coordinating these various angles of push and pull, he stood up on the sloping, slippery slab.

Pat Ament one-arm handstand atop Castle Rock, August 1981.

Royal had created a bold and formidable sequence, involving every hand, foot, and limb. I doubt he realized the magnitude of what he had done. Modern climbers through the decades would rate these moves solid 5.11. Even with the help of chalk for the hands and the tremendous friction of modern rubber soles, and as people employ more and more sophisticated training, this short pitch has remained a remarkable challenge. Royal gave the route a 5.10 grading. Nevertheless, apart from Gill's routes in the Needles, *Athlete's Feat* and *Final Exam* were possibly the first 5.11s in the country,.

Royal led in a straightforward way the second pitch, though he took one short fall at the crux. He led Rearick's infamous third pitch, without the wild nose-dive. Royal began to realize he had gotten away with hogging the first three leads and insisted I take the next one. Easy-looking, the fourth pitch turned out to be 5.10 as well. As I led, Royal asked what was taking so long. When he followed, he was amazed at how difficult it was. He praised me for the lead.

Later in the day I showed Royal *Country Club Crack*. The first section, a smooth wall, had been the site of bolt wars, where incompetent climbers had drilled holes, and others had chopped them, and bolts had been replaced and chopped again. A shoulder stand,

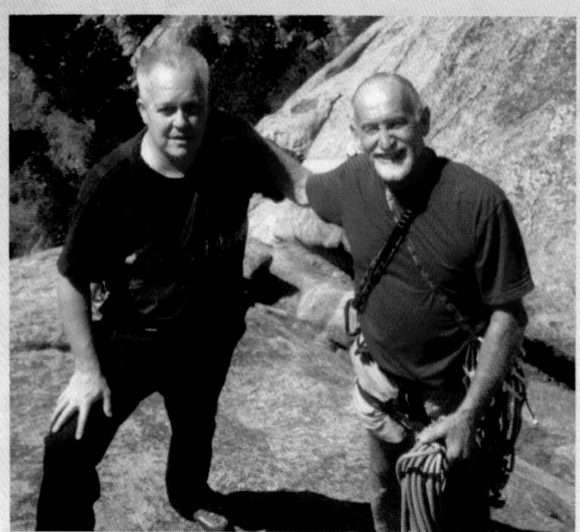
Pat Ament (left) and Royal Robbins after an ascent of The Dome in the mid-1990s. Photo Ament collection.

followed by only one bolt, was used to negotiate this initial wall on the first ascent. Royal was ready to apply his skills. To see if any bolts were necessary, he made a delicate aid lead of the first pitch, using no bolts. He then lowered from a piton and climbed the pitch free, with the protection of the rope through the piton. I followed the difficult moves free. He then hurriedly led the final pitch, as the sun set. This is one of the most aesthetic hand cracks anywhere, a long sweep up absolutely vertical rock. The crack arrives at a roof that is climbable by a hidden hold above. The final hand-finger crack was difficult in near-dark and by that time Royal had expended energy on the crack below. The sun went down on Castle Rock, and Royal ran out of both light and energy. He placed a piton or two and held onto them to finish the final crack. I followed fast, to avoid being caught in total dark.

That fall of 1964, I led the first free ascent of *Curving Crack*. Snow fell, as I moved up the steep, slippery layback to a sloping mantel. I was in good shape, and my partner Rearick couldn't see how I did the route under those conditions. In the spring of 1967, I led the free ascent of *Country Club Crack*. I had no illusions of grandeur, however, and no doubt Royal could have led the entire route free.

A few years after Royal and I did *Athlete's Feat,* two climbers attempted the route, thinking they would make a first ascent. The leader, fifteen feet up the first pitch, stood in aid slings from a bolt he had placed. He began to drill a second bolt above the bulge. I was appalled by the desecration of this free-climbing masterpiece. As the fellow hammered on the drill, I commented, "Do you know that has been done free?" The guy turned to me, as he hammered, and replied, "Sure, yeah."

Instead of turning *Athlete's Feat* into a battleground of holes, as was *Country Club,* I left the bolts in. I already had gone up, soon after my ascent with Royal, and made my own unprotected lead of that first pitch. The first bolt was later either removed or pulled out, but the upper bolt remained and was replaced by a thicker, high-quality bolt. Few climbers today will realize the difference between doing such a lead the way the master had and with the protection of a bolt, almost to create a toprope.

We owe much respect to those who precede us, namely those who set the standards and who so facilitated today's rise in consciousness and ability. Since people were going to allow the highest bolt to exist, I viewed it as a tribute to Royal. The bolt was a community admission of his remarkable spirit.

Christa Cline on *The Owl* 5.7, Dome Rock (next page). Photo Ron Olsen.

THE DOME 0.5 miles

Approach time: 10 minutes.
Exposure: East, south and west.

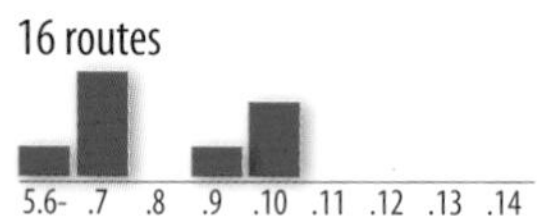

Easy access, great routes in the moderate range, and east, south, and southwestern exposure add up to a great experience a mere 10 minutes from downtown Boulder. Popular on the weekends, the Dome can get crowded — especially the easier trad routes. Be aware of other climbers and show common courtesy and respect.

Access: Park in a large pullout on the left side of the road 0.5 miles from the bridge, cross the road and access the Boulder Creek Trail, cross the footbridge and turn right along a trail for a 100 feet to a trail on the left leading up to the Dome.

The routes on the Dome require a standard rack.

❶ Evening Stroll 5.10c R ★ ☐
Starts just left of the descent gully. Somewhat of an obscure route with an old bolt that protects the crux. If you've done everything else in the area, go for it.
Pitch 1: 5.10b. Start left of the gully on the far left side of the rock near a pine tree, climb up blocky rock to the slab, past an old bolt and veer left to a belay on the left edge of the rock.
Pitch 2: 5.10c. Traverse right a little down to a flake, gain the flake and then reach a crack, follow the crack to the top.
Gear to 2 inches.

❷ Left Edge 5.7 ★★ ☐
As the name suggests, climb the left edge just left of the low point of the wall up to a large roof, skirt the roof on the left and head straight up the corner to the top.
Gear to 3 inches.

❸ Prelude to King Kong 5.9 ★ ☐
Climbs just left of the black streak. End at the belay for *Gorilla's Delight* or continue up and left to the top in one long pitch. Also used for accessing several routes to the right.
Gear to 2.5 inches.

❹ Black Plague 5.10c R ★ ☐
Climbs the right-facing corner just left of the obvious black streak. Committing moves with dubious gear.
Gear to 3 inches.

❺ Gorilla's Delight 5.9+ ★★ ☐
Somewhat of a sandbag at the grade and the site of several bad accidents. Feel solid or don't do it.
Pitch 1: 5.9. Start with *Left Edge* and belay below the large roof.
Pitch 2: 5.9+. From the belay, climb into a left-facing corner, make a hard move out of the corner then up a crack to the top.
Gear to 3 inches.

❻ Super Squeeze 5.10d+ ★★ ☐
If you like gauging your progress by inches, this is the route for you. The site of humiliation for climbers of all abilities.
Pitch 1: 5.9. Climb the first pitch of *Prelude to King Kong*, belay just below the A-shaped roof.
Pitch 2: 5.10d+. Jam a right-leaning hand and finger crack in the roof and grunt, squeeze, or hyperventilate through the crux.
Gear to 3 inches.

❼ The Umph Slot 5.10d ★★★ ☐
Pitch 1: 5.8. Take any route that gets you to the right side of the large roof.
Pitch 2: 5.10d. Belay below the roof and then climb up and right into the slot. The route was rated 5.8+ on the FA but that is only for those who haven't eaten in at least a week.
Variation: Familiar Face 5.10d ☐
Once out of the slot go left up a thin crack to a face and then the top.
Gear to 4 inches.

❽ The Owl 5.7 ★★★ ☐
A route that demands respect for the grade. Bring long slings for the first pitch. Photo previous page.
Pitch 1: 5.7. Start right of the huge roof trending left on nice face climbing, go right on chicken heads and then climb a hand crack to a belay above the large roof.
Pitch 2: 5.7. Follow the *Cozyhang* finish to the top.
SR.

❾ Direct 5.10d R ☐
A committing line that sees little traffic on the lead. At the low point of the rock is a small buttress, climb either side and follow the black groove to the first belay of *Cozyhang*.
Gear to 4.5 inches.

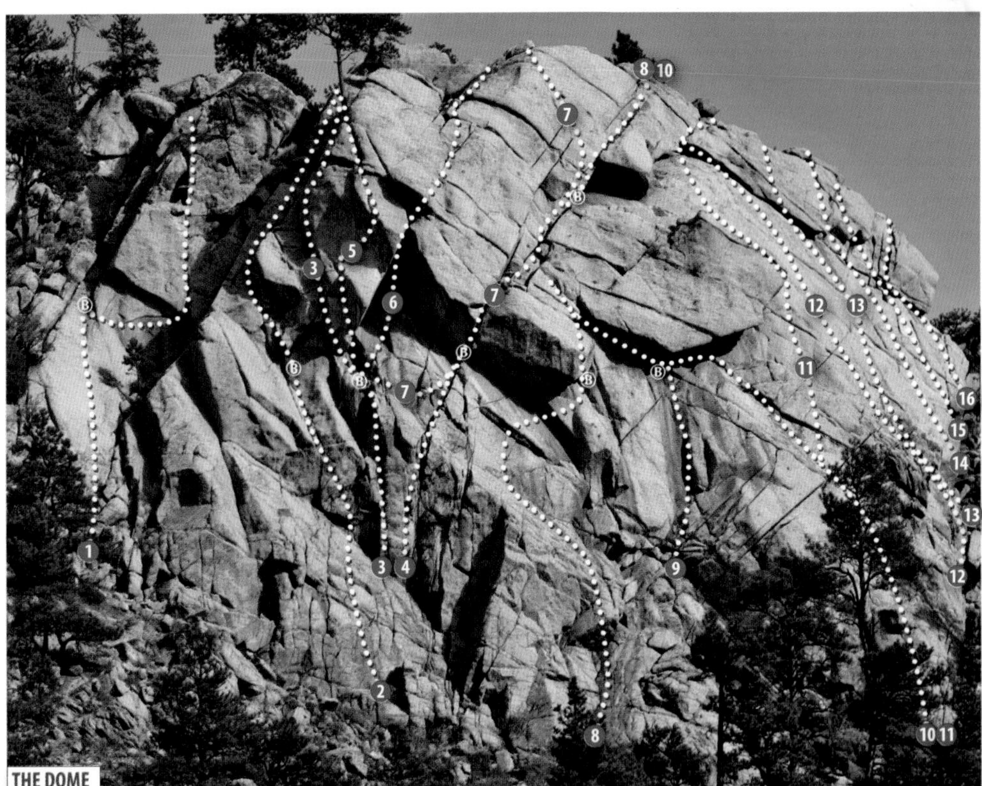

⑩ Cozyhang 5.7 ★★★ ☐

Pitch 1: 5.7. Start up and right of the low point of the rock. Follow cracks up and left to a series of small roofs, tackle the upper roof and then left up a ramp to the cozy belay under a large roof.

Pitch 2: 5.7. Go left then straight up through a slot to a ramp and belay.

Pitch 3: 5.7. Climb over the roof to a belay and the top.

Variation 1: Cozy Overhang 5.10d ★ ☐ Turn the big roof on the left.

Variation 2: Groove 5.10d ★ ☐ Just above the first belay climb the roof at a groove/dike.

Gear to 2.5 inches.

⑪ East of the Sun 5.7 ★★★ ☐

Pitch 1: 5.7. Follow the first pitch of *Cozyhang*, gain the ramp above the overhangs and go right up a right-leaning corner (pin) to a belay.

Pitch 2: 5.6. Climb just right of the chimney and then left on a ramp. Follow face holds up to a belay below roofs on a ramp.

Pitch 3: 5.7. Go over the roof about ten feet left of *East Slab* to the top.

SR.

⑫ East Slab 5.6 ★★★★ ☐

One of the finest routes in the Boulder area for the grade. Can be done in one pitch.

Pitch 1: 5.6. Start up and right of *Cozyhang* at a V-corner. Climb the corner and trend left. Gain the slab and enjoy blissful climbing up a crack to a roof and belay.

Pitch 2: 5.4. Climb right out the roof and reach a pine tree at the top.

Gear to 2.5 inches.

⑬ East Slab East 5.6 ★★ ☐

As the name suggests, the route starts east of the *East Slab*. Start right of the V-corner and climb into a slot and bulge, continue up a crack and over the final roof.

Gear to 2.5 inches.

⑭ East of East Slab East 5.7 ★★ ☐

Start at the upper, easier start to East Slab. Climb up to a right-angling finger crack then move up and left into a groove with a bucket. Climb the slab aiming for a black streak. Surmount the overlap on the left (easier) or on the right via a hand crack.

SR.

⑮ East Slab Far Right 5.7 ★★ ☐

Begin in the steep corner 30 feet up and right of the standard East Slab route. Climb the awkward dihedral (crux) to gain the slab. Meander up ramps and cracks to an overlap with two exits. Take the right exit on great hand jams.

⑯ East Face, Farthest Right 5.7 ★ ☐

Climb the same awkward dihedral as the previous route to gain the slab. Climb cracks near the right arete to a right-leaning offwidth. Climb this to the top.

ELEPHANT BUTTRESSES 0.5 miles

Approach time: 10 - 15 minutes.
Exposure: East, south and north.

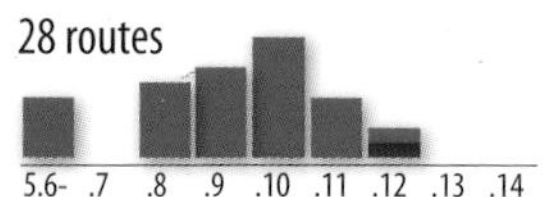

The Elephant Buttresses are a series of towers that lie right of the Dome. Many good climbs exist here with easy access and south, west and north exposure. The Buttresses are named in order with the First being to the climber's left and the Fourth is the farthest right.

Access: Park in a large pullout on the left side of the road 0.5 miles from the bridge. Cross the road and the footbridge, then turn right along a trail and follow it for 100 feet to a trail leading left up to an aqueduct. Follow the trail along the aqueduct to a large water pipe. Most climbs on the Third and Fourth Buttresses start from the pipe.

Descent: To descend from any of the Buttresses, head northwest towards the Dome and take a steep trail down between the First Elephant Buttress and the Dome.

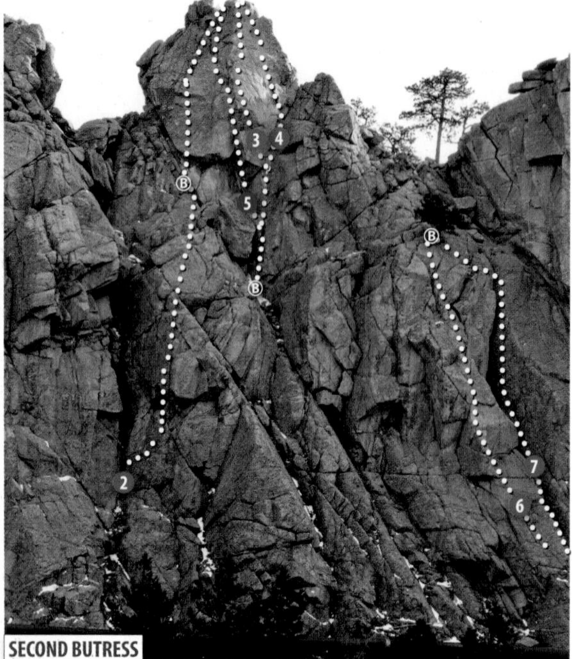

FIRST BUTTRESS

❶ Flash Dihedral 5.6 ☐

On the left side of the First Buttress find a corner/OW and climb the crack that lies to the right of it.

Gear to a 3.5 inches.

SECOND BUTTRESS

❷ Elephantiasis 5.11c R ☐

Pitch 1: 5.9. Climb the gully between the First and Second Buttress to an obvious flake on the right, climb the flake and then up a crack to a ledge below *Tough Situation.*

Pitch 2: 5.11b/c R. Climb up to a new bolt on the left (crux) and then follow a thin seam that joins *Tough Situation* near the top.

Gear to 2.5 inches.

❸ Tough Situation 5.10a ★★ ☐

Climb the 4th-class gully in the middle of the buttress to a ledge and thin crack out a roof.

Gear to 2 inches.

❹ Classic Finger Crack 5.9 ★★★ ☐

Climb the 4th-class gully and then trend right up to a thin crack splitting the clean wall above. Climb the crack to top.

Gear to 2 inches.

❺ Avalon Rising 5.12b ★ ☐

Somewhat of a strange route. Climb the fourth class gully and trend right towards *Classic Finger Crack*. Look straight up for bolts up a blunt arête and climb it.

3 bolts and gear to 2 inches.

❻ Pine Tree Route 5.6 ★ ☐

Start just left of the gully between the Second and Third Buttresses. Climb a slab to a short dihedral. Climb the dihedral and continue up cracks to a pine tree.

Gear to 3.5 inches.

❼ Chimney 5.6 ☐

The obvious chimney just right of the *Pine Tree Route*. Go left at the top to the pine tree.

Gear to 3.5 inches.

Tony Everhart on *FM* 5.11c, next page. Photo Jimmy Farrell.

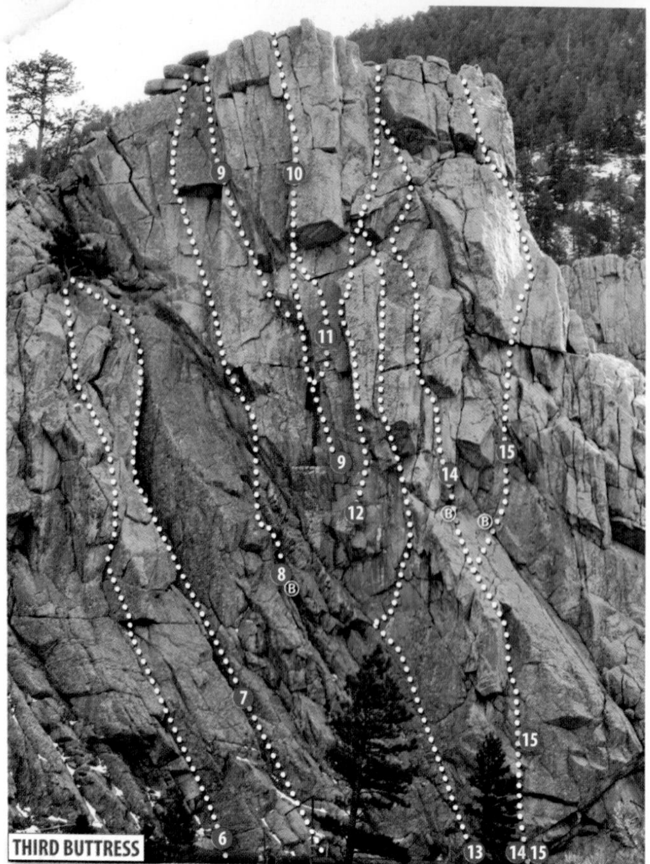

THIRD BUTTRESS

8 Wingtip 5.10c/d ★

Scramble up the gully/slab on the left side of the Third Buttress to the base of a left-leaning dihedral near a tree. Belay at the tree. Traverse right to a left-facing dihedral and climb it to the top of the rock.

Gear to 2 inches.

9 Left Wing 5.10c ★★★

Scramble up the gully for 70 feet to the obvious ledge on the right. Belay here. Climb a short face up past two bolts to reach the main corner below a roof. Climb through the left side of the roof to the top.

Variation: Misdirected 5.11b/c

past the second bolt go into a groove on the right and climb over a roof and meet the upper part of *Pegasus* to the top.

Gear to 2 inches.

10 What's Up 5.10d ★★

Climb up to the first bolt on *Left Wing* and then fire up a short corner to a roof on the right side and then make a few face moves to reach a small pillar that forms a roof, turn the roof on the left and then up to the top.

Gear to 2.5 inches.

11 Pegasus 5.11c

Scramble up the gully for 70 feet to the obvious ledge on the right. Belay here. Climb the first section of *Left Wing* past the bolts, veer a little right to a thin crack going through an overhang on the right. Fire the crack and race your arms to the top.

Gear to 2 inches.

12 FM 5.11c ★★★

Begin down and right of *Left Wing* aiming for the left facing dihedral above an A-shaped roof on the right. Move left a little and then fire up the corner to the top.

Gear to 2 inches, mostly small to medium wires.

13 Kangaroof 5.11c

Pitch 1: 5.9. Start down and right of *FM* and climb the short face to a west facing ramp. Belay at the top of the ramp.

Pitch 2: 5.11c. Fire up the thin crack through the overhang just right of *FM*. Reach the upper section of *FM* and follow it to the top.

Gear to 2 inches..

14 Mojo Rising 5.9 ★★

Start as for *Standard Route* and belay at the ramp. Climb the shallow corner to a roof, go left out the roof and follow a crack to another roof going left to the top.

Gear to 2.5 inches.

15 Standard Route 5.8- ★★★

Pitch 1: 5.7+. Start off the pipe and climb up a short dihedral then up the left side of a ramp, belay after 50 feet.

Pitch 2: 5.8-. Traverse right to a short overhanging corner, climb the corner, then fire up a crack in a ramp/corner. Go left at the top of the corner and then straight up a short crack to the top.

Gear to 2.5 inches.

16 Monster Woman 5.9- ★★

Start right of the *Standard Route*. Head up a short corner with an old eyebolt and turn the roof on the left. Finish as for the *Standard Route.*

Gear to 2.5 inches

17 Ah Maw 5.10a R ★

Climb the slab right of *Monster Woman* to a roof, pass the roof in the middle and then finish as for the *Standard Route*.

Gear to 2.5 inches..

⑱ **West Face** 5.8- ★★ ☐

Pitch 1: 5.7+. Start in a shallow dihedral about 25 feet right of *Monster Woman*. Climb the dihedral then cracks to a shelf just right of the *Standard Route*.

Pitch 2: 5.8-. Go left to the *Standard Route* and finish on that.

Gear to 2.5 inches.

FOURTH BUTTRESS

⑲ **Flake** 5.10c ★★ ☐

On the left side (north) of the buttress climb the overhanging flake/crack to a bolt on the right, then up to a small roof with a pin. Climb the roof and then straight up the steep face.

Gear to 2 inches..

⑳ **Zolar Czakl** 5.9+ ★★ ☐

Step off the pipe and climb a shallow left-leaning dihedral. At the top of dihedral climb and finish for the *Flake Route.*

Direct Finish: 5.9+ ☐

After the roof trend slightly right up the steep face.

Gear to 2.5 inches

㉑ **Northwest Face** 5.8 ★★★ ☐

Begin on top of the water pipe at the mouth of the tunnel and pull across to the horizontal crack. Climb the crack to a nice vertical crack and follow this to the top.

Gear to 2.5 inches, long slings.

㉒ **The Heartland** 5.9+ ★★ ☐

Pitch 1: 5.9+. Traverse the horizontal crack at the start of Northwest Face, going right to a thin crack. Climb the crack to a nice belay.

Pitch 2: 5.9 Go left from the belay and climb the crack left of a dihedral.

Gear to 2.5 inches.

㉓ **Southwest Chimney** 5.4 ☐

The obvious chimney on the southwest face. Not pleasant.

Gear to 2.5 inches.

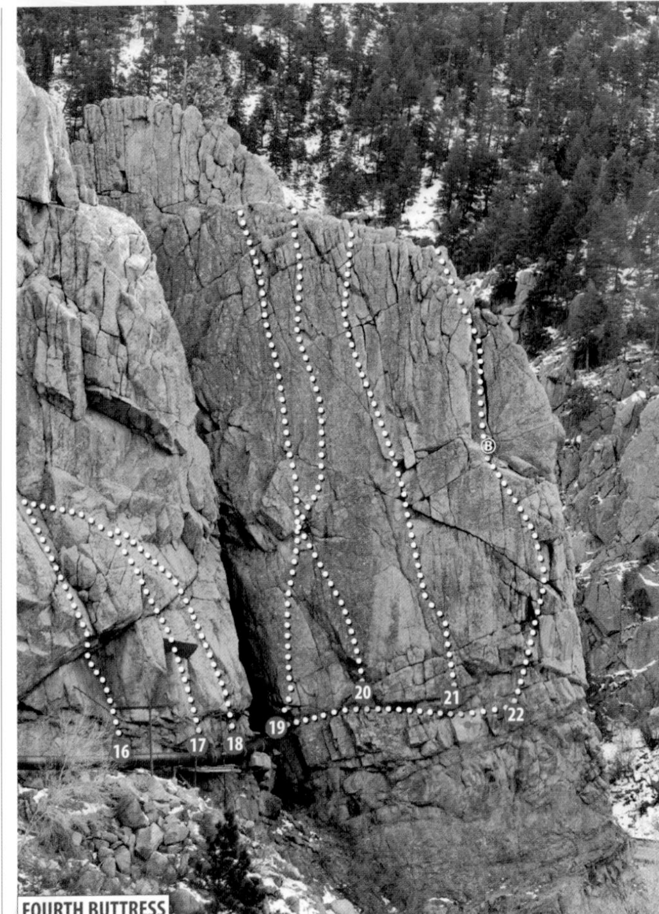

㉔ **Mickey Mantel** 5.10b/c ★ ☐

Pitch 1: 5.9. Start at a right-facing corner at the end of a grassy ramp, climb the corner or the face to the right aiming for a left-facing dihedral. Climb the dihedral and then left to belay at a recess.

Pitch 2: 5.10b/c. Move up and left doing a strange mantel move gaining a ramp. Climb a nice crack to a higher ramp, follow another crack to the top.

Gear to 2.5 inches.

㉕ **Azimuth** 5.10b/c ☐

Climb the obvious finger crack up and right of the start of *Mickey Mantel*.

Gear to 2 inches.

㉖ **Mr. Atrophy** 5.12a ☐

Start as for *Mickey Mantel* but go left at the roof and then climb the right of two flaring cracks to the top.

Gear to 2 inches.

㉗ **Wait Until Dark / After Dark** 5.10d ★★ ☐

Pitch 1: 5.10d. About 50 feet right of *Mickey Mantel* and the grassy ramp is a short hand crack. Climb it.

Pitch 2: After Dark 5.10a ☐

Scramble up to two thin cracks and a ramp, climb the roof at the top of the ramp and continue to the top.

Gear to 2.5 inches.

㉘ **Cloddy Corner** 5.6 ☐

Climb an obvious left-facing corner on the upper east side of the south face.

Gear to 2.5 inches.

FROGMAN PINNACLE 0.5 miles

Approach time: 5 minutes.
Exposure: South.

2 routes

5.6- .7 .8 .9 .10 .11 .12 .13 .14

A nice option if you want a hard climb close to the road.

Access: Park in a large pullout on the left side of the road 0.5 miles from the bridge, cross the road and gain the footbridge, turn right along a trail for 20 feet to a trail leading up and left to the Pinnacle.

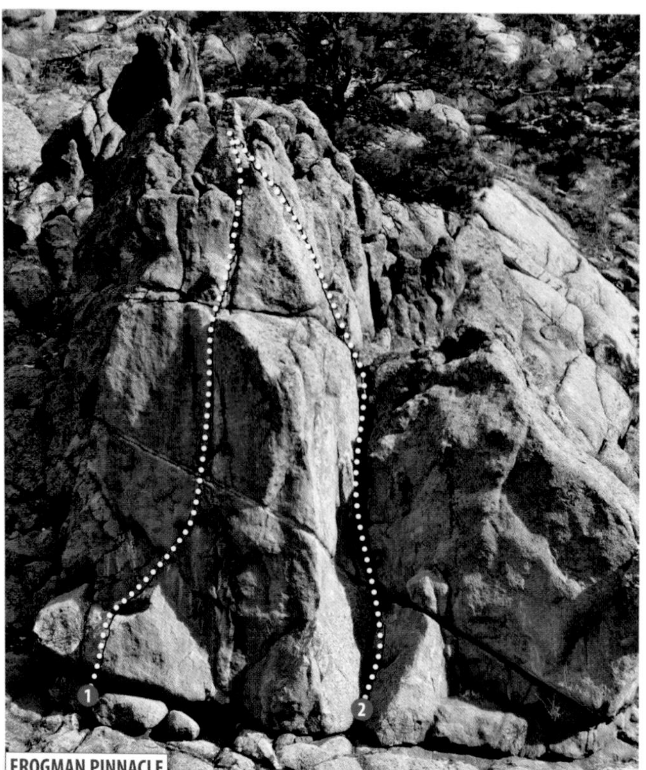

FROGMAN PINNACLE

❶ **Frogman** 5.12a ★★
Climb up the center of the south face. Hard face moves gain a short finger crack and the top. Can be easily top-roped. Funny the things you remember, I first did this route with the late Charlie Fowler, led it and Charlie followed, one of the few times we roped up together.
Gear to 4.5 inches.

❷ **Chimney** 5.6 ★★
Climbs the obvious chimney on the southeast part of the rock.
Gear to 3.5 inches.

ROCK ISLAND 1 & 2 0.5 miles

These roadcuts are located 0.5 miles up the canyon near the Dome. Park in the large parking area for the Dome and then cross the road. Just before the footbridge is Rock Island 1. Several topropes up to 5.11 can done on this somewhat dubious looking rock. Approach the top from the east.

Rock Island 2 is located up canyon about a two tenths of mile from Rock Island 1. A short crack (*Candelaria's Crack* 5.11d) splits the west face. There is a small parking area on the east side of the rock.

LITTLE CRAG 1.0 miles

Approach time: 10 - 15 minutes.
Exposure: North and southwest.

4 routes

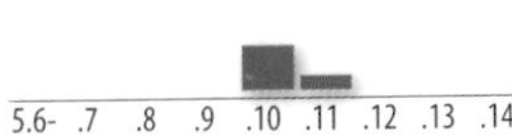

A small rock that seldom sees traffic, maybe due to the runout nature of the existing routes. Worth a trip if only to top rope or practice your headpointing skills.

Access: Park in a small pullout on the left side of the road 0.9 miles up the canyon, cross the road, and head about 200 yards uphill to the crag.

1 Belladonna 5.10a ★ ☐
Climb the obvious left-angling crack on the northwest side of the rock.
Gear to 2.5 inches.

2 Short but Cute 5.10c R ★ ☐
On the left side of the west face is a small right-facing corner. Groundfall potential.
Gear to 2 inches.

3 Nothing to Fear 5.10d R ☐
Start for *Short but Cute* and angle up and right to a horn and safety. Continue up on easier climbing to the top.
Gear to 2 inches.

4 Cool Operator 5.11d R/X ★ ☐
On the southwest face is this short, vicious problem. Better done as a top-rope or head-point. The R/X rating depends on how high you get and where you fall.
Gear to 4.5 inches. RP's.

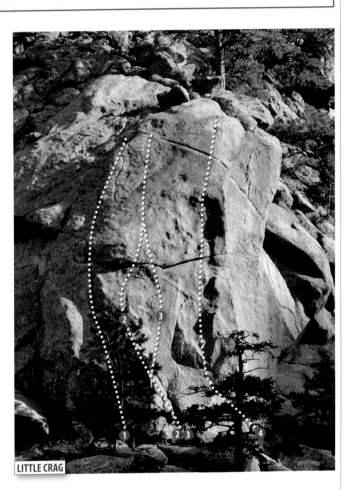

LITTLE CRAG

ISLAND ROCK 4.2 miles

Approach time: 10 - 15 minutes.
Exposure: Northwest.

4 routes

5.6- .7 .8 .9 .10 .11 .12 .13 .14

A good size chunk of granite that looks way better than it is on closer inspection. Only a few routes exist on the rocks. There is potential for more with cleaning.

Access: Park in a large pullout on the left side of the road 4.2 miles from the bridge at an island of rock with a large parking area. Drop down to the creek and cross on rocks or wade. The crossing can be quite dangerous during runoff. Follow a faint trail uphill to the rock.

Descent: Walk off to the east or west from the top back to the base of the rock.

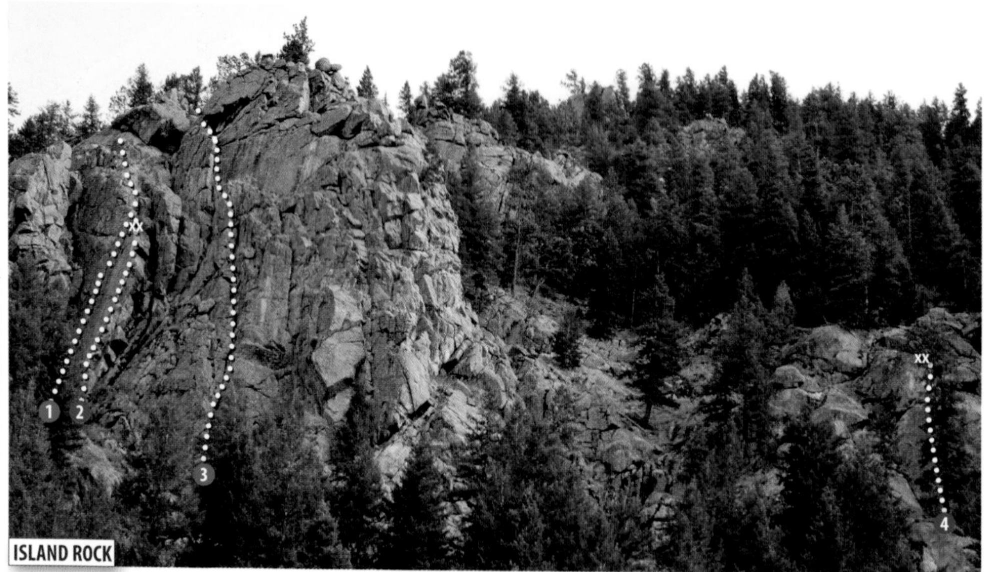

❶ Cracks are for Kids 5.8 ★
Start just left of the bolted arete and climb the handcrack to the top of the rock.
SR.

❷ No Man Is An Island 5.11a ★★
Climb the obvious arete making some dicey, technical moves. Lower from a two bolt anchor.
7 bolts.

❸ Lost Ring 5.7
Start about 25 feet down and right of *No Man Is An Island* at a right facing corner/crack. Dirty climbing leads to more dirty climbing.
SR.

❹ Miss Mantel 5.11a ★★★
A very good slab climb that is located west of the main rock. Head west from the main rock for 100 yards to the obvious bolted slab at a large pine tree. Climb the slab making hard moves at every bolt.
6 bolts.

BRICK WALL 4.6 miles

Approach time: 30 seconds.
Exposure: South.

5 routes

A popular rock with easy access. Bolts and trees on top make for easy top-roping. Most, if not all, of the routes have been led and are rated R or X.

Access: Park in a small pullout on the right side of the road 4.6 miles from the bridge at the rock, hop out of your car and start climbing.

Descent: Walk off to the east.

❶ **The Perfect Route** 5.9 ★★ ☐☐
Start on the left side of the rock, climbing into a dish/bowl. Reach a crack with gear and climb just left of the arete. Move left and reach the top.
SR.

❷ **Living on the Edge** 5.11b R ☐☐
Start as for *The Perfect Route*. Reach the dish and then head straight up through a small roof and gain the arete to the top.
SR.

❸ **Direct** 5.11a/b ☐☐
Climb the blank wall just left of center at a faint yellow streak.
Toprope.

❹ **Crease** 5.11a ★★ ☐☐
As the name suggests, climb near a seam/crease right of the center of the rock. Join the *South Face* about 20 feet from the top.
Toprope.

❺ **South Face** 5.10c R ★★★ ☐☐
This route has been led and soloed, most will want to top-rope it. On the right side of the rock, climb up 25 feet to an obvious face leading up to parallel cracks, reach a break and then climb a hand crack to the top.
SR. Toprope.

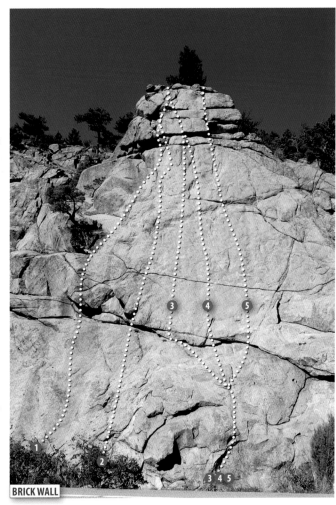

BRICK WALL

SPASMODIC ROCK 4.6 miles

Approach time: 1 minute.
Exposure: South.

2 routes

5.6- .7 .8 .9 .10 .11 .12 .13 .14

A small and short chunk of granite lying right off the road and 100 feet west of the Brick Wall.

Access: Park in a small pullout on the right side of the road 4.6 miles from the bridge. Hop out of your car and walk 100 feet west to the rock.

Descent: Walk off to the west.

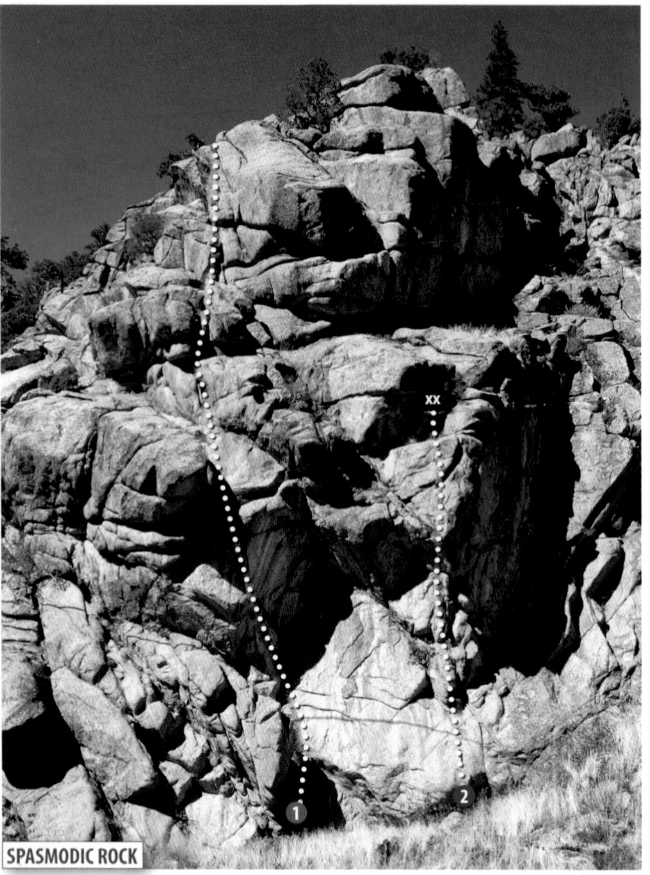

❶ **The Joker and the Thief** 5.11d ☐☐
Start about 15 left of *Lily* at a thin overhanging crack. Strenuous climbing leads to a ledge and a belay. Climb easier rock to the top.
Gear to 2 inches.

❷ **Lily and the Jack of Hearts** 5.11a ★☐☐
Start on the right side of the rock. Follow a line of bolts up the steep wall to a ledge and the anchor. A bit dirty but should clean up with more ascents.
5 bolts.

Sheyna Button on *Thumb Tack* 5.11d at The Bihedral, page 86. Photo: Topher Donahue

MENTAL ROCK 4.8 miles

Approach time: 10 - 15 minutes.
Exposure: Northwest.

4 routes

5.6- .7 .8 .9 .10 .11 .12 .13 .14

A nice piece of granite with several hard crack climbs. Maybe the hardest 5.11+ in the world lies on this rock. All the routes have been led but it has become quite popular to toprope them.

Access: Park in a small pullout on the right side of the road 4.8 miles from the bridge. Drop down to the creek and cross on rocks on wade or use the old bridge to cross the creek. Can be quite dangerous during spring runoff. Follow a trail west to the rock.

Descent: Walk off to the west from the top back to the base of the rock.

1 Love or Confusion 5.11c ☐
Climb a flake/crack up to a small roof on the left side of the crag. Strenuous and hard for the grade.
Small to medium gear.

2 Obsessive-Compulsive 5.12b ★ ☐
Climb a thin seam leading to a roof, make a series of hard moves over the roof, and reach the top. Hard climbing with good, but difficult-to-place, gear.
Small to medium gear.

3 Manic-Depressive 5.11d ★★★ ☐
Start at the obvious chalked crack with some fixed pins, trend right at the roof and use flaring jams to gain a ledge. Hard for the grade.
Small to medium gear.

4 Sleeper 5.12b ★★ ☐
Like the rest of the routes on this crag, this baby is a fight to the finish. On the right side of the crag climb up thin seams through two small roofs to a ledge and the top.
Small to medium gear.

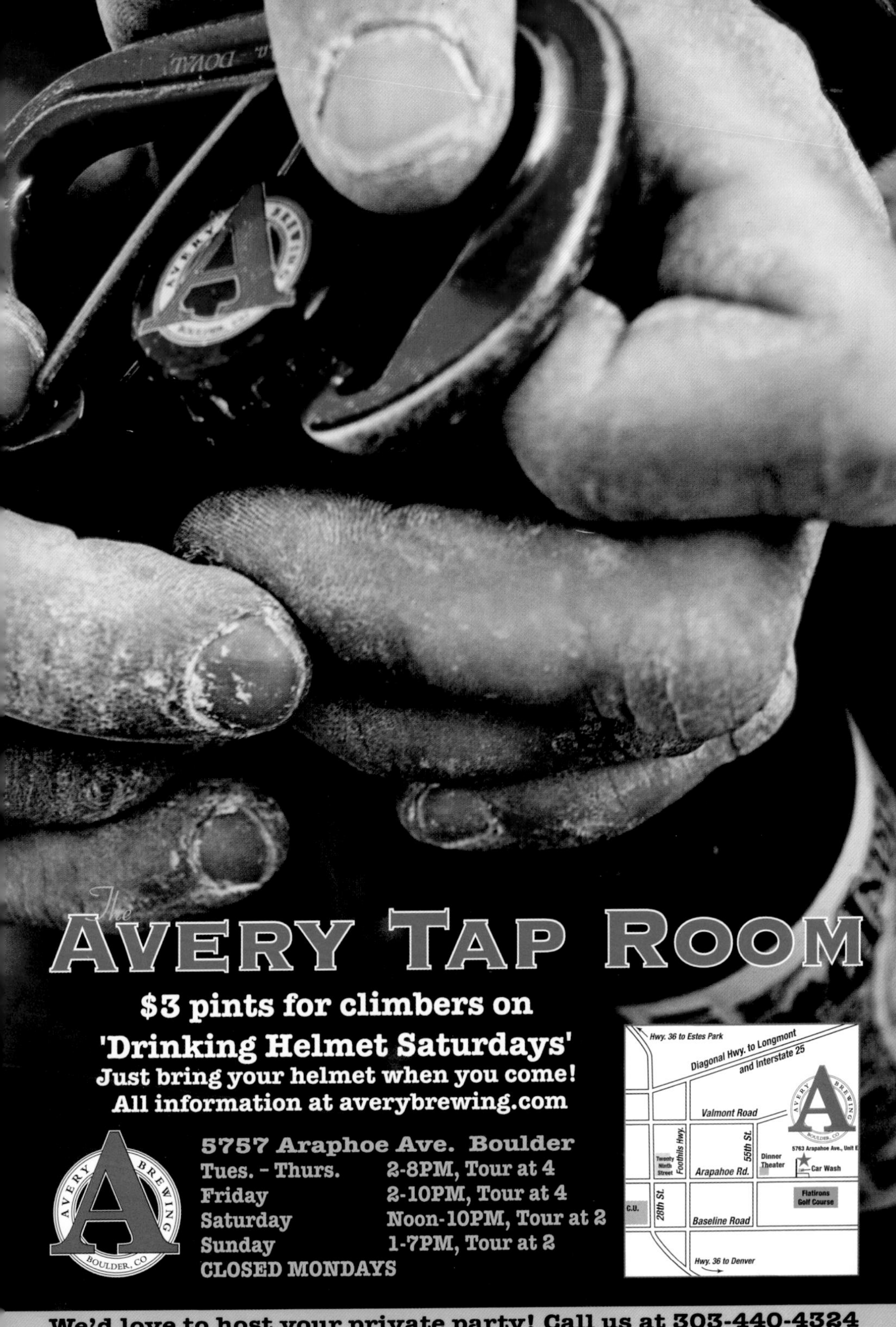

The AVERY TAP ROOM
$3 pints for climbers on
'Drinking Helmet Saturdays'
Just bring your helmet when you come!
All information at averybrewing.com
AVERY BREWING
BOULDER, CO
5757 Araphoe Ave. Boulder
Tues. - Thurs. 2-8PM, Tour at 4
Friday 2-10PM, Tour at 4
Saturday Noon-10PM, Tour at 2
Sunday 1-7PM, Tour at 2
CLOSED MONDAYS
Hwy. 36 to Estes Park
Diagonal Hwy. to Longmont and Interstate 25
Valmont Road
Foothills Hwy.
55th St.
Twenty Ninth Street
Arapahoe Rd.
Dinner Theater
5763 Arapahoe Ave., Unit E
Car Wash
C.U.
28th St.
Baseline Road
Flatirons Golf Course
Hwy. 36 to Denver
We'd love to host your private party! Call us at 303-440-4324

CANYON BLOCK aka THE MILK DUD

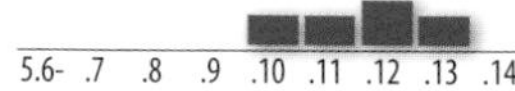

Approach time: 10 - 15 minutes
Exposure: East, south and west.

9 routes

5.6- .7 .8 .9 .10 .11 .12 .13 .14

This is a beautiful piece of granite in a wonderful setting in the woods high above the road. It has several hard routes. There are also a few boulder problems along the wash/trail that leads to the rock.

Access: Park in a small pullout on the right side of the road at 4.8 miles, look right to find a trail leading up the hillside. Follow the trail/wash/slabs marked with cairns for about 10 minutes and then angle right to the rock. Several of the old routes have been re-equipped with modern gear.

Descent: Walk off to the west or east from the top back to the base of the rock.

CANYON BLOCK LEFT

CANYON BLOCK RIGHT

1 Ament Crack 5.11b ☐
Climb a low overhang on the left side of the rock and gain a ledge, then follow the thin seam/crack to the top.
Gear to 2 inches.

2 Seam 5.11d ☐
Start as for *Ament Crack* and climb the seam a few feet right. Thin gear protects the crux.
Gear to 4.5 inches.

3 Scorcher 5.10a ☐
Climb the crack 10 feet right of *Seam*.
Gear to 3.5 inches.

4 Wallflower 5.12b/c ★★ ☐
Hard and devious climbing. Start as for Scorcher and follow the flake past a bolt and join *Damaged Goods* near the top.
4 bolts, few small cams.

5 Damaged Goods 5.13a ★★★ ☐
Climb the overhanging arete on southwest face to a thin crack/seam, make several hard moves to gain and climb the crack. Really hard and devious.
Small TCUs and RPs

6 Rude Boys 5.12b/c ★★★ ☐
Classic, a must do at the grade. Climb the right-leaning corner/crack up to a small overhang and the crux mantel. Gain a crack and scamper to the top.
Gear to 4.5 inches.

7 Blues for Allah 5.13a ★★ ☐
Climbs the obvious slab just right of *Rude Boys*. Hard moves past the second bolt to gain a short crack and the top.
Small gear and quickdraws.

8 Tricks Are For Kids 5.12a/b ★★★ ☐
Devious slab climbing that will keep you thinking. Start on the right side of the rock, just left of *Shallow Jam*. Climb steep rock to gain the first bolt, make hard moves to gain the second bolt, make a harder move and gain a ledge and some gear, pop to the top.
2 bolts, 1.5 and 4 inch cams

9 Shallow Jam 5.10a ★★ ☐
A nice little crack climb on the right side of the rock.
Gear to 2 inches.

EAGLE ROCK 6.2 miles

Approach time: 10 - 15 minutes.
Exposure: West.

17 routes

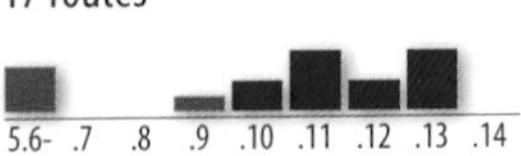

Eagle Rock is a large piece of granite looming above the highway and Boulder Creek. Almost forgotten by trad climbers, the wall now has several great sport routes and has become quite popular. Eagle Rock also has a couple of hard classic boulder problems, see page 256

⃠ This cliff may be closed due to raptor nesting between February and August (see page 17).

Access: Park in a pullout on the right side of the road at 6.2 miles. Cross the road and drop down to the creek. Locate the Tyrolean traverse just downstream or cross the creek on rocks or wade during low water.

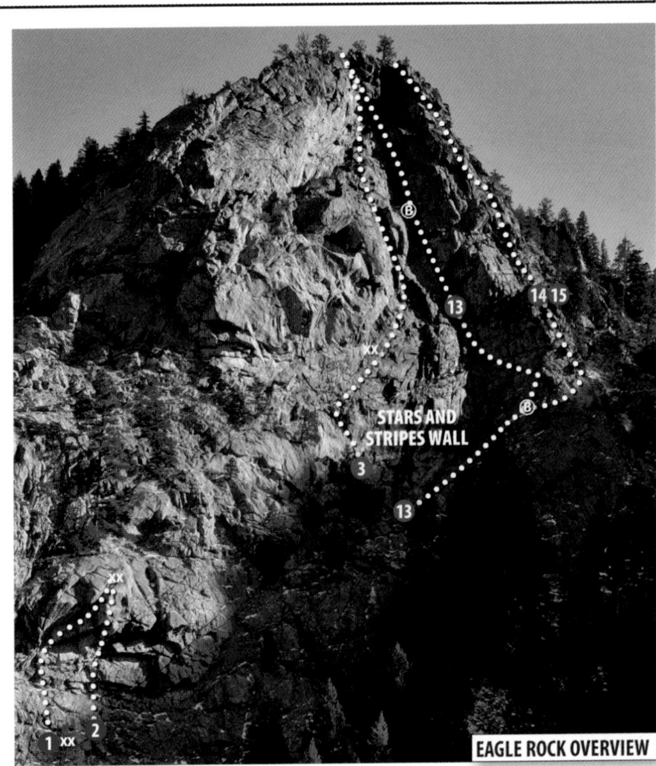

EAGLE ROCK OVERVIEW

1 Iggle 5.11c ★ ☐

Look for an obvious right-slanting corner system about midway up the left side of Eagle Rock. Belay at a pine tree and pass one bolt to get to a two-bolt belay at the start of the corner. Climb into the corner and then make some interesting moves out right.

7 bolts.

2 Iggle Direct 5.11c ★ ☐

This climb takes a direct line out an overhanging crack/corner to an anchor just right of the finishing anchors on *Iggle*.

7 bolts.

3 Gros Vogel 5.9 A2 ☐

Pitch 1: 5.8. Climb the long angling ramp that starts on the left side of the wall that cuts above the overhanging Stars and Stripes Wall. Belay at a bolted anchor just right of orange lichen streaks.

Pitch 2: 5.8 A2. Climb a short face leading into a overhanging corner, continue up and belay below roof. This may have been free climbed at 5.10d.

Pitch 3: 5.9. Climb out the left side of the roof and then up easier rock to top. Walk off to the east.

SR.

See next page for Stars and Stripes Wall.

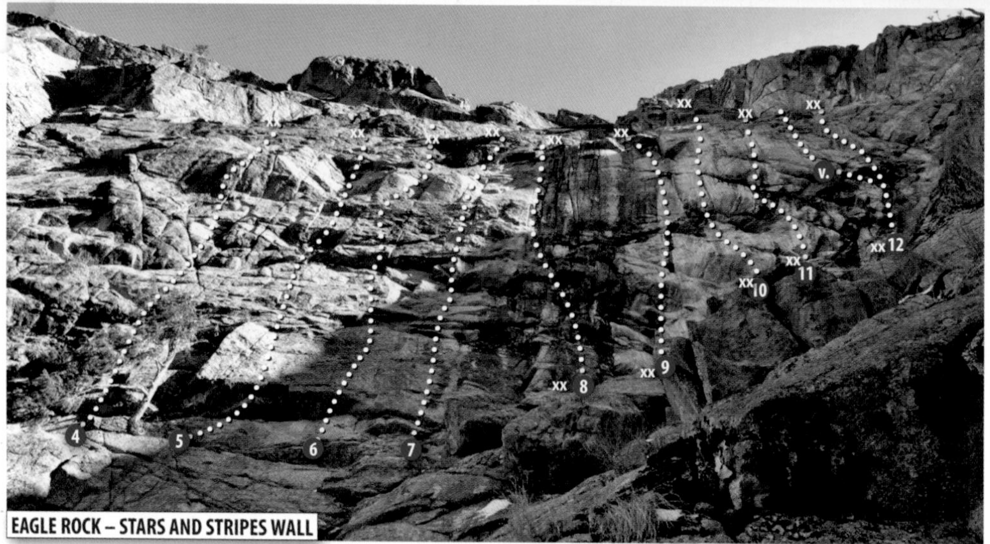

EAGLE ROCK – STARS AND STRIPES WALL

STARS AND STRIPES WALL

This is the overhanging black-streaked wall in the middle of the lower wall.

❹ Eagle Tricks 5.12a ★ ☐
Start left of a tree on the left side of the wall. Climb easy rock to thin cracks that shoot through a small roof. Crank the roof and gain the anchor.
8 bolts.

❺ Eagle Snacks 5.10d ★★ ☐
A nice warm up on really good stone. Climb up a clean slab through overlaps to a short corner and engage the crux. Finish on jugs that lead to the anchor.
9 bolts.

❻ Eagle Chicks 5.10d ★ ☐
The second route right of the pine tree. Climb over a roof and up vertical rock to a second roof. Go slightly left over the roof and then back right to a short corner and then up to the anchor.
10 bolts.

❼ Eagle Eyes 5.12a ★★ ☐
Belay from a bolt anchor at the start of the ramp. Climb the steep face on good holds to a thin seam, fire the crux seam and then over a roof to the anchor.
10 bolts.

❽ Eagle Hardware 5.11b/c ★★★ ☐
Belay from a two-bolt anchor. Climb the obvious black streak past several bolts to a short crux and then up easier rock to the anchor.
10 bolts.

❾ Golden Eagle 5.11c/d ★★ ☐
Belay from a bolt anchor on the ramp. Gain an easy ramp and then head up the steep wall past a hard move to reach a left facing corner. Climb the corner and pass the crux to reach a short corner that leads to the anchor. See photo page 52.
10 bolts.

❿ Eagle Warrior 5.13b ★ ☐
Climb the steep wall past an unusual hold to gain a handcrack. Climb the crack and then fire the boulder problem crux to gain the anchors.
11 bolts.

⓫ Buddha Belly 5.13a ★★★★ ☐
See description opposite.

⓬ Green Panther 5.12d ★★ ☐
The right-most route bolted route on the ramp. Fire up a short face to hard moves over a series of small roofs to a short corner that leads to the anchor.

Variation: Stoner Homeland 5.13a ★★ ☐
From the fourth bolt on *Green Panther* undercling left and then up a flared seam to the anchor.
7 bolts.

⓭ Great Dihedral 5.5 ★★ ☐
Pitch 1: 3rd Class. Climb the easy ramp past the sport routes to a belay on a pedestal below the obvious large dihedral.
Pitch 2: 5.5. Climb the dihedral to a good belay ledge just left of the roof.
Pitch 3: 5.5. Continue up the dihedral to the top of the rock. Walk off to the west.
SR.

⓮ To the Sun 5.5 ★★ ☐
Pitch 1: 3rd Class. Climb the gully and belay on the pedestal for the *Great Dihedral.*
Pitch 2: 5.4. Angle right under a roof and gain a ledge with a tree and belay.
Pitch 3: 5.5. Climb straight up the buttress in a long pitch to the top.
SR.

⓯ Right Face 5.5 ★★ ☐
Pitch 1: 3rd Class. Same as #15.
Pitch 2: 5.4. Same as #15.
Pitch 3: 5.5. Move right from the belay and gain a large left-facing corner. Climb the corner to easy rock and the top.
SR.

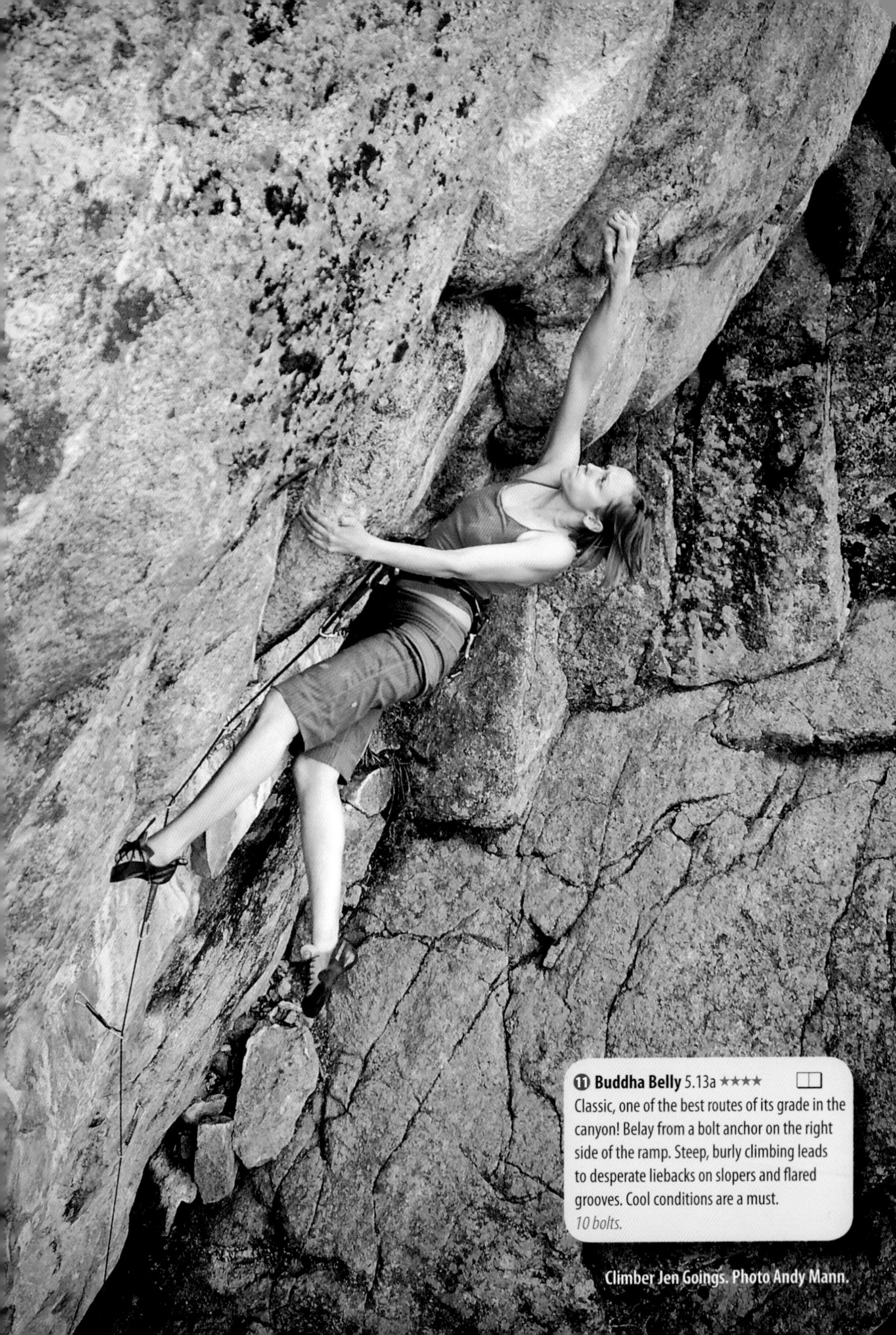

⑪ Buddha Belly 5.13a ★★★★

Classic, one of the best routes of its grade in the canyon! Belay from a bolt anchor on the right side of the ramp. Steep, burly climbing leads to desperate liebacks on slopers and flared grooves. Cool conditions are a must.

10 bolts.

Climber Jen Goings. Photo Andy Mann.

THE ARENA 6.3 miles

Approach time: 10 minutes.
Exposure: East and south.

5 routes

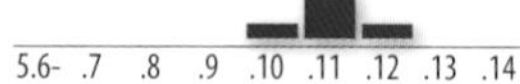

This short orange and gold wall offers several bolted routes on good in-cuts and edges. The wall sits on a steep hillside directly across from Eagle Rock and receives good mid-morning to mid-afternoon sun.

Access: Park in a pullout on the right side of the road at 6.2 miles. Walk up canyon for 100 feet and then up the steep hillside on the right to the wall.

THE ARENA

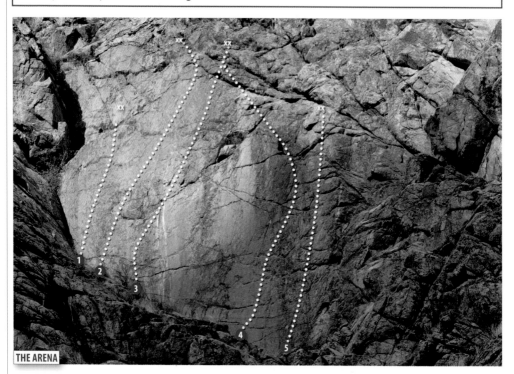

❶ **Sucker Punch** 5.11d ★ ☐
A really short route that packs a big punch. On the far left side of the wall.
2 bolts.

❷ **Standing Eight Count** 5.11c/d ★★ ☐
Start 10 feet right of *Sucker Punch*. Getting past the first bolt is the crux. Lower from a two-bolt anchor.
3 bolts.

❸ **Contender Direct** 5.11c/d ★★ ☐
Great route that takes a direct line up a steep face. Expect a hard move at the second bolt.
4 bolts.

❹ **Contender** 5.12a ★★ ☐
On the right side of the wall. Climb to the first bolt, crank the crux, pass the second bolt and trend left (green alien). Clip the third bolt and continue up left to the finish on *Contender Direct*.
6 bolts, 0.5 or 0.75 micro-cam

❺ **First Round** 5.10c ★ ☐
A good indicator for if you can at least reach the second round. Climb the steep face on the right side of the crag past three bolts. A red Camalot can be placed before reaching the anchors.
3 bolts.

ONE SHOE MAKES IT MURDER 6.4 miles

Approach time: 10 - 15 minutes.
Exposure: South.

5 routes

5.6- .7 .8 .9 .10 .11 .12 .13 .14

A fun south-facing cliff that has several good routes in a pleasant setting a short distance east of the Cob Rock parking area. There is only one pure sport route so bring a small rack if you plan on climbing several routes.

Access: Park at the Cob Rock parking area at 6.6 miles and head down canyon for 200 yards. Find a faint trail on the left (north) side of the road angling up and right to the obvious crag.

1 Russian Bride 5.11d ★★★

This is the beautiful almost-vertical slab on the left side of the cliff. Start near a tree and climb up on good holds to a tricky move past the second bolt. Reach a small ledge and fire up the slab making several tenuous moves (crux) on small holds. Reach a good hold at the sixth bolt and climb over a small roof to a ledge and the anchor.

7 bolts.

2 Dating Game 5.12b ★★

Start just left of a pine in the center of the face. Powerful moves lead up past several bolts. Tackle the overhang right of *Rockin' Horse*, then up a short groove.

6 bolts, light rack tp 2" cams.

3 Rockin' Horse 5.12a/b ★

Start as for *Pale Horse* but angle left on steep face, technical moves. Tackle the roof left of *Dating Game* and then up a short crack to the anchors.

4 bolts and gear to medium.

4 Pale Horse 5.11d

The obvious right-leaning corner on the right side of the rock. Strange climbing up the corner, trend left at the top of the corner and meet *Rockin' Horse* for the crux roof.

3 bolts, pins, gear to medium.

ONE SHOE MAKES IT MURDER

5 Blind Date 5.11a ★

This route begins on the right side of the crag. Start near a blocky corner with a bolt. Climb up the corner on good holds and go left near the third bolt into a right-facing corner. Follow the corner (small gear) to the large roof. Clip the bolt and make some cool moves over the roof. Reach a good rest and climb up on good holds to a ledge. Move left and up to the anchor.

6 bolts, gear to medium.

COB ROCK 6.6 miles

Approach time: 5 - 15 minutes.
Exposure: North, east and west.

Cob Rock is a large north-facing buttress with several classic moderate routes in a pleasant setting just above Boulder Creek. Cob Rock is a great place for aspiring trad leaders and those who are just getting into multi-pitch routes to hone their skills. From the top of the rock walk off to the west and down a steep trail along the west side of the wall back to the base. The routes on the northwest and west face start right off the descent trail. Cob Rock also has good bouldering, see page 256.

Access: Park in a pullout on the left side of the road at 6.6 miles. Locate the Tyrolean traverse just downstream, cross the creek on rocks, or wade during low water.

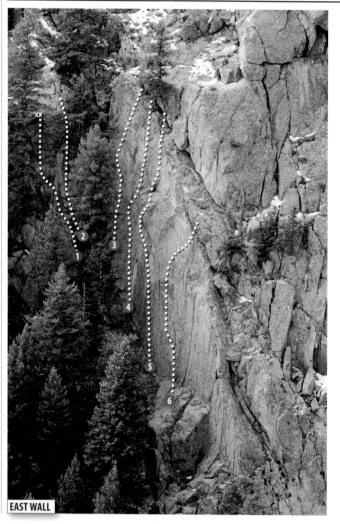

EAST WALL

EAST WALL

This seldom-visited wall is located on the upper left side of the rock on a steep hillside.

❶ **Scratch** 5.12a ★ ☐

One of the few sport routes on the wall. On the left side of north facing wall climb past four bolts to the anchor.
4 bolts.

❷ **Leave it or Lead it** 5.12b ★ ☐

A nice toprope problem right of *Scratch*. Climb the steep concave face just right of *Scratch*.

❸ **Racing the Sun** 5.11c R/X ☐

Climb parallel seams on the left side of the wall up past a lone bolt to a steep, hard-to-protect face.
Gear to 2 inches.

❹ **Devil's Dream** 5.9 ★ ☐

Climb a thin crack near the center of the wall to a bulge and then up to a tree.
Gear to 2 inches.

❺ **Body Talk** 5.9+ ★ ☐

Climb the left-angling crack to a short right-facing corner just right of *Devil's Dream* to the ledge. Walk off to the east
Gear to 2.5 inches.

❻ **Othello** 5.10b ★ ☐

Climb a left-angling crack up to a left-leaning dihedral and then right to a ledge.
Gear to 2 inches.

NORTH FACE

7 Ms. Fanny Le Pump 5.11c ★★ ☐
This and the next two routes are located just off the trail on the lower left side of the north face below the huge rock fall/scar. Climb the left of three cracks with tenuous moves up the shallow corner. Walk off to the east.
Gear to 2 inches.

8 Indistinction 5.8 ★★ ☐
Climb the center crack up a right-facing corner to lower-angle, easier climbing. Walk off to the east. Be careful of loose rock on the descent.
Gear to 2.5 inches.

9 Right Crack 5.7 ★★ ☐
Climb the crack in the short left-facing corner up to a wide crack and then the top. Be careful of loose rock on the descent.
Gear to 4 inches.

The next four routes are single-pitch lines on a short buttress at the base of the North Face Expect stout grades.

10 East Crack 5.10a/b ★★★ ☐
Pitch 1: 5.7. Climb easy rock on the right side of the lower buttress to the base of the steep wall and belay.
Pitch 2: 5.10a/b. Classic Grade Climb a shallow left-facing corner then veer left up the thin crack splitting the wall to ledge and belay.
Pitch 3: 5.7. Step slightly right and climb the corner crack to the top.
SR.

11 Night Vision 5.10b ★★ ☐
Pitch 1: 5.10a. Start left of the obvious wide crack climbing up to high bolt and then up past a second bolt to a ledge and belay.
Pitch 2: 5.10b. Climb straight to the left side of small overhang, clip fixed gear then climb just right of the arete to a belay on a large ledge.
Pitch 3: 5.7. Step slightly right and climb the corner/crack to the top.
Gear to 2.5 inches.

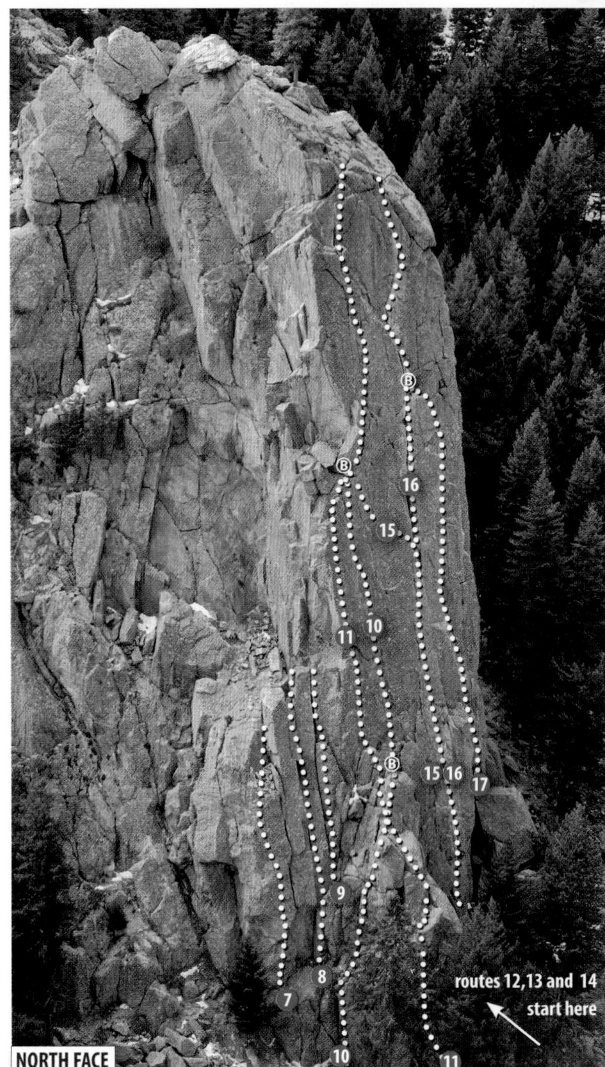

12 Huston Crack 5.9 ★★ ☐
A sandbag at 5.8, I have no problem calling this route 5.9. The obvious wide crack on the left side of the wall.
Gear to 4 inches.

13 Aid Crack 5.10d ★★ ☐
The thin crack splitting the wall. Sustained and somewhat hard to protect. A great pitch.
Gear to 2 inches.

The following routes start to the right of the short buttress at the base of the North Face.

14 Face Route 5.11 ☐
Toprope the face just right of the crack.

15 North Face Left 5.8+ ★★ ☐
Pitch 1: 5.8+. Start as for *North Face Center* and climb 50 feet to where the crack goes right, go left and climb a short face, and traverse left to a ledge and belay.
Pitch 2: 5.7. Step slightly right and climb the corner crack to the top.
SR.

COB ROCK, NORTH AND WEST FACES

16 North Face Center 5.7+ ★★★ ☐
See description opposite.

17 Empor 5.7+ ★★★ ☐
Classic, another great moderate route, start about 25 feet right of *North Face Center.*

Pitch 1: 5.7+. Climb 10 feet up a short face to the left of a huge boulder. Climb the corner and then follow a flake up to the start of large right-facing corner and belay on a nice ledge.

Pitch 2: 5.7. Climb the large right-facing corner to the base of a slot. Belay.

Pitch 3: 5.7+. Fire up the polished zig-zag hand crack to the top.

SR.

18 Northwest Corner 5.8 ★★ ☐

Pitch 1: 5.7. Start on top of the huge boulder then gain a right-facing corner. Climb the corner to a steep face, move right to the arete and belay by a small pillar.

Pitch 2: 5.8. Climb straight through a roof to the top.

SR.

WEST FACE

19 Hurley Direct 5.10a ★★ ☐
The thin crack just right of the large boulder, climb it to a ledge and finish with *Empor* or *Northwest Corner.* This was my first route in Boulder Canyon in 1974.

SR.

20 Brownies In The Basin 5.9+ ★ ☐
Once a vague trad route, someone went back and placed bolts and an anchor on the lower section of the route. Climb the steep face just right of *Hurley Direct* up past two bolts to an anchor (a lower first bolt has been chopped). You can continue up and then left to the top in a long pitch with gear.

3 bolts, gear to 2 inches.

21 West Cracks 5.9 ★★ ☐

Pitch 1: 5.9. Start right of *Brownies in the Basin* and go up a somewhat hard-to-protect crack to start and continue up for another 50 feet to a small roof, step left then up good jams to a belay at a pillar.

Pitch 2: 5.8. Climb straight up over a small roof to the top.

SR.

22 West Rib 5.8 ★★ ☐

Pitch 1: 5.7. Start near a large boulder uphill from *West Cracks,* climb the obvious crack above the boulder, move left when the crack ends and belay as for *Northwest Corner*.

Pitch 2: 5.8. Climb straight through a roof to the top.

SR.

23 West Dihedral 5.8 ★★ ☐

Pitch 1: 5.8. Hand and fist jam the obvious dihedral, belay for *Northwest Corner.*

Pitch 2: 5.8. Climb straight up through a roof to the top.

24 Thunder Road 5.12a ★★ ☐

Pitch 1: 5.3. The west face of Cob Rock is a steep gold and brown wall. *Thunder Road* fires up the center of this beautiful wall. Climb up to a large crack/corner on the left side of the west face. Belay here with gear.

Pitch 2: 5.12a. Traverse right and clip the first bolt. Crank up and clip the second bolt, make a series of weird layaways and then crank on good holds to a difficult mantel. Steep climbing veers right and then straight up on good holds to the anchor.

6 bolts and light rack to 2 inches.

25 Corn on the Cob 5.10c ★ ☐
Climb the obvious bolted route right off the descent trail on the west face.

6 bolts.

⑯ North Face Center 5.7+ ★★★

Maybe the best route on the rock. A Kor classic, enjoyable and engaging climbing for the grade.

Pitch 1: 5.7. Start between two boulders and fire up the obvious crack over a small roof to a ledge, climb to another ledge to a belay at a notch just left of the large corner.

Pitch 2: 5.7+. Climb the polished and steep zig-zag hand crack to the top. Walk off to the west.

SR.

Climber Ben Egbers. Photo James Beissel.

WALL OF VOODOO 6.7 miles

Approach time: 10 - 25 minutes.
Exposure: Southeast.

3 routes

5.6- .7 .8 .9 .10 .11 .12 .13 .14

The Wall of Voodoo is a secluded wall just below the Bitty Buttress area offering three good sport climbs on steep rock. The rock gets great morning sun - all routes on the wall face southeast.

⃠ This cliff may be closed due to raptor nesting between February and August (see page 17).

Access: Park in a pullout at 6.7 miles on the right side of the road. This is the same pullout for Blob Rock (page 59). Take the Blob Rock trail for 100 yards uphill to where the trail splits at a boulder. Take the right fork past the boulder and angle along the side of a steep hill past the Wall with Three Cracks, continue right to the Bitty Buttress area. From the downed tree at the start of the Bitty Buttress route take a trail downhill to the wall on the right.
A shorter and more direct approach to the wall is to park at 6.6 miles for Cob Rock and walk down canyon for 200 feet and take a steep gully that leads to the wall. Approach time is 10 minutes. Be careful of loose rock.

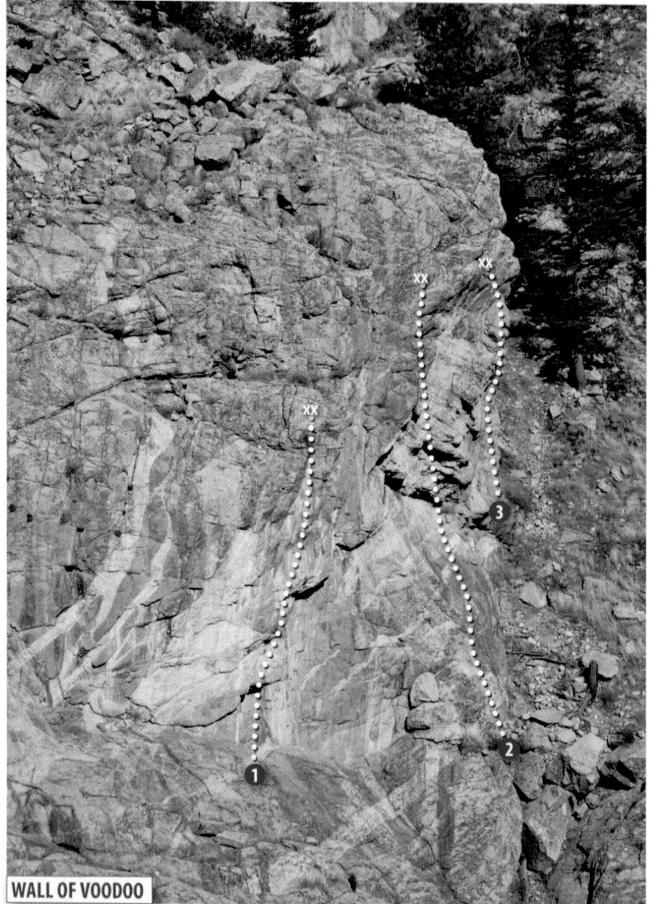

WALL OF VOODOO

❶ Voodoo Child 5.12a/b ★★ ☐☐
Scramble up a short 3rd Class ramp to reach the start. Climb the steep face on the left side of the wall. Steep and deceiving; save some ammunition for the top.
9 bolts.

❷ Porch Monkey 5.12b/c ★★★ ☐☐
Climb a nice face on jugs to below a roof. Crank the roof and then continue up the wall on steep rock to the anchor.
8 bolts.

❸ Suffering Succotash 5.11d ★★ ☐☐
The obvious line up the corner on the right side of the wall. The crux is near the top over a small roof.
6 bolts.

Sheyna Button on *Golden Eagle* 5.11c, Eagle Rock, page 43. Photo Andy Mann.

BITTY & PEAPOD BUTTRESSES 6.7 miles

Approach time: 15 - 25 minutes.
Exposure: South.

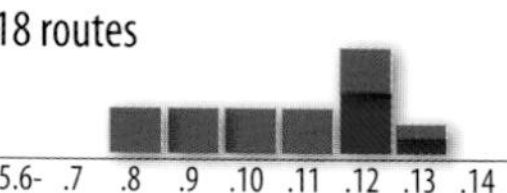

The Bitty and Peapod Buttresses offer great climbs in a remote area just right (east) of the Main Blob Rock area. The routes vary from steep faces, to technical slabs, cracks, and severely overhanging sport routes. A great place to get away from the crowds.

⊘ This cliff may be closed due to raptor nesting between February and August (see page 17).

Access: Park in a pullout at 6.7 miles on the right side of the road. This is the same pullout for Blob Rock. Take the Blob Rock trail for 100 yards uphill to where the trail splits at a boulder. Take the right fork past the boulder and angle along the side of steep hill up to the base of Wall with Three Cracks (page 58). Continue east and then up to the base of the wall.

PEAPOD BUTTRESS

❶ Treetop Landing 5.9 ★ ☐
On the left side of the wall climb a short face to a thin crack, then angle right at the top of the crack to the top.
Gear to 2 inches.

❷ Razor Hein Stick 5.12c ★★ ☐
Climb a thin, short corner (RP's) up to the first bolt. Make several hard moves getting past the next two bolts. Angle right at the fourth bolt and then up a short crack to a two-bolt anchor.
4 bolts, RPs and few small cams.
Variation: Palm Saturday 5.12b/c ☐
Top rope the face just left of *Razor Hein Stick* and join it at the fourth bolt.

❸ Peapod 5.11c ★★★ ☐
The obvious flaring crack up a slot. Looks easy, but… Turn the roof on the right then up a nice crack to the top, or stop at the anchor on the left.
Variation: Split Pea 5.11d ☐
Go left at the roof, laybacking past a pin and bolt to the finish for *Razor Hein Stick*.
Gear to 2 inches.

❹ Holy Ascension 5.13a ★ ☐
The thin seam just right of *Peapod*. Thin laybacks and thin jams will get you to a good rest about 25 feet up. Follow nice cracks to the top.
Toprope.

❺ The Hand is Quicker Than the Eye 5.11b/c ★★ ☐
Start as for Jaguary, then trend left past two bolts. Climb up steep cracks to the top.
Gear to 2 inches.

❻ Jaguary 5.11a ★★ ☐
The left of three cracks on the right side of the wall. Tricky start leads to better gear and the crux. Follow a nice crack past the crux to the top.
Gear to 2 inches.

❼ Left Crack 5.9+ ★★ ☐
The nice middle crack with good hand jams.
Gear to 2.5 inches.

❽ Right Crack 5.10a/b ★★ ☐
The right most crack on the right side of the wall. Nice route with good protection.
Gear to 2.5 inches.

❾ Welcome Home 5.12a/b ★ ☐
A bizarre little route that looks way easier than it is. Down and right of *Right Crack* is a short east-facing wall. Climb it.
3 bolts.

❿ Electricity 5.12a ★ ☐
Pitch 1: 5.12a. Climb a dirty 4th Class corner just right of *Welcome Home*, aiming for a crack on the left wall around the level of the *Welcome Home* anchor. Step left and up, climbing a steep wall into a short, thin corner, which leads to the anchor.
Pitch 2: 5.11a. Step right from the belay and clip a bolt, gain a thin crack in a dihedral and climb it to the top.
12 quickdraws and gear to 3.5 inches.

BITTY BUTTRESS MAIN WALL

The main area of Bitty Buttress starts just right of Electricity in a large corner and most of the easier trad routes follow a series of right-facing corners.

⓫ A Day at the Crags 5.8 ☐
More like a day of gardening.
Pitch 1: 5.7. Start as for *Electricity*, but continue up the dirty corner to a large ledge and belay.
Pitch 2: 5.8. Climb a flake above the belay and then veer left on a ramp to a big ledge. Walk off to the west.
SR.

⓬ A's Jax 5.8 ★ ☐
Pitch 1: 5.8. Start in the right-facing orange corner just left of a slab with bolts. Climb the corner through bushes into a wide section and reach a large ledge.
Pitch 2: 5.7. Follow a short face to a right facing corner. Continue up the corner, bypassing a large roof system on the left to a large ledge. This is the second pitch of *South*. Walk off to the west.
Gear to 4 inches.

⓭ Return To Sender 5.12a/b ★★★ ☐

A gem in the rough.

Pitch 1: 5.11a. Climb the nice slab just right of *A's Jax*. Veer left to the corner then rail out left (hard move) to a stance below a slab. Climb the nice slab to the anchor.

Pitch 2: 5.12a/b. Move left and climb the steep, obvious east-facing gold wall past several hard moves to the anchor.

12 quickdraws.

⓮ South 5.8 ★ ☐

Pitch 1: 5.8. Start in the dirty right-facing corner just right of *Return to Sender*. Grovel through bushes and some lichen and veer left to the upper section of *A's Jax*.

Pitch 2: 5.7. Follow a short face to a right-facing corner. Continue up the corner bypassing a large roof system on the left to a large ledge. Walk off to the west.

Gear to 4 inches.

⓯ Bitty Buttress 5.9- ★★★★ ☐

A classic and one of the best routes in the canyon at the grade. Excellent rock, good protection, and great position make for a wonderful outing.

Pitch 1: 5.8+. Start at a dead pine lying at the base of the wall. Climb up shallow cracks following the obvious line to a good ledge, then climb up and right to a better ledge below a small roof.

Pitch 2: 5.8. Climb over the roof, then up a shallow corner, trend a little left and then climb a flake/crack to a good ledge with a small juniper tree.

Pitch 3: 5.9-. Climb up and a little left to a crack. Reach left to a flake and then head up a crack making a weird move left to a good hold, then veer left to a good ledge. One can also climb a short roof (5.8) just before the traverse to the belay. Walk off to the west.

SR.

Variation 1: Rob's Way 5.9 R/X ☐

Climb the faint crack just left of the first pitch, meeting the normal route about 100 feet up.

Variation 2: Orange Dihedral 5.8 ☐

Climb the dirty corner to the right of the normal start passing an old bolt, then veer left into the normal route about 70 feet up.

PEAPOD BUTTRESS

BITTY BUTTRESS MAIN WALL

BITTY BUTTRESS, THE AMPHITHEATRE

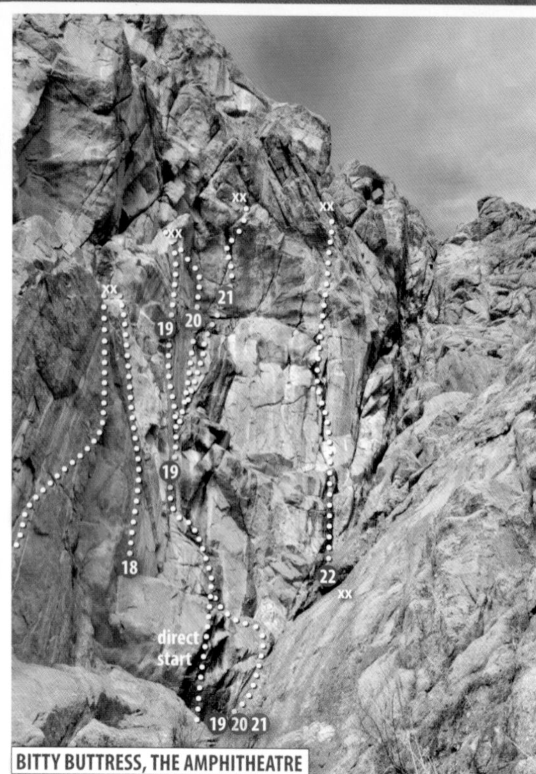

BITTY BUTTRESS, THE AMPHITHEATRE

BITTY BUTTRESS/ THE AMPHITHEATRE

To reach the Amphitheatre, go right and up a short hill past the Bitty Buttress, the first route you reach is The Buzz on the left side of the obvious orange wall.

⑯ The Buzz 5.12d ★★★ ☐

Classic and steeper than it looks. Climb the left side of the obvious orange wall working a thin seam past hard underclings and small crimps to a short arete and the anchor.
8 bolts.

⑰ The Spins 5.12c ★★ ☐

Climb the obvious crack right of *The Buzz*. At the top of the crack veer right and clip the first bolt and then up and right toward the arete with a hard move gaining the arete proper.
5 bolts, gear to 2 inches..

Variation: 5.14? ☐

Instead of going right at the cracks end, continue up the steep holdless face to the anchor.

⑱ The Jitters 5.12c ★★ ☐

Start right of the wide crack/chimney on the right side of the orange wall, make a hard move to gain a ledge, then climb up the steep face to gain another ledge and then past two bolts to the anchor.
8 bolts.

⑲ Rise and Shine 5.12a ★★★ ☐

Another classic – steeper than it looks. Start on the left side of a steep overhanging striped wall. Climb up blocky rock to reach a short left-facing corner. Climb the corner to a ledge and then fire up the steep face to the anchors. Expect a hard move getting off the ledge.

Direct Start: 5.13a/b? ☐

Just left of the normal start is a short wall with two bolts.
12 bolts.

⑳ Reveille 5.10d ★★ ☐

Climb *Rise and Shine* to the fifth bolt, then veer right into a corner. Follow the corner up to the anchor on *Rise and Shine*.
5 bolts, gear to 3 inches.

㉑ The Aid Roof 5.10 A3 ☐

Climb *Rise and Shine* to the fifth bolt, step right, then up the corner for *Reveille*. Step right, then aid up the large roof to the anchors.
5 bolts, gear to 3 inches.

㉒ The Lorax 5.13b ★★★★ ☐

See description opposite.

㉒ The Lorax 5.13b ★★★★

One of the steeper routes in the canyon. On the far right side of the wall, scramble up to a one bolt anchor. Step left and clip a bolt, reach a ledge and clip the second bolt, unclip the first bolts and fire up the thin flaring crack via laybacks, crimps and flaring jams to below a roof. Crank the roof and then reach the anchors.

10 bolts.

Climber Justen Sjong. Photo Dan Hare.

WALL WITH THREE CRACKS 6.7 miles

Approach time: 15 - 20 minutes.
Exposure: South.

4 routes

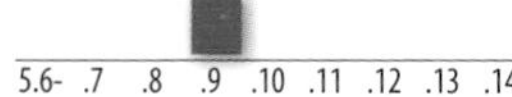

A short south-facing wall that offers a few nice lines in a nice setting high above canyon.

⊘ This cliff may be closed due to raptor nesting between February and August (see page 17).

Access: Park in a pullout at 6.7 miles on the right side of the road. This is the same pullout for Blob Rock (page 59). Take the Blob Rock trail for 100 yards uphill to where the trail splits at a boulder. Take the right fork past the boulder and angle along the side of a steep hill up to the base of the rock.

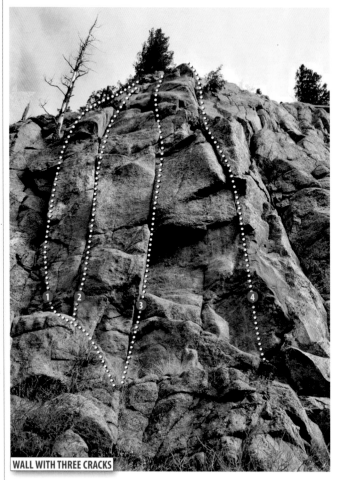

WALL WITH THREE CRACKS

1 Far Left 5.9 ★ ☐
Climb the left-most crack that is just right of a dead tree about 40 feet up.
Gear to 2.5 inches.

2 Catalyst 5.9+ ★★ ☐
The nice finger crack on the left side of the wall.
Gear to 2 inches.

3 Hesitation 5.9+ ★ ☐
The middle of the three cracks. Nice climbing.
Gear to 2 inches.

4 Mirage 5.9 ★ ☐
The right of the three cracks.
Gear to 3.5 inches.

BLOB ROCK 6.7 miles

Approach time: 10 - 20 minutes.
Exposure: South, east and west.

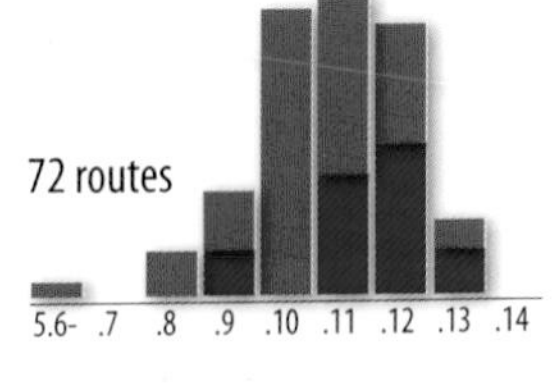

This large, complex rock offers some of the best routes in Boulder Canyon on excellent granite with great views up and down Boulder Canyon. The area is broken into six different areas - Little Blob, West Blob, Central Area, Gully Area, Lower Slab and East Blob.

⃠ This cliff may be closed due to raptor nesting between February and August (see page 17).

Access: Park in a pullout on the right side of the road at 6.7 miles. Walk up the hill to the rock.

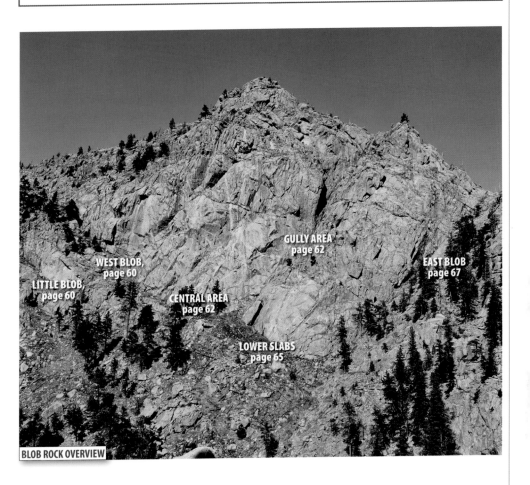

GULLY AREA page 62
WEST BLOB, page 60
EAST BLOB page 67
LITTLE BLOB, page 60
CENTRAL AREA page 62
LOWER SLABS page 65

BLOB ROCK OVERVIEW

LITTLE BLOB

Once at the main Blob Rock go left and down to this short piece of granite right below the *Divine Wind* dihedral.

❶ Two Minute Warning 5.11c/d ★ ☐
Climb a short slab on the left side of the wall up and over a small roof to the anchor.
5 bolts.

❷ Lost and Found 5.12a ★★ ☐
Climb a short corner up to a steep slab. Reach a flake and then a hard move getting over a roof to reach a short corner and the anchors.
7 bolts.

❸ Take Five 5.12a ★★ ☐
Climb the arete on the right side of the wall with a tricky clip at the third bolt.
5 bolts.

❹ Slow Death 5.11a/b ★★ ☐
Climb up an unprotected slab to gain a crack in a roof. Veer left at the roof and then to the top or over to the anchor for *Take Five*.
Gear to 2 inches.

WEST BLOB

Once at the main Blob area go left and up past the obvious dihedral system of *Divine Wind* to reach the following routes.

❺ The Far Side 5.11d ★★ ☐
As the name suggests, this route is about as far west on Blob Rock that you can go. Climb a short gold face up to a black streak and the anchors.
5 bolts.

❻ Tears of a Clown 5.12d ★ ☐
Climb the thin steep face just right of *The Far Side* with the crux coming just before the anchor.
5 bolts.

❼ Comedy Works 5.11a ★ ☐
Climb blocky rock right of *The Far Side* and *Tears of a Clown* to the upper face of *True Comedian*.
6 bolts.

❽ True Comedian 5.12b ★ ☐
Climb a difficult slab past bolts to gain a ledge. Go left on the ledge to easier climbing that leads to the anchor.
7 bolts.

❾ Night Stalker 5.9 ★★ ☐
Climb the obvious left-facing corner on the left side of the huge roof past a thin section into a wide fist crack near the top. Rap from an anchor or walk off to the west.
Gear to 4 inches.

❿ Nightwind 5.12b ★ ☐
Climb *Night Stalker* for 25 feet, move right to gain a flake and bolts, and then up the arete to the anchors.
2 bolts, gear to 3 inches.

⓫ Wind Walker 5.12d ★ ☐
Climb the left side of the huge roof system via small holds to a steep face and the anchor.
7 bolts. An open project continues above the anchor.

⓬ Bad Girls Dream 5.10a ★ ☐
Climb the large flake out the middle of the roof system making a hard move to gain the face.
2 bolts, light rack to 1 inch.

⓭ Divine Intervention 5.12a/b ★ ☐
Climb the first 30 feet of *Divine Wind*, then veer left to clip a bolt and gain the face that leads to the arete and the anchor for *Divine Wind*.
7 bolts.

⓮ Divine Wind 5.11b ★★★ ☐
Pitch 1: 5.11a/b. Climb a short crack and gain the obvious right-facing corner. Stemming moves get you to a strange crux move left to the arete then up to the anchor.
Pitch 2: 5.11b. Hard, unprotected moves up a corner get you to a ledge and gear; easier climbing gets you to the top. Walk off to the west.

Variation:

Avoiding Wounded Knee 5.11b

Step right from the belay on the first pitch of *Divine Wind* and gain a right-facing corner. Stem the corner then reach an easy slab to anchors on the right. Rap or walk off to the west.

Gear to 2 inches.

15 Wild Cat 5.11a ★★

Just right of *Divine Wind* is a short bolted line. Climb nice steep rock to a two-bolt anchor. An open project second pitch has yet to redpointed.

4 bolts, couple of medium stoppers for the start.

16 Wounded Knee 5.11b ★★

More like wounded hands for the crux roof.

Pitch 1: 5.11a. Climb *Wild Cat* to the anchor or start with *Bearcat Goes to Hollywood*, climbing to the second bolt and moving left to the *Wild Cat* anchor.

Pitch 2: 5.10d. Climb a crack in a right-facing corner to a ledge (*Divine Wind*). Continue up the crack/corner, moving right to the anchor for Bearcat below the roof.

Pitch 3: Jam out the roof and gain easier climbing that leads to the top. Walk off to the west.

7 quickdraws and gear to 3.5 inches.

17 Bearcat Goes to Hollywood 5.12a/b ★★★★

Classic slab climbing...one of the top five slab routes in the canyon. Start right of *Wild Cat*, climbing easy rock up shallow corners to reach the first bolt. Follow the line of bolts up the steep slab to a difficult move before the anchor. *Bearcat* was Mark Rolofson's old house cat. One may also climb *Wild Cat* and move right from the anchor to make this a pure sport route.

9 bolts and light rack to 2 inches.

18 Central Chimney 5.6

This is the large chimney system that splits West Blob from the Central Blob. Climb the chimney in three pitches to top. Good belays and gear are found on this moderate route.

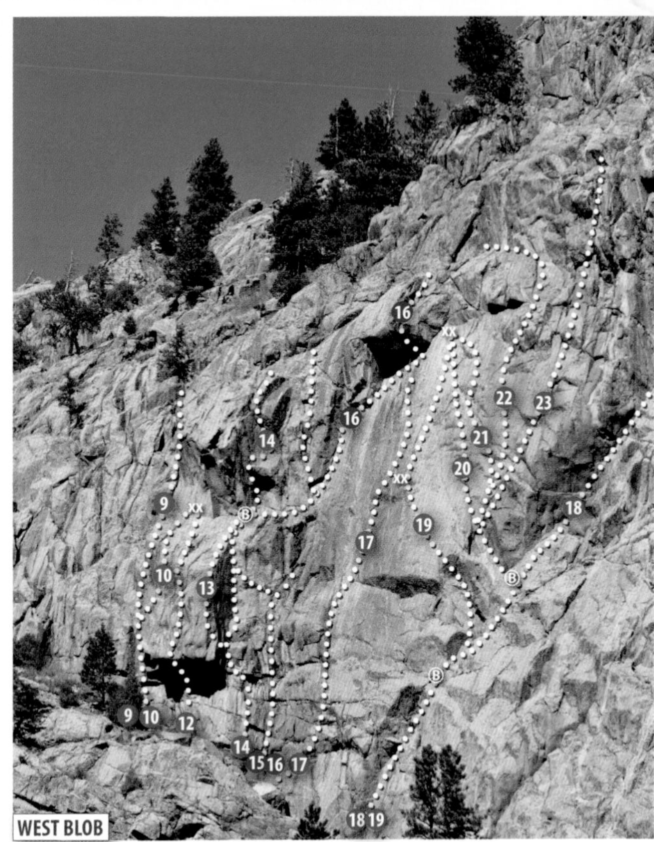

19 Radlands of Infinity 5.13a ★★★

Classic and a must do for the slab meister.

Pitch 1: 5.13a. Start up *Central Chimney*, then veer left into a short corner leading to a roof. Climb the left side of the roof to gain the slab and then left on tenuous slab moves to the anchor.

Pitch 2: 5.12a/b. Climb a thin seam up the steep slab to a two-bolt anchor.

9 quickdraws and rack to 2.5 inches.

The next four routes all share a common start.

20 Silent Running 5.11a/b R+ ★

A long and serious pitch. Start off a huge flake about 60 feet up *Central Chimney*. Climb over a roof and then up and left following shallow grooves to a flake. Climb the flake and then move left to the anchor for the second pitch of *Radlands*.

Gear to 3.5 inches.

21 Kamikaze 5.10c ★

Start as for *Silent Running* and get established over the roof. Make a move right and then gain a left-leaning dyke. Climb the dyke to a short left-facing corner, climb the corner, then follow the ramp left to the upper anchor on *Radlands*.

Gear to 3.5 inches.

22 Gathering Storm 5.10c R+ ★

Climb *Kamikaze* to the dyke. Gain a shallow left-facing corner and then climb left and follow shallow cracks to the top.

Gear to 3.5 inches.

23 Tempest 5.10c/d ★★

Climb the roof and then angle right, following a ramp that leads to crack/corner system. Follow the crack to the top.

Gear to 3.5 inches.

CENTRAL AREA/MAIN WALL

24 Cold Fusion 5.10b ★ ☐

Climb the crack/face just right of Central Gully to a bolted anchor.

2 bolts, 0.5 and 0.75 micro-cams.

25 Under the Eagle's Wing 5.12b ☐

Pitch 1: 5.9. Start right of a large boulder and climb a right-facing corner to a good belay below two right-facing corners.

Pitch 2: 5.10d. Climb the right corner and make a hard move past a bolt to gain the Central Gully and move up and right to belay below three cracks.

Pitch 3: 5.12b. Climb the middle crack past three bolts to gain a corner and then the top.

Gear to 3.5 inches.

Descent: Rap or walk off to the west.

Variation: Erickson Crack 5.10b/c ☐

Climb the left of the three cracks from the third belay. A difficult start leads to good jams and the anchor on the right.

Variation: One Way Out 5.10c/d ☐

Climb the right of the three cracks from the third belay.

26 Charisma 5.11a/b ★★ ☐

Pitch 1: 5.10a. Climb a small roof past two bolts to gain a dyke and the arête. Climb the tricky arete and then up shallow cracks to a small roof. Turn the roof on the left past a bolt and then up to a ledge with anchors.

Pitch 2: 5.9+. Climb up a short crack and then move left to a left-facing corner. Follow the corner to the Central Gully to a two-bolt belay.

Pitch 3: 5.11a/b. Climb the obvious, well-bolted corner to the anchor.

10 quickdraws, gear to 2.5 inches.

27 On Ballet 5.9 ★★★ ☐

A really nice route that climbs moderate terrain to gain the summit of Blob Rock.

Pitch 1: 5.9. Climb a long right-facing corner just right of *Charisma* to the bolted belay.

Pitch 2: 5.9. Move right from the belay and then gain a left-facing corner that leads to a short face and then the *Central Gully.*

Pitch 3: 5.7. Climb a nice crack in the face just right of the finish for *Central Gully*.

Gear to 3 inches.

28 The Throne Crack 5.13b/c ★★★ ☐

Access the route by climbing the *Central Chimney* or *On Ballet* to the start of the third pitch of *On Ballet*. Climb the obvious overhanging crack on the southeast wall. The crux is getting past the face/seam to gain the thin finger and hands crack.

2 bolts, gear to 2 inches.

29 The Reamer 5.11c/d R ★ ☐

Start just right of where the approach trail meets the wall.

Pitch 1: 5.7. Climb easy ramps up to a block and belay below an orange overhanging wall.

Pitch 2: 5.11c/d. Go left from the belay and gain a spike of rock. Stand on the spike, place gear, and then climb the overhanging face to easier slab climbing and a ledge below the *Throne Crack*.

Pitch 3: 5.7. Finish with the third pitch of On Ballet.

SR.

30 Lichen to Like 5.10d R ★★ ☐

Start just right of where the approach trail meets the wall. Photo page 66.

Pitch 1: 5.7. Climb easy ramps up to a block and belay below an orange overhanging wall.

Pitch 2: 5.10d R. Climb up from the belay and tackle the overhang wall via a leftward traverse on flakes that leads to a slab and easier climbing.

Pitch 3: 5.7. Finish with the third pitch of *On Ballet.*

SR.

31 Shimmer 5.9 ★ ☐

Start right of *Lichen to Like* climbing a short face that leads to a high first bolt. Clip the bolt, then veer left to below a small roof. Go right over the roof and then up easier rock to the anchor.

4 bolts, gear to 1 inch.

32 Slimmer 5.10a/b R ★ ☐

Climb shallow cracks/seams just right of *Shimmer* to a roof. Tackle the roof with bad gear and then easier climbing to the anchor on *Shimmer*.

Gear to 1 inch.

33 Simmer 5.8+ ☐

Climb shallow cracks just left of *Bolt Cola* to a roof with a bolt. Fire the roof on good holds and then up and left to the anchor for *Slimmer*.

4 bolts, light rack to 1 inch.

34 Astrophysics 5.12a/b ★★ ☐

Pitch 1: 5.10a/b. Start just left of *Bolt Cola* and climb a shallow crack to a left-facing corner. Climb the corner then move right to the anchor for *Bolt Cola*.

Pitch 2: 5.9+. Climb straight up from the anchor past an old bolt and pin to gain a ledge with a large right-facing corner just left of an orange streak and at a huge eagle's nest.

Pitch 3: 5.12a/b. Climb the corner past bolts and then veer left up a left-facing corner to the top.

SR.

35 Bolt Cola 5.9+ ★★ ☐

A nice bolted pitch that climbs bulletproof granite. Start off a flake and climb shallow corners up to a good ledge. Move right to gain a dyke and then up a crack to the anchor.

7 bolts and a medium piece for the crack.

36 Get Shorty 5.10a/b ★ ☐

Start 15 feet right of *Bolt Cola*. Climb up a nice clean section of rock past two bolts. Angle up and slightly right to a horizontal crack. Climb up past a small, short left-facing corner, passing two bolts to a good ledge. Angle up and a little right to some short corners, clip a high bolt a step left onto a slab. Continue straight up past three more bolts to the anchor.

8 bolts and few small pieces.

xx
29
25
28
B
34
B eagle's nest
30
29
B
B
xx
43
44
45
B
xx
large ledge
46
47
xx
xx
xx
39
40
42
41
xx
38
xx
37
31
32
33
34
35
36
29
30
53
54
55
56
57
58
xx59
BLOB ROCK CENTRAL AREA

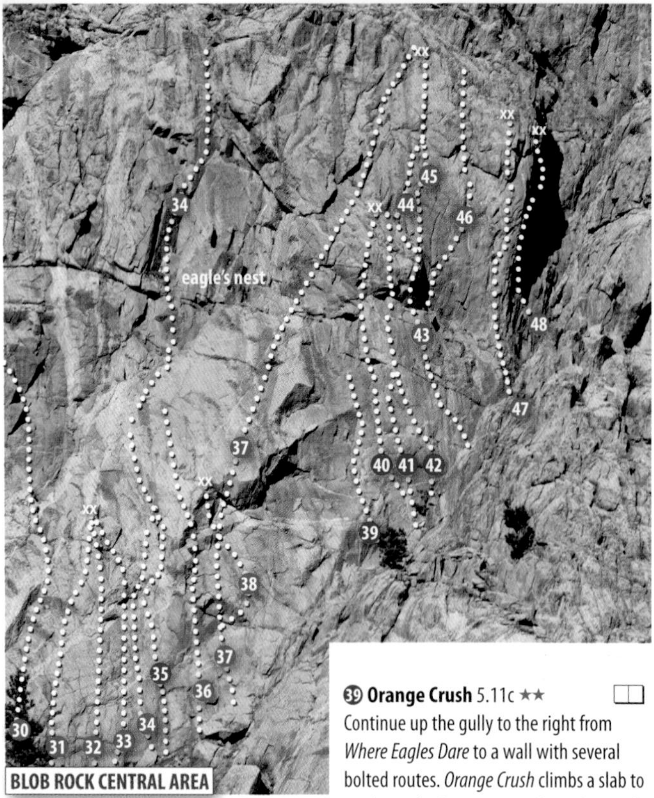

BLOB ROCK CENTRAL AREA

37 Where Eagles Dare 5.10b R ★★★

A great route that zig-zags to the summit.

Pitch 1: 5.10b. Climb a slab up to a small tiered roof, then through a V-shaped roof/corner to a bolted belay.

Pitch 2: 5.8+. From the belay, angle up and right along a thin right-facing corner to a belay.

Pitch 3: 5.9+. Step right and climb a right-facing flake to a crack and then the belay.

Pitch 4: 5.9-. Climb a short face to reach a corner/crack. Follow the crack up to where it turns wide at the top. Walk off to the west.

Gear to 3.5 inches.

38 Orange Corner 5.8 R ★

Climb the first 40 feet of #37 but veer right on thin edges to approach the thin namesake corner. Traverse 10 feet right under an overhang, up a little, then back left into the corner. Climb it to its top, mantel, and ascend 15 feet to a two-bolt anchor.

Nuts and cams to 2 inches.

39 Orange Crush 5.11c ★★

Continue up the gully to the right from *Where Eagles Dare* to a wall with several bolted routes. *Orange Crush* climbs a slab to reach a right-facing corner through a small roof to the anchor.

9 bolts.

40 Respite 5.11d/12a ★★

Start right of *Orange Crush*, clipping the first three bolts on *Jolt Cola*. Stem left into a weird corner, then over a small bulge to a stance at two bolts. Continue up the steep face past several bolts to an anchor on the top pitch of *Where Eagle Dare*. Rap 100 feet to descend.

14 bolts.

41 Jolt Cola 5.12a ★★★★

Classic.

Pitch 1: 5.12a. A great pitch with continuous climbing. Start as for *Respite*, then go up and right, making difficult moves to gain thin seams, follow them to an anchor.

Pitch 2: 5.12a. Continue straight up from the anchor over an overhang and then reach a thin crack that leads to a ledge and the anchor. Can be done in a long pitch.

12 bolts.

42 Ginseng Rush 5.12a ★★

Start up the gully just before a boulder. Climb a left-facing corner to steep face, veer left to the first anchor on *Jolt Cola*.

6 bolts.

43 Little Juke 5.10a/b ★

Continue up the gully past a boulder and locate a lone bolt on the left. Climb past the bolt and then gain a ledge and crack. Follow the crack up to a large ledge and belay. Walk off to the right.

Gear to two inches.

44 Decade Dance 5.11a/b ★★

Continue up the gully and then traverse left on a large ledge to the base of a corner. The next three routes start from this belay.

Pitch 1: 5.9. Climb a short corner and reach a ledge and bolted anchor.

Pitch 2: 5.11a/b. Climb the left of two cracks. It starts hands and then thins down. Step right to a short corner on *Aging Time* before struggling to the anchor. Rap to the ledge.

SR.

45 Aging Time 5.11b/c ★★★

Pitch 1: 5.9. Climb a short corner and reach a ledge and bolted anchor.

Pitch 2: 5.11b/c. Climb the right of two cracks. Hands quickly turns to a thin seam and the crux. Gain a short, difficult corner and then move slightly right at the top and back left to reach the anchor.

SR.

46 Limits of Power 5.12b R ★★

Spectacular and bold. From the belay, go right and up, making a strange mantel move to gain a ledge and thin seam. Climb the seam with increasing difficulty and then move left over a small roof and easier climbing to the top. Traverse left to rap anchor.

SR.

47 Vasodilator 5.13a ★★★★

Classic climbing and the benchmark for .13a in the canyon. Start on the right side of the traverse ledge and power up the face to a blunt arête, moving left to the anchor.

11 bolts.

48 Hypertension 5.12b R ★★ ☐
Climb up the gully past *Vasodilator* to this steep route that climbs the right side of the prow. Climb into a corner and past a tricky crux move at the top to gain the anchor.
8 bolts.

To reach the next five climbs continue up the gully past a huge chockstone (squeeze under it) and reach a small ledge. The climb Erki Nool has a bolted belay anchor at its base.

49 Perspective 5.10b/c ★★ ☐
Start left of *Erki Nool* and climb a crack through a short roof and into a corner that leads to the top. Walk off to the east and then down the gully back to the base.
Gear to 2.5 inches.

50 Erki Nool 5.11d ★★★ ☐
From the bolted anchor on the ledge, climb the spectacular orange wall up past several bolts on good incuts to the anchor.
8 bolts.

BLOB ROCK CENTRAL AREA

51 Extreme 5.11d ★★ ☐
Climb the left of two thin cracks on the right side of the ledge. Thin gear at the start leads to a hard move and then easier climbing moving right near the top to *Conan*.
Gear to 2 inches.

52 Conan 5.11d ★★★ ☐
Climb the thin crack just right of *Extreme. Continuous* with quite the pump. Great route.
Gear to 2 inches.

53 Devil's Rain 5.10c/d ★ ☐
Climb the thin flake/crack just right of *Conan* through orange lichen. Gain a ledge and move up and left to *Conan's* anchor.
Gear to 2 inches.

LOWER SLAB

To reach the lower slab hike east and slightly downhill from the main Blob area to this nice piece of granite. See photo on page 59.

54 Left Roof 5.8 R ★ ☐
Start just right of a huge boulder and climb the slab up to and over a small roof. Walk off to the west or use the anchor on the right.
Gear to 1.5 inches.

55 The Old Route 5.8 R ★ ☐
Start just right of *Left Roof* and gain a short corner. Climb the corner, turning a small roof on the right, then up the slab to the ledge. Walk off to the west or use the 2-bolt anchor.
Gear to 1.5 inches.

56 A Hike with Ludwig Dude 5.10a R ★★ ☐
Climb a short face to gain a short corner about 10 feet up. Place gear and then move up and right to a dyke (aim for a bolt), and then up the easier climbing to the anchor.
1 bolt, gear to 1 inch.

57 Out of Limits 5.10b/c R/X ★★ ☐
Start right of *Ludwig Dude* near the low point of the slab. Climb a thin seam/crease up to a small roof and then up through a black streak to the anchor. A smart climber would traverse left to the bolt on *Ludwig Dude* to finish the route.
Gear to 1 inch.

58 Crack Tack R 5.10a ★★ ☐
Start as for *Out of Limits* but angle up and right to a bolt and make a hard move to gain a small ledge. Move left and then up discontinuous cracks to the anchor. One can start on the right and climb a left-leaning crack to gain the bolt to lower the grade and increase the safety factor.
1 bolt, gear to 1.5 inches.

59 Of Human Bondage 5.10a/b R+ ★★ ☐
Start as for *Crack Tack* and then right from the first bolt up a blank face aiming for a second bolt. Continue straight up past the bolt and then slightly right to a third bolt that protects a hard move to gain the ledge.
3 bolts, gear to 2 inches.

60 A Hike For Y2K 5.11c ★★ ☐
A great route and a pleasant outing compared to the other run-out routes on the wall. Climb a short gully to gain a bolted belay right of *Crack Tack*. From the belay, climb the obvious bolted slab over a bulge to easier climbing above that leads to the anchor.
7 bolts.

The late great Derek Hersey ropeless on *Lichen to Like* 5.10d R, Blob Rock, page 62.
Photo: Dan Hare.

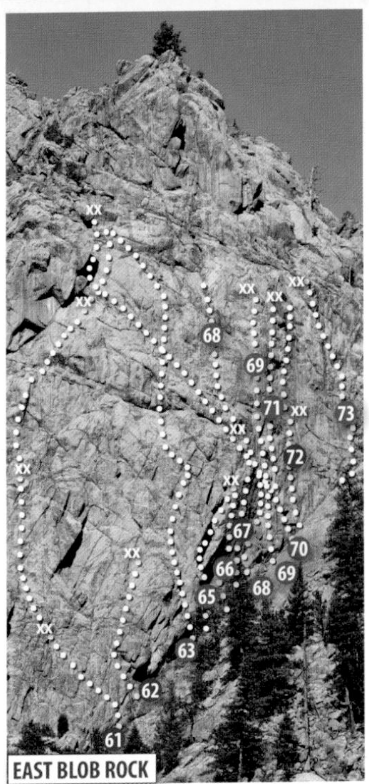

EAST BLOB

From the lower slab, continue east and then up a gully on the left that leads to the following routes.

61 The Young and the Rackless 5.9+ ★★★ ☐
Popular, and for good reason. One of the best moderate multi-pitch sport routes in the canyon. This route start about 100 feet up the gully just left of dead pine tree.
Pitch 1: 5.9+. Climb a right-angling seam and then veer to the left and up a short slab to the anchor.
Pitch 2: 5.9+. Climb cracks up to a steep face and then reach the anchor.
Pitch 3: 5.9+. Climb a bolted hand crack on the right or take the left line up past bolts that lead to a short arête. Gain a ledge and make tricky moves out a small roof to reach the anchor.
Pitch 4: 5.9. Step right from the anchor and then climb up the nice slab to anchors.
Descent: Rap the route or walk off to the east.
14 quickdraws.

62 DH 1 5.9+ R ★ ☐
Start right of the *Young and the Rackless*. Climb a steep face past three bolts and then up and right to the anchor.
3 bolts, light rack to 1 inch.

63 Gray Elk's Big Rack 5.11a ★ ☐
Pitch 1: 5.10a/b. Start uphill from the *Young and the Rackless* and climb a short, steep overhanging wall that leads to an angling crack. Climb the crack to the anchor.
Pitch 2: 5.9. Climb right past a bolt and then up a corner to the anchor. Watch for a loose block on the right.
Pitch 3: 5.11a. Climb over a small roof and gain a crack. Continue up to a ledge and the anchor. One can easily avoid the crux move at the overhang by stepping right and then back left.
Pitch 4: 5.11a. A short, steep face leads to a big ledge and then easier climbing to the anchor for the *Young and the Rackless*. Rap or walk off to the east.
6 quickdraws and gear to 3 inches.

64 Blind Trust 5.10c R ★ ☐
Climb a short, steep wall past two bolts to gain a right-leaning corner. Climb the tricky corner and then go left to the anchor for *Gray Elk's Big Rack*.
3 bolt, gear to 1.5 inches.

65 Nighthawk 5.10a/b ★ ☐
Climb the obvious wide, dark crack just uphill from *Blind Trust* to the anchor for *Mile High Comic Crack*. Dirty.
Gear to 4 inches.

66 Mile High Comic Crack 5.12a ★★★ ☐
Depending on your pain threshold and finger size, this route could be easy or hard for the grade. Climb the thin crack just right of *Nighthawk*. After 20 feet the crack becomes handsize and easier. Rap from the anchor.*Gear to 2.5 inches.*

67 The Enlightment 5.13b ★★ ☐
Climb the severely overhanging wall just right of *Mile High Comic Crack*. Technical and devious.
8 bolts.

68 Shock Therapy 5.12a/b ★ ☐
Pitch 1: 5.12a/b. Climb a short corner that leads to a left-angling flaring crack. Climb the crack past a bolt to a good ledge and the anchor.
Pitch 2: 5.11c. Climb straight up over a small roof and then reach a bolt. Continue up the face to reach a second bolt and the anchor.
6 quickdraws and gear 2.5 inches.

69 Schizofrantic 5.11b ★★ ☐
Climb a face past two bolts and then reach a right-angling seam. Follow the seam past two bolts and then gain a ledge, move right and then back left up a short corner that gains a large ledge and optional anchors. Climb past the anchors and then up the face past bolts to the higher anchors.
10 bolts, light rack 2.5 inches.

70 Saturday Treat 5.9- ★ ☐
Climb the handcrack just left *The Ticket*. Angle left to a good ledge and then follow the path of least resistance to top.
Gear to 3 inches.

71 Vicious Rumors 5.11b/c ★ ☐
Start for *Saturday Treat* and then go right to the first bolt. Climb the steep face past bolts to gain a ledge, then climb the obvious handcrack and a steep short face to reach the anchors.
6 bolts and gear to 3 inches.

72 The Ticket 5.12a ★★★★ ☐
Classic and one of the best routes in the canyon. Climbs the obvious black streaked wall. Start for *Saturday Treat* and move right to the first bolt, climb a thin seam and reach a good ledge, rest and then fire up the steep face with a hard move and then a short corner to reach the anchor.
10 bolts, 1 pin.

73 Long Live Rock 5.10d ★★ ☐
Climb right of *The Ticket*, following a corner and discontinuous cracks to top.
Variation: Direct Finish 5.11a ☐
After 60-70 feet, head straight up past three bolts to the anchor.
3 bolts and gear to 2.5 inches.

Richard Rossiter

I moved to Boulder from graduate school in the summer of 1977, which made me a newcomer to a climbing scene that had been developing here for 70 years, though I was not a beginner. I had climbed in Yosemite, the Pacific Northwest, Canada, The Tetons, The Sawtooths and City of Rocks since my last year of high school. As a newcomer to Boulder I was struck by the fantastic physical resource, the awesome variety and quality of rock, and the very high standard of climbing that had developed here over those 70 years.

I rented a house near 18th and Mapleton. I had no sooner parked the car than I began solo climbing in the Flatirons and Eldorado Canyon and was lucky to connect with the likes of Steve Monk, Jean Ruwitch, Roger Briggs, Bob Rotert, Jim Erickson and Pat Ament. I found a little shop called the Boulder Mountaineer tucked back in a corner at Broadway and University (the current location of Dot's Diner on the Hill) and bought a copy of *High Over Boulder* from a clerk named Dan Hare. I thereafter acquired a copy of *5.10, A Rock Climber's Guide To Boulder, Colorado* by Pat Ament and Jim Erickson, all of which set the stage for the next three decades of my life.

My first climb in Boulder Canyon was the route *Empor* on Cob Rock during the summer of 1977 and from that day on I was hooked. I was accustomed to driving a couple of hours and hiking several more just to reach a good climb. Some destinations required several days before you could set down your pack and get out the rope. Moving to Boulder changed all that and Boulder Canyon had the shortest lead-time of all the local options. Just one minute from town you could park the car or your bicycle and climb at the Dome and the Elephant Buttresses. A few minutes farther up the canyon and this amazing granite gymnasium opened up, split down the middle by the cascading waters of Boulder Creek. There were already a hundred or so established climbs on a dozen crags in the twelve miles between the City of Boulder and Castle Rock. The canyon was so beautiful, convenient and bursting with potential for adventure ... what was one to do?

I worked my way through the canyon's repertoire with a variety of partners, not the least of which was Joyce Bracht (later my wife). We climbed everything we could find in the guidebook and then broke off on our own and started climbing everything that wasn't. We went everywhere: Mickey Mouse Wall, Eldorado Canyon, the Flatirons, Boulder Canyon, Lumpy Ridge, the High Peaks (RMNP), The Tetons, Wind River Range, Mount Rainier and Index Town Wall. I learned how to place expansion bolts from Roger Briggs in 1977. Ten years later Joyce and I felt we had run out of new cracks to climb (which wasn't actually so) and my wrists were inflamed from drilling by hand (*The Radlands of Infinity* for example). I purchased a Bosch Bull Dog from the Boulder Mountaineer in 1988 and we got serious about new routes on crackless terrain.

Our first new route in Boulder Canyon (I think) was *The Slit* on Wall of The Winter Warmth, 1981. Then *On Ballet*, Blob Rock, 1983, neither of which had any fixed protection. To make a long story short, by 1986 Joyce and I were committed to developing new climbs requiring bolts or not. *The Radlands of Infinity*, 1988, was our first foray into semi-crackles face climbing in Boulder Canyon, though we had already done *Misses Clean Gets Down* and *Sunrider* in Eldorado Canyon, *Zen Effects, Life Stream and Asahi* on Mickey Mouse Wall. By the end of that summer we had also completed *Birds of Fire* on the Northwest Face of Chiefs Head Peak, Rocky Mountain National Park.

Joyce and I went separate ways in 1990, but my obsession for new routes continued through the summer of 2008. In 1996 I was "fortunate" to find a variety of crags in Boulder Canyon that had gone almost completely unnoticed. These included Avalon, Watermark, Sleeping Beauty and the whole of Upper Dream Canyon, which consisted of another dozen crags. I spent the next decade of my life developing every good crack and face climb I could find on these features. Hundreds of routes, thousands of hours and thousands of dollars (for stainless steel bolts) later I felt I had fulfilled the vision, done everything worth doing and retired from setting new routes in the canyon.

A few more lines yet beckoned me from Rocky Mountain National Park, mostly on Arrowhead. *Full Metal Jacket, Ripsaw* and *Sidewinder* I thought, surely must be the final exams, after which I could move on to other neglected aspects of my life. So let's say I have retired from the quest for new routes, or that's the theory anyway, but that is not to say I have retired from climbing. As for Boulder Canyon, I'll see you there.

HAPPY HOUR CRAG 6.8 miles

Approach time: 10 - 15 minutes.
Exposure: South.

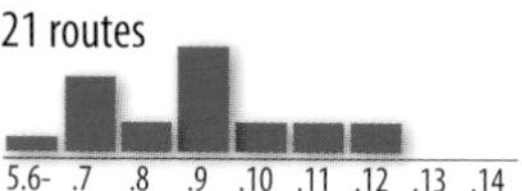

A popular cliff that see a lot of climbing traffic during weekends when the weather is nice. A wonderful selection of great moderate routes that can be easily top-roped or led.

Access: Drive 6.8 miles up the canyon to a pullout on the left. It gets full very quickly on nice days. Cross the road and then walk up a steep trail that dumps you at the east end of the wall.

Descent: To descend from the top, walk west down a steep gully leading back to the base. To set top-ropes, do the opposite, walk up the steep gully and then right to the top. Several trees lie close to the edge of the cliff but try to find natural gear before slinging the trees.

❶ Left Side 5.5 ★★ ☐
On the left side of the wall, start below a triangle-shaped block, climb past it and then take a short handcrack to the top.
Gear to 2.5 inches.

❷ I, Robot 5.7 ★★ ☐
The obvious right facing corner that starts right behind a tree.
Gear to 2.5 inches.

❸ Are We Not Men 5.7 ★ ☐
Start 5 feet right of *I, Robot*. Head up an easy crack to small roof, then to the top.
Gear to 2 inches.

❹ Twofers 5.8 ★★★ ☐
Climb a right facing corner that leads to a roof about 30 feet up, turn the roof on the left and then fire up to the top.
Variation: Twofers Bypass 5.8 ☐
Turn the roof on the right and then to top.
Gear to 2 inches.

❺ The Big Spit 5.9 ☐
Start right of a dirty section at a short right-facing corner leading to the left side of a large roof. Climb the corner then pass the roof on the left, angle slightly right into a good crack and follow it to the top.
SR.

❻ Rush Hour 5.12a ★ ☐
Not the 5.10 it used to be. Start on the right side of the roof. Climb a flake to below the roof, angle left to center of the roof, clip a bolt and pull like mad, then follow the cracks of *Last Call* to the top.
1 bolt. SR.

❼ Last Call 5.9 ☐
Start as for *Dementia*, but head left after 15 feet and follow thin cracks to the top.
SR.

❽ Dementia 5.10a ★★★ ☐
Start beneath the obvious left leaning V-slot roof near the middle of the crag. Climb up to and into the V-slot, thin finger moves get you to good locks. Move right at the top to the anchors.
Gear to 4.5 inches.

❾ Malign 5.7 ★ ☐
Start just right of *Dementia* and climb a left-facing corner just right of a knobby face to the top.
Gear to 2 inches.

❿ Thrill of the Chase 5.10a ★★★ ☐
Climb the first 25 feet of *Malign*, then climb the bolted knobby face on the left to the top.
2 bolts, gear to 2 inches.

⓫ Tipsey 5.9 ★ ☐
Climb the first 50 feet of *Malign*, then head left to a crack and take it to the top.
Gear to 2 inches.

⓬ Nightcap 5.9 ★★ ☐
Start 15 feet right of *Dementia*. Climb up a short corner aiming for higher left facing corner. The crux is getting through the upper corner.
Gear to 2 inches.

⓭ Skid Row 5.9+ ☐
Start as for *Grins*, but angle left up to *Nightcap* and then up and left to the finish of *Malign*.
Gear to 2.5 inches., long slings.

⓮ Grins 5.8 ★★★ ☐
A really good route with excellent protection and great hand jams. Climb up to a tooth, follow the crack and good jams past the tooth then onward to the top.
Gear to 3.5 inches.

⓯ Last Laugh 5.11a ★★ ☐
Start as for *Grins* and climb to the top of the tooth, clip a bolt on the left and then climb past two more bolts to the top.
3 bolts, gear to 2.5 inches..

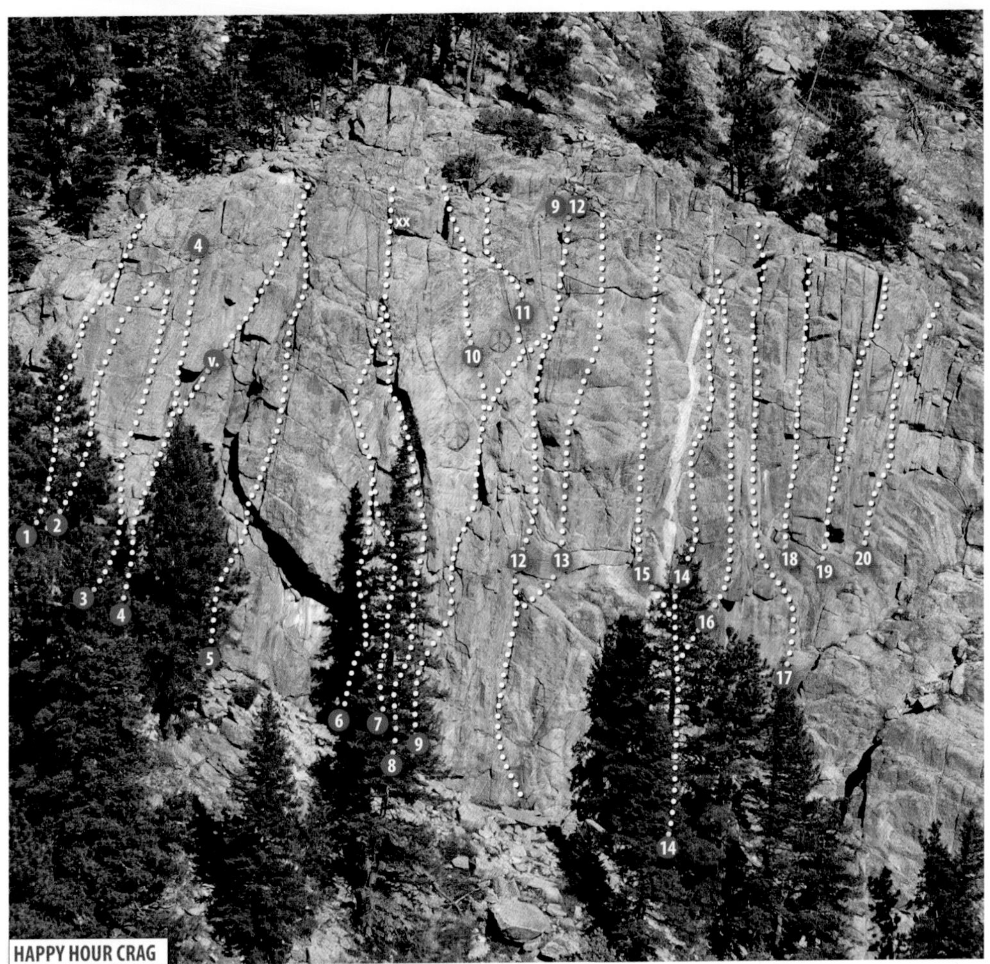

⑯ Teetotaler 5.11a ★★ ☐

Up and right from *Grins*, this route climbs up to the obvious flake/arete passing four bolts to the top.

4 bolts, a small piece for the start.

⑰ Hands Off 5.7 ☐

Right of *Teetotaler* is a large right facing dihedral, climb it!

Gear to 2.5 inches.

⑱ The Great Race 5.9+ ☐

The corner system to the right of *Hands Off.* Short but worth the effort.

Gear to 4.5 inches.

⑲ Baby Aliens 5.12a R ★★ ☐

A route that seems out of place on this cliff. Just right of *The Great Race* is a thin seamy wall.

Small gear to 0.75 micro-cam.

⑳ Cruel Shoes 5.9 ★ ☐

The last corner system on the right side of the rock, short.

A few small and mid-size pieces.

㉑ Bent Faith 5.7 ★ ☐

Down and right of the main wall is this right arching crack.

A few pieces to mid-size.

SECURITY RISK CRAG 6.8 miles

Approach time: 20 - 35 minutes.
Exposure: South and west.

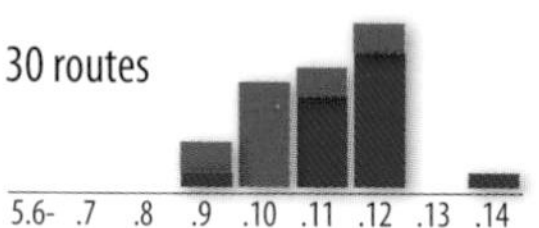

Nestled high above the road on a forested slope, Security Risk Crag is actually three separate cliffs offering great routes in a beautiful setting. The steep uphill hike brings you to the lower right side of the lower buttress.

⊘ This cliff may be closed due to raptor nesting between February and August (see page 17).

Access: Drive 6.8 miles up the canyon to a pullout on the left. It gets full very quickly on nice days. Cross the road and then walk up the trail that leads to Happy Hour Crag. The trail will veer left towards Happy Hour after 100 yards; instead go right and up following a faint trail to the base of Lower Security Risk.

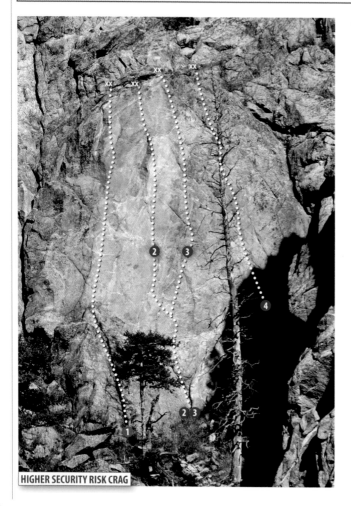

HIGHER SECURITY RISK CRAG

HIGHER SECURITY RISK CRAG.

To approach this crag walk past the Lower and Upper Security Risk Crags, going uphill to a clean, white, southwest-facing wall.

1 Gimme 3 Steps 5.11b ★

Start on the left side of the wall and climb up thin cracks to below a steep face. Crank the face moves and reach a short crack and then the anchors.

2 bolts, gear to 4.5 inches.

2 Evolution 5.11b ★

Start as for *Cold Shot* and then veer left up a thin seam past several bolts. Continuous climbing leads to the anchor.

6 bolts.

3 Cold Shot 5.11a ★

In the center of the wall, climb the thin crack angling right to the anchor – thin and a little devious.

5 bolts.

4 Turmoil 5.11d ★

On the right side of the wall, climb a very thin seam past several bolts to a stopper move around the fourth bolt. Continue up the steep face to the anchors.

7 bolts.

UPPER SECURITY RISK CRAG

The middle buttress with several good routes.

5 The "S" Buttress 5.10a ★ ☐

Superceded by the bolts of *Pup* on the upper half, the lower section is hard and worth a go if you brought gear. Start up the left-facing corner and tackle the crux overlap/bulge down low. Continue up the corner to below a roof, go right and join *Pup*.

6 bolts, SR.

6 Pup 5.9+ ★★ ☐

The bolted line on the left side of the wall. Start with a hard move to clip the first bolt then follow the line of bolts up the step wall. Nice warm up.

8 bolts.

7 Crash Test Blondes 5.11c ★★ ☐

Start right of *Pup* and fire up the vertical slab below a large roof, clip the bolts and then veer right and over the roof to the anchor.

8 bolts.

8 Led Astray 5.11a ★ ☐

Start right of *Crash Test Blondes* and climb the right-facing corner past two bolts to a ledge. Fire the face along a dyke to below the roof and the anchor.

8 bolts.

9 Crossfire 5.9 ★ ☐

Pitch 1: 5.9. Climb the large pointed flake then head left over a roof to a right-leaning dihedral. Climb the dihedral and step left at its top to a belay.

Pitch 2: 5.9. Climb the crack to the top.

SR.

10 Cracking the Code 5.11b ★ ☐

Pitch 1: 5.11b. Start right of *Crossfire* in a right-facing corner and stay right of the dyke to below a small roof and belay.

Pitch 2: 5.10b/c. Climb past two roofs then up a nice corner to a short arete and the top.

10 bolts.

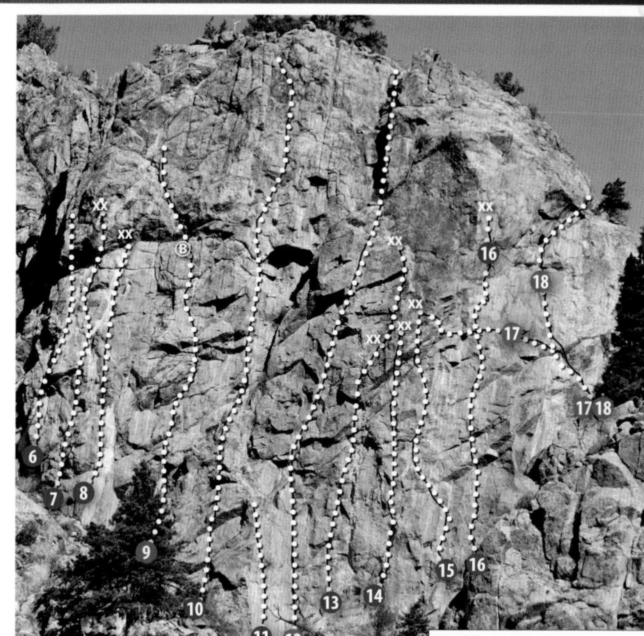

11 Just a Little Insecure 5.12a ★ ☐

Start just left of a wide crack and climb just right of a sharp arete. The crux comes low.

3 bolts.

12 Get Smart 5.10d ★★ ☐

Climb the obvious wide crack up through several small roofs and then angle right up a thin crack in a corner that leads to anchors at 100 feet. Rap.

Gear to 4 inches.

13 Plan B 5.12b ★★★★ ☐

Classic, one of the best routes in the canyon. Climb the obvious bolted line up the steep face just left of the dyke. There are two anchors: one at 75 feet and one at 100 feet.

12 bolts to the second anchor.

14 The Juice 5.12d ★★★ ☐

Classic. Start just right of the dyke and left facing corner. Climb a nice steep face with continuous moves to below a small roof. Fire the roof (hard), gain a face, and make another hard move before the anchor. See photo page 75.

10 bolts.

15 Hot Flyer 5.12a ★★★ ☐

Once a forgotten scary trad route, now retro-bolted and quite popular. Climb a series of short right-facing corners on the right side of the wall. Continuous and somewhat devious with a hard move getting to the anchor.

9 bolts.

16 Hot Wire 5.12c ★★ ☐

Climb the steep face just right of *Hot Flyer* to a small roof (crux), then continue up on good holds till a hard move to reach the anchor.

12 bolts.

17 Cappuccino 5.10d R ☐

Start up the gully near a block, go left to a bolt and reach a roof, turn the roof on the left and then reach a short overhanging crack with a fixed piece, go left and somehow make your way to *Hot Flyer's* anchor. Probably unrepeated.

SR.

18 Espresso 5.10d R ☐

Start for *#17* and climb to the bolt and roof, turn the roof on the right and angle left to a ledge and small roof, go right and then to the top.

SR.

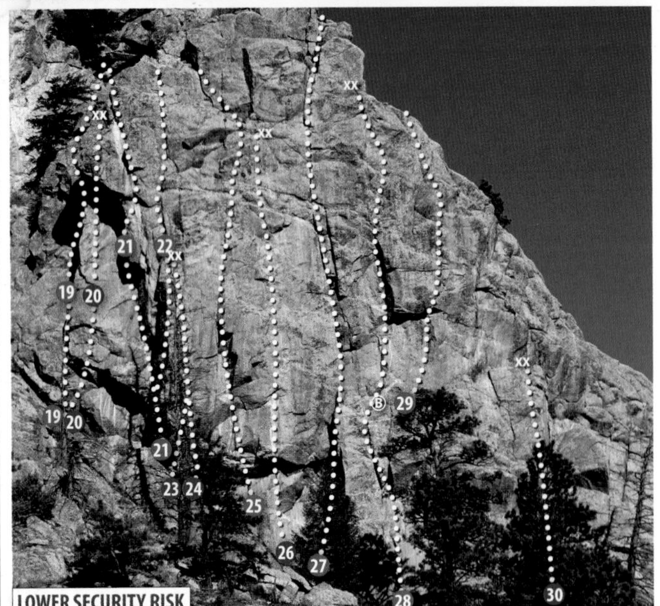

LOWER SECURITY RISK

This beautiful west facing rock offers several excellent routes, both trad and sport, on solid compact granite in a nice setting high above the canyon.

⑲ Scraping By 5.10a ☐

On the left side of the crag is a large left-facing dihedral with a bolted line just right. Start from a block to gain the main upper corner, cruise to the top. The crux comes low.

SR.

⑳ Eldo of the People 5.12b ★ ☐

Start as for *Scraping By* (gear) then go right over a roof to a steep slab trending left to a blunt arete and a large roof. Fire over the large roof (hard) to the anchors. One can easily avoid the upper roof by stepping left to *Scraping By* and then to the anchors.

8 bolts, two medium cams (for the start) and 0.5 micro-cam for below the roof.

㉑ The Prism 5.9 ★★ ☐

The obvious corner just right of *Eldo of the People*. Encounter some funky rock to gain the main corner. Stem, layback and jam your way up and left to the anchor.

SR.

㉒ Maximum Security 5.10a ★ ☐

Follow *The Prism* to below the first roof, step right and gain a thin crack, follow it to a good stance and then face climb to the top.

SR.

㉓ Ecstasy of the People 5.12d ★★★ ☐

Start just left of the arete and climb right on a steep face to gain the arete and a thin seam, continue up the arete to the anchor.

7 bolts.

㉔ The Agony and Ecstasy 5.14a ★★ ☐

The direct start to *Ecstasy of the People*. Three bolts of V10 climbing leads directly to the arete. One of the harder routes in the canyon and the time of writing hasn't seen a second ascent.

8 bolts.

㉕ Enemy of the People 5.12b ★★★ ☐

Start right of *Ecstasy of the People* below a small roof. Climb up past bolts into a shallow corner below a roof, crank the roof and gain good jams, climb to a fixed pin then up and left to the anchor for *Ecstasy of the People.*

2 bolts, Gear to 2 inches, RP's.

㉖ Central Insecurity 5.12d ★★★ ☐

Classic - crack the roof and you're almost home free. Start down and right of *Enemy of the People*, climb over a roof and then up the beautiful steep face to the anchor. Classic hard face climbing.

9 bolts.

㉗ Security Risk 5.10c/d ★★★ ☐

The 5.10 start is a much better way to do the route.

Pitch 1: 5.10c/d. The obvious right-facing corner on the right side of the wall, harder than it looks. Climb it to a good ledge at a large horn.

Pitch 2: 5.9. Follow twin cracks to the top.

Variation 1: 5.7. Start right of the corner up a nice crack to the ledge.

Variation 2: 5.10b. Climb the thin crack right of *Variation 1*.

SR.

㉘ Men Are From Mars 5.11a ☐

Pitch 1: Climb one of the starts for *Security Risk* to gain the ledge and a two-bolt anchor.

Pitch 2: 5.11a. Climb up a shallow stemming dihedral past several bolts to the anchors.

5 bolts, SR.

㉙ Comfortably Numb 5.12a/b ★★★ ☐

Pitch 1: Climb one of the starts for *Security Risk* to gain the ledge and a two-bolt anchor.

Pitch 2: 5.12a/b. Climb just right of the anchor up a shallow dihedral to below a roof, crank the roof and follow a thin crack up to the anchor.

Gear to 2 inches, RP's.

㉚ Enema of the People 5.12a ★ ☐

The obvious arete (with unobvious moves) on the right side of the crag.

5 bolts.

SOLAR DOME aka THE LIGHTHOUSE

This short blob of granite is located just north of Upper Security Risk crag. The routes (5.10 to 5.12) are short, well-protected and sunny. Continue uphill from Security Risk to the obvious blob of rock on the ridgeline.

Ted Lanzano squeezes *The Juice* 5.12d, Upper Security Risk Crag, page 73. Photo Adam Brink.

WITCHES TOWER 6.8 miles

Approach time: 15 minutes.
Exposure: Northwest.

10 routes

Tucked away on a nice forested slope, Witches Tower offers a good option to beat the heat in the summer. It has several worthwhile sport routes and, along with the Garden Party Wall and Sherwood Forest, provides a good selection of routes in a nice shaded setting.

Access: Park in a pullout on the left side of the road at 7.0 miles. Walk down canyon for a tenth of a mile to a Tyrolean traverse located on a big boulder coming out of the creek. Once on the south side, walk 100 yards downstream on a quaint path through the forest. The wall on the right below Sherwood Forest is Witches Tower, only 100 feet or so from the creek.

1 It's My Swamp 5.8 ☐

A three-pitch route that wanders up the left side of the north face. Be on the lookout for some loose rock.

Gear to 3.5 inches.

2 Panic Attack 5.12a ★★★ ☐

AKA *BOB... Bombs Over Baghdad*. Start just left of the boulder on the north face. Sequential moves from the ground to the fifth bolt.

7 bolts, 0.5 micro-cam.

3 War is Love 5.11b/c ★★★ ☐

One of the better routes on the wall. Start on top of a big boulder that leans against the north face of Witches Tower. Make a high first clip and power up laybacks to a series of technical face moves (crux). Reach the third bolt and move right to a short left-facing corner. Climb up, passing two more bolts to the anchor. You can place a small stopper or Alien before reaching the anchor.

5 bolts, medium stopper.

4 Tipskin Jihad 5.12a/b ★★★ ☐

Thin face just right of *War is Love*. Excellent route. Stick-clip the first bolt then power layback a seam system to the complex crux face move, stretch right then straight up to a tricky move before the anchor.

5 bolts.

5 Teenage Terrorists 5.12b ★★★ ☐

Thin, steep and devious. Really good climbing on nice granite. Power-layback up a good rail to the bizarre crux moves, then race your arms up to the anchor.

6 bolts.

6 Romancing the Stone 5.9 ★ ☐

The route starts on the northwest face of Witches Tower. Climb up to the first bolt on good holds. Good face moves on knobs and edges get you to the second bolt. A red Alien can be placed in between bolts here. Veer a little left and place gear to gain a ledge and the third bolt. Fire up past the third bolt using a hanging, weird block. Reach the arete and climb up past three more bolts to a two-bolt anchor. A purple Camalot can be placed before reaching the anchor.

6 bolts, medium gear.

7 Nala 5.10a ★ ☐

Start just left of *Tese*. Make a committing move up to a flake/horn, sling the horn and step up to a good crack system, follow the left-leaning crack to the roofs (bolt here), stem and make wild moves into a shallow corner, and follow the nice corner to the anchor of *Tese*.

1 bolts, gear to red Camalot.

8 Tese 5.10a ★★★ ☐

Start right of *Romancing the Stone*. Climb up a cool face, making nice moves on edges and knobs past two bolts. A yellow Alien can be placed before the third bolt. Make cool moves stemming up and over several small overhangs, then up an arete to the anchor.

11 bolts, 0.75 micro-cam.

9 No Direction Home 5.11a/b ★★ ☐

Start just right of *Tese*. Climb up fun layback moves to a small roof. Clip a bolt and make a strenuous move up to the next clip. Power up and over the larger roof to good holds. Follow bolts to the anchor.

10 bolts.

10 Scarecrow 5.9- ★ ☐

Start right of *No Direction Home*. The crux is the first 20 feet of weird crack climbing and then a move getting past the lone bolt. Lower from a two-bolt chain anchor.

1 bolt, gear to medium.

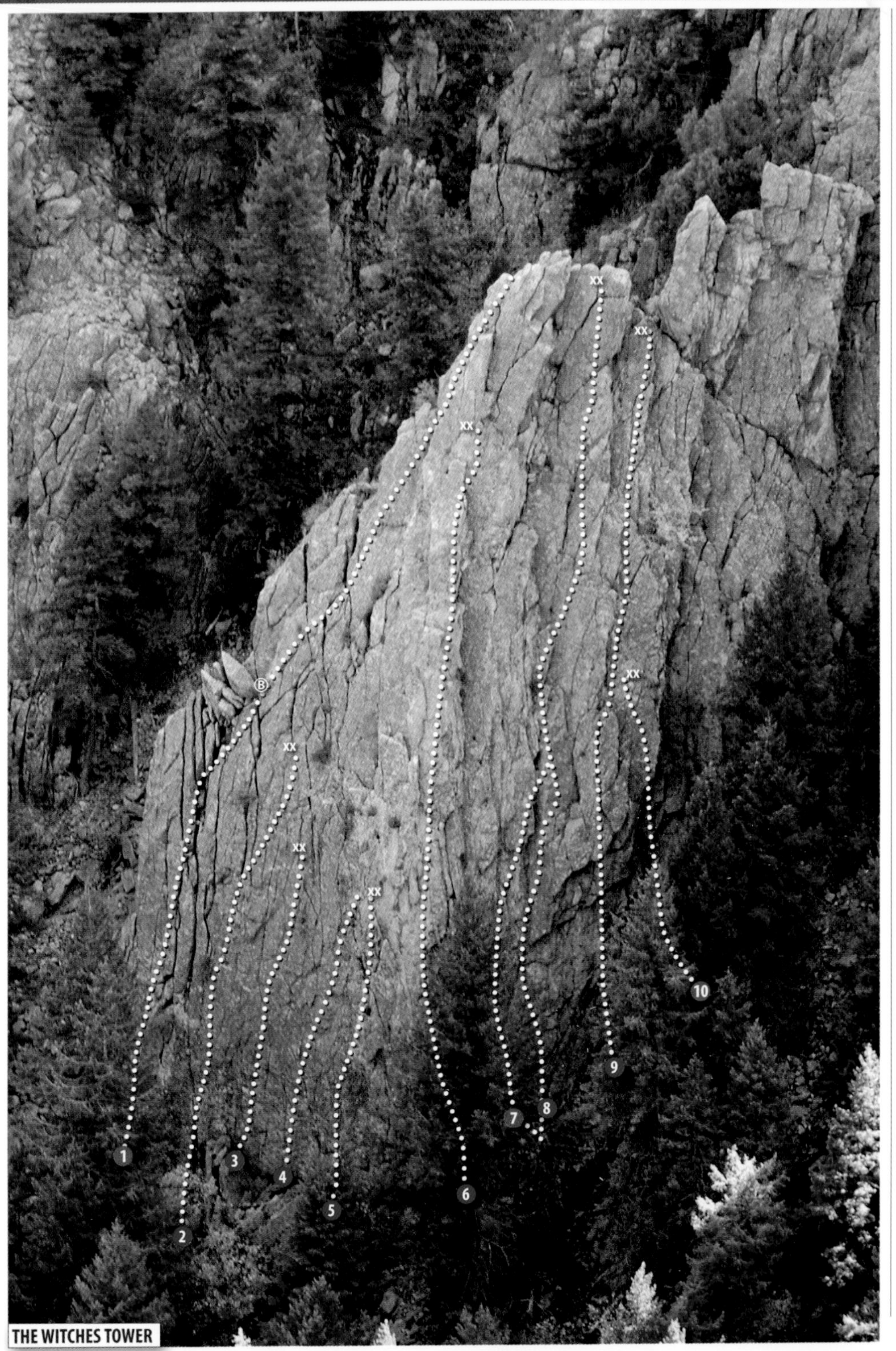

THE WITCHES TOWER

SHERWOOD FOREST 6.8 miles

Approach time: 15 minutes.
Exposure: Northwest.

11 routes

Tucked away on a nice forested slope, Sherwood Forest offers a good option to beat the heat in the summer. The crag has several worthwhile sport routes and, combined with the Garden Party Wall and Witches Tower, it offers a great selection of routes in a nice shaded setting.

Access: Park in a pullout on the left side of the road at 7.0 miles. Walk down canyon for a tenth of mile to a Tyrolean traverse located on a big boulder coming out of the creek. Once on the south side, walk 100 yards downstream on a quaint path through the forest, then head south up the very steep hill for five minutes, passing Witches Tower along the way.

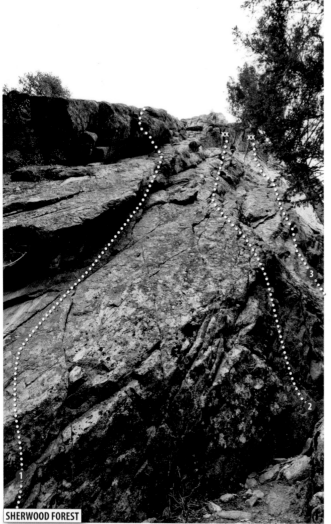

SHERWOOD FOREST

❶ Boyz From The Hood 5.10a ★ ☐
On the far left side of the wall. Climb up to the first bolt and make a weird move reaching the second bolt. Climb past the bolt and move left into the corner passing the third and fourth bolt. Make a cool move left to the arete/face and climb up the face on good holds, slinging a horn for protection to the anchor.
6 bolts.

❷ The Prince and the Pauper 5.10a ★ ☐
Start 10 feet right of *Boyz,* climbing dubious-looking rock past six bolts to the anchor.
6 bolts.

❸ Merry Men 5.11a ★★ ☐
One of the better routes on the wall. Nice climbing up a faint groove/arete feature.
7 bolts.

❹ Robbin' The Hood 5.11c ★★★ ☐
The classic route on the wall. The crux comes low (gaining the shallow corner) and then some nice moves above get you to the anchor.
6 bolts.

5 Prince Of Thieves 5.12b ★★ ☐

Start 10 feet right of *Robbin'*, climbing up through two small overhangs (crux); another hard move comes just before the anchor. The third clip is hard.

11 bolts.

6 Sheriff's Tariff 5.11c ★★ ☐

Start on the middle of the wall just right of the small roof. Crank the face and climb the roof; make a hard move getting past the last bolt on the headwall.

9 bolts.

7 Tuckered And Fried 5.10c ★★ ☐

Just right of *Sheriff's Tariff* is a nice face that leads to several juggy roofs.

8 bolts.

8 Men In Tights 5.10b/c ★★★ ☐

A really good route that climbs a clean slab just left of *Little John's Big Stick*.

8 bolts.

9 Little John's Big Stick 5.9+ ★ ☐

A route with history. Established in the early 1990s, cleaned intensively and climbed at least a thousand times. Still, someone felt the need to remove the bolts on the bottom corner.

Bring some cams to2 inches and QD's for the top.

10 Tony Bubb's Little Stick 5.10c ★★ ☐

In retaliation for the removal of the bolts, Alan Nelson came back and added this route a mere three feet from *Little John's*. Shouldn't be hard to figure out who chopped/removed the bolts.

8 bolts.

11 Maid Marian 5.9 ☐

The last route on the wall; nice warm-up.

6 bolts.

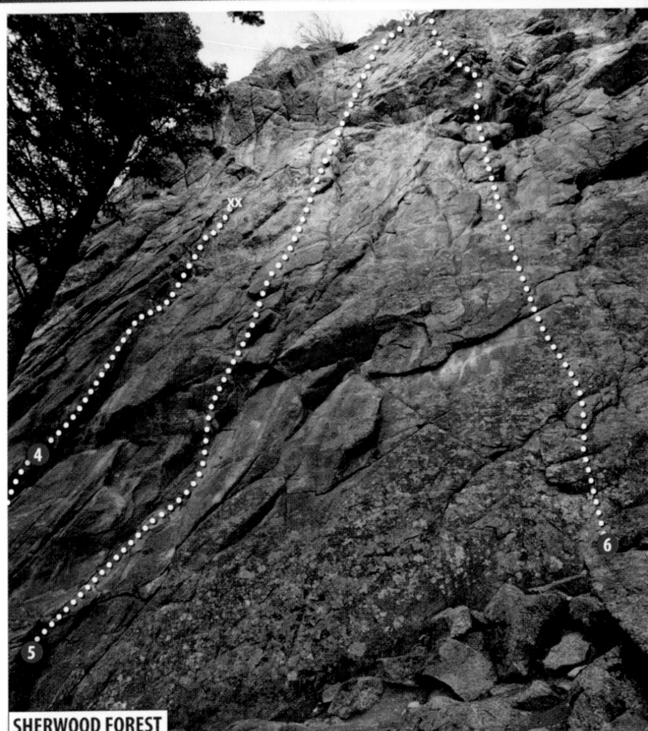

GARDEN PARTY WALL 6.8 miles

Approach time: 20 minutes.
Exposure: Northwest.

7 routes

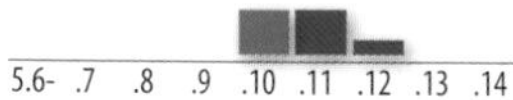

Tucked away on a nice forested slope the Garden Party Wall offers a good option to beat the heat in the summer months.

Access: Park in a pullout on the left side of the road at 7.0 miles. Walk down canyon for a tenth of a mile to a Tyrolean traverse located on a boulder coming out of the creek. Once on the south side of the creek walk 100 yards down stream on a quaint path through the forest and up to the Sherwood Forest crag. At the south, or upper end, of the Sherwood Forest crag follow a trail uphill to the right, avoiding a wet area.

Climbs listed from left to right.

❶ Arete 5.10a ★ ☐
Scramble up to a ledge on the far left side of the wall. Climbs the obvious cracks/arete.
Gear to 2 inches.

❷ Dirty Love 5.10c ★ ☐
Climb up towards the arete but head straight up to climb the left crack of a double crack system.
Gear to 2 inches.

❸ Right Crack 5.10c ★ ☐
Start as for *Dirty Love* but take the right crack to the top.
Gear to 2 inches.

❹ Excalibur 5.11d ★ ☐
Climb a short slab then steep face in the center of the rock. Identify the route by weird bolts and pins.
5 bolts, 2 pins.

❺ The Illusionist 5.12a ★★★ ☐
A really good route that takes a direct line up and over the roof right of *Excalibur*. Climb the short face/corner to below the roof, decipher the crux moves and then fire straight up to the anchor on steep climbing.
8 bolts, 1.5 inch cam.

❻ Topiary 5.11c/d ★★ ☐
Start up a shallow corner right of the *Illusionist*. Surmounting the roof is the crux.
7 bolts.

❼ Can't Please Everyone 5.11a ★★ ☐
The last route on the right side of the cliff. Short and good.
5 bolts.

THE RIVIERA 7.0 miles

Approach time: 10 - 15 minutes.
Exposure: South and west.

15 routes

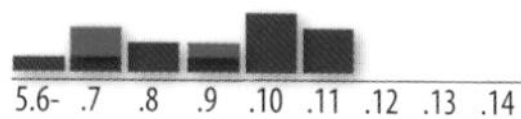

This is the lower-right side of the Bihedral area. It has a nice collection of sunny sport routes in a very safe setting. The routes are well protected and all have anchors for lowering.

Access: Travel 7.1 miles up the canyon to a pullout on the left side of the road. Walk back down canyon and take a trail that shoots up and left at a cement post marked 430.

❶ Dancing Hippos 5.7 ☐
On the far left side of the rock, climb vague cracks up to the start of the *Bihedral Arete*.
Gear to 2.5 inches.

❷ Lease Agreement 5.10b ★★ ☐
Climb a short finger crack up to a bolted face dyke.
3 bolts, small cams for the crack.

❸ New Lease on Life 5.10a ★★ ☐
Climb a clean face up to a black streak and angle left to the anchors for *Lease Agreement*.
6 bolts.

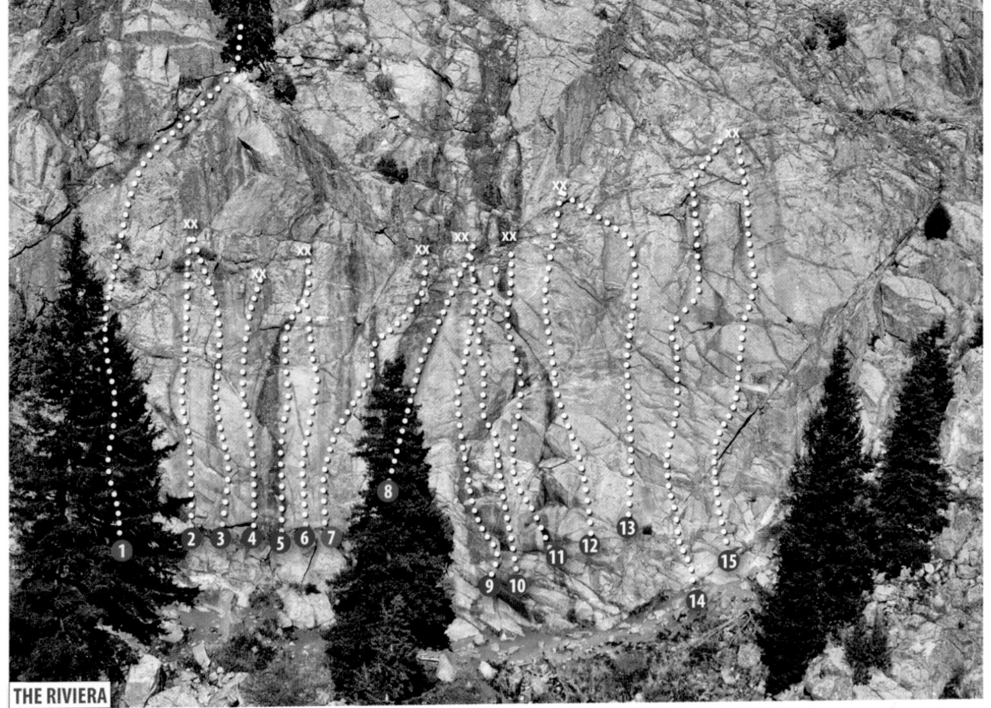

4 Abandonment 5.8 ☐

The third bolted route from the left. Climb up and right past overlaps between two black streaks. After the fourth bolt, continue straight up to a higher anchor, or angle left along a quartz dike to a lower anchor shared with the routes on the left.

4 bolts, 0.75 micro-cam.

5 Sea Breeze 5.11a ★★★ ☐

Fourth bolted route from the left. Thin face moves up the black streak.

6 bolts.

6 The Minstrel 5.11a ★ ☐

Somewhat close to *Sea Breeze*. Meet *Sea Breeze* at the fourth bolt.

5 bolts.

7 Au Natural 5.7 ★★ ☐

The left of two corners. Good gear. Traverse left to *The Minstral* anchor or right to *Devin's Dihedral* anchor.

Gear to 2.5 inches.

8 Devin's Dihedral 5.9+ R ★★ ☐

Good route that climbs a nice dihedral with tricky pro. At the top of the corner clip a bolt and then straight up to the anchor.

1 bolt. Small to medium gear.

9 Birthday Suit 5.10a ★ ☐

The next bolted route right of the corner.

5 bolts, 2 inch cam.

10 Silver Glide 5.11b ★★ ☐

Depending on how you use your feet, the grade of this climbs varies. Just right of *Birthday Suit*, up to and over a small roof to the anchor.

6 bolts.

11 Bosch Blanket Bingo 5.9 ★ ☐

Just right of *Silver Glide*, climb up to a roof and turn it on the left, follow bolts to the anchor.

6 bolts.

12 Topless Etiquette 5.8 ★★ ☐

Nice route with good moves all the way to the anchor.

6 bolts.

13 Le Nouveau Riche 5.10a ★★ ☐

Third bolted route from right the side of the cliff. Nice climbing up featured granite.

3 bolts, small to medium cams.

14 Chouette 5.6 ★★ ☐

Climb the right side of a large flake and then up on good holds to the anchor. Good route on very nice granite.

4 bolts, small to medium cams and few stoppers.

15 Splash 5.7 ★★ ☐

Climb up featured rock to a high first bolt. Great climbing on wonderful holds get you to the anchor.

4 bolts, small to medium cams.

THE BIHEDRAL 7.0 miles

Approach time: 10 - 20 minutes.
Exposure: South and west.

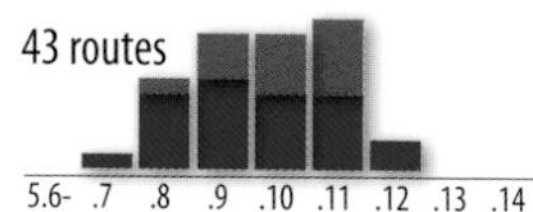

This large south and west facing rock offers many good routes in a nice setting high above the road. The cliff has become quite popular and can be quite crowded on weekends. I have split the rock into three different sections for clarity: The Left Side, Lower Tier and the Upper Tier.

Access: Park in a pullout on the left side of the road at 7.1 miles. Walk down stream for a short distance and then access a trail leading up and left to the rock.

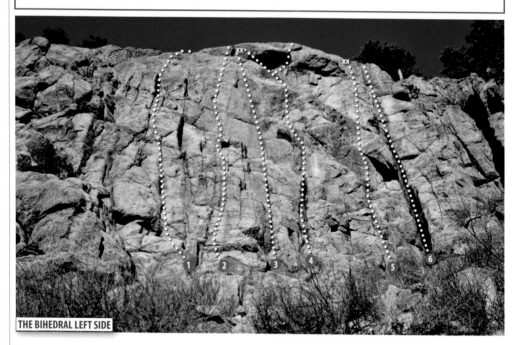

THE BIHEDRAL LEFT SIDE

THE BIHEDRAL LEFT SIDE.

Once at the main the main Bihedral rock, skirt the cliff going left on a faint trail that will bring you to the Left Side. Several nice mixed routes climb this south and west facing rock and give solitude when the main area is crowded.

❶ Most of the Time 5.8+ ★ ☐
On the left side of the cliff, follow shallow cracks and a short right-facing corner near the top.
Gear to 2 inches.

❷ Slight of Hand 5.11b ★★ ☐
Start as for *Don't Ask*, then head left up to an obvious thin flake/crack. Fire past the flake, then nice moves reach the anchor.
2 bolts, gear to 2 inches.

❸ Don't Ask 5.10a ★★ ☐
In the center of the cliff, follow a corner up to an obvious, short left-facing corner. Gain a ledge and make cool face moves left past a bolt to a short right-facing corner. Follow cracks up to the anchor.
1 bolt, gear to 2 inches.

❹ Calling All Trad Climbers 5.10a ★★ ☐
This route follows a series of short corners just left of *What's Wrong With Parents Today*. Follow short corners with good gear up to a steep section with a bolt. Crank past the bolt and gain a ledge below a steep, short finger crack. Power up the crack and angle left past the crack following good cracks with good gear to the anchor.
2 bolts, gear to 2 inches.

5 What's Wrong with Parents Today 5.11a ★★ ☐

On the right side of the rock and just left of a chimney, climb up a short corner with two bolts. Reach a steep section and crank through the roof (crux) and up to a ramp. Clip a bolt and make cool moves up the arete/face on great holds past the last bolt and into a nice crack system.

4 bolts, gear to 2 inches.

6 Twisted 5.9 ★ ☐

The obvious chimney on the right side of the wall.

Gear to 4 inches.

THE BIHEDRAL LOWER TIER

These next climbs start right where the trail meets the main rock.

7 Like a Wonk 5.9 ☐

Pitch 1a: 5.9. Begin just left of *The Unknown*, solo up easy rock and place a yellow & green Alien in a diagonal crack. Climb past 2 bolts to a 2-bolt anchor.

Pitch 1b: 5.9+. Climb the line just left of pitch 1a following 3 bolts to the same anchor.

NB: When lowering off pitch 1a or 1b, keep the rope out of the notch between the two routes or it will shred your rope.

Pitch 2: 5.8. Move right past the anchor for *The Unknown* and wonk your way straight up placing gear until the bolts are reached. The crux is the short traverse right at the 2nd bolt.

Variation: Wonky 5.11a ☐

The obvious arete. Climb the arete with a hard move down low, then easier rock to the anchor of *Like a Wonk*.

10 quickdraws and a few finger size pieces.

8 The Unknown 5.9 ☐

Just right of *Like a Wonk*. Nice climbing.

4 bolts.

9 Leave No Trace 5.11a ★ ☐

The overhanging flat face just right of *The Unknown*. Hard start leads to good climbing above to the anchor of *The Unknown*.

4 bolts, small cams.

THE BIHEDRAL LOWER TIER

10 Free at Last 5.11c ★★ ☐

A long pitch. Climb up into the obvious V-dihedral, make several hard moves in the corner, then reach the anchor at the top of the corner.

2 bolts, gear to 2 inches.

11 Beer Dog 5.10a ★ ☐

Three short routes start just left of the rappel gully and they all share a common start. *Beer Dog* is the left route.

7 bolts.

12 Hound's Tooth 5.10a ★ ☐

Climb to the third bolt of *Beer Dog* then straight up to the tooth and then to the anchor.

7 bolts.

13 Canine Corner 5.10a ★ ☐

Climb the right-facing corner past the third bolt of *Beer Dog*.

7 bolts.

THE BIHEDRAL UPPER TIER

Where the trail meets the rock, head right up broken 4th Class climbing to the main ledge right below the Bihedral Arete. To reach the routes on the far left side traverse an exposed easy 5th Class ledge to a nice flat area.

⑭ Tool King 5.8+ ★★ ☐

On the far left side of the of the main ledge on a separate pinnacle is the start of this route. Follow 3 bolts on well-featured rock to a ledge that leads to a finishing crack with good gear to the anchor.

3 bolts a few mid-size cams.

⑮ A Fly in the Ointment 5.10a ★ ☐

Layback past 3 bolts (crux) to a big bucket. Place a small cam to protect a move to a big ledge. Follow the final crack of *Tool King* to anchors.

3 bolts, gear to 2 inches.

⑯ Edge of Reality 5.12a/b ★ ☐

The obvious arete. Several awkward clips up the left side of the arete.

6 bolts.

⑰ Case of the Fags 5.11d ★★ ☐

The obvious thin crack on the east face of the pinnacle. Could be harder for those with big stubs. Climb up easy rock and gain a ledge near a wide crack, then fire the obvious thin crack above.

Gear to 3.5 inches.

⑱ It's Time for Change 5.8+ ★★ ☐

Start as for *Night Moves* and move left after the third bolt, stem up a slot, move left to the arete and follow it to the anchors.

8 bolts.

⑲ Night Moves 5.7 ★ ☐

Climb the obvious corner to a two-bolt belay.

5 bolts and few small cams.

⑳ Daydreaming 5.10c ★★ ☐

Climb to the anchors of *Night Moves*, step left, and fire up the steep finger crack to an anchor.

Gear to 2 inches.

㉑ Oh Boy 5.10c/d ★★ ☐

Climb to the anchors for *Night Moves* and then veer right up the steep right-facing corner to a hard move to reach the anchor. Great Position.

6 bolts, light rack to 2 inches.

㉒ Diamonds and Rust 5.9 ★★ ☐

Step up and clip a bolt on the right and traverse right to a right-facing corner. Climb the corner to a ledge at its top. Climb a tricky slab past an overlap (crux), and continue straight up to the anchor.

9 bolts.

㉓ Heterohedral 5.9 ★ ☐

A huge right-facing corner splits the west face. The first pitch of *Heteroherdral* climbs this feature.

Pitch 1: 5.8. Angle up and right, stepping right at the top of the corner to a belay.

Pitch 2: 5.9. Climb up and right to a short corner that leads to a crack, follow the crack to the top.

Gear to 4 inches.

㉔ Fat Tuesday 5.11a/b ★ ☐

Start just right of *Heterohedral* at the rap anchor. Climb a short slab and then reach a short overhanging corner. Crack the crux and gain the upper slab. Climb a thin crack and then move left to the anchor for *Diamonds and Rust*.

4 bolts, RP's, and a few thin cams.

㉕ Blood Diamond 5.11d ★★ ☐

Start on the left side of the traverse ledge at a two-bolt belay. Climb the nice slab up to the obvious overhanging corner, make a hard move to catch the lip of the roof, then up to the anchor for *Diamonds and Rust*. Great pitch.

7 bolts.

㉖ High Hard One 5.9+ ★★ ☐

On the left side of the main ledge is a rappel anchor. The route starts from the anchor. Climb about 20' left along a low-angle ramp to the first bolt. Clip the bolt and crank up a short wall to an easy slab. Climb the slab to a good ledge where the wall steepens. Climb a pillar with a hairline crack past five more bolts. Climb up on small holds past three more bolts and traverse right to the anchor.

9 bolts.

㉗ Group Therapy 5.8 ★★ ☐

The obvious bolted line on the left side of the main ledge. Well protected and friendly. Perfect for the 5.8 sport leader.

10 bolts.

㉘ Dan's Line 5.8 ★★ ☐

The next bolted route to the right. Good moves on excellent rock. Go up center of slab.

8 bolts.

Optional Pitch 2: Puff Daddy 5.10a ★★ ☐

Climb straight up from the belay to a high bolt, follow the line of bolts to the top and an anchor.

8 bolts.

㉙ Trick or Treat 5.8 ★★ ☐

Start as for *Dan's Line* at a flat boulder. Climb straight up the slab past two bolts and continue to a steep headwall. Move right and surmount the headwall. Continue up to a right-angling crack. Climb the crack and then angle left past two more bolts to the anchor shared with *Dan's Line*.

7 bolts and a couple of medium cams for the crack.

㉚ Sun Spot 5.7 ★ ☐

Climb the obvious right-facing corner just left of *Hold the Line*. Bring several large cams.

2 bolts, gear to 4 inches.

㉛ Hold The Line 5.9 ★★ ☐

Really good slab climbing on flawless granite. Climb the slab just right of the large right-facing corner.

9 bolts.

㉜ Rhodian Shores 5.10b ★★★ ☐

Maybe the best slab pitch on the rock. Excellent rock and protection. Fire up the center of the slab just left of the *Bihedral*.

9 bolts.

THE BIHEDRAL UPPER TIER

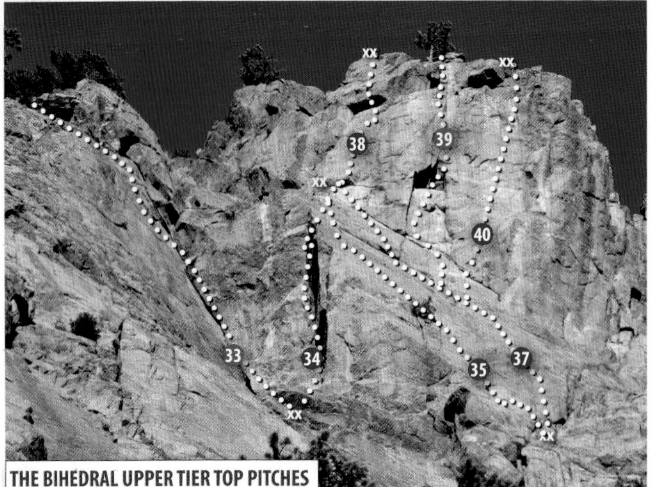

THE BIHEDRAL UPPER TIER TOP PITCHES

33 Bihedral 5.9- ★★ ☐

The namesake of the rock and good climbing at the grade, you should feel solid on 5.9.

Pitch 1: 5.7. Follow the obvious corner, climbing past the anchor of *Rhodian Shores* to a ledge about 20 feet higher.

Pitch 2: 5.9-. Climb a smaller left-facing corner with scant gear; the holds get better and so does the gear. Rap from one of the sport anchors.

Gear to 3 inches.

34 The Vortex 5.11c ★★ ☐

Access this pitch by climbing the first pitch of *Rhodian Shores*. From the belay, climb up the obvious dihedral with bolts to the anchor of the second pitch of *Bihedral Arete*. Well protected.

9 bolts.

35 Bihedral Arete 5.10a ★★★ ☐

See description opposite.

Variation: **Dihedral Variation** 5.9+★★☐

Climb the corner left of Bihedral Arete past two bolts and join Bihedral Arete after its third bolt.

2 bolts, great to2 inches.

36 Where's Ray? 5.8 ★ ☐

Start right of *Bihedral Arete* on a nice face. Climb past four bolts to the anchor.

4 bolts.

37 Flags of Our Fathers 5.10b ★★★ ☐

Pitch 1: 5.10b. Walk right from *Where's Ray?* along a ledge to a yellow/orange lichen corner. Place a green Alien and traverse right and up on easy rock to the first bolt. Place a blue Alien before the 2nd bolt and clip three more bolts as the rock gets steeper.

Pitch 2: 5.9+. Face climb up past 2 bolts and follow easy climbing to a 3rd bolt (crux). A small wire may be placed and climb up and left to 4th bolt and anchors above. Can be combined with Pitch 1.

Pitch 3: 5.9. When doing the 3rd pitch, you should belay at the 2nd belay of the *Bihedral Arete*. Climb just right of the belay (red Alien and small wire to protect a hard start), then follow 6 bolts to the anchor.

12 quickdraws and small cams.

38 Sands of Iwo Jima 5.11d ★★★ ☐

Climb the first two pitches of *Bihedral Arete* or *Flags of Our Fathers*. From the belay head right and fire up the steep headwall past 6 bolts to the anchor.

12 quickdraws and few small pieces.

39 Thumb Tack 5.11d ★★★ ☐

Great position and technical finger jamming. Photo page 39.

Pitch 1: 5.9+. Climb the first pitch of *Bihedral Arete.*

Pitch 2: 5.11d. From the belay angle up and right along a seam/crack aiming for the obvious crack splitting the upper headwall. Gain the crack to pod, struggle up and right to thin jams and the crux, then power to the top.

10 quickdraws and gear to 3.5 inches.

40 Pariah 5.12b/c ☐

This pitch climbs the right side of the impressive upper head wall above the second pitch of *Bihedral Arete*. The best way to access the route is by doing:

Pitch 1: 5.9+. Climb the first pitch of *Bihedral Arete* and belay.

Pitch 2: 5.12b/c. Start up the last pitch of *Flags of Our Fathers* and break right after the third bolt. Go across the slab to the arete on the right side of the upper head-wall. *Pariah* starts here. Work up the left side of the arete past eight bolts to a 2-bolt anchor with hangers but no lowering rings.

11 bolts, a few small and medium cams.

41 Flesh Eating Flies 5.11a ★ ☐

Climbs an arete and face located on the far right side of the headwall of the *Bihedral*. The best approach is to take the Happy Hour Crag trail to its end and then traverse the hillside to the left. Be very careful here — the Riviera climbing area is below.

6 bolts to a two-bolt anchor.

BITTY BIHEDRAL SLAB

Just right of where the trail splits to the Riviera is this short but pleasant slab.

42 Quick Work 5.7 ☐

Climb the slab/blunt arete on the left side of the wall to a two-bolt anchor.

3 bolts and 0.5 and 0.75 micro-cams

43 Git 'er Done 5.10d ★ ☐

Start down and right of *Quick Work* at a pine tree. Climb up easy rock to a bulge, then follow bolts up the steep slab to the anchor.

3 bolts, 0.75 micro-camn, 3.5 inch cam.

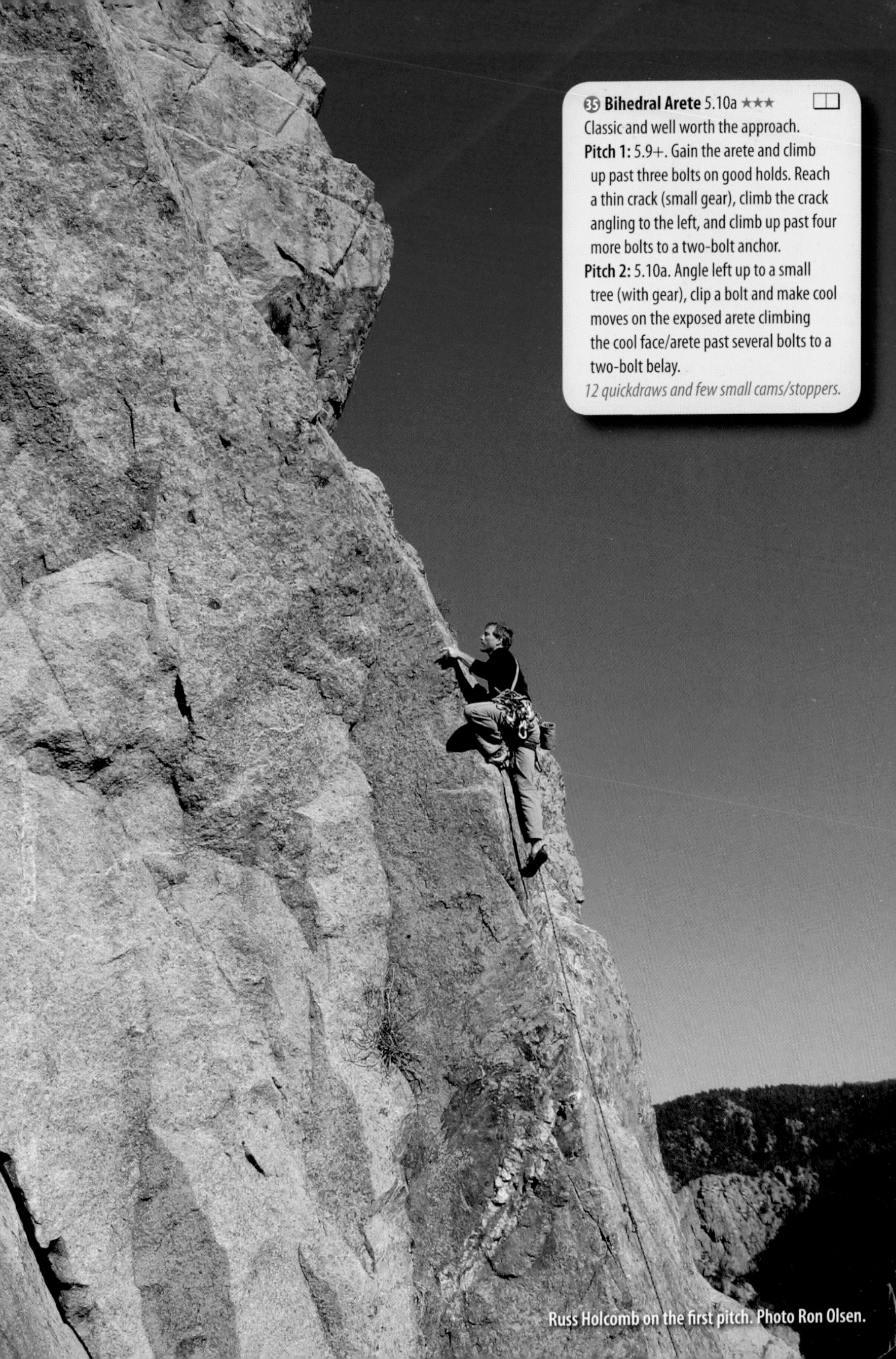

35 Bihedral Arete 5.10a ★★★
Classic and well worth the approach.
Pitch 1: 5.9+. Gain the arete and climb up past three bolts on good holds. Reach a thin crack (small gear), climb the crack angling to the left, and climb up past four more bolts to a two-bolt anchor.
Pitch 2: 5.10a. Angle left up to a small tree (with gear), clip a bolt and make cool moves on the exposed arete climbing the cool face/arete past several bolts to a two-bolt belay.
12 quickdraws and few small cams/stoppers.

Russ Holcomb on the first pitch. Photo Ron Olsen.

HILLBILLY ROCKS 7.2 miles

Approach time: 10 - 35 minutes.
Exposure: South and west.

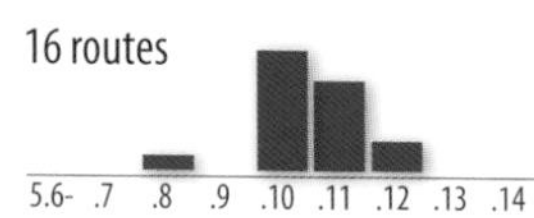

Sitting above several old mines, these seldom-visited crags have a number of good climbs with great southern exposure. The routes are short but offer a good alternative on busy weekends.

Access: Drive 7.1 miles up the canyon to a pullout on the right side of the road at the double-passing lane. Go straight up the steep gully from the pullout. The lower rock, Hillbilly Rock #1, can be reached by hiking up a steep drainage/ravine directly above the parking area for about 5 - 10 min. The upper rocks, Hillbilly Rocks #2 and #3, are about another 20 minutes up and to the left. However, the best approach to Rocks #2 and #3 is from above, by continuing west past the Solar Dome (see page 74) and then dropping down to the Hillbilly Rock #3. The rocks can be seen from the lower end of the pull-out across from the Inca Stone at mile 7.2. Hillbilly Rock #3 has a distinctive slender pine, with no low branches, right in front of it. Rock #2 is 300 feet down and left (approximately southwest) from Rock #3.

HILLBILLY ROCK #1

HILLBILLY ROCK #1

HILLBILLY ROCK #1

1 I Reckon 5.12a ★★ ☐
On the far left side of the rock, climb a black face on thin holds past four bolts to the anchor. Short and continuous.
4 bolts.

2 Boy Howdy 5.11c ★ ☐
Do a tricky move to gain a right-angling ramp. Follow the ramp, cut back left at a horizontal seam, and then struggle over the small roof.
4 bolts.

3 Like Water for Bob 5.10b ★ ☐
Climb up to a ledge; move up and left making a reach move to gain easier climbing.
5 bolts.

4 I'll be Dipped 5.10b ★ ☐
On the far right, a large tree can be seen projecting out of the cliff, up high. Climb past 5 bolts below the tree and finish just to the right of the tree. Tread lightly up high.
5 bolts.

5 Square Dance 5.10b ★ ☐
Climb to the first bolt of *I'll be Dipped*. Move up and right on a ramp past two more bolts. Then go straight up past a small left-facing-corner to a two-bolt belay.
5 bolts.

6 Hoo-doggy 5.8 ★ ☐
Climb past the first three bolts of *Square Dance*. Continue on the large right-angling ramp until you can move up and left to the anchor of *Square Dance*.
6 bolts.

HILLBILLY ROCK #2

7 Dagnabitol 5.10d ★★ ☐
Climb a left-facing corner to gain a large ledge. Move left to the leftmost of two small right-facing corners. Follow this past two bolts, step left to a bolt, and then back right into a crack to the top.
6 bolts.

8 Heavy Cipherin' 5.11a ★★ ☐
Start as for *Dagnabitol*. From the big ledge, ascend the rightmost of the two small corners. Move left to join the last two bolts of *Dagnabitol*.
7 bolts.

9 By Cracky 5.11b ★★ ☐
Ascend the nice-looking left-facing corner in the middle of the rock. Exit right, and save a little strength for the finishing moves.
7 bolts.

10 Hankerin' in the Midsection 5.10b ★ ☐
At the right end of the cliff, climb past three bolts to a ledge. Move up the corner past one more bolt to the anchors.
4 bolts.

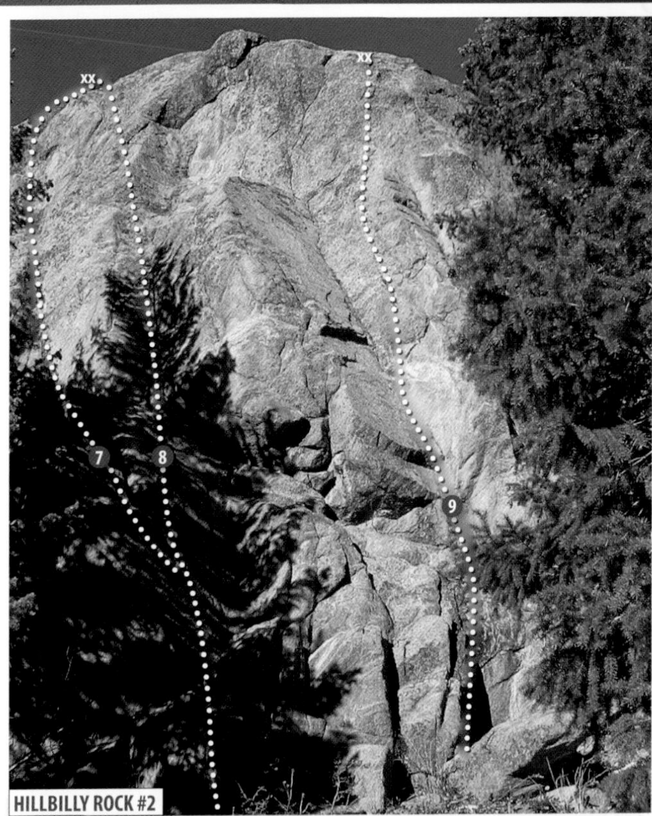

HILLBILLY ROCK #2

HILLBILLY ROCK #3

11 Pesky Varmints 5.11b ☐
On the far left side of the cliff, move up and right on overhanging rock past 4 bolts.
4 bolts.

12 Moonshine 5.11a ☐
Balance up the face past 4 bolts.
4 bolts.

13 Edge-a-macation 5.12a ★★ ☐
Between the large left-facing corner and *Moonshine*, climb up the face on small edges, past 5 bolts.
5 bolts.

14 Book Learnin' 5.10d ★★ ☐
Ascend the beautiful left-facing corner in the middle of the cliff, past 4 bolts, moving left at the end.
4 bolts

HILLBILLY ROCK #3

15 Jethro 5.10d ★ ☐
On the right side of the cliff, step up to a sloping ramp below a roof. Move left around the roof and up to the anchors.
4 bolts.

16 Ellie May 5.10d ★ ☐
Begin just right of *Jethro*. Climb directly over the roof and continue straight up to another interesting section over a bulging corner.
4 bolts.

THE INCA STONE 7.3 miles

Approach time: 5 minutes.
Exposure: South.

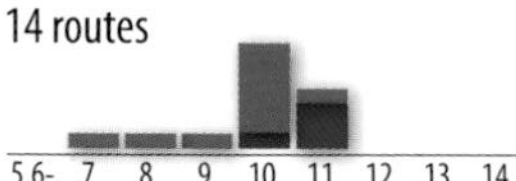

This is another seldom-visited crag with a number of short, difficult routes just a few hundred feet from the road.

Access: Drive 7.3 miles up the canyon to a large pullout on the left and cross the road. Head a little east and then up, following rock cairns to the base of the rock. The trail ends at the far left side of the wall. You can also park as for Hillbilly #1 (previous page) and walk west up the road to the cliff.

Descent: To descend from the top, walk east or west and then back down to the base.

THE INCA STONE

❶ Left Side 5.10b/c R
Boulder up to the first bolt, clip and relax; fire up to the ledge and then to the top. Seems hard for the grade.
2 bolts, gear to 2 inches..

❷ The Treadmill 5.11a PG-13 ★★
A little dirty near the start but still a nice route that heads up a thin crack to a flake/crack and then easier climbing to the top.
Gear to 4.5 inches.

❸ Ruins 5.10d/11a
The bolted line. Strenuous, but easier if you stay right.
5 bolts.

❹ The Alter 5.11a/b ★★
Climb up easy rock to access the first bolt located on the left edge of the main wall. Follow a right-leaning flake/crack up a steep wall. Hard for the grade.
4 bolts.

❺ Jamie 5.10c
Start on the lowest part of the main wall just left of a tree. Climb up to a short broken corner to a ledge; take the left of two leaning cracks to bolt anchors.
Gear to 2.5 inches.

❻ Elegant Pleasure 5.10a/b ★★
Start right behind a tree, climb unprotected rock to reach a black crack and gear. Continue up to the ledge, veer a little left into a right-facing corner (crux) to top.
Gear to 2 inches.

❼ Sacrificial Virgin 5.11b ★
Start as for *Inca Stone*. Climb to the second bolt, but go left up the arete to the anchor.
6 bolts.

❽ Inca Stone 5.11d ★★★
Technical and devious, hard for the grade. Climb just right of the first bolt, clip it and make a hard move left. Veer right at the third bolt, making several hard moves to gain the anchor.
5 bolts and cams to 5 inches.

❾ Speak Softly 5.10d
Up and right of *Inca Stone* is a shorter wall, *Speak Softly*. Climb the right-leaning dirty crack.
Gear to 2 inches.

❿ Prayer Wheel 5.8
A short rock juts out from the base of this climb. Stand on the rock and climb the crack above it.
Gear to 2 inches.

⓫ Unknown 5.11a
The two-bolt route just right of *Prayer Wheel.*
2 bolts.

⓬ Truth Serum 5.7
Near the center of the wall is a right-leaning crack.
Gear to 2 inches.

⓭ Venom 5.10a ★
On the right side of the wall at some black streaks is a short dirty crack leading to grooves.
Gear to 2 inches.

⓮ Masquerade 5.9
On the far right side of the wall is a short thin crack just left of a tree.
Gear to 4.5 inches.

4
5
6
THE INCA STONE

xx
xx
7
8
9
THE INCA STONE

10
11
12
13
THE INCA STONE

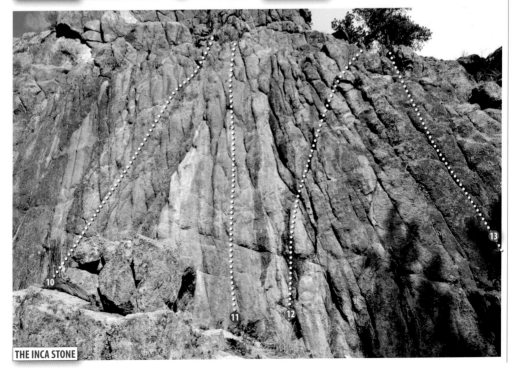

LOWER DREAM CANYON 7.6 miles

Lower Dream Canyon lies above (north) of the popular tourist attraction of Boulder Falls. A short paved path leads from the Boulder Falls parking area at 7.6 miles to the Falls themselves. Tourists flock to this area, making for hectic scenes on weekends and frequent injuries.

Beyond the Falls is a different world: Tourists rarely venture into the Canyon and, other than fellow climbers, you're unlikely to see anyone except the occasional fisherman or adventure runner. It's amazing that a place like this exists so close to a major highway and city. Bring your gear, but leave any bad vibes in the car.

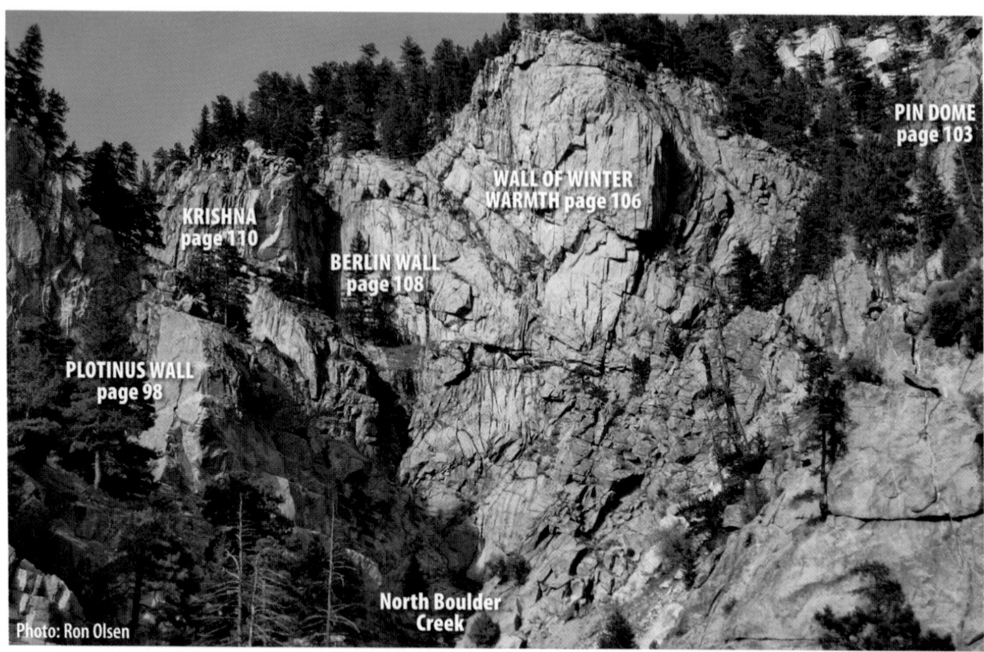

Access: This area currently has access issues.

Climbers have traditionally approached the Canyon from the Boulder Falls parking area. This involves following the paved trail toward the Falls and scrambling up a steep slope over gabions (caged rocks) on the left about 100 feet before the Falls. Above this angle up and right, pass through a notch/hole, and drop back down to the creek on the backside of the Falls. Climbers, hikers, fishermen and others have used this approach for over 30 years. Unfortunately, Boulder Open Space and Mountain Parks (OSMP) has posted signs closing the area above and behind the gabions, apparently due to potentially unsafe conditions and the number of tourists who have been injured at the Falls over the years. Local climbers and The Access Fund are negotiating with OSMP and hopefully this access issue will be resolved soon, however, at the time of writing, **this approach is illegal and you risk being ticketed for travel above and beyond the gabions.**

Currently, the only legal access to Lower Dream Canyon is via Upper Dream Canyon. Drive 3.9 miles up Boulder Canyon to Sugarloaf Rd, turn right and travel 3.1 miles to Lost Angel Road, turn left and continue for 1.5 miles on Lost Angel Road to a parking area on the left. Keep in mind that the area surrounding the Canyon is private property and show respect by not speeding, littering or parking along the road or in private areas and driveways.

From the parking area head southeast and down to a small gulch avoiding private property on the left, cross the gulch and then angle right following cairns that lead to the top of the Wall of Winter Warmth, take the gully down the south side of the Wall to the Creek. Approach time is 15 to 20 minutes to the Creek. See map opposite.

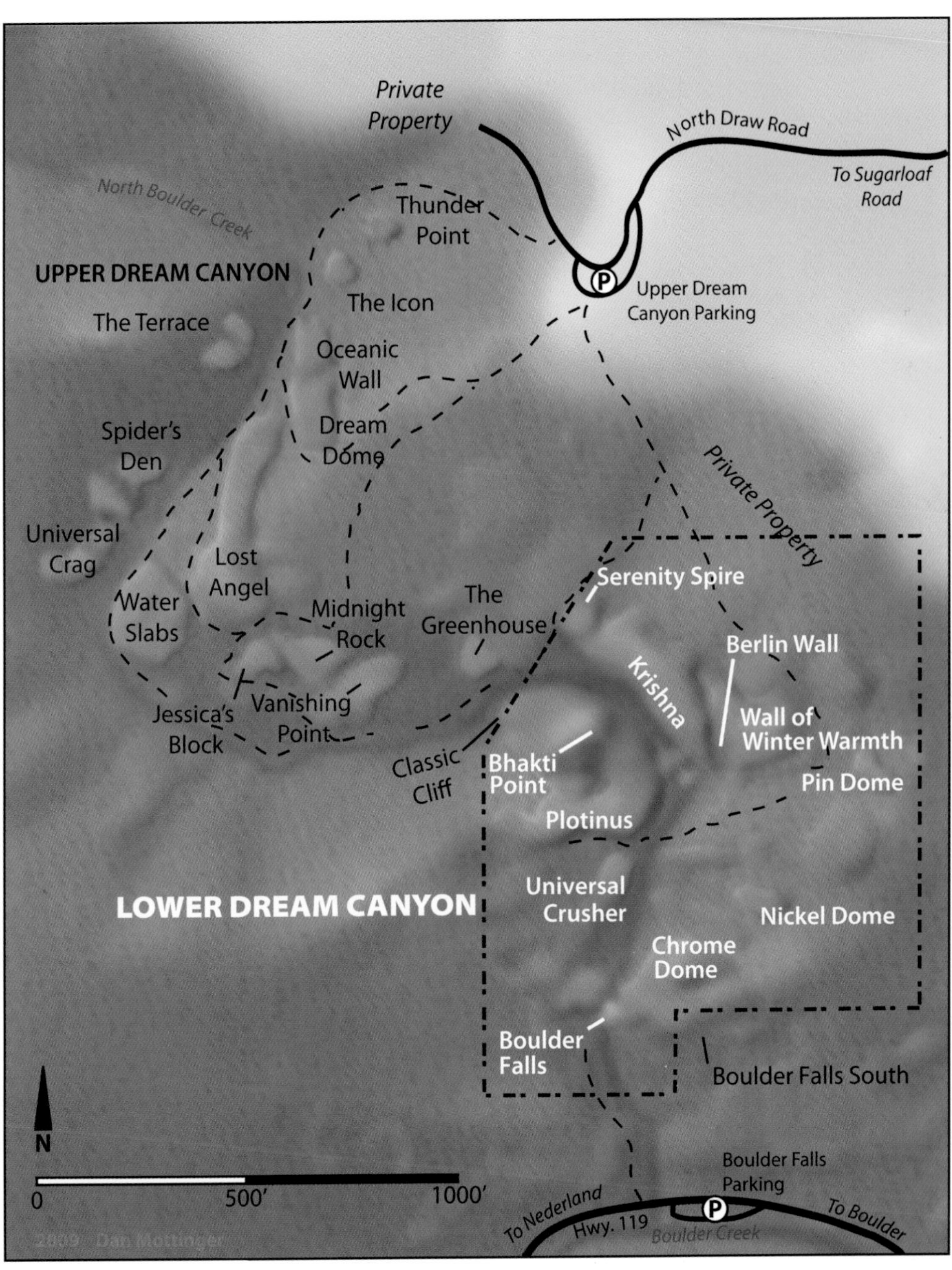
Private
Property
North Draw Road
To Sugarloaf
Road
North Boulder Creek
Thunder
Point
UPPER DREAM CANYON
Upper Dream
Canyon Parking
The Icon
The Terrace
Oceanic
Wall
Spider's
Den
Dream
Dome
Private Property
Universal
Crag
Lost
Angel
Serenity Spire
Water
Slabs
Midnight
Rock
The
Greenhouse
Berlin Wall
Krishna
Jessica's
Block
Vanishing
Point
Wall of
Winter Warmth
Classic
Cliff
Bhakti
Point
Pin Dome
Plotinus
Universal
Crusher
LOWER DREAM CANYON
Nickel Dome
Chrome
Dome
Boulder
Falls
Boulder Falls South
N
0
500'
1000'
Boulder Falls
Parking
To Nederland
Hwy. 119
Boulder Creek
To Boulder
2009 Dan Mottinger

CHROME DOME 7.6 miles

Approach time: 15 - 20 minutes.
Exposure: Northwest.

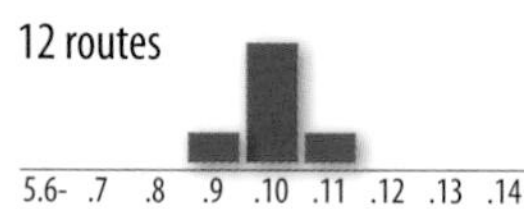

This secluded, dark piece of granite is located just upstream of the falls on the east side of the creek. The routes are slabby in nature and tend to be run-out with old, poor fixed gear.

Access: See page 92.

❶ Splendor in the Grass 5.9 R ★ ☐
On the far left side of the cliff, gain a short right-facing corner and climb right following the sparsely protected dyke.
Gear to 2 inches.

❷ Headstrong 5.10a R ★ ☐
Start down and right from *Splendor* in the Grass at a faint corner. Climb up to the dyke, then veer right and up shallow cracks to the top.
Gear to 2 inches.

❸ Platinum Blond 5.10d R ★★ ☐
Start just left of the dyke and climb up to a tree and roof. Turn the roof and gain a thin seam and follow it to the top.
Gear to 2 inches.

❹ The Sheen 5.10d R ★★ ☐
Start as for *Platinum Blond*. Climb past the tree; veer right to a flake to gain a thin crack that leads to the top.
Gear to 2 inches.

❺ Steel Blue 5.11c R ★ ☐
Traverse the ledge from the start of *The Sheen* to a two-bolt belay to gain the start. Climb a shallow, left-facing corner leading to a lone bolt. Make a difficult move past the bolt and then go straight up to the top.
Variation: Blue Sheen 5.10d R ☐
Go left from the bolt and gain the upper crack on the *Sheen*.
Gear to 2 inches.

❻ Left Side 5.10a ★★ ☐
On the left side of the lower wall climb the slab past a lone bolt to the ledge.
9 bolts.

❼ Cold-Rolled Steel 5.10b/c ★★ ☐
One of the better-protected climbs on the wall. Start right of *Left Side*, climbing the slab past three bolts to the ledge.
3 bolts, a few small cams.

❽ Point Blank 5.11b ★★ ☐
Climb right of a small corner to a bolt, trend right and up to another bolt, then fire up the face to the ledge.
2 bolts, gear to 1.5 inches.

❾ Acrophobia 5.10d R ★ ☐
Pitch 1: 5.10d. Start right of *Point Blank* to gain a face and bolt. Climb right of a small roof then up cracks to the ledge.
Pitch 2: 5.10. Climb a short thin crack then veer right up a groove to the top.
8 bolts.

❿ Tumbling Dice 5.9 R ☐
Gain a flake on the right side of the wall and then head up a groove that leads to the ledge.
Gear to 1.5 inches.

⓫ Mean Streak 5.10a ★ ☐
Start on the flake of *Tumbling Dice* and go right to the obvious black streak, following it to the ledge.
Gear to 1.5 inches.

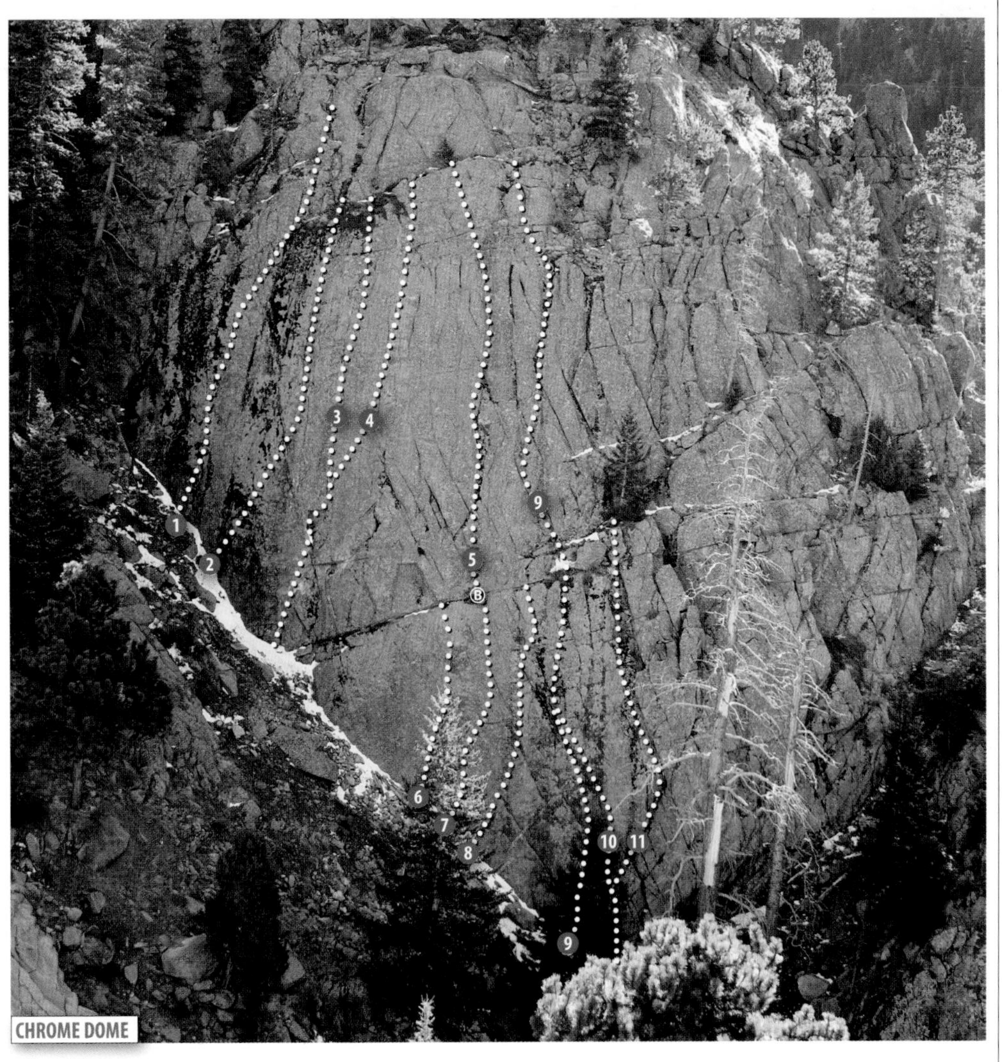

CHROME DOME

NICKEL DOME 7.6 miles

Approach time: 15 - 20 minutes.
Exposure: South.

5 routes

5.6- .7 .8 .9 .10 .11 .12 .13 .14

Nickel Dome is a hidden little crag that sits uphill just past Chrome Dome and near the scenic Boulder Falls.

Access: See page 92.

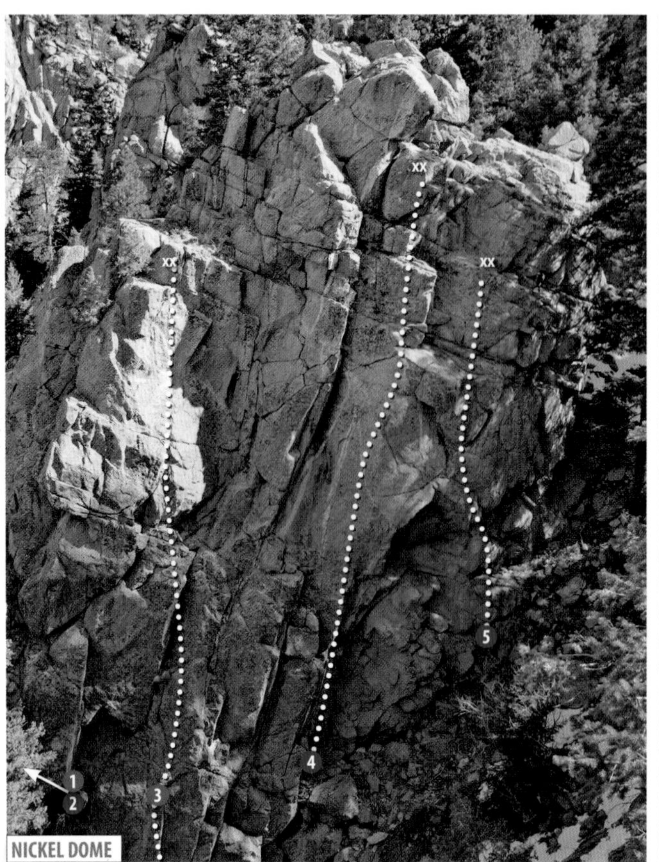

❶ Eye Opener 5.11a ★ ☐

On the left side of the crag is a slanting, tiered roof. Climb over the roof then up the face to the anchor.

4 bolts, a light rack to 2 inches.

❷ Bob the Builder 5.11a ★ ☐

Start right of *Eye Opener* at a short right-facing corner. Climb the face to a small roof, then straight up to the anchor.

6 bolts.

❸ Oversleeping 5.10a ★ ☐

Climb up the corner passing two bolts to a small ledge. Clip the fourth bolt and head left into a crack system. Follow the crack around a small roof and up to a steep face. Crank up cool moves past two bolts to a two-bolt anchor.

7 bolts, light rack to medium.

❹ King Slopers 5.11c ★ ☐

At the right side of the cliff is an overhanging section of rock. *King Slopers* starts at the left side of this section at a right-facing corner. Stem around some dubious-looking rock past two bolts to gain a ledge. Climb up a scoop and then move sharply right to finish on the blunt arete.

7 bolts.

❺ Engineering Marvel 5.11c ★ ☐

On the far right side of the Nickel Dome is a square-cut overhang 15 feet off the ground. This is *Engineering Marvel.* Climb past the first two bolts. Avoid the block on the left and power up the overhang, make a hard move over the overhang and then another one to gain a good hold and the end of the hard climbing.

4 bolts.

UNIVERSAL CRUSHER ROCK 7.6 miles

Approach time: 15 - 20 minutes.
Exposure: South and north.

3 routes

5.6- .7 .8 .9 .10 .11 .12 .13 .14

This block/boulder sits right off the trail directly opposite the old Universal crusher mining equipment sitting in the creek.

Access: See page 92. The wall is just left of the start of the uphill trail to Plotinus Wall.

1 Fly Off The Handle 5.12b/c ★★ ☐
The obvious bolted route on the south side of the block. Power moves and a big lunge will get you to the anchor.
4 bolts.

2 Seamingly Left Out 5.11a ★ ☐
On the left side of the north face of the block, climb to a short crack and power up the seam to the top.
Gear to 1 inch, 2 nad 2.5 inch cams to belay.

3 Universal Crusher 5.11a ★ ☐
A nice short route up the right side of the block past four bolts.
4 bolts.

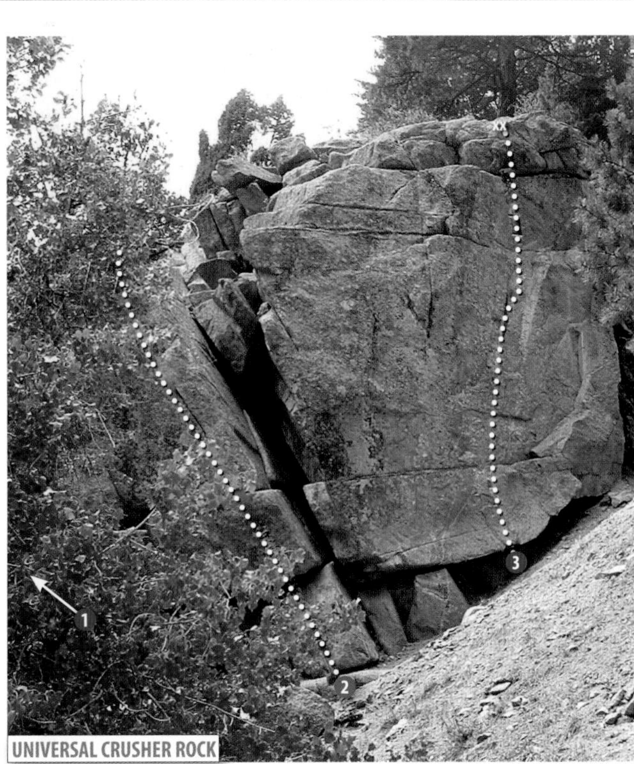

UNIVERSAL CRUSHER ROCK

PLOTINUS WALL 7.6 miles

Approach time: 20 minutes.
Exposure: East and South.

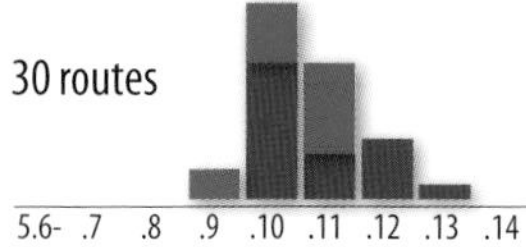

One of the best walls for moderate sport routes along the Front Range. Great winter sun in the late morning and nice shade in the afternoon during the summer months. Bring gear, as several routes require the odd piece and there are also a few good trad climbs.

Access: See page 92.

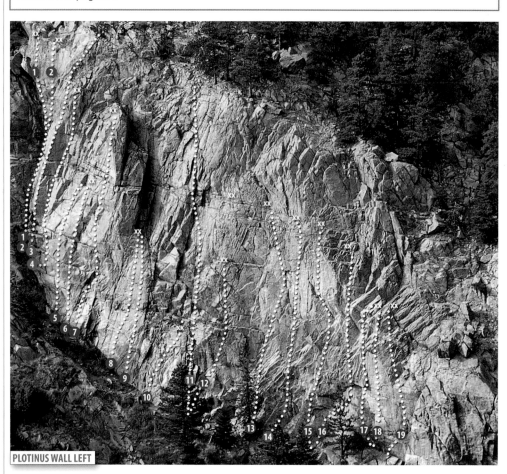

PLOTINUS WALL LEFT

❶ My Buddy 5.10c

On the far left side of the cliff, start as for *Bedtime Story* (just past the fourth bolt) and then head left, following a line of bolts up the steep slab. There is an optional belay.
12 bolts.

❷ Bedtime Story 5.10b ★

Nice start leads to good face climbing. Long pitch.
11 bolts.

❸ Sleepless Child 5.9 ★★

Nice route that climbs up to a pine tree and then to the top. Walk off to the west.
Gear to 2 inches.

4 Morpheus 5.11b ★★
A nice long pitch that follows the obvious corner to a steep face. Small gear for the lower section. A 60-meter rope is critical.
8 bolts and gear to 4.5 inches.

5 Wake Up Call 5.10a/b ★★★★
Really good slab climbing on almost perfect granite. Do this route.
7 bolts.

6 Snooze Button 5.10a/b ★★★
Another great slab route on perfect granite..
9 bolts.

7 Chore Boy 5.10c ★★★
An excellent long pitch that climbs a beautiful headwall. Watch when lowering – this was the scene of bad accident. A 60-meter rope is critical.
10 bolts.

8 Smell the Coffee 5.10a ★★
Another good route that climbs a steep wall on excellent granite. **Option:** From the anchor, trend right and follow the bolts up a dirty but nice face.
8 bolts.

9 The Daily Grind 5.10d ★★
Just right of *Smell the Coffee.* Climb up the steep face to a seam, make a devious move over the small roof and prance up the steep face, then angle left to the anchor for *Smell the Coffee*. **Option:** From the anchor, trend right and follow the bolts up a dirty but nice face.
8 bolts.

10 Napster 5.10a ★★★
If only it was 100 feet longer. The obvious right-leaning flake. Climb a short face to reach the flake. Layback and then make a hard move to reach the anchors.
4 bolts.

11 Something Obscure 5.10a
The shallow crack 10 feet right of *Napster. Shallow* jams lead to a ledge and broken rock. Climb to the top and walk off to the west.
Gear to 2 inches.

12 Tooth Fairy 5.11a ★★
Hard moves at the start lead to pleasant climbing above. The FA party went straight over the roof then into the upper corner, grading it 5.11c. Most climbers now step left below the roof and then right to the upper corners.
8 bolts.

13 Mr. Sandman 5.10a ★★★
Start at a large pine and climb beautiful featured granite to the anchor. Classic.
10 bolts.

14 Golden Slumber 5.10d ★★★
Another classic on featured granite. Bring some small gear for the middle part of the climb and the bat flake.
8 bolts, medium gear.

15 Sleepless in Boulder 5.11b ★★
Excellent steep start leads to fun jug climbing above. A large flake was removed from the start, making this climb much safer.
11 bolts.

16 The Art of Dreaming 5.12b ★★
Starts just right of *Sleepless in Boulder.* Climb up steep rock and then make a rising traverse to the right. The crux is gaining a ledge, then crank the roof and fire straight up to the anchor.
11 bolts.

17 The Bobsled 5.11d ★★★
A classic pitch. Start on ledge right of *The Art of Dreaming*. Climb up to the first bolt, make a committing move, clip the second bolt, and trend right to reach a good stance below a roof. Fire up and out the roof (tricky) on better holds to the anchor.
8 bolts.

18 War on Freedom 5.13a ★★
Start down and just right of *The Bobsled*. Strenuous moves to start lead to some long reaches on the upper wall. Great route. You can also climb the first few bolts and link into *The Bobsled* at 5.12.
12 bolts.

PLOTINUS WALL, LUCID DREAMING

19 Lucky Strikes 5.12b ★★★
Another classic route - steep climbing past the first two bolts leads to continuous climbing up the face. Fight the pump to the anchor.
9 bolts.

20 Corner Pocket 5.9
The obvious corner splitting the two walls.
Gear to 3 inches.

21 Nerve Damage 5.11a
Start just right of the corner and climb up to an old bolt. Make hard moves left to *Corner Pocket* and then scramble to the top. Traverse right at the top and rap from *The Scientist* anchor.
Gear to 3 inches.

The following routes begin from a ledge down and right from Nerve Damage.

22 The Scientist 5.11a ★★★★
One of the best slabs in the Boulder area. Looks impossible from the ground but is a classic on good holds. Climb up the blank face to the second bolt. . .teeter over to a crack and then fire straight up over a roof and clean face to the anchor. Photo page 105.

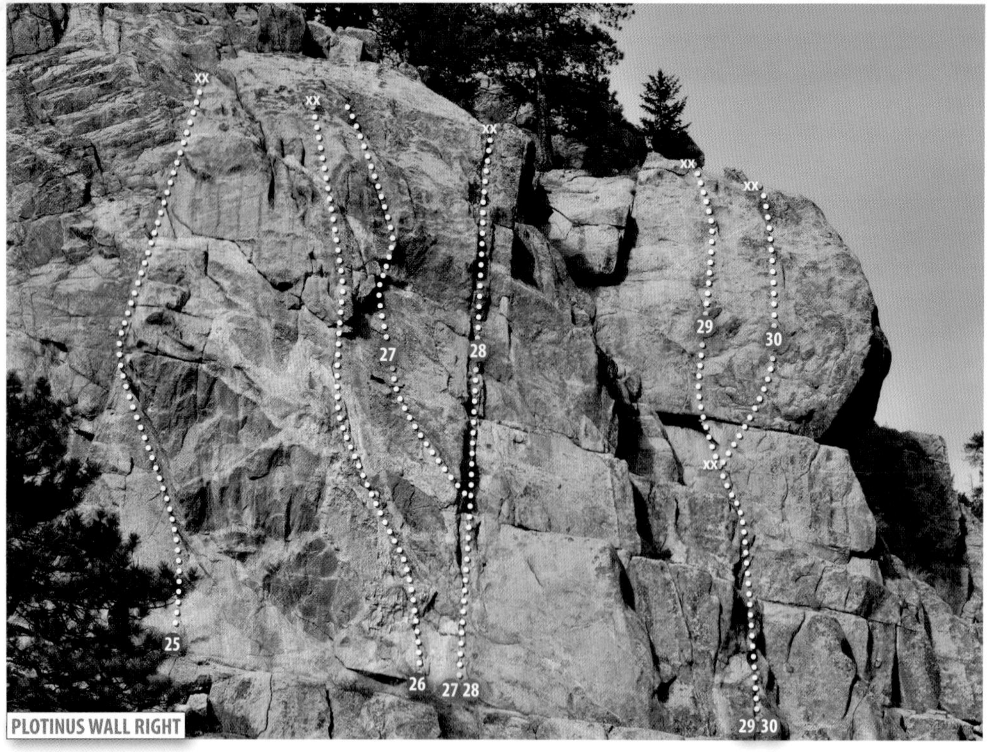

PLOTINUS WALL RIGHT

23 Plotinus 5.10a/b ☐

The namesake route of the crag and a strange one at that. Start right of *The Scientist* and follow the crack left across the wall.

Gear to 3 inches.

24 Rama 5.10c ☐

The obvious V-corner just left of the arete. See cover photo.

3 bolts, gear to 3 inches.

25 Lucid Dreaming 5.12d ★★★★ ☐

See description opposite.

The following routes are around to the right on a ledge overlooking the creek: be careful on this ledge. There is an anchor, so use it!

26 Boulder Quartz System 5.12a ★★★ ☐

Another soon to be classic on wild quartz-featured rock. The quartz-filled corner right of *Lucid Dreaming*. Stem up the corner with increasing difficulty to a small roof, turn the roof and reach the anchor.

8 bolts.

27 Tooth and Nail 5.11a ★ ☐

Same start as *Counting Sheep*, then left up to a steep face with bolts.

6 bolts, gear to 2 inches.

28 Counting Sheep 5.11a ☐

Start just right of *Boulder Quartz System*. Climb up the thin crack with good gear and then go right up into the corner past some bolts to the anchor.

3 bolts, gear to 2 inches.

Fifteen feet right of the Boulder Quartz System *is a 20-foot hand crack leading to a large ledge with a clean 50-foot slab above. This is the start of* Sominex *and* Sleep Deprivation.

29 Sominex 5.11a ★★ ☐

Pitch 1: 5.7. Climb the crack using small-to-medium gear, gaining the ledge after 25 feet. Belay at a 2-bolt anchor. You can avoid this pitch by scrambling in from the right.

Pitch 2: 5.11a. Climb up a short left-facing corner (with gear) stepping right to clip the first of several bolts. Make a hard move and follow the line of bolts up the clean slab to a two-bolt anchor. Alternately, one can start on *Sleep Deprivation* and move left into *Sominex*, requiring no gear.

8 bolts, gear to 2 inches.

30 Sleep Deprivation 5.10d ★ ☐

Pitch 1: 5.7. Climb the crack using small-to-medium gear, gaining the ledge after 25 feet. Belay at a 2-bolt anchor. You can avoid this pitch by scrambling in from the right.

Pitch 2: 5.10d. Climb past two bolts on the right to reach a horizontal crack (crux). Continue up past 4 bolts at the right side of the face and move back left to the anchor of Sominex. Great slab climbing on excellent rock.

6 bolts, gear to 2 inches.

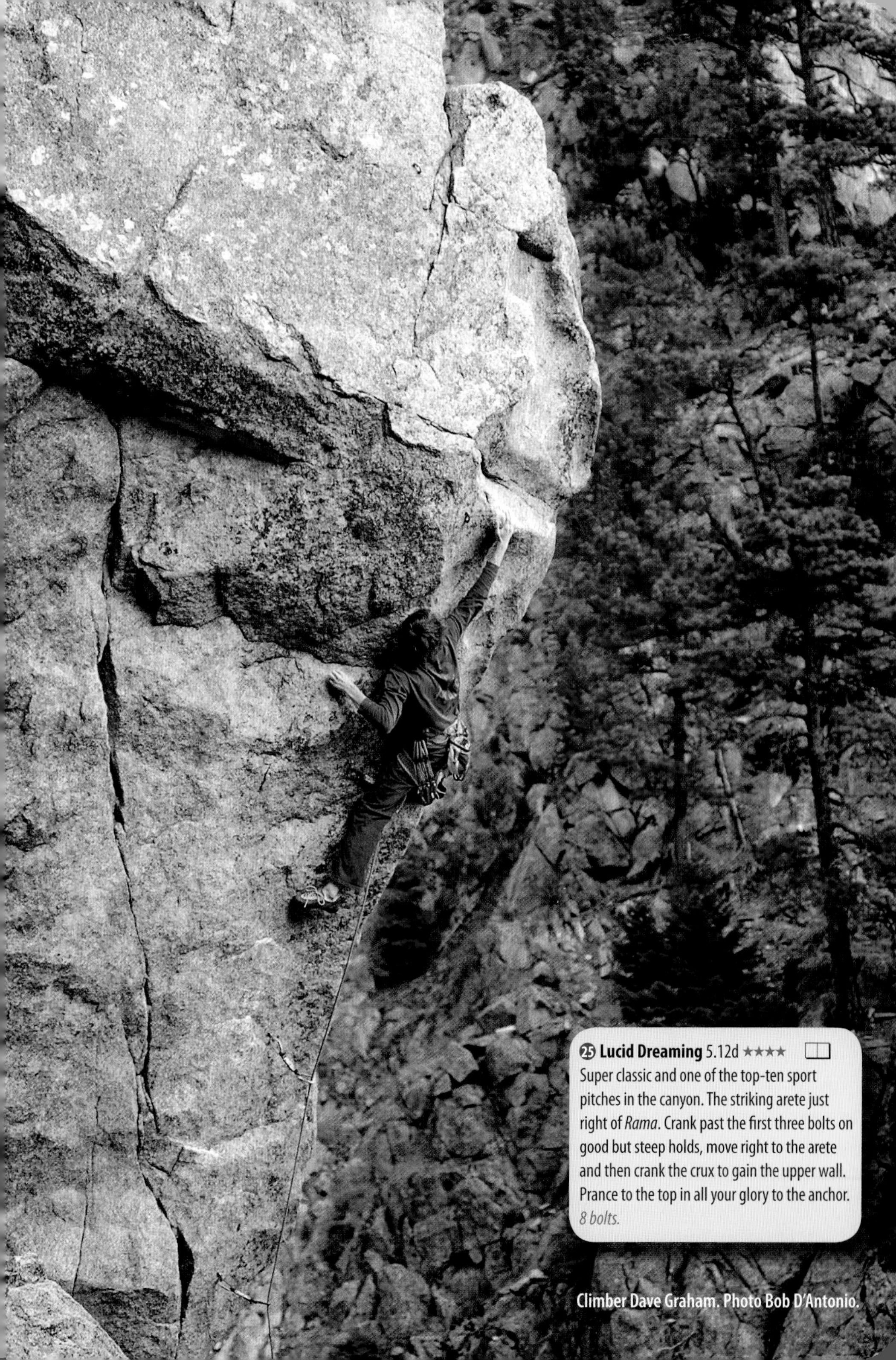

25 Lucid Dreaming 5.12d ★★★★

Super classic and one of the top-ten sport pitches in the canyon. The striking arete just right of *Rama*. Crank past the first three bolts on good but steep holds, move right to the arete and then crank the crux to gain the upper wall. Prance to the top in all your glory to the anchor. *8 bolts.*

Climber Dave Graham. Photo Bob D'Antonio.

BHAKTI POINT 7.6 miles

Approach time: 25 - 35 minutes.
Exposure: East and south.

5 routes

5.6- .7 .8 .9 .10 .11 .12 .13 .14

Bhakti Point is a nice summit knob high above Boulder Creek in Lower Dream Canyon. A few good sport routes exist on the wall and the view into Upper Dream Canyon makes the approach worthwhile.

Access: See page 92. Head to the Plotinus Wall. Skirt the wall on the left and then reach a steep gully leading to the notch on the right. Gain the notch and then up a steep fourth-class wall to gain a large ledge. Follow the ledge east to the climbs.

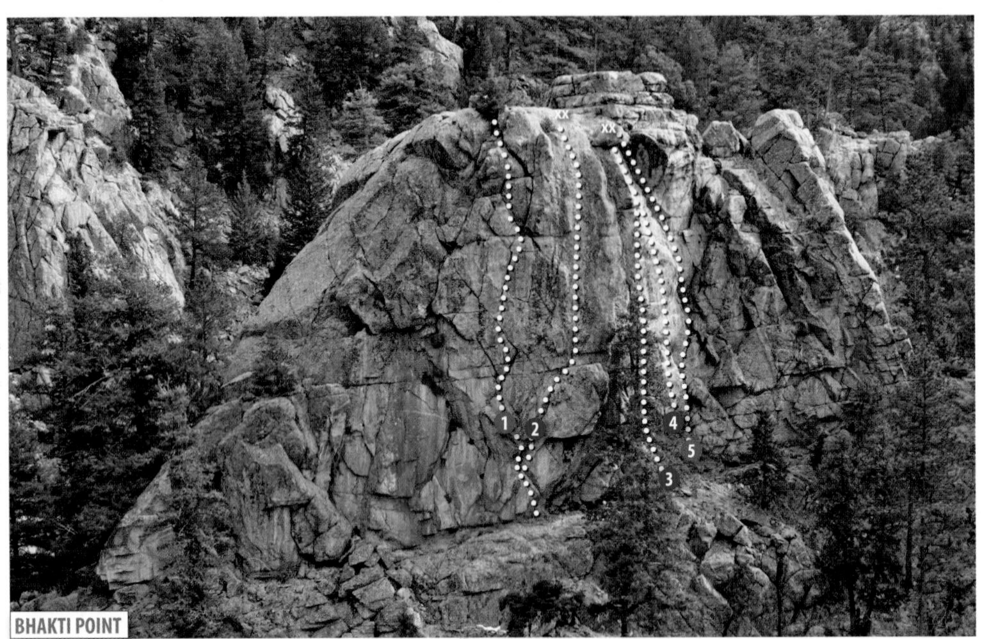

❶ The Talon 5.10b/c ★
Climb a short fist crack on the left side of the wall to a thin crack that leads to the summit.
Gear to three inches.

❷ Sport Crystal 5.11a/b ★
Start just right of *The Talon* and climb a nice face into a black groove studded with cool crystals.
7 bolts.

❸ English Immersion 5.12a ★★
Start 15 feet right of *The Talon* and *Sport Crystal*. Begin in an overhanging flared crack just right of a pine tree. Climb up to a quartz crystal filled vein and then exit right to the short slab finish of *Flight of the Bumbly.*
7 bolts.

❹ Flight of the Bumbly 5.11c ★★
Start about 20 feet right of *English Immersion*. Climb up to a left-angling ramp. Exit the ramp onto the face and make a series of difficult moves to gain the slab above.
7 bolts.

❺ West Ride 5.6 ★
Climb the obvious hand and fist crack on the right side of the wall.
Gear to 3 inches.

PIN DOME 7.6 miles

Approach time: 30 - 40 minutes.
Exposure: South and southwest.

4 routes

5.6- .7 .8 .9 .10 .11 .12 .13 .14

This secluded piece of rock lies just south of the Wall of Winter Warmth up on a ridge. There are a couple really good routes and maybe the best stemming corner (*Big Sky Corner*) in Boulder Canyon.

Access: See page 92. Cross to the east side of the creek just past the Plotinus Wall. Hug the creek passing the Lower Buttress of the Wall of Winter Warmth then head up the steep gully just right of the south face of Wall of Winter Warmth.

1 Big Sky Corner 5.12c/d ★★★★ ☐
Classic, top ten in the canyon. Start just right of the mine hole and climb up a groove to a good ledge below a short corner. Climb the corner, then veer a little left into the main corner to below an overhang. Go left under the roof and then up to the anchor.
10 bolts, a couple of 1 to 1.5 inch cams.

2 Big Sky Arete 5.12a ★★★ ☐
Start right of a hobbit hole (mine hole) up a steep slab and over a small roof to a good ledge below the arete. Climb the arete using a crack and a strange move to gain the anchor.
10 bolts, 0.75 micro-cam and few small cams.

3 Sweetest Taboo 5.10c R ★ ☐
Start right of *Big Sky Arete*, climbing poor rock to below a small roof. Fire up past the roof and then a short face up to a right-facing corner and then to the anchor.
2 bolts, gear to medium.

4 Mine all Mine 5.10a ★★ ☐
About 300 feet right of *Sweetest Taboo* is a nice arete up a steep slab. *Mine all Mine* climbs the face, slab, and arete to an anchor.
6 bolts.

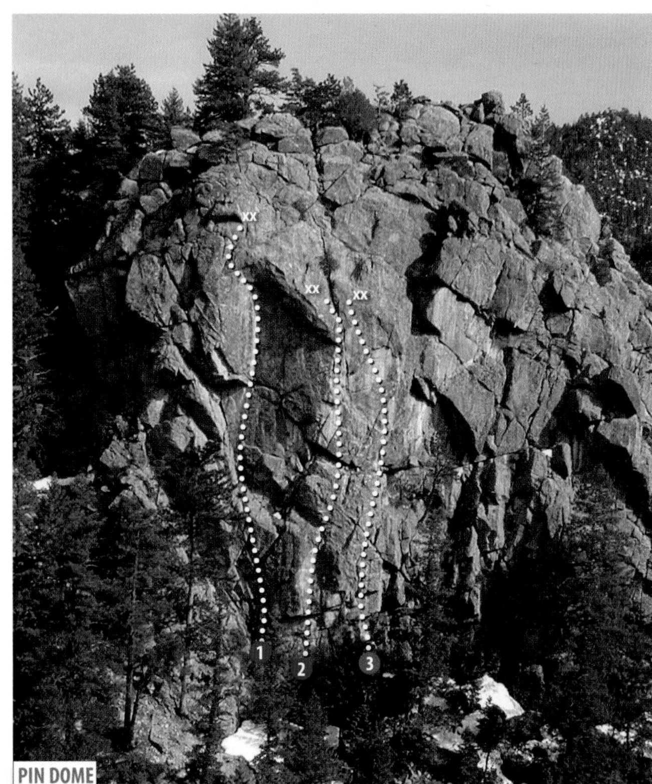

WALL OF WINTER WARMTH LOWER BUTTRESS 7.6 miles

Approach time: 20 - 30 minutes.
Exposure: East, south, and west.

6 routes

5.6- .7 .8 .9 .10 .11 .12 .13 .14

The impressive Wall of Winter Warmth dominates the area above Boulder Falls. The lower buttress contains several worthwhile routes on really good granite.

Access: See page 92. Cross the east side of the creek just past the Plotinus Wall. Hug the creek to reach the Lower Buttress.

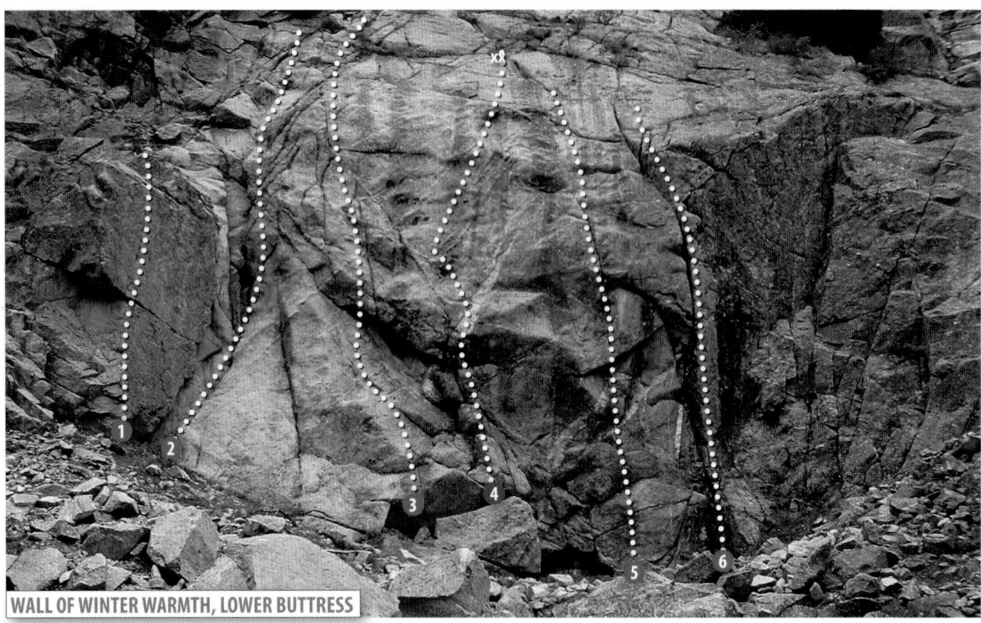

WALL OF WINTER WARMTH, LOWER BUTTRESS

❶ Escutcheon 5.10b ★ ☐
Climb the obvious crack in the large boulder just left of the Lower Buttress.
Small to medium gear.

❷ Mini Moe 5.2 ☐
Mini Moe climbs the easy crack/chimney on the left side of the rock just right of the *Escutcheon* boulder.
Gear to 2.5 inches.

❸ Closed Open Space 5.9 ★ ☐
A nice climb that takes small gear to supplement the bolts.
5 bolts, gear to 0.75 micro-cam.

❹ Alpha-Bob 5.12a ★★ ☐
On the left side of the slab, climb up to a small overhang, clip the first bolt, and make a hard move onto a small ledge. From the ledge angle up and right making a hard smear move (crux) with the feet and small crimps for the hands. Clip the last of the bolts and mantel up onto a ledge with the anchor.
6 bolts.

❺ Leader of the Pack 5.11d ★★ ☐
Start right of *Alpha-Bob* and climb up to the first bolt on good edges. Climb up to a small overhang, clip the second bolt and smear up on balancy moves reaching a finger crack (crux). Layback and jam (with gear) up the crack to good holds and the anchor.
4 bolts, gear to 0.75 micro-cam.

❻ The Slit 5.10a ★★ ☐
The obvious hand and wide crack on the right side of the wall. Holds moisture and is a little dirty. . . still a nice route and good approach pitch for routes on the main buttress.
Gear to 3.5 inches.

Dan Brockway on *The Scientist* 5.11a, Plotinus Wall, page 99. Photo Bob D'Antonio.

WALL OF WINTER WARMTH 7.6 miles
MAIN BUTTRESS

Approach time: 20 - 35 minutes.
Exposure: East, south, and west.

12 routes

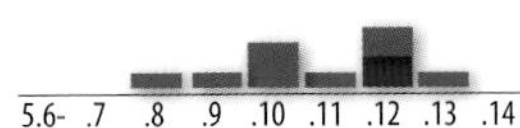

The impressive Wall of Winter Warmth dominates the area above Boulder Falls. The wall gets winter sun (*duh*) and has a fine collection of trad and sport routes in a beautiful setting above Boulder Creek.

Access: See page 92. Cross to the east side of the creek just past the Plotinus Wall. Hug the creek to reach the Lower Buttress. Skirt the lower buttress on the left and make your way up to the main wall.

❶ On The Bough 5.12a ★★ ☐

Access the start by climbing the first pitch of Left Side or by hiking down a steep gully from the top of the rock just above the Berlin Wall. A new two-bolt anchor has been placed at the start for a better and safer belay. This route starts just left of *Angle of Repose* on the Wall of Winter Warmth. Clip the first bolt and make a hard move (crux) on a very rounded hold to gain a flared crack. Make a series of strenuous moves up the overhanging face past several bolts angling right to the first belay of *Angle of Repose*. Rap to the ground or climb the second pitch of *AOR*.

7 bolts.

❷ Angle of Repose 5.12a ★★★★ ☐

One of the best two-pitch climbs in the canyon. Access the start by climbing the first pitch of *Left Side* or by hiking down a steep gully from the top of the rock just above the Berlin Wall. A new two-bolt anchor has been placed at the start for a better and safer belay.

Pitch 1: 5.12a. Follow a line of bolts up a steep wall. The first moves off the ground are the crux (lunge) and lead to steep continuous climbing up past a "tooth" to good holds and the end of the first pitch. *7 bolts.*

Pitch 2: 5.12a. The repose pitch! Climb up on good holds to a small overlap. Crank past the overlap making technical moves into a shallow corner. Stem up the corner moving left on extremely thin holds (crux) into another shallow corner. Make hard layback moves up into a shallow corner over a steep section that leads to a good rest. Follow bolts up to the anchors on great holds with spectacular exposure. *12 bolts.*

Descent: Rappel.

❸ Left Side 5.10b ★★★★ ☐

An amazing outing on mostly solid granite in a pristine position high above Boulder Creek.

Pitch 1: 5.9+. Climb *The Slit* (previous page) to access the main buttress or scramble up and left aiming for the black grooves on the left side of the wall.

Pitch 2: 5.10b. Climb the obvious black cracks/grooves to a belay at a tree. The crux of the climb.

Pitch 3: 5.9. From the belay tree, work right out onto easy climbing on the edge of an overhang. Continue up following good cracks and then trend left to a finger crack in a slot. Climb the slot up to a belay on the left. Spectacular position.

Pitch 4: 5.9. Work left from the belay climbing over a small roof. Aim straight up to a roof and skirt it on the right and reach the top.

SR.

Descent: Rap from the AOR anchors or walk off to the south.

❹ Cop Out 5.9 R ★ ☐

Hike up to the Wall of Winter Warmth and start the climb on a ledge right near a pine tree below the wall.

Pitch 1: 5.9. Angle right and reach a wide crack, place a large Friend, and traverse left up into a shallow crack. Follow the crack up to an old 1/4" bolt and a new 3/8" bolt.

Pitch 2: 5.9 R. Angle up and left to a corner and surmount a roof. Climb up and slightly right to a belay.

Pitch 3: 5.8. Climb up to a small corner and then follow the path of least resistance to the top.

SR.

Descent: Walk off to the south.

❺ Direct Cop Out 5.10c ★★★ ☐

Hike up to the Wall of Winter Warmth and start the climb on a ledge right near a pine tree below the wall.

Pitch 1: 5.9+. Start near the pine tree and angle up and left to a bolt. Clip the first bolt and climb up and over the roof on cool holds. Continue up the face to the belay. Bring some small gear.

Pitch 2: 5.10c. Follow a shallow crack up to old 1/4" bolt and angle right up steep, shallow cracks into a sentry box. Clip the first of two bolts (placed on lead) up to a shallow right-facing corner. Clip the second bolt and make cool moves up to a ledge (watch out for loose block) and belay.

Pitch 3: 5.9-. Climb up to an old bolt and climb straight into a shallow right-facing corner. Great moves up the corner lead to a small overhang. Climb straight up through the overhang and follow shallow cracks with good gear to the top of the wall.

Gear to 2 inches. Walk off to the south.

6 Direct 5.10d ★★ ☐

As the name suggest. . . a direct line up the south face. Hike up to the Wall of Winter Warmth and start the climb on a ledge right near a pine tree below the wall.

Pitch 1: 5.10b. Start about 30 feet right of the pines and follow cracks up to an old bolt and belay.

Pitch 2: 5.10d. Climb over the roof and follow discontinuous cracks on easier terrain to the top.

SR.

Descent: Walk off to the south.

7 The Titleist 5.11b/c ★★ ☐

aka The Alicia Golembeski Memorial Route

Pitch 1: 5.11b/c. Start on the *Regular Route* to a ledge about 25 feet up. Climb up to a "tooth," clip two bolts and head up to a roof. Climb the roof to a seam, and then climb a second roof. Head straight up to a notch and climb it on the right, making a hard mantel move, and up to a two bolt anchor.

Pitch 2: 5.11a. Follow a line of bolts up between *Direct* and the *Regular Route*.

SR.

Descent: Rap the route from the end of the 2nd pitch. **A 60m rope is critical.**

8 Regular Route 5.8 ★ ☐

Pitch 1: 5.8. The obvious slot on the right side of the wall, climb to a belay.

Pitch 2: 5.7. Continue up the slot to the top.

Gear to 3.5 inches.

9 Right Side 5.10a ★★ ☐

Pitch 1: 5.10a. Climb the *Regular Route* to just below the belay, angle left out the large roof on good holds to a ledge.

Pitch 2: 5.9. Follow cracks to the top.

Gear to 3.5 inches.

10 Mordor 5.12b/c ★★★ ☐

Three-star climbing with four-star position! The second pitch of *Mordor* is one of the most spectacular in the Boulder area.

Pitch 1: 5.11a. Start 50 feet right of the *Direct Route* on a ledge with several pine trees. Climb up a dog-leg crack (tricky start and gear) to a ledge. Follow a thin seam past two bolts up to a two-bolt-anchor.

Pitch 2: 5.12b/c. Climb up to the first bolt and make committing moves out left towards the arete. Make a hard, technical move past the second bolt and reach a good incut hold. Follow the bolts up the face and move left at the fourth bolt. Reach the arete and 500 feet of air below your feet. A spectacular spot! Climb the arete up to a two-bolt-anchor.

Gear to 0.75 micro-cam and 11 quickdraws

Descent: Rappel the route to the ground.

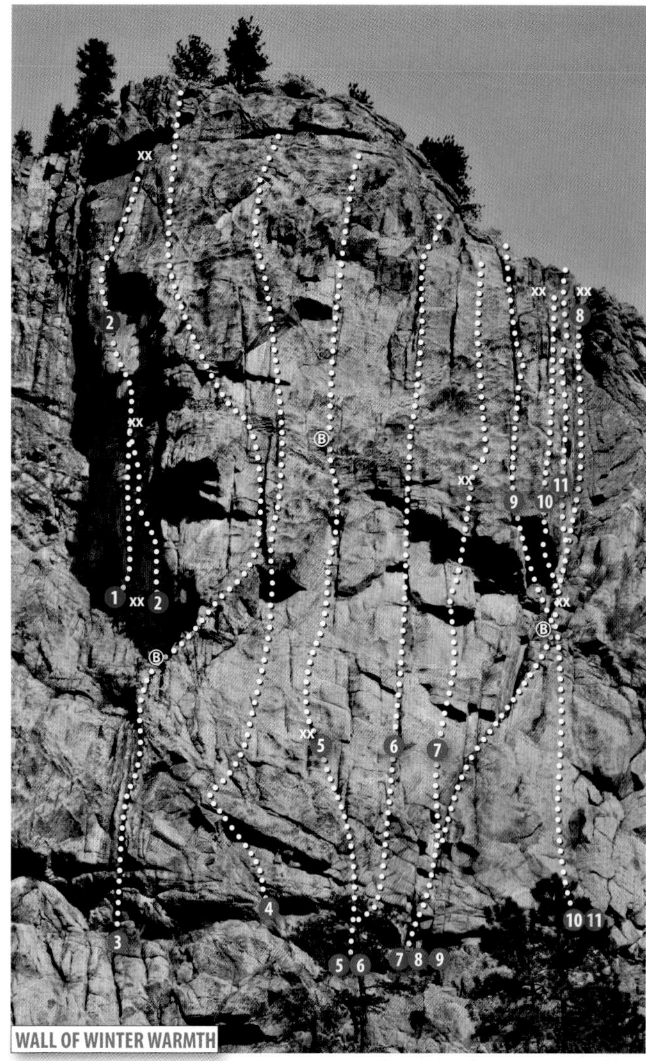

WALL OF WINTER WARMTH

11 The Prisoner 5.12b ★★★ ☐

Climb the first pitch of *Mordor* or scramble right of the wall and then angle in on good ledges to the base of the climb. The business: climb up into a pod, exit the pod, angle right and then up a crack/corner to the top.

Gear to 2 inches.

12 Bed Hog 5.13b ★★★ ☐

Start as for *The Prisoner* but go right and up the steep bolted face. Lower or rap from a two bolt anchor. Sandbag for the grade.

5 bolts, gear to 4.5 inches.

BERLIN WALL 7.6 miles

Approach time: 20 - 35 minutes.
Exposure: South and west.

14 routes

5.6- .7 .8 .9 .10 .11 .12 .13 .14

The impressive Wall of Winter Warmth dominates the area above Boulder Falls. Just left of the upper wall is this chunk of granite sitting high above the creek. In the early 1980s a handful of trad routes (mostly R-rated) were done on the wall, but it never became popular due to the runout nature of the routes. In the early 2000s that changed as several well-protected sport routes were completed, offering good climbs with better protection. The 2008 season saw more great sport routes added, too.

Access: See page 92. Cross to the east side of the creek just past the Plotinus Wall. Hug the creek and then reach the Lower Buttress. Skirt the lower buttress on the left and climb up the steep gully (easy fifth class) to a shelf below the hanging wall.

1 Walpurgisnacht 5.11b ★★ ☐
On the far left side of the wall, climb a steep black face past several bolts to a two-bolt anchor. This route was retrobolted with the FA party's permission.
7 bolts.

2 Dachau 5.11a ★ ☐
Start just left of a right-facing corner that starts about 20 feet off the ground. Climb up to just below the left side of the corner/flake, place gear and angle left past an old bolt, climbing a steep face to the anchor.
Gear to 2 inches.

3 Iron Curtain 5.10d ★★ ☐
Start right of *Dachau*, climbing up a steep ramp to the corner/flake; follow the corner to the top.
Gear to 2.5 inches.

4 Fall of the Wall 5.12b ★★★ ☐
The obvious black-streaked wall 20 feet right of *Iron Curtain*. Climb straight up the black streak with a crux down low, reach a small roof and trend to the left then up.
7 bolts.

5 East Germany 5.12d ★★★ ☐
Climb a short pillar just right of *Fall of the Wall* and then up the steep wall, laybacking to below a small roof; climb the roof and easier rock to the belay.
11 bolts.

6 Stalingrad 5.11c R/X ☐
I don't know of anyone other than the FA party who has done this route on lead. Near the center of the wall is a block/pedestal behind a tree. Place gear then launch into the dark, aiming for a double flaring crack that leads to the top.
Gear to 2.5 inches.

7 Waterboarding 5.12b/c ★★★ ☐
A really good route with some engaging crux moves. Start on a gold blocky wall aiming for a black streak. Climb the steep wall just left of the black streak to the anchors.
10 bolts.

8 Interrogation 5.12c ★★★★ ☐
The best route on the wall in my opinion. Start right of *Waterboarding*, climbing blocky rock to below a small roof. Veer right past the roof, milk a rest then fire up the steep layback cracks on the right side of the black streak.
10 bolts.

9 Blitzkrieg 5.11 R ☐
Left of *Eastern Promises* is steep wall leading to a roof. Climb up the face past an old bolt to the roof, then veer right into a left-facing corner, climbing it to the top.

10 Eastern Promises 5.13b ★★★ ☐
Start just right of two low black streaks. Climb blocky rock to just below a roof, continue up via weird power moves through the bulge/roof, and then follow easier rock to the top. The hardest route on the wall and the fine work of Dan Levison and Matt Samet.
10 bolts.

11 Weinachtsfest 5.11 R ☐
Start on the far right side of the wall. Climb a short pillar and veer left to a thin hand crack through a bulge. Now move right and follow a crack to the top.
Gear to 2.5 inches.

12 Himmelbrunch 5.10d R ☐
Start just right of *Weinachtsfest*, climbing straight up to a roof; veer left over the roof and finish as for *Weinachtsfest*.

13 Checkpoint Bravo 5.10d ★ ☐
Climb blocky rock up over a small roof to the anchors.
6 bolts.

14 Checkpoint Charlie 5.10 ☐
On the far right side of the wall, climb the obvious left-facing dihedral.
Gear to 2.5 inches.

xx
xx
xx
xx
xx
xx
1
2
3
4
5
6
7
8
9
10
11
12
13
14
BERLIN WALL

KRISHNA 7.6 miles

Approach time: 20 - 30 minutes.
Exposure: South and southwest.

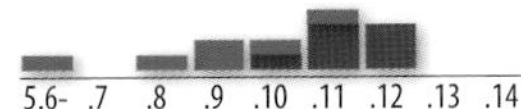

The impressive Wall of Winter Warmth dominates the area above Boulder Falls. The lower buttress contains several worthwhile routes on really good granite. The Krishna Spire lies just north of the main wall holding a commanding position high above the creek offering several good routes in a remote setting.

Access: See page 92. Cross to east side of the creek just past the Plotinus Wall. Hug the creek passing the Lower Buttress of the Wall of Winter Warmth and the gully to the Berlin Wall to the wall on the left coming out of the creek.

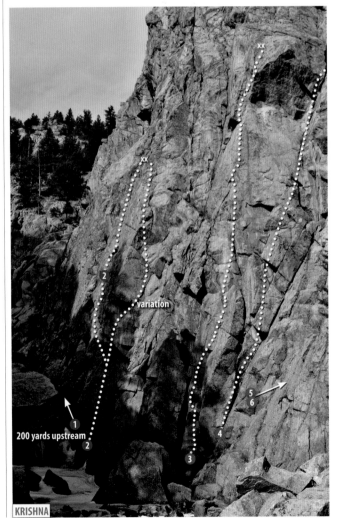

❶ Full Circle 5.12b ★★ ☐
Hike past the small water fall and reach a short corner below a large roof about 200 feet left of *Black Pool*. Scramble up to a ledge system above a narrow gully (200 feet above the creek). Climb straight up 50 feet of moderate rock up to a massive triangular two-tiered roof. Pull through the roof (crux) via throws to a small edge and dish to good holds and the anchor above.
7 bolts.

❷ Black Pool 5.11c ★★ ☐
Start out of the creek just right of the waterfall and left of a large detached block. Climb up to a small roof and then left up a steep face to the anchor.
Variation: 5.11c. At the roof go over the roof and into a short corner, then left up to the anchor.
8 bolts.

❸ Diving for Kipper Snacks 5.11a ★★ ☐
Start right of the detached block and head up a crack/corner veering left up the face arete to the anchor.
5 bolts, gear to medium.

❹ Helix 5.9+ ★ ☐
Start as for *Kipper Snacks* but continue up into a right-facing corner to the top.
Gear to 3 inches.

5 Old and Easy 5.6 ★ ☐
Climb the long left facing dihedral to the upper wall.
Gear to 3 inches.

6 Eat my Lichen 5.8 ★ ☐
Climb the next corner right of *Old and Easy* finishing on the same ledge.
Gear to 3 inches.

UPPER LEDGE OF KRISHNA

To reach the Upper Ledge of Krishna, follow the obvious gully system to the base of the Berlin Wall, go left on a narrow ledge, and belay.

7 Shiva the Destroyer 5.11c ☐
This climb is located just left *Prajna* below and left of an obvious cave/overhang. Start left of the cave and head up a face that leads to cracks and then the anchors.
10 bolts.

8 Cave Traverse 5.12b/c ★ ☐
Start right of the cave and make a rising traverse past several bolts to reach the upper part of *Shiva the Destroyer* and the anchors.
12 bolts.

9 Prajna 5.10b ★ ☐
Climb the obvious orange arete past a bolt and several loose looking flakes.
1 bolts, gear to 3 inches.

10 Higher Rites 5.11b ★★ ☐
Climb the bolted face just right of the arête. Steep climbing on good edges.
6 bolts.

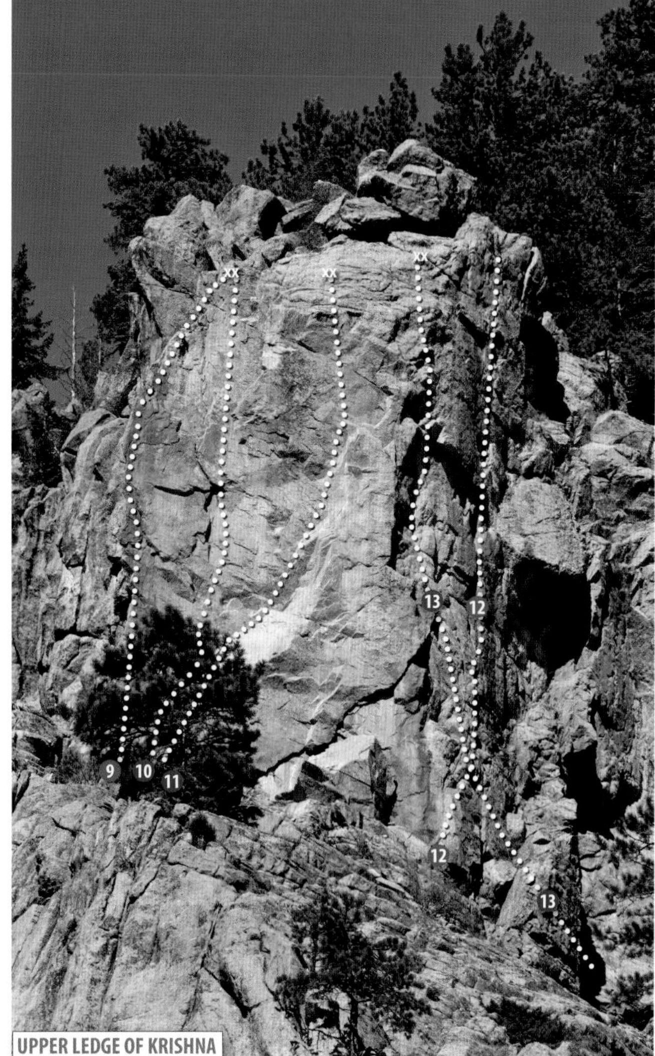

UPPER LEDGE OF KRISHNA

11 Vishnu 5.11d/12a ★★★ ☐
Vishnu climbs the obvious sloping ramp system in the center of the wall with hard moves near the top. A great route in a commanding position. Two stars for the climbing and add another for the position.
8 bolts.

12 Krishna Orange 5.9 ★★ ☐
Climb the obvious handcrack just right of *Vishnu*. Cool route in a great position.
Gear to 3 inches.

13 The Coug 5.10d ★ ☐
The Coug starts down and right of *Vishnu* on a short grey face just left of the Berlin Wall. Scramble about 30 feet to a ledge below a small grey face. Clip two bolts here, step right, chase two bolts up the right side of a nice arete and then join the crack *Krishna Orange* for 20 feet (thin-fingers and hand-sized gear here). One could just start up on the big ledge on *Krishna Orange* and link into the last 5 bolts on *The Coug*.
9 bolts, 0.5 micro-cams, and 2 inch cam.

SERENITY SPIRE NORTH FACE 7.6 miles

Approach time: 20 - 30 minutes.
Exposure: North and west.

2 routes

5.6- .7 .8 .9 .10 .11 .12 .13 .14

This secluded spire is tucked away in a steep gully just west of Krishna and the Wall of Winter Warmth.

Access: See page 92. Cross to the east side of the creek creek just past the Plotinus Wall. Hug the creek passing the Lower Buttress of the Wall of Winter Warmth and the Krishna formation, staying close to the creek. Hike past the main Serenity Spire and reach a gully on the right. Go up the gully to the obvious wall on the right.

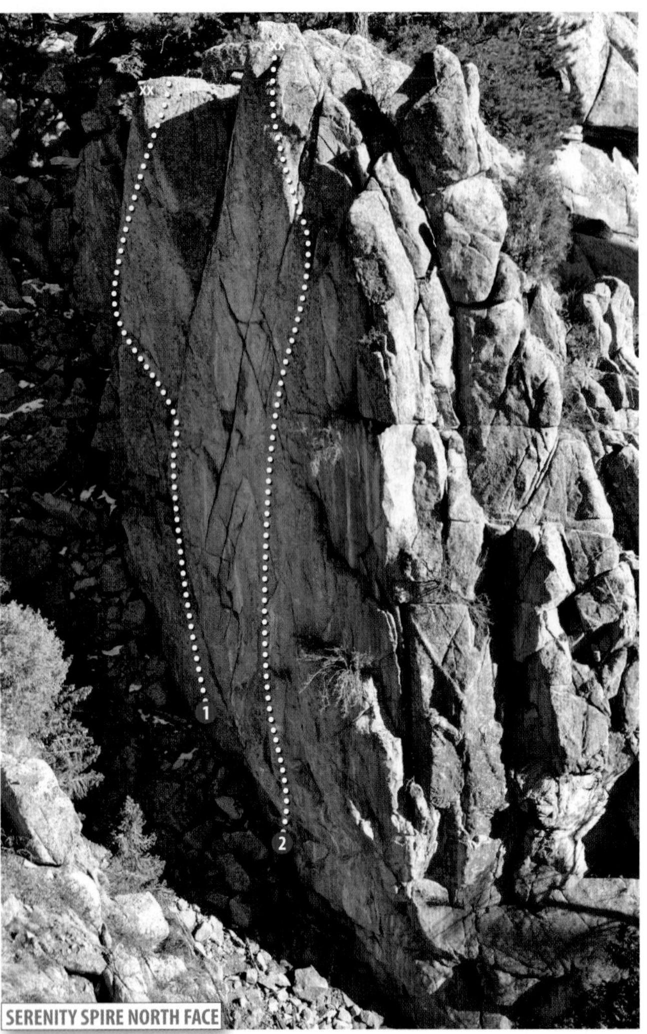

SERENITY SPIRE NORTH FACE

1 Adam's Arete 5.10d ★★ ☐
Climb a short corner and then up a face following bolts to the arete. Climb the arete and then reach the anchors. Nice route in a very cool location.
5 bolts.

2 Bobby's Wall 5.10c ★★ ☐
Follow the line of bolts up the center of the wall to the anchor. Nice climbing on solid granite.
9 bolts.

Dan Levison

Boulder Canyon (aka Bo-Can, Bo-Co, Bolted Canyon, etc.) is unsexy to many; apparently it lacks the name-dropping status of Rifle, Indian Creek, or even Eldorado. It has always been the modern-day whipping boy of Front Range climbers. The routes are soft, over bolted, and too slabby say the masses who would rather squander seven roundtrip hours doing the I-70 shuffle to Rifle and back. Yet this disjointed crucible of granite continues to yield V14 boulder problems, hard sport routes, and headpoint established testpieces. Just when you think Bo-Can will fall into obscurity, it continues to reinvent itself, from the time Jerry Moffat flew across the pond to send area testpieces (later to be downgraded by Tommy Caldwell) to modern cutting-edge problems established just last month. This prolific, unregulated arena constantly produces new lines, seemingly on a weekly basis; there is always a route to do from a Rolofson classic to a new D'Antonio 5.12.

I can honestly say that I've spent over 1000 days here in the last decade projecting, developing new lines, or replacing fixed hardware. The memories are endless, but what stands out for me is when I developed The Berlin Wall in Upper Dream Canyon during 2003 – 2008. This beautiful southwest-facing crag, sandwiched between The Wall of Winter Warmth and Krishna Buttress, was first established in the early 1980's by Dan Hare and Dale Goddard, who did a handful of sparsely protected traditional and mixed lines on the intimidating black streaked wall. Berlin now hosts several modern sport routes in the 5.12 – 5.13 range, mega-classics include *Interrogation* (12c), *East Germany* (12d), and *Eastern Promises* (13b). Establishing and eventually sending *Eastern Promises* with Matt Samet was quite memorable. While cleaning the line, Matt got stung in the neck twice by two angry wasps. A few weeks later, while on the cusp of redpointing; I severed my left adductor tendon while attempting the crux sequence, which features a bizarre Donkey Kong move. A depressing 6 weeks sans climbing ensued. Shortly after my healing hiatus, I came back and sent.

Berlin Wall is one of the many slices of Boulder Canyon, a place that truly has it all: sport, traditional, and bouldering in a four-season playground just minutes from downtown. Despite what my friends say, I do branch out and climb in Eldorado or The Flatirons. But, for the most part, you know where to find me.

DAN'S BO-CAN FAVORITES:

Jolt Cola 12a, Blob Rock.

Joy Ride 12b, Coney Island

Interrogation 12c, LDC - Berlin Wall

Lucid Dreaming 12d, LDC - Plotinus Wall

Vasodilator 13a, Blob Rock

Eastern Promises 13b, LDC - Berlin Wall

China Doll 5.13c-5.14a, UDC - Lost Angel Wall

BOULDER FALLS EAST/WEST 7.6 miles

Approach time: 10 minutes.
Exposure: West, east, and south.

11 routes

5.6- .7 .8 .9 .10 .11 .12 .13 .14

A nice crag with several good routes on featured granite. The falls area is a zoo of tourists during the summer months. Climb earlier in the morning or later in the afternoon to avoid the crowds.

Access: Drive 7.6 miles up the canyon to a large parking area on the left for Boulder Falls. Cross the road and follow the trail to the falls, cross in low water near the falls to the east side.

Descent: To descend from the top walk east or west and then back down to the base.

BOULDER FALLS EAST

BOULDER FALLS EAST

1 Dari Design 5.11c ★ ☐
On the left side of the wall, boulder up to the first bolt, clip and relax, then angle left into a dish and then up to the anchor.
3 bolts.

2 Hubris 5.11c R/X ☐
Pitch 1: Staying on the original line makes this a very severe climb. Start just right of *Dari Design*, climb the smooth slab to knobs and edges, veer left to the anchor on *Dari Design*.
Pitch 2: Climb a short corner to an arete; follow the arete to a right angling crack leading to tree with sling. Rap.
Gear to 2 inches.

3 Into Temptation 5.10a R ★ ☐
Climb the obvious crack just behind a large pine tree, go left on a ledge to horizontal crack with pins, fire up the sparsely protected face to the tree with slings. Rap.
Gear to 2 inches

4 Cold Plunge 5.10a R ★ ☐
Start as for *Into Temptation*; reach a good horizontal crack with a horn and climb the steep face just left of crack up to a tree with slings.
Gear to 2 inches.

5 Sleepwalker 5.10b ★★ ☐
Start as for *Cold Plunge* and climb to the horizontal and then the obvious crack to the tree with sling.
Gear to 2.5 inches.

6 Somnambulist 5.10b/c ★ ☐
Start as for *Sleepwalker* and climb the right crack, traverse back to *Sleepwalker* at the crack's end and then up to the tree.
Gear to 2.5 inches.

7 Vertical Stall 5.10c/d R ★ ☐
Start as for *Somnambulist* and then go right into a flaring right leaning crack, follow the crack till it ends and then step left up an unprotected face to the tree with slings.
SR.

8 Flight Deck 5.11a ★ ☐
Start as for *Vertical Stall* climbing the crack on the right up to a face with a bolt, then angle left into a corner with a horn. Go straight up the corner to the top. Walk off to the south.
1 bolt, gear to 2.5 inches.

BOULDER FALLS WEST

Follow the tourist path all the way to the falls and a bench. Boulder Falls West is the orange wall facing you.
Exposure: East and south facing.

9 Orange Dihedral 5.11a ☐
Climb the obvious corner/flake/crack up to a ledge. Walk off to the west.
Gear to 2 inches.

10 Diagonal Crack 5.10a ☐
Climb the left leaning crack that starts near the creek.
Gear to 2 inches.

11 Midnight Dari 5.12a ★★ ☐
The bolted route on the right side of the wall.
4 bolts.

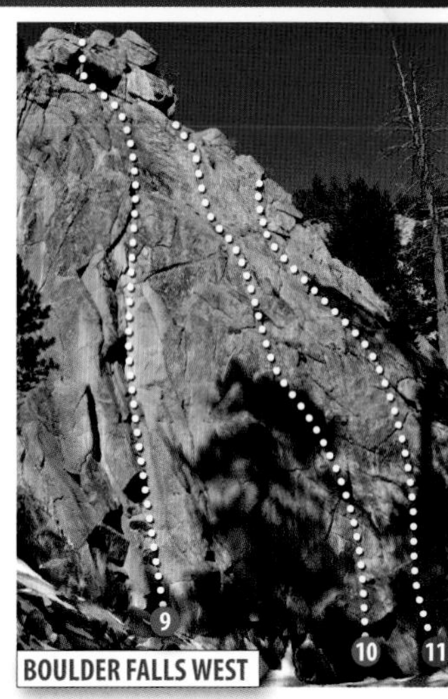

BOULDER FALLS WEST

BOULDER FALLS SOUTH 7.6 miles

Approach time: 10 - 15 minutes.
Exposure: West.

3 routes

5.6- .7 .8 .9 .10 .11 .12 .13 .14

A nice crag with several good routes on featured granite. The falls area is a zoo of tourists during the summer months. Climb earlier in the morning or later in the afternoon to avoid the crowds.

Access: Drive 7.6 miles up the canyon to a large parking area on the left for Boulder Falls. Cross the road and cross the creek near the bridge. Take the first major gully on the east side of creek until you are below the wall. Easy fifth class climbing leads to an anchor on a good ledge at the base of the wall.
Descent: Rap from the anchors

1 Prodigal Summer 5.11d ★★★ ☐
Prodigal Summer is the leftmost route on the wall and climbs a blunt arete. Clip the first bolt and begin a series of technical and balancy moves past five more bolts to a large ledge. Sling a large horn and make delicate slab moves up a beautiful face.
10 bolts.

2 Crocodile Smile 5.12a ★★ ☐
Crocodile Smile lies 10 feet right of *Prodigal Summer*. Climb steep rock past two bolts with a tricky move to reach the "Croc Teeth", milk the rest, then and power past a steep bulge to a layback seam. Continue up the delicate slab with a faith-and-friction move to reach the anchor.
8 bolts.

3 Doctor Patient 5.11b ★ ☐
Start on the right side of the angling ramp. Stem/lieback up to reach a blunt arete. Make some difficult moves over a bulge to reach the obvious sharper arete and then the anchor.
6 bolts.

BOULDER FALLS SOUTH

TONNERE TOWER 7.6 miles

Approach time: 5 - 15 minutes.
Exposure: North and east.

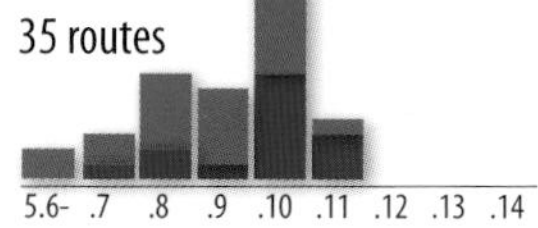

Tonnere Tower is the large crag across Boulder Creek and slightly upstream from the Boulder Falls parking area. It rises more than 450 feet from the creek to the summit, making it one of the tallest crags in Boulder Canyon. The large summit area provides great views of Lower Dream Canyon and Boulder Falls. The tower now hosts a number of very good moderate sport and trad routes in a nice setting along the creek.

Access: Drive 7.6 miles up the canyon to the large parking area for Boulder Falls on the left. Park here and walk upstream a short distance to the tower on the left. A Tyrolean traverse can be used to cross the creek when the water is too high to hop rocks or wade. It is located about 60 yards upstream from the Boulder Falls parking area. The far end of the Tyrolean is right by the path heading up to Sport Land, Treasure Wall, and The Garden. If the water level is low enough, you can wade the creek or hop rocks about 15′ upstream from the Tyrolean. Wading or hopping rocks can be done from late July until mid-May.

Routes are listed from left to right, starting at Sport Land and ending at Creekside. All routes have two-bolt anchors (some with lowering hooks), and can be climbed and descended with a 60m rope.

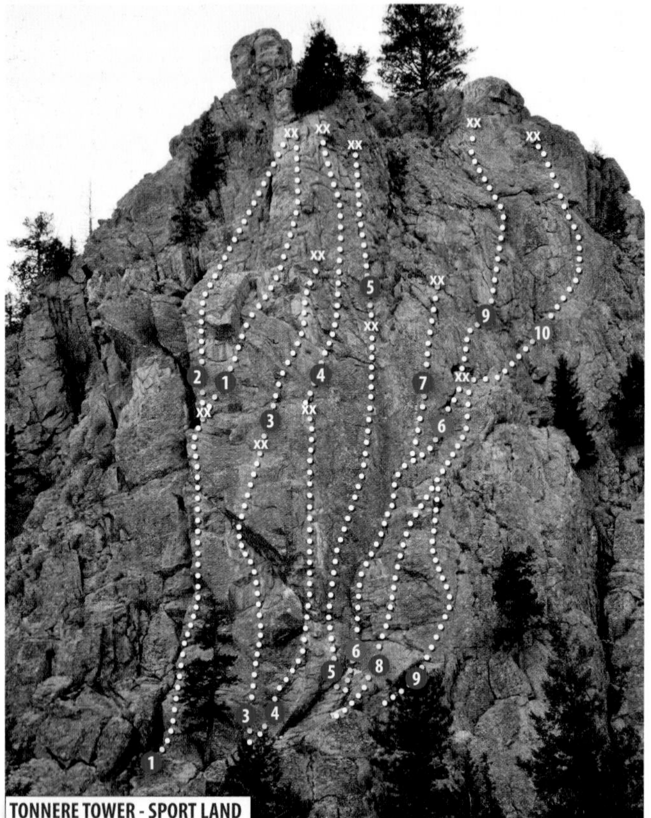

TONNERE TOWER - SPORT LAND

EAST FACE AKA SPORT LAND

From the far side of the Tyrolean, follow a path up left through the woods, go up a talus field, and follow a path up around the left side of the rock. Continue up to the prominent east arete, then traverse right on a ledge to access the routes. There are belay anchors at the start of each route.

❶ Toe The Line 5.10b ★★ ☐

Pitch 1: 5.10b. Climb straight up the east arete to a small stance.
9 bolts.

Pitch 2: 5.10a. Traverse right around a steep headwall. Climb a slab, traverse right, and continue up to the anchor.
11 bolts.

❷ Generous Donation 5.11a ★ ☐

Start atop the first pitch of *Toe The Line.* Climb the steep headwall directly above.
8 bolts.

❸ Tag Team 5.10d ★★ ☐

Pitch 1: 5.10c. Climb a slab and a short corner, then crank right past an overhang.
7 bolts.

Pitch 2: 5.10d. Climb a slab and a tan dihedral capped by an overhang.
8 bolts.

❹ Total Eclipse 5.10a ★★ ☐
Pitch 1: 5.9. Climb a slab and a right-facing corner, traverse right under a roof, and continue straight up to the anchor.
Pitch 2: 5.10a. Climb a short headwall, go up a slab, traverse right, and continue up and right to the anchor.
12 bolts.

❺ Sidekick 5.10d ★★★ ☐
Pitch 1: 5.10d. Climb the steep face right of *Total Eclipse*. May be the best pitch at the crag; continuous climbing at the 5.10 level.
11 bolts.
Pitch 2: 5.9. Climb straight up on big features.
6 bolts.

❻ Nick Of Time 5.6 ★ ☐
Climb a corner with a wide crack right of *Sidekick*.
Gear to three inches.

❼ Hard Times 5.11c ★ ☐
Climb *Face Off* to a ledge, then continue up the steep face on the left.
9 bolts.

❽ Face Off 5.7+ ★ ☐
Climb the face right of *Nick Of Time*.
6 bolts.

❾ Stayin' Alive 5.10a ★★★ ☐
Pitch 1: 5.8. Climb the arete right of *Face Off.*
7 bolts.
Pitch 2: 5.10a. Climb up and right to a V-corner. Climb the corner, move left to an arete, and continue up and right to the anchor. Good route with consistent moves.
13 bolts.

❿ Clean Sweep 5.9 ★★ ☐
Start atop the first pitch of *Stayin' Alive*, or atop the second pitch of *Buried Treasure*. Traverse 30' right and climb steep cracks.
Gear to 3 inches.

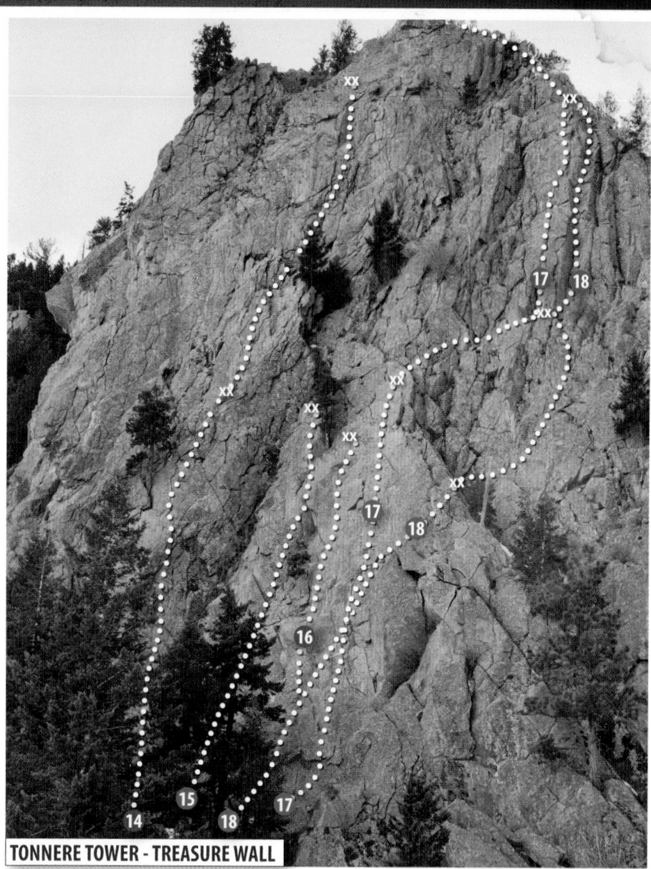

TONNERE TOWER - TREASURE WALL

TREASURE WALL

Treasure Wall is the left side of the north face of Tonnere Tower. From the far side of the Tyrolean, follow a path up left through the woods, then go up a talus field to the rock wall. The routes are just up to the right.

The routes from left to right:

⓫ Tree Line 5.8+ ☐
Climb a face just left of a big pine tree.
4 bolts.

⓬ Twilight Time 5.9+ ★★ ☐
Climb the steep face just right of a big pine tree. Nice route with clean moves.
6 bolts.

⓭ Bobby's Back 5.10d ★ ☐
Climb straight up a steep thin face. Staying left of the bolts ups the grade.
5 bolts.

⓮ Buried Treasure 5.8+ ★★ ☐
Pitch 1: 5.8+. Climb a slab just left of a big left-facing corner. Step left and continue straight up to the anchor on a pedestal.
10 bolts.
Pitch 2: 5.7. Step right, angle up right to an arete, and continue up to a good ledge.
6 bolts.
Optional Finish Buried Alive 5.10a.
Continue with the last pitch of *Stayin' Alive* (#9). One of the best moderate multi-pitch sport routes in Boulder Canyon.
13 bolts.

⑮ Join The Party 5.9+ ★★ ☐
Climb a left-facing corner and flake just right of *Buried Treasure*. Nice crack and corner climbing.
Gear to 2 inches.

⑯ The Twilight Kid 5.11a ★★ ☐
Steep face and shallow corner. Maybe the second best pitch at the crag. . . using the tree to gain the upper face lowers the grade.
9 bolts.

⑰ Fields of Gold 5.10a ★★★ ☐
Fun mixed route that can be done as a 1, 2, or 3-pitch climb. The best multi-pitch route at the cliff; all three pitches are worth the effort.

Pitch 1: 5.10a. Start by a big pine tree. Traverse right and climb a slab and a left-facing corner, then traverse right to a ledge. Continue up a steep slab and finger crack to an anchor at 100 feet. Lower from here if you're just doing the first pitch. If you're doing the upper pitches, continue another 35 feet up and right to a higher anchor by a dead pine tree.

Pitch 2: 5.9. Climb a left-facing corner, then step right and climb a hand and fist crack. Climb a steep buttress past two bolts to a good ledge. You can rappel the route from here, or continue to the top of the crag and walk off the back.

Pitch 3: 5.5. Climb a finger crack and a short wall with hand cracks to the summit area. Belay from a pine tree.

12 quickdraws and gear to 3 inches.

Descent: walk south to a notch at the back of the crag, then follow a path down to the left (east).

⑱ Workingman's Blues 5.10c ★ ☐
Start as for *Twilight Kid.*

Pitch 1: 5.9. Climb up to a high first bolt then move right into shallow corners. Veer right and gain a small point of rock above a dead pine. Go right across a ramp to a two-bolt anchor.

Pitch 2: 5.10c. Climb up a small thin flake, clip a bolt and make a hard move to gain a ledge. Continue straight up and then left to a good ledge and a two-bolt anchor by a dead tree. (This is the same anchor as for *Fields of Gold*).

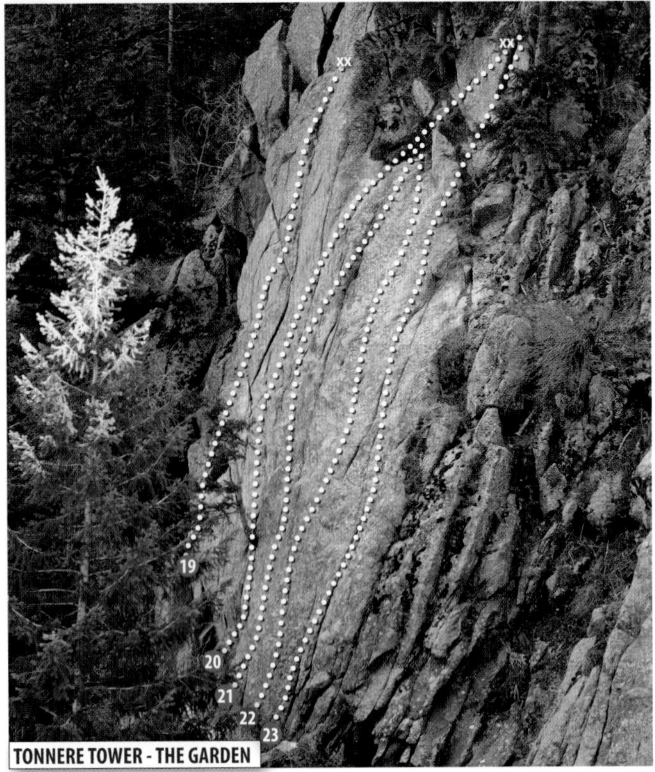

TONNERE TOWER - THE GARDEN

Pitch 3: 5.10b/c. Climb up short corners and step right to a perfect hand and fist crack. Climb the crack till it ends. Directly above is the buttress with two bolts on *Fields of Gold*. Step right of the buttress into a shallow corner with tricky gear. Make a hard move to another shallow corner then straight up doing chimney-type moves. The angle eases and climb up to a pine tree and belay. Be careful of loose rock.

Pitch 4: 5.6. Climb cracks straight above the pine and reach the top of Tonnere Tower and belay.

8 quickdraws and gear to 3 inches.

Descent: Walk south to a notch at the back of the crag, then follow a path down to the left (east).

THE GARDEN

The Garden is in the center of the north face in a secluded spot hidden from the road by large pine trees. From the far side of the Tyrolean, follow a path up left through the woods. Just before the talus field, cut back right about 50′ to the wall.

Routes from left to right:

⑲ Just Do It 5.8 ★★ ☐
Face and cracks on the left side of the wall. Lowering anchor with hooks.
2 bolts and gear to 2 inches.

⑳ Fine Fir 5.7+ ★ ☐
Climb past a pine tree 15 feet up the wall and angle right up a slab to the anchor.
2 bolts and gear to 1 inch.

㉑ Storm Warning 5.10a ★ ☐
The face just right of *Fine Fir*.
Toprope.

㉒ Before The Deluge 5.10a ★ ☐
The bolted face in the center of the wall. Nice face climbing on clean rock.
5 bolts.

㉓ Crackdown 5.9 ★ ☐
The finger crack on the right side of the wall.
1 bolt and gear to 1 inch.

The following routes start from the common anchor atop routes 20-23. Rap from the top of pinnacle to the anchors on B-Boys *and then to the ground.*

24 Showtime 5.8+ ★★★ ☐

Step right from the anchor, climb up to a steep wall with a bolt, and move right onto an arete. Climb hand cracks up the left side of the pinnacle to its top. There is an intermediate anchor halfway up the pitch if you want to do the route in two short pitches instead of one long pitch.

1 bolt and gear to 2 inches.

25 Dutch Treat 5.8 ★★ ☐

Start on *Showtime* and move right to cracks in the center of the pinnacle.

1 bolt and gear to 2 inches.

26 Border Crossing 5.8 ★ ☐

Start on *Showtime*, and move right to a left-facing corner right of *Dutch Treat*.

1 bolt and gear to 2 inches.

27 The B Boys 5.10d ★★ ☐

Two good pitches with technical moves at the crux.

Pitch 1: 5.10d. Traverse right, climb up a steep face past a bolt, and move right to the anchor.

Pitch 2: 5.10d. Stem up a steep corner past three roofs, and continue up a left-facing corner to the top of the pinnacle.

8 quickdraws and gear to 2 inches.

28 Smooth Operator 5.11d ★★ ☐

Starts after pitch 1 of *The B Boys* and merges with *Local Hero*. Intense face moves off the belay...then you cruise. Worth doing.

8 bolts and gear to 2 inches.

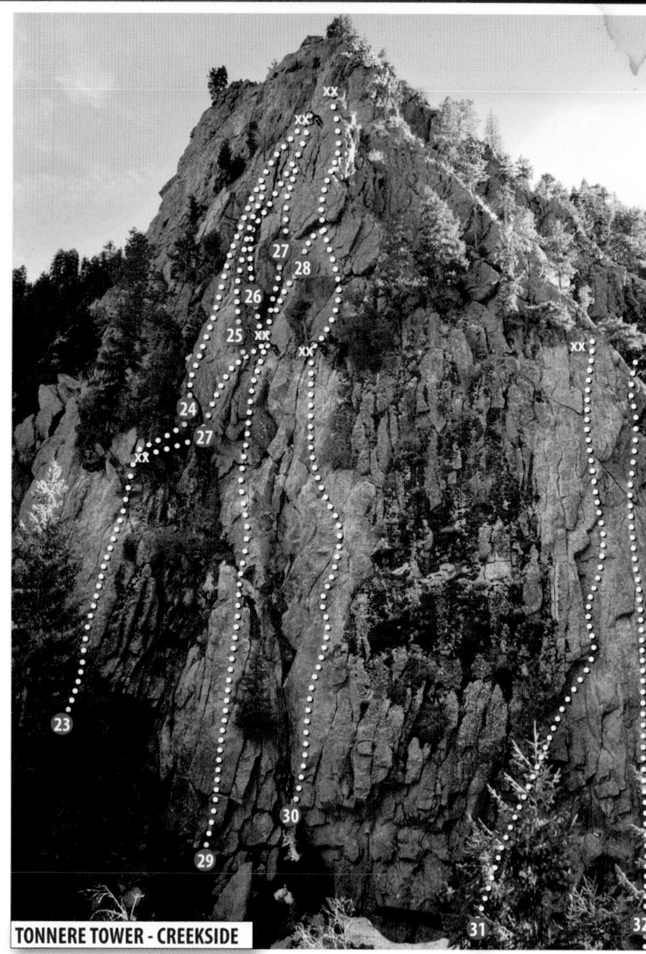

TONNERE TOWER - CREEKSIDE

CREEKSIDE

Creekside is on the north face of Tonnere Tower, down by the creek. This is one of the most magical and beautiful places to climb in all of Boulder Canyon. Enjoy the unique ambience of this special place.

From the far side of the Tyrolean, go upstream about 100' to a clearing just before the rock wall comes all the way down to the creek. *Curtain Call* and *Local Hero* start here. The remaining routes start right next to the creek, and are accessible only if the water level is low enough (late summer to mid-spring).

From the start of *Curtain Call* and *Local Hero*, a dirt path heads left and up to The Garden.

Routes from left to right:

29 Curtain Call 5.8+ ★ ☐

Pitch 1: 5.8. Climb a short headwall just left of a gully. Continue up low-angle slabs to a steep corner. Traverse left under a roof and up cracks to the anchor.

Pitch 2: 5.8+. Step left and climb an arete that merges with *Showtime*.

7 quickdraws and gear to 3 inches.

30 Local Hero 5.10a ★★★ ☐

Slab, roof, and exposed arete. Another classic worth the effort. The crowds will love you for climbing this one....just remember to smile for the camera.

Pitch 1: 5.9. Start up the gully just right of *Curtain Call*, and move right onto the wall. Continue up the face and cracks to an anchor by a pine tree.

Pitch 2: 5.10a. Step right, then climb up and left to a roof with a hand crack. Turn the roof and continue up the right side of the pinnacle to its top.

9 quickdraws and gear to 3 inches.

Donna DuBois on the second pitch of *Stayin' Alive* 5.10a, Tonnere Tower, page 116. Photo: Ron Olsen.

31 Creekside Cruise 5.7 ★ ☐☐

Start on a pointed boulder by the creek, about 20' right of *Local Hero*. Climb a bulge with a fist crack and traverse right beneath two pine trees. Climb cracks and a right-facing corner with a bolt. Turn a roof on the left and continue up to a slab. Angle up right to a flake, and follow it to a ledge at its top. Rap or lower back to the start. Be careful pulling the rope to try to keep it out of the creek.

Gear to 3.5 inches.

The following routes start right by the creek, and are not accessible when the water level is very high (from mid-May to the end of July):

32 Liquid Therapy 5.10b ★ ☐☐

Start about 20 feet right of *Creekside Cruise*. Climb a water-polished bulge, a corner, and flared cracks to a roof. Traverse left under the roof and continue up to the anchor.

Gear to 2 inches.

33 Spirit on the Water 5.9 ★★★ ☐☐

Classic stemming and face climbing. Very few climbs offer the setting and belay as this one does. Start at an alcove next to the creek, about 15 feet right of *Liquid Therapy*.

Pitch 1: 5.9. Step left from the alcove and climb a corner to a roof. Step right and climb up a face and cracks to an anchor just above a large tree.

Pitch 2: 5.8. Step left and climb a slab to a ledge. Continue up a thin crack to the anchor.

11 quickdraws and gear to 2 inches.

34 Los Pinos (The Pines) 5.9 ★★ ☐☐

Can be climbed all the way to the summit. One of the longer routes in Boulder Canyon and quite the adventure to a true summit. The second pitch offers cool slab climbing between three little pine trees. Start at the alcove by the creek as for *Spirit on the Water*.

Pitch 1: 5.8. Climb out the right side of the alcove and straight up to a bolt anchor shared with *Spirit on the Water*.

Pitch 2: 5.9. Climb a thin crack up the right side of the slab, past three small pine trees, and climb a short wall to a bolt anchor shared with *Spirit on the Water*. You can rappel from here or continue up three more pitches to the summit. There are no fixed anchors beyond this point.

Pitch 3: 5.6. Climb moderate cracks to a ledge with a pine tree. Can be combined with Pitch 2.

Pitch 4: 5.6. Angle up left to a buttress with hand cracks. Watch for loose rock. Continue up moderate rock to a ledge with a pine tree.

Pitch 5: 5.6. Climb a hand crack on the right side of a buttress, and move up right to hand cracks on a short wall. Climb the wall and continue to the summit area.

10 quickdraws and gear to 3 inches.

Descent: Walk south to a notch at the rear of the crag and descend to the left (east).

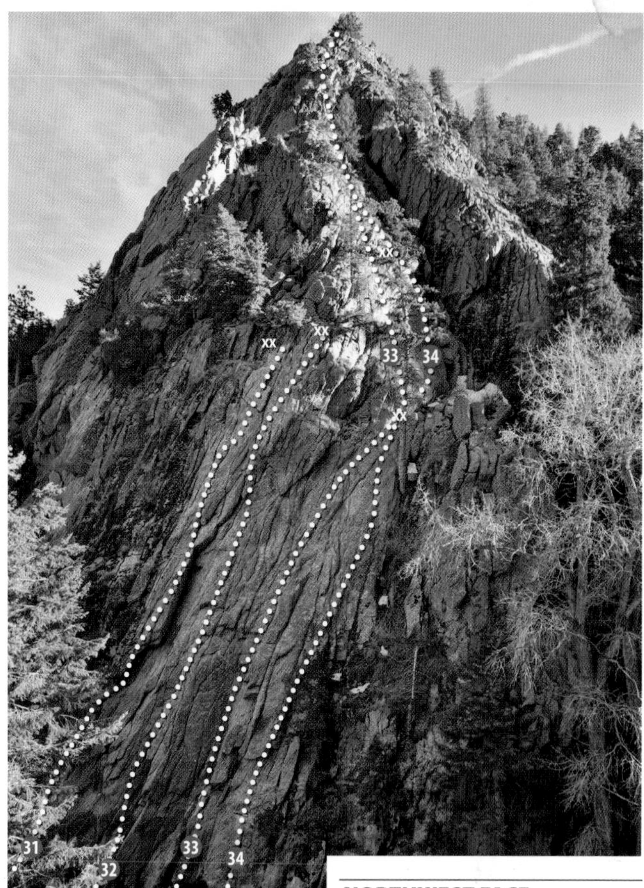

TONNERE TOWER - CREEKSIDE RIGHT

NORTHWEST FACE

The Northwest Face is on the right hand side of the north face, and is relatively untouched, with moss, lichen, and loose rock. There is one old trad route here (Northwest Ridge) that was first climbed many years ago, but doesn't see much traffic from climbers today.

35 Northwest Ridge 5.6 ☐☐

Adventure route to the summit of the tower. Little is known of this route. Expect dirty cracks and somewhat run-out sections. Cross the creek and go up a short steep gully on the right side of the north face. Move left onto the rock and climb up the rounded northwest ridge for three pitches, belaying from trees on good ledges.

SR.

Descent: Walk south to a notch at the rear of the crag and descend to the left (east).

BOULDER SLIPS 7.7 miles

Approach time: 1 - 5 minutes.
Exposure: South and west.

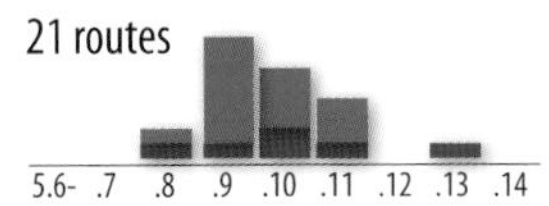

Boulder Slips is an obscure crag just west of the trail to Boulder Falls. Access is right next to the road, but until recently the cliff saw very little activity. The crag faces south and gets good sun well into the afternoon. Beware loose rock and tourists. This is a great crag to get a workout if you are short on time or to find midday sun.

Access: Drive 7.6 miles up the canyon to the Boulder Falls parking lot on the left, or continue just past the falls to a pullout on the right, below the cliff. The climbs start about off the road, on the north side. To access the far left side of the crag, you must hike up a steep, loose hillside that is covered in poison ivy from May through October.

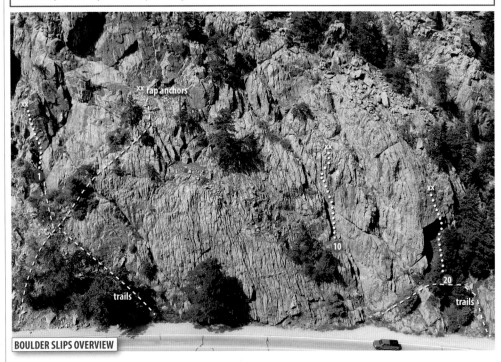

BOULDER SLIPS OVERVIEW

❶ Edges and Ledges 5.8 ★★ ☐
A fun, popular route on the very left side of the wall.
8 bolts.

❷ Brand New Bosch 5.9 ★★ ☐
Start as for *Edges and Ledges* and traverse right after 15 feet; good warm-up for the other routes. Follow a corner to overlaps and then to the anchor.
6 bolts.

❸ Party Time 5.9 ★ ☐
Corner, arete, finger crack, hand/fist crack. Varied for such a short route.
5 bolts and light rack to 3 inches.

❹ Minutiae 5.8 ★★★ ☐
Hand crack. Classic crack climbing for the grade and arguably one of the better pitches in the canyon for the grade.
Gear to 3 inches.

❺ Minutiae Arete 5.9+ ★ ☐
Toprope the arete just right of the crack.

❻ Pumpkin Corner 5.9 ☐
When you've done the rest of the routes . . . this will be waiting for you. Climb the obvious corner just right of *Minutiae*.
Gear to 2 inches.

7 La Lune 5.13a ★★ ☐

Once a trad route done by Bob Horan, it saw little to no traffic. Horan went back and retro-bolted it. Overhanging thin crack out the large roof. Looks extremely painful.

5 bolts.

8 Sunlight Arete 5.10b ★★ ☐

Nice arete climbing at a moderate grade, well worth the effort. Scramble up to the right of the *Minutiae* area to reach it. There is a rap anchor for descent.

5 bolts.

9 Useless One 5.10b ☐

Start about 50 feet right of *La Lune,* climbing thin cracks to the top.

Gear to 2 inches.

10 Colorado Senior Open 5.10b ★★ ☐

Greg Hand's claim to fame: He is a one-handicap golfer. Face-climb up and into the black crack, with cool moves to reach the anchor.

6 bolts and medium gear.

11 Family Guy 5.11a ★★ ☐

Cool face moves lead to an arete and hand crack. Continuous and fun. Some thin flakes.

6 bolts and few medium pieces.

12 Same As It Ever Was 5.11a/b ★ ☐

Crimpy crux down low to nice climbing above.

6 bolts and a few small pieces.

13 Giggity-Giggity 5.10c ★ ☐

Climb the face leading to flake, solve the crux and continue straight up the shallow corner/crack to the anchors.

6 bolts and 3.5 inch cam.

14 Quagmire 5.9+ R ★ ☐

Start at a thin crack that leads to a ramp and another thin crack to the top.

Gear to 2 inches.

15 The Throttle 5.11b R ★ ☐

Scary start. Better holds and gear above.

Gear to 2.5 inches.

16 The Threshold 5.11a ★★ ☐

Another route with the crux down low and some thought-provoking moves up high. Old school: be prepared for a little spice.

Gear to 2.5 inches.

17 My Way 5.9+ ★★ ☐

Start just left of *Boulder Slips*. Climb a left-angling wide crack to a stance, and continue up the arete and face above to a bolt anchor.

4 bolts, gear to 2.5 inches

18 Boulder Slips 5.9 R ★ ☐

You should feel confident at the grade before attempting this one. Climb a right-facing corner to a roof, traverse left under the roof, and continue up slabs to a bolt anchor shared with *My Way*.

Gear to 2 inches.

19 Where's Bob? 5.10b ★★ ☐

Face to overhang. Bob is everywhere . . . you just have to look. Great face climbing. Shade in the afternoon.

5 bolts, plus two 1 inch cams.

20 The Ride 5.10a ★ ☐

Face and cracks. You might take the ride at the start, but after that it's a cruise.

5 bolts and a few small pieces.

TOWER OF BABEL 7.7 miles

Approach time: 2 - 5 minutes.
Exposure: North and west.

3 routes

5.6- .7 .8 .9 .10 .11 .12 .13 .14

A true pinnacle located on the banks of Boulder Creek. The Pinnacle is popular with the swimming/cliff jumping crowd in the summer months.

Access: Drive 7.7 miles up the canyon to a pullout on the right and pinnacle on the left. Cross the creek to the pinnacle.

Descent: Walk off to the west.

❶ Pinnacle 5.9 ☐
On the north side of the pinnacle is a route first done by Larry Dalke in 1965. It seems to have slipped into complete obscurity.
Gear to 3 inches.

❷ Babylon Is Burning 5.12a ★★ ☐
Belay about 20 feet above the creek on a good ledge. Follow the crack to a stance below a small overlap, crank the crux and following a line of bolts up the steep wall to the anchor.
7 bolts and gear to 3.5 inches.

❸ Ziggurat 5.11b/c ★ ☐
Start from the creek during low water. Follow the line of bolts up the northwest face.
11 bolts.

Cliff diving, The Tower of Babel. Photo: Ron Olsen.

Jim Erickson

When I came to Boulder in 1967, Castle Rock was the epicenter of hard free climbing in Colorado. I had been climbing for five years and had led a couple of easier 5.10 climbs (the hardest grade at the time) on-sight at Devil's Lake and the Gunks, and I hoped to have some success climbing in Boulder. Boulder Canyon soon handed me a heavy dose of humility.

My first experience at Castle Rock was less than fulfilling. I struggled up *Cussin' Crack* and decided to try a 5.9 called *Coffin Crack.* After three or four falls I gave up. I decided to lower my ambitions a bit and started up *Bailey's Overhand* (5.6), but chickened out 20 feet off the ground, well below the 5.6 crux. I was thoroughly disgusted at myself for being so inept. I had no idea that my failures were mostly due to lack of "cross-pressure" technique.

By then I was climbing well in Eldo, where these techniques were not so critical. Eventually I realized that if I wanted to be an excellent, well-rounded free climber, I would have to learn these techniques: finger and hand and fist jamming, chimneying, offwidthing, stemming, laybacking, and pure friction. As distasteful as it was to me, I started forcing myself to climb in Boulder Canyon to try to learn these techniques.

Within a year, I was able to barely on-sight *Skink Crack* (5.8) and *Curving Crack* (5.9) and other similar 5.9 routes. The real 5.10 plums, *Athlete's Feat*, and *Country Club Crack,* were still way out of the question. The second pitch of *Athlete's Feat*, billed in the guidebook as "probably the most difficult 5th Class (free) pitch in the entire Boulder region," beckoned me.

Climbing in Yosemite, South Platte and Boulder Canyon helped improve my technique immensely, and by 1969 I was ready to try *Athlete's Feat*. Bob Poling and I took a few falls on the first pitch (called 5.10 then, realistically solid 5.11) and failed, but we were very close. A few months later I was able to do *Final Exam* (rated 5.10 then, now 5.11a), possibly the first on-sight of it. (John Gill free soloed it about the same time, I believe.)

I went back to *Athlete's Feat* with Bob. He led the first pitch (thank God) and I was able to follow it free. I psyched up and launched into pitch two, laybacking and placing pitons, getting a kneebar semi-rest, and hand jamming past the crux. Success! It was a very big moment in my climbing career — I felt (rightly or wrongly) I had finally arrived as a force in the free climbing scene. I had learned to love Boulder Canyon.

A year or so later, in the fall of 1971, Steve Wunsch and I did the second free ascent of *Country Club Crack*. Steve flashed pitch one, an impressive feat, although his height and newfangled chalk made a difference on this pitch. I tried to follow because I wanted to lead pitch two, but I fell off a couple of times. So I cheated. I used a little of Steve's chalk at the start and was able to immediately follow it free (in the 1960s, chalk had only been allowed on boulder problems). It is still the only roped pitch in Colorado that I completed using chalk.

In 1972 in Boulder Canyon, I started my perhaps-unprecedented career of unroped, on-sight first ascents. My first route of many in Boulder Canyon was an old aid route called *Boulder Slips*. I wanted to do these solos as purely as possible, so I always used my road bike instead of a car to approach the routes, and I used no aid other than a pair of EB climbing shoes. Although I did many difficult routes, within a year my minimalist ethics nearly cost me my life. I am a very lucky man.

MINDLESS CLIFF 7.8 miles

Approach time: 10 - 15 minutes.
Exposure: South.

3 routes

5.6- .7 .8 .9 .10 .11 .12 .13 .14

A nice wall with three really good routes in a nice setting just down and left of the Mind Shift Cliff.

Access: Drive 7.8 miles up the canyon and park in a large pullout on the right at the entrance to old closed-off mine. From the parking area go to the far west end of the parking area and follow a faint trail straight up to this nice clean south-facing wall.

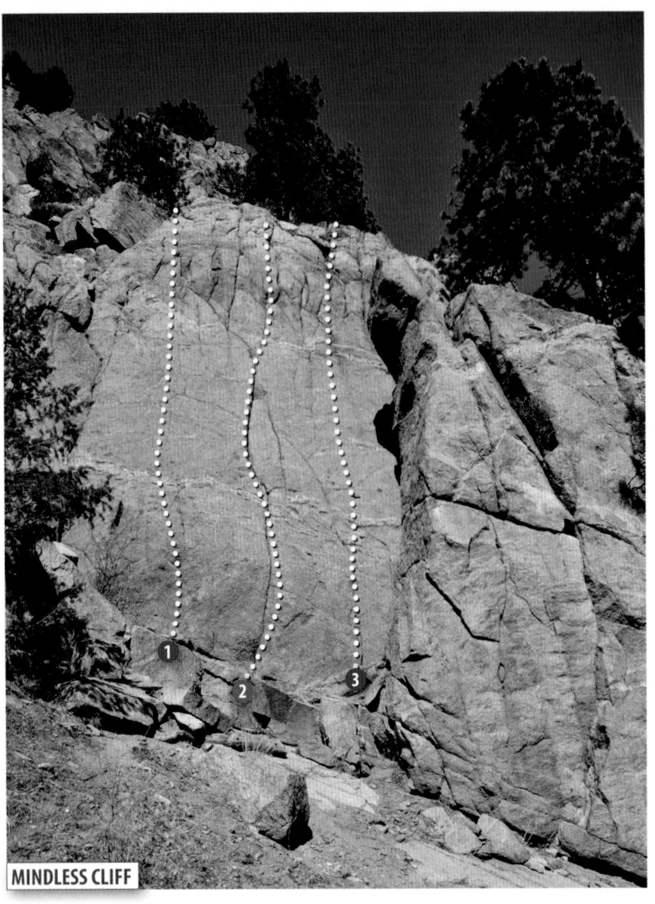

❶ Ground Swell 5.10a ★★ ☐

On the left side of the cliff, climb a nice clean face past four bolts.
4 bolts.

❷ Quick Chill 5.9 ★★ ☐

The obvious thin crack that splits the center of the wall.
Gear to 2 inches.

❸ Aqua Regia 5.11a ★★ ☐

On the right side of the wall climb a beautiful near vertical wall past four bolts.
4 bolts.

MIND SHAFT CLIFF 7.8 miles

4 routes

5.6- .7 .8 .9 .10 .11 .12 .13 .14

Approach time: 30 seconds.
Exposure: South.

Three short cracks located right off the road, just left an old mine opening/shaft.

Access: The Mind Shaft Cracks are located eight miles up Boulder Canyon, just past Boulder Falls. Park at the pullout on the right at the obvious mine shaft.

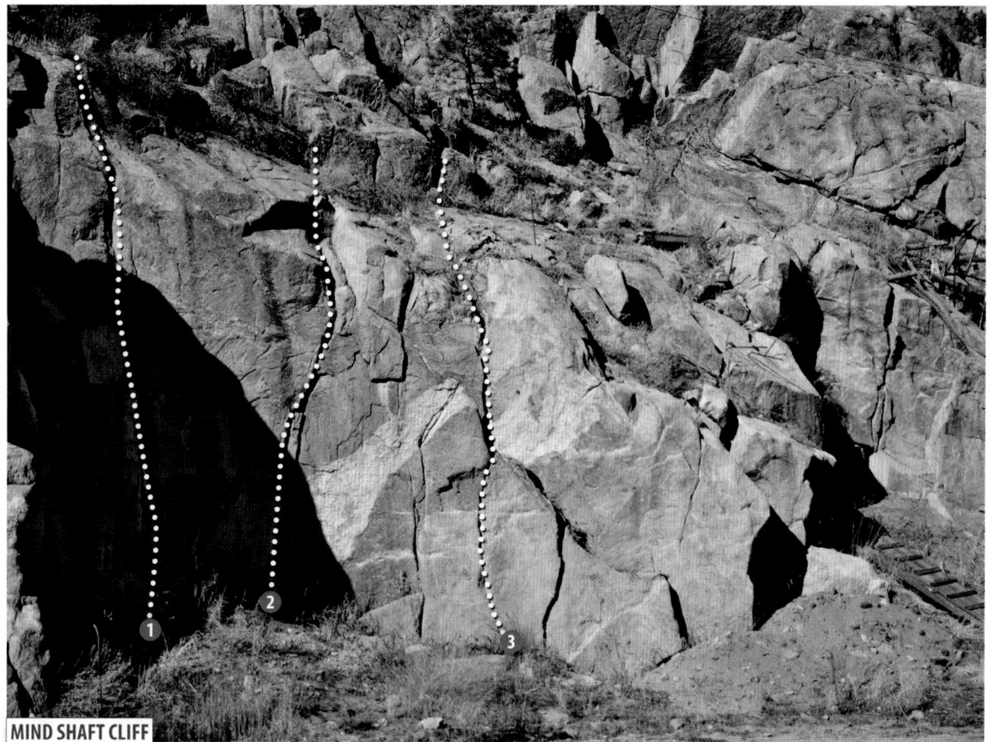

MIND SHAFT CLIFF

❶ **Mind Shaft Crack Left** 5.8 ★ ☐
The left of the three cracks.
Gear to 3.5 inches.

❷ **Mind Shaft Crack Middle** 5.7+ ★ ☐
The middle fist size crack.
Gear to 3.5 inches.

❸ **Mind Shaft Right Crack** 5.7 ☐
The right crack.
Gear to 2.5 inches.

ACROSS FROM THE MIND SHAFT CRACKS

This route is located directly across the road and creek from the cracks.

❹ **I Looked at That** 5.11a/b ☐
Climb the obvious clean slab past six bolts to the anchor.
6 bolts.

MIND SHIFT CLIFF 7.8 miles

Approach time: 10 - 15 minutes.
Exposure: South.

8 routes

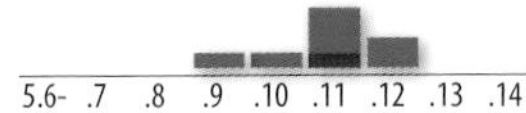

Sitting above several old mines this seldom-visited crag has a number of good climbs with great southern exposure. The ratings seem quite stiff here.

Access: Drive 7.8 miles up the canyon and park in a large pullout on the right at the entrance to an old closed-off mine. Skirt the mine on the right, then head up left passing another open mine to the cliff.

Descent: For all routes that top out, walk off to the east to then back west to the base of the wall.

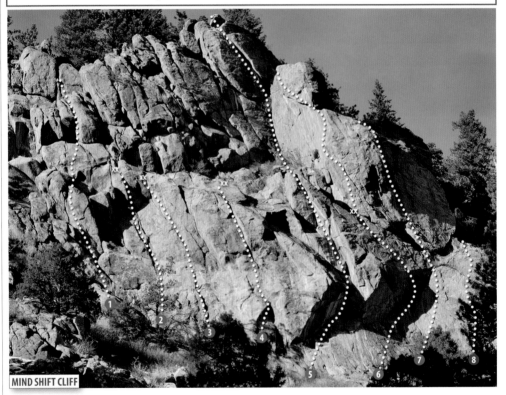

MIND SHIFT CLIFF

1 Goin' Down Slow 5.9+ ☐
On the far left side of the crag. Climb the obvious arch and then over a roof, angle right to an anchor.
Gear to 3.5 inches.

2 Stickshift 5.11c ★ ☐
A thin crack starts 20 feet off the ground. Make hard moves past the bolt to gain the crack, continuous climbing leads flaring and hard moves to the anchor.
Gear to 2.5 inches.

3 Spellbound 5.11c ★★ ☐
Pitch 1: 5.11c. Start just left of a huge block on the left side of the wall. Climb a flake up to and past the first bolt, then clip the second bolt and go right to a left-leaning crack. Climb the crack to an anchor on the left. Most will want to rap from this three-bolt anchor.

Pitch 2: 5.10c. Angle right and then up corners to the top.
Gear to 3.5 inches.

4 Downshift 5.12a/b ★★

In the center of the wall is a short right facing corner. Climb the right side of the corner past bolts using layaway holds to a nice finger and hand crack on the right that leads to a belay.
Gear to 2 inches..

5 Elixir 5.10d R ★

Two large roofs lie low on the right side of the wall. *Elixir* starts on the left side of the left roof.

Pitch 1: 5.10d. Angle up and right to a notch between the overhangs, make hard and serious moves out the overhang, then angle right to a corner and up a hand crack to a ledge.

Pitch 2: 5.10a. Climb a left-facing corner past a bush to a small overhang; turn the overhang on the left then up a steep fist crack to the top.
Gear to 3.5 inches.

6 Pale and Thin 5.11a R

Pitch 1: 5.11a. Climb up the right side of the roof and belay.

Pitch 2: 5.10c. Angle right into a left facing dihedral and belay at the top on a ledge.

Pitch 3: 5.9. Climb a short thin crack to the top.
Gear to 2.5 inches.

7 Brainstorm 5.12b ★★

Pitch 1: 5.11b. Climb up the obvious face on the right side of the crag past two bolts. Go left over the roof passing two bolts and then up to a belay.

Pitch 2: 5.12a/b. Angle right to a bolt and flake, climb the flake, and then head up and right past two bolts, a hard move, and on to the anchor.

Pitch 3: 5.12b. From the belay, move down and left, then traverse along a left leaning crack to a belay on top of a block. Rap the route or climb the top pitch of *Elixir*.
Gear to 2 inches, lots of quickdraws.

8 Mental Imbalance 5.11b ★★

Start right of *Brainstorm* up a steep face to a ledge. Climb the face left of the arete and then head right near the top.
5 bolts. Rap from a two bolt anchor.

VALOR 7.9 miles

Approach time: 10 minutes.
Exposure: South.

5 routes

5.6- .7 .8 .9 .10 .11 .12 .13 .14

A short wall located above the Mind Shift Cliff.

Access: Park in a large pullout on the right side of the road 7.9 miles up the canyon. Hike right of the obvious mine and then uphill passing the Mind Shift Cliff on the right to reach the wall.

1 Valor 5.8 ★

Climb the nice face up the center of the wall.
Gear, top rope . . . soloed on the FA.

2 Limited Partnership 5.9 ★

Climb the diagonal crack on the right side of the wall.
Gear to 2 inches.

3 Discretion 5.8 ★

Climb the diagonal crack on the right side of the wall.
Gear to 2 inches.

4 Schizophrenia 5.11c/d ★★

Climb a short arch on the right side of the wall to gain an arête. Climb the arete past bolts to the anchor.
4 bolts.

5 Pinnacle of Success 5.11b/c

Down from the main wall is a short pinnacle located just off the approach trail. Climb the short face and then gain a finger crack that leads to the anchor.
2 bolts, light rack to 1.5 inches.

LAW OF PHYSICS 7.9 miles

Approach time: 10 minutes.
Exposure: South.

3 routes

5.6- .7 .8 .9 .10 .11 .12 .13 .14

A short wall located above the Mind Shift Cliff.

Access: Park in a large pullout on the right side of the road 7.9 miles up the canyon. Hike right of the obvious mine and then uphill passing the Lion Den's Crag on the left, then up a short hill to the wall.

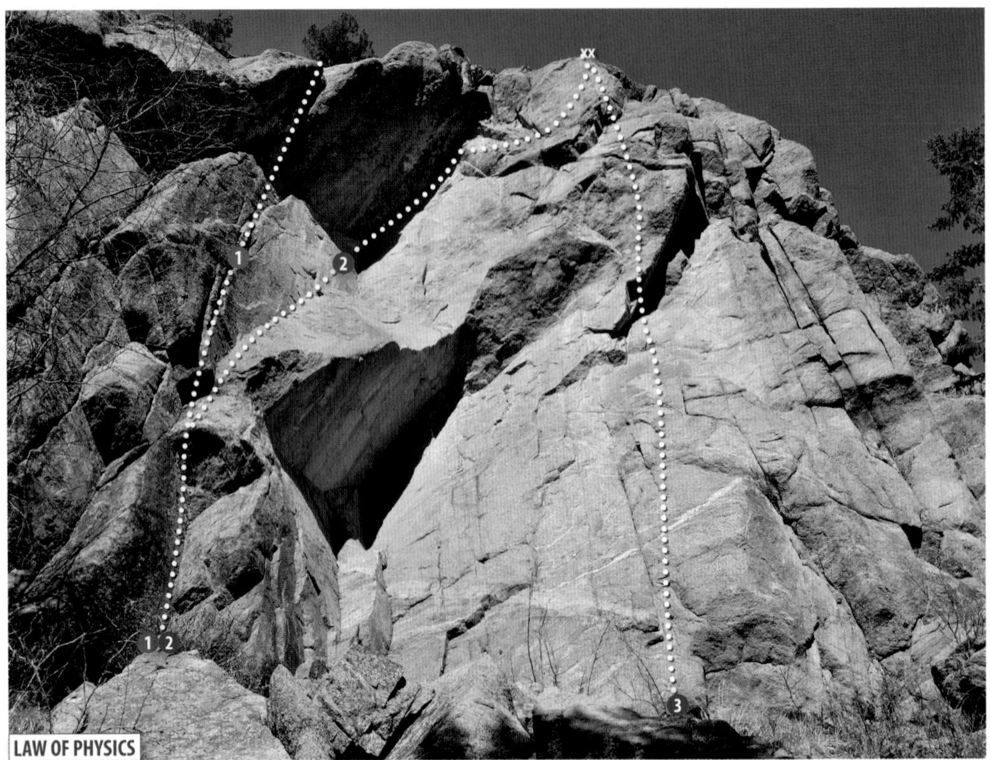

LAW OF PHYSICS

❶ If Six Were Nine 5.9+ ★ ☐
Climb a short face past a bolt to a crack in a black streak to a roof. Go left out the roof to a tree. Rap.
1 bolt, gear to 2 inches.

❷ The Law Comes Down 5.12a ★ ☐
Climb the obvious seam/ramp to gain a steep corner. Go right at the top of the corner and join *Trouble with the Law*, following it to the anchor.
8 bolts.

❸ Trouble with the Law 5.11c/d ★ ☐
Climb a short slab over a small roof and then follow the arete to the anchor.
7 bolts.

LION'S DEN 8.0 miles

Approach time: 10 minutes.
Exposure: South.

5 routes

5.6- .7 .8 .9 .10 .11 .12 .13 .14

A short, south-facing crag with five routes of fair to good quality.

Access: The Lion's Den is located eight miles up Boulder Canyon just past Boulder Falls. Park at the pullout on the right at the mine shaft. Climb up the steep hill to the right of the mine to access the wall.

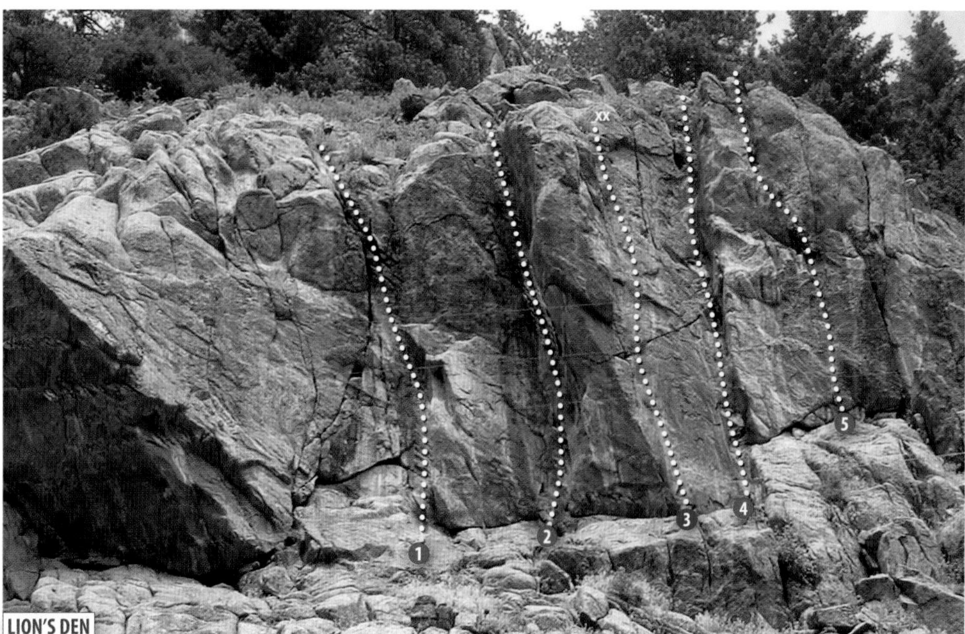

1 Gray Panther 5.10b ★ ☐
Start just right of the big roof on the left side of the crag. Climb the overhanging hand and finger crack. Walk off to the west.
Gear to 3.5 inches.

2 Simba 5.10b ☐
Near the center of the wall is a left facing dihedral.
Gear to 3.5 inches.

3 Tall Talking Midget 5.11d ★★★ ☐
Really good route that offers some powerful technical moves up bottoming seams.
5 bolts.

4 Skin and Bones 5.9 ★ ☐
The obvious short offwidth crack.
Gear to 3.5 inches.

5 Lion's Den 5.9 ★ ☐
The short hand crack on the right side of the wall.
Gear to 3.5 inches.

LOWER BOWLING ALLEY 8.1 miles

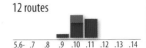

Approach time: 1 - 3 minutes.
Exposure: East, south and southwest.

12 routes

Easy, accessible and great for a quick workout. The Bowling Alley has some wonderful routes in a nice setting close to the road.

Access: Drive 8.1 miles up the canyon to a pullout on the right side of the road just east of Bell Buttress. The Lower Bowling Alley lies just north of the road.

LOWER BOWLING ALLEY

❶ Hareless in Boulder 5.10b ★ ☐
From the parking area, take the short trail up and left to upper left side of this first wall. On the left side of the wall is this short overhanging crack.
Gear to 2 inches. Rap from Dry Run anchor.

❷ Dry Run 5.9 ★ ☐
Climb the short, slightly overhang wall to the anchor below a ledge.
3 bolts.

❸ Happy Ending 5.10a/b ★ ☐
Start just right of *Dry Run,* making a long reach to good rail. Continue up the faint seam to good ledge and tackle the crux up a short headwall to the anchors.
8 bolts.

❹ Father Figure 5.11a/b ★★ ☐
Start 10 feet right of *Happy Ending,* aiming for the blunt arete. Gain the arete and then fire past the crux to a good ledge, and then finish with the headwall of *Happy Ending*.
8 bolts.

❺ Shady Deal 5.11b/c ★★ ☐
Behind the huge tree. Climb the obvious left-facing corner via stems, palming and a tenuous slab move to the anchor.
7 bolts.

❻ Splitting Hares 5.10a ★★ ☐
Start just right of the Ponderosa tree, gaining a shallow corner up to a good ledge. Climb the headwall to the anchor.
8 bolts.

7 A Tall Cool One 5.12a ★★ ☐☐
The obvious steep, well-chalked face just right of *Splitting Hares*. Technical pulls and a devious crux move make this one of the better routes on the wall.
9 bolts.

8 Centennial 5.11d ★★ ☐☐
A good route just right of *Tall Cool One*. Climb a shallow corner up to a steep face, power past the crux and gain a big ledge and optional anchor. Continue up the upper slab past four bolts to the anchor.
11 bolts.

9 Fin 5.10d ☐☐
Somewhat of a pile. Start as for *Curb Service* then veer left to the arete, climb the arete/face and then reach the anchor for *Curb Service.*
3 bolts, a few small cams.

10 Curb Service 5.10a ★★ ☐☐
Climb the center of obvious face on the fin of rock facing the road.
4 bolts.

11 Just Like Nebraska 5.11d ★ ☐☐
Start up right of the fin at the base of the broken slab. Climb the slab up to a left-facing corner to an overhang, fire right over the roof and up a short face to the anchor.
9 bolts.

12 Zee Eliminator 5.10c ★ ☐☐
Up and right of *Just Like Nebraska*, climb a finger crack, gaining a left-leaning, left-facing corner.
Gear to 3 inches. Walk off to the east.

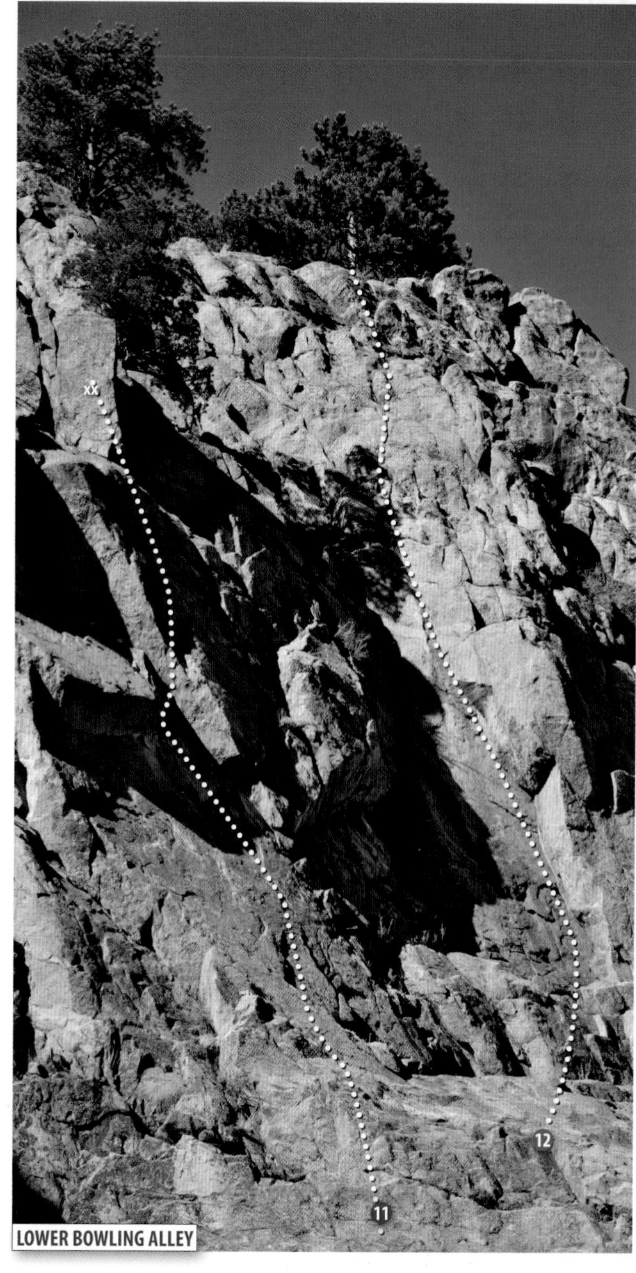

LOWER BOWLING ALLEY

UPPER BOWLING ALLEY 8.1 miles

Approach time: 5 - 8 minutes.
Exposure: East, south and southwest.

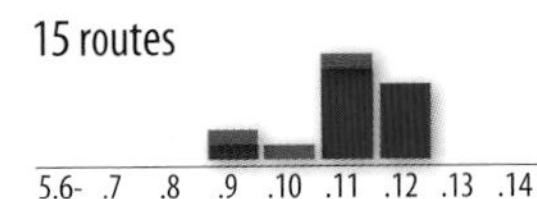

Easy, accessible and great for a quick workout. The Bowling Alley has some good routes in a nice setting close to the road.

Access: Drive 8.1 miles up the canyon to a pullout on the right side of the road just east of Bell Buttress and right below Practice Rock. Take the trail right of Practice Rock, crossing over some mine tailings, and head uphill to the obvious west-facing wall.

❶ Lucky Strike 5.11b ★ ☐
On the far left side of the wall, start on broken rock, climbing past a small bulge on bad holds and then up to the anchor.
11 bolts and 60m rope.

❷ Frothing Green 5.11b ★ ☐
Start just right of a tree and climb blocky rock past several ledges to gain the upper slab that leads to the anchor.
12 bolts and 60m rope.

❸ Next to Nothing 5.12b ★★ ☐
Pitch 1: 5.12b. Climb a short corner to a steep face, then struggle past three bolts to gain a ledge.
Pitch 2: 5.11d. Climb straight up past the first bolt, making a hard move, and gain the upper face, with a difficult move to gain the anchor.
12 quickdraws.

❹ Amazing Face 5.12c ★★★ ☐
Pitch 1: 5.12c/d. Climb a clean face on nice holds to a hard moves (most will lunge) to gain the anchor.
Pitch 2: 5.11c. Stem your way up a steep, shallow corner to the anchor.
12 quickdraws.

❺ Meteor Roadblock 5.12a/b ★★★ ☐
An excellent route with interesting moves. Climb the corner/crack system just left of an arete in the middle of the wall.
7 bolts.

❻ Super Bon Bon 5.12c ★★ ☐
Things get a little congested in this area. Climb up a steep wall to gain an arete about 30 feet up. Difficult moves moving right over the arete get you to the anchor.
7 bolts.

❼ Shiny Dog 5.12c ★ ☐
The crux is figuring out what holds to use and what bolts to clip. The second route from the right side of the wall.
8 bolts.

❽ Take the Termites Bowling 5.11c ★★ ☐
The rightmost route on the wall. Climb on good holds to a seam/crack and crux. Continue up steep rock to the anchor.
5 bolts.

❾ Bloodstone 5.11c ★★ ☐
This route starts on the left side of a ledge above the Main Wall. From *Take the Termites Bowling*, scramble up the gully to a good ledge, the traverse left to the start of the route.
Climb a thin stemming dihedral with tricky protection past a bulge and then follow easier but runout climbing to the *Amazing Face* second-pitch anchor. Rap.
Gear to 2 inches, extra RP's.

❿ Oil Pan Service 5.11a ★ ☐
Climb the first bolted route right of *Bloodstone* on the upper ledge. Tricky moves to start lead to easier climbing to the anchor.
7 bolts.

⓫ Bowling Ball and Chain 5.9+ ★ ☐
On the right side of the ledge, start off a block and wander upwards to the anchor.
7 bolts.

⓬ Digital Divide 5.10c ★ ☐
Down and right of the main wall is a short west-facing wall split by a crack. Climb it. Walk off to the north.
Gear to 2 inches.

The next three routes start on a separate wall down and right from the main wall, just above the Lower Bowling Alley.

⓭ Midge Squadron 5.11b/c ★ ☐
Start just left of the obvious corner, clipping two bolts, and then veering left up the face/arete to the anchor.
11 bolts.

⓮ Bad Girls Get Spanked 5.11b/c ★ ☐
Start as for *Midge Squadron* but continue straight up after the third bolt. Deceptive climbing; watch for a loose block halfway up. So what do good boys get?
11 bolts.

⓯ Mosquito Burrito 5.9 ★★★ ☐
Climb the bolted slab just right of the corner. Nice enjoyable climbing on good rock. It's 5.10a if you stay left of the bolts.
9 bolts.

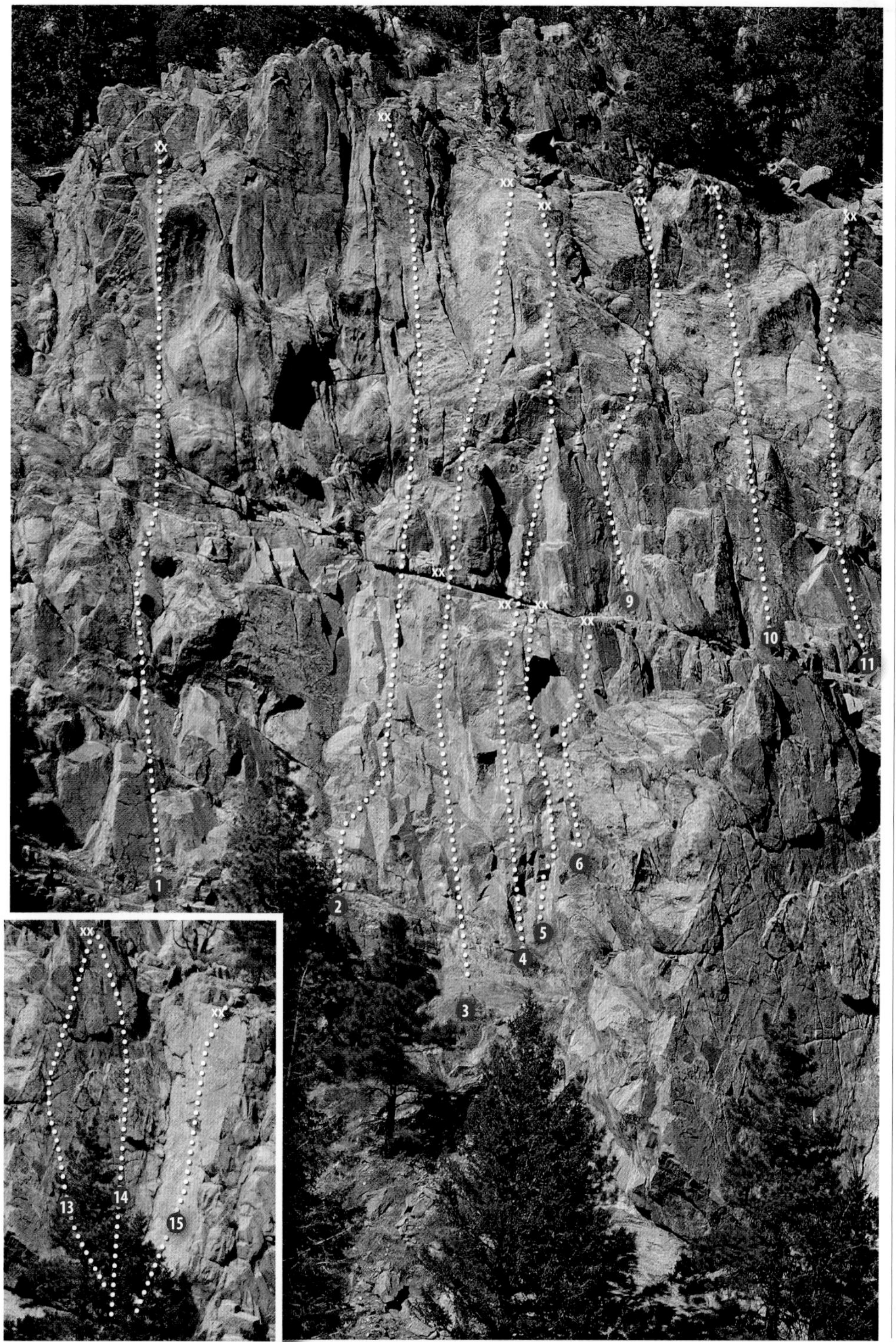
1
2
3
4
5
6
9
10
11
13
14
15

TUNGSTEN MINE SHAFT 8.1 miles

Approach time: 5 - 10 minutes.
Exposure: South.

2 routes

5.6- .7 .8 .9 .10 .11 .12 .13 .14

Some would call this piece of rock a pile but it's steep, offers a couple of really good routes, and some worthwhile bouldering.

Access: Park in a pullout on the right side of the road at 8.1 miles up the canyon. Hike up on the right side of Practice Rock to the Bowling Alley; go left along the base of the Bowling Alley, following a trail that leads to the base of the wall.

TUNGSTEN MINE SHAFT

The left side of the wall offers some good bouldering on solid granite.

❶ **Heart of Darkness** 5.13b ★ ☐

Climb the obvious overhanging wall on the left side of the wall. Getting past the fifth bolt is the crux.

7 bolts.

❷ **Neuromuscular Toxin** 5.12a/b ★★ ☐

Not a bad route that packs a good punch in 25 feet of climbing. Climb the arete/crack on the right side of the wall.

6 bolts.

PRACTICE ROCK 8.1 miles

Approach time: 2 to 3 minutes.
Exposure: South and west.

3 routes

5.6- .7 .8 .9 .10 .11 .12 .13 .14

A nice clean piece of granite a mere two minutes from the road. It also holds one of the best finger cracks in the area.

Access: Park in a pullout on the right side of the road at 8.1 miles up the canyon. Eat an energy bar and get ready for the arduous two-minute approach to the rock just uphill from the parking area.

PRACTICE ROCK

❶ **Thin Crack** 5.9+ ★ ☐
Climb the obvious crack on the left side of the rock. Walk off to the west or east. Another variation is marked.
Gear to 2 inches.

❷ **Regular Route** 5.11b ★★★★ ☐
Climb the beautiful thin crack that angles right near the top. The bigger your fingers, the harder it will feel. Classic!
Mostly thin finger sized gear.

❸ **LieBack** 5.10b ★ ☐
The obvious lieback flake on the right side of the rock.
Gear to 2 inches.

THE CORNERSTONE 8.1 miles

Approach time: 10 - 15 minutes.
Exposure: South.

6 routes

5.6- .7 .8 .9 .10 .11 .12 .13 .14

A nice clean piece of granite just uphill from the Practice Rock. Worth a visit due to the quality of rock and the well protected nature of the routes.

Access: Park in a pullout on the right side of the road at 8.1 miles up the canyon. Start about 100 feet up the road from Practice Rock and then go right up the steep hill, passing a stone wall, and then through a narrow walled section to the base of the rock.

❶ The Forgiven 5.9 ★ ☐
Start on the far left side of the rock, clipping a bolt just below a bush. Head up past the bush and climb the face or corner till the last bolt and then straight up to the anchor.
5 bolts.

❷ Repo Man 5.11d ★ ☐
Climb a short slab into a short corner/seam and then easier rock to the anchor.
6 bolts.

❸ Victory in De Feet 5.11a ★ ☐
Start just right of *Repo Man*, climbing just right of black streak.
7 bolts.

❹ The Good Book 5.10b ★★ ☐
Climb a short face up to the obvious right-facing dihedral, following it to the anchors.
6 bolts.

❺ Assault on the Earth 5.10c/d ★★ ☐
Climb the obvious bolted arete on the right side of the rock.
7 bolts.

❻ The Mustard Seed 5.8 ★★ ☐
The right-most route on the wall. A face leading to left-facing dihedral.
5 bolts.

ELECTRA GLIDE 8.1 miles

Approach time: 3 - 5 minutes.
Exposure: East and south.

3 routes

5.6- .7 .8 .9 .10 .11 .12 .13 .14

A nice, short piece of granite right off the road. It seems to be popular, as booty always seems to show up in the main crack.

Access: Park in a pullout on the left side of the road at 8.1 miles up the canyon. Walk two minutes up canyon to the rock on the right side of the road.

❶ **Bloody Monday** 5.10c ☐
Start around left on the west face and climb up shallow cracks to a bolt, clip the bolt then face climb and meet *Electra Glide*.
1 bolt, gear to 2 inches.

❷ **Electra Glide** 5.9- ★ ☐
The obvious crack on the left side of the rock. The hardest moves seem to be getting to the roof. Climb the roof to tree.
Gear to 2 inches.

❸ **Catch You Later** 5.9+ ☐
Start as for *Electra Guide*, then angle right taking a direct line to the tree. The roof is the crux.
Gear to 2 inches.

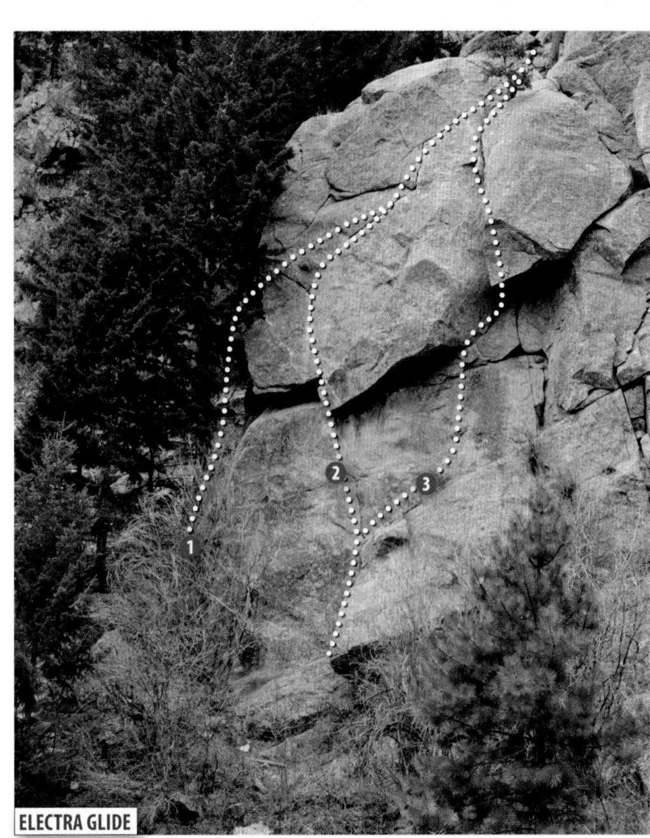

ELECTRA GLIDE

THE HIDEOUT 8.1 miles

This obscure crag is located just north of the upper Bowling Alley and sees little traffic. It has routes ranging in difficulty from 5.9 to 5.13. Go explore.

Access: Follow a faint trail on the left side of the Upper Bowling Alley (page 134) that leads to the crag.

ROAD ROCK 8.1 miles

Approach time: 3 - 5 minutes.
Exposure: South and east.

5 routes

This piece of granite is located close to the road and has four routes on its southeast-facing wall.

Access: Park in a pullout on the right side of the road at 8.1 miles up the canyon as for Practice Rock. Walk up canyon for about 150 yards to the rock on the right.

ROAD ROCK

1 Motorcycle Diaries 5.10b ★★ ☐
This climb starts on the far left side of the wall.
Pitch 1: 5.10b. Climb up a 5-easy slab to a bulge with a good hand crack. Climb the crack and reach a thin RP crack. Make a weird move past the crack and climb up the shallow corner to two small trees. Move right to a large tree and belay.
Pitch 2: 5.7. Climb up a shallow crack to a large tree.
Gear to 2.5 inches.

2 Magic Bus 5.12b/c ★★ ☐
Climb up easy corners on the right side of the wall to a right-slanting overhang with a thin crack splitting it. Fire through the roof and then up the slab to the anchors for Road Trip.
5 bolts and gear to 2 inches.

3 Road Trip 5.10b ★★★ ☐
The obvious mossy, left-facing corner on the right side of the rock. Climb up easy rock to gain the corner, step left to the arete and then up the steep slab to the anchor.

4 Tailspin 5.9 ★ ☐
Start as for *Road Trip* but go straight up the shallow corner past several trees to the top.
Gear to 2.5 inches.

5 Roadrash 5.10b ★★ ☐
Climb the obvious slab right of *Tailspin*. Thin with a cool upper crux.
5 bolts.

Vaino Kodas

I first saw Boulder Canyon during a trip to Colorado around 1987. I was living on the East Side of the Sierra Nevada in California and had been climbing on the sweeping flat granite faces of Yosemite and various domes in the Southern Sierras. As I drove down Boulder Canyon that day I kept my eyes peeled for some of the good rock climbing that I had heard about. I never saw it, and I drove right through, feeling a little disappointed in what looked like broken-up rock with maybe a few good short climbs. I think the only climb I noticed was *The Regular Route* on Practice Rock. I didn't visit Colorado again until I moved to Boulder in 1999.

The intervening years had seen the growth of "sport-climbing" and I had done my share of it. When I saw Boulder Canyon again, it looked different! One of the first experiences I remember was being taken to the Lighthouse (aka Solar Dome) by veteran climber Greg Hand. Greg would later introduce me to the indefatigable Bob D'Antonio with whom I would eventually do many new routes. We hiked up from the road, past the Security Risk area. I didn't learn until later that the best approach was from the top but it was a great warm up and gave us a beautiful view of the canyon. It was a cold February day, but the climbing was relatively warm and very enjoyable. That experience stands out as the one that opened my eyes to the possibilities in Boulder Canyon. After that, every trip into the canyon felt like a little adventure. Hidden among the trees were numerous gems that were not apparent from the road. I began hiking in the canyon with my favorite dog Lucky, looking for new routes, and was slightly surprised by what had *not* been climbed yet.

By the time I left Boulder in 2005 I had climbed countless enjoyable routes, did the first ascent of many, and never felt close to having "climbed out" Boulder Canyon. I had the fortune of climbing with many excellent partners and meeting many people who just plain love the sport, including the occasional climbing legend hobnobbing it with the little people. Considering the ease of access combined with rapidly obtained solitude, beautiful settings, fun people, and quality routes, I have to say Boulder Canyon stands out as the most enjoyable place I have ever climbed.

When I think of Boulder Canyon now, I see a picture of Lucky — he has enthusiastically run up ahead to a pine-shaded bend contouring the steeply rising granite. He's looking alternately at the scene ahead of him, and back at me, wondering what's taking me so long. I can't wait to get there and see what he sees. That moment of anticipation, potential discovery, and adventure epitomizes Boulder Canyon for me and will always live fondly in my imagination.

For me it's difficult to separate a route from the entire experience of climbing it, but here is a list of some of the routes that I remember as being very pleasurable (in alphabetical order):

- *Animal Magnetism,* 5.11c, Animal World
- *Bihedral Arete,* 5.10a, The Bihedral
- *Boulder Quartz System,* 5.12a, Plotinus Wall
- *East Slab,* 5.6, The Dome
- *Empire of the Fenceless,* 5.12a, Easter Rock
- *Global Gorilla,* 5.12c, Animal World
- *Jolt Cola,* 5.12a, Blob Rock
- *North Face Center,* 5.7+, Cob Rock
- *Plan B,* 5.12b, Security Risk Crag
- *The Ticket,* 5.12a/b, Blob Rock

AQUARIUM WALL 8.0 miles

Approach time: 5 - 10 minutes.
Exposure: North and northwest.

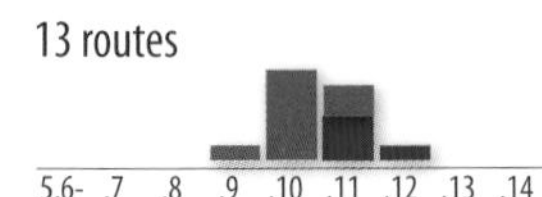

A nice piece of granite that rises out of the creek offering several good sport and trad routes. The wall faces north and stays cool during the summer months. Many of the trad routes start from the water and are inaccessible during runoff or high water.

Access: Park in the pullout on the left side of the road 8.1 miles up the canyon. Head back down canyon for 100 feet, cross the creek and then to the wall.

The first four routes are accessed by the same first pitch (5.9). They all start off a wide ledge with a tree on the right side. Gain the first pitch by crossing the creek near the left side of the wall and scramble up to the base.

❶ Lichen Has Feelings Too! 5.11d ★☐

Pitch 1: 5.9. Climb past three bolts on a dirty moss-covered ledge to a two-bolt anchor.

Pitch 2: 5.11d. A short crux section at the start leads to a corner then the anchors.

9 bolts.

❷ The Future Of Life 5.11d/12a ★★★☐

Pitch 1: 5.9. Climb past three bolts on a dirty moss-covered ledge to a two-bolt anchor.

Pitch 2: 5.11d/12a. Climb up a short ramp and clip the first of six bolts on a slightly overhanging wall. Power up on good sharp edges to a funky move past the fourth bolt. Gain a small ledge, make a technical move past the fifth bolt and cruise to the anchor.

6 bolts.

❸ Huck Finn 5.11d/12a ★★★ ☐

Pitch 1: 5.9. Climb past three bolts on a dirty moss-covered ledge to a tree on the right.

Pitch 2: 5.11d/12a. Start just left of *Nowhere Man* and reach for a big knob. Clip the first bolt and make a series of cool slab moves on wonderful knobs trending left past several bolts. Gain a small ledge and make some thin, devious moves up thin seams. Reach the "Finn" and make more thin moves to a bucket and a good ledge. Crank up on good holds to the anchor.

8 bolts.

❹ Nowhere Man 5.11b/c ★★ ☐

Pitch 1: 5.9. Climb past three bolts on a dirty moss-covered ledge to a tree on the right.

Pitch 2: 5.11b/c. Climb up past the first bolt on amazing knobs. Reach a good finger pocket by the third bolt and make a hard move to gain a ledge. From the ledge fire straight up a thin seam past three more bolts to the anchor. Great slab climbing on excellent rock.

8 bolts.

5 Parallel Development 5.10d ★ ☐
Start out of the creek directly below a pine tree and just left of stepped dihedral. Climb up to the roof, clip an old bolt and veer left out a handrail then up and slightly right to a finger crack, follow the crack and make a hard move to gain the ledge.
1 bolt and gear to 2 inches.

6 Filet of Soul 5.10d ★★ ☐
Start out of the creek directly below a pine tree and small roof. Climb up to the roof, clip an old bolt and then right up a steep finger crack to the tree or continue up *Weed Killer* to the top.
SR.

7 Convergence Corner 5.10c/d ★ ☐
Start out of the creek at the bottom of a stepped dihedral, climb it to the ledge and tree or continue up *Weed Killer* to the top.
SR.

8 Weed Killer 5.9 ★★ ☐
This is actually a pretty good route. It climbs a nice crack with good gear just to right of *Convergence Corner*. Climb the crack to the ledge at a pine tree; continue up (easier) to the top. Walk off to the east.

9 Jerome Webster Memorial 5.11d/12a ★★ ☐
Another good route that sees little traffic. Start for *Weed Killer* but head right up a thin crack with sustained climbing, there's a definite crux about 40 feet up, the crack and climb trend left and meet back with *Weed Killer* near the top.
Lots of small and medium pieces. SR.

10 Justin Alf Memorial Route 5.10c/d ★ ☐
Start just left of *Gish* on the Aquarium Wall. Climb a short slab past two bolts to good rest. Climb up past four bolts (a long reach at the fifth bolt is the crux) and gear, passing a small pine tree up to a ledge. From the ledge, go left up to a small pine tree and shallow crack, place small gear and crank past three more bolts up a steep face to a good crack and ledge. Place a Friend and go right to the *Gish* anchor
11 bolts and a few small to medium pieces.
A 60-meter rope WILL NOT get you back to the ground.

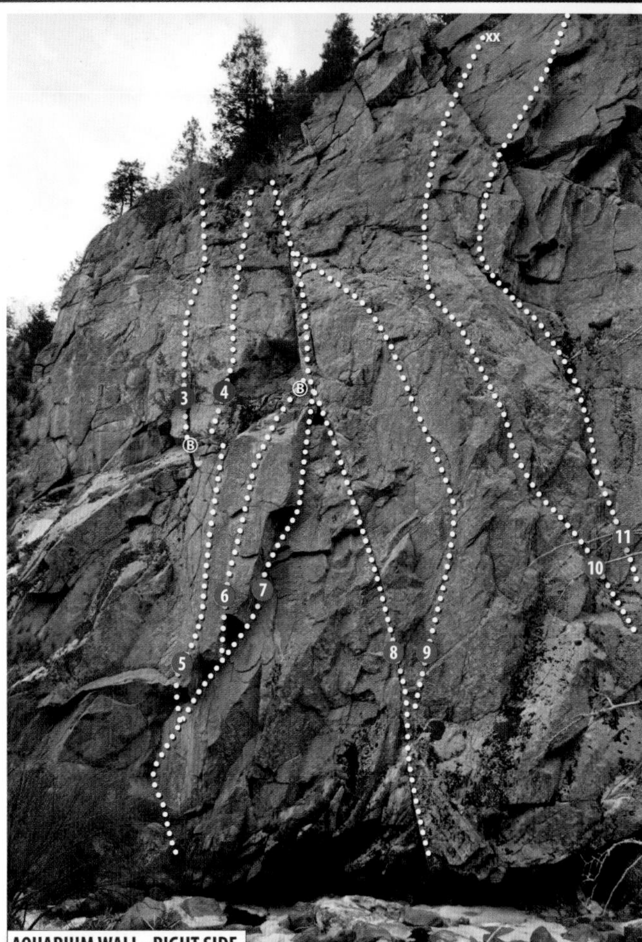

AQUARIUM WALL - RIGHT SIDE

11 Gish 5.10c ★★★ ☐
Just left of *Pigs in Space* where the wall meets Boulder Creek is a two-bolt anchor 15 feet off the ground. Climb up to the anchor and belay from here. Angle left past the anchor and climb up on good holds to a ledge just past the sixth bolt. The bolts continue straight up into a shallow corner past a small overhang to a two-bolt anchor. Be careful when lowering!!!
10 bolts and a few small to medium pieces.
70-meter rope required to lower.

12 Pigs In Space 5.10c/d ☐
Pitch 1: 5.10d. Start as for *Gish*, but climb straight up the dirty moss-covered corner. Belay on the left below a steep right facing corner.
Pitch 2: 5.10c. Climb the slightly overhanging corner, step right to an arete and then straight up on easier climbing to the woods.
SR.

13 Eur-A-Peon 5.11d ☐
Start on the clean face at the right margin of the wall, climb a difficult slab then right into some dirty corners and up to the woods. The quality of climbing decreases greatly after the initial face.
4 bolts, SR.

Roger Molina working *Times of Blindness* 5.13b, Bell Buttress (next page). Photo: Adam Bove.

THE PATIO 8.1 miles

Approach time: 5 minutes.
Exposure: North and northwest.

10 routes

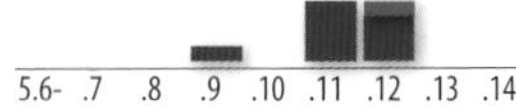

Once no more than a popular bouldering traverse, The Patio now has about eight sport routes gracing the wall above the traverse.

Access: Park in a pullout on the left side of the road at 8.1 miles up the canyon. Cross the road and hike downhill to the creek. Cross the creek at a log crossing and go uphill to the obvious wall just slightly right of the trail.

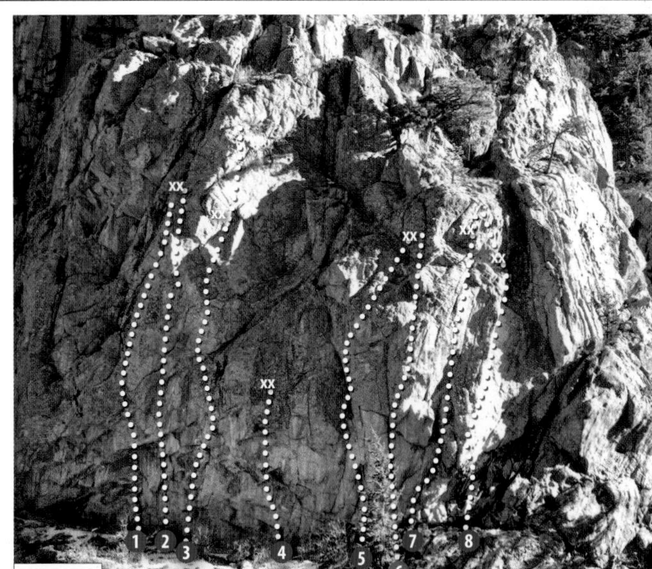

❶ **Carrying Futons** 5.11c ★ ☐
On the far left side of the wall. Stick clip the 1st bolt and climb up steep rock through a bulge. Crack the crux and follow bolts up the steep face to a 2-bolt anchor.
6 bolts.

❷ **Clyde's Big Adventure** 5.12a ★ ☐
The second route on the left side of the wall. Named after Matt Samet's dog. Climb through the roof staying on the right side of the arete.
6 bolts.

❸ **War on Peace** 5.12a ★★★ ☐
Stick clip the first bolt (or boulder up to it), then fire up a series of difficult moves to a good stance. Shake out, then continue up on 5.10 moves to the top and the anchors.
8 bolts.

❹ **Poolside** 5.12b/c ★ ☐
Power up through the roofs just right of *War on Peace.* Short route.
3 bolts.

❺ **Underbelly** 5.11c/d ★ ☐
The obvious left-facing corner, boulder up to the first bolt then gain the corner, stem, then head right at the top to anchors.
3 bolts and few small to medium pieces.

❻ **Antebellum** 5.12a ★★ ☐
At the right side of The Patio traverse is a flaring hand-size crack that turns thin below a roof. Climb the crack with good gear (crux) to a roof. Undercling right and up a face (hard) past 3 bolts.
3 bolts, 1.5 - 3 inch cams.

❼ **Bottom Feeder** 5.11a/b ☐
Climb the slot (gear), then climb seams/cracks past four bolts to the top and a 2-bolt anchor.
4 bolts, 0.5 and 0.75 micro-cams.

❽ **For Whom the Bell Tolls** 5.11a/b ☐
The slanting, right-facing corner on the far right side of The Patio. The crux is getting past the first bolt; enjoyable stemming leads to the anchor.
7 bolts.

The next two climbs are located down and right of The Patio close to the creek.

❾ **Bell Bottom** 5.9 ☐
The route on the left side of the wall. Climb 20' or so (no pro) up a slab (5.4-ish) to the 1st bolt where the wall turns to vertical. Head up this clipping 4 bolts along the way until the wall kicks back. Head easily up and right to the anchors.
4 bolts.

❿ **Bell Bottom Blues** 5.11a ★★ ☐
A nice, short, and sweet climb on a slightly overhanging wall. Easy slab climbing up to the 1st bolt. There is a hard move to get started and it stays challenging till the wall kicks back just above the 4th bolt.
4 bolts.

BELL BUTTRESS 8.1 miles

Approach time: 10 - 15 minutes.
Exposure: North and west.

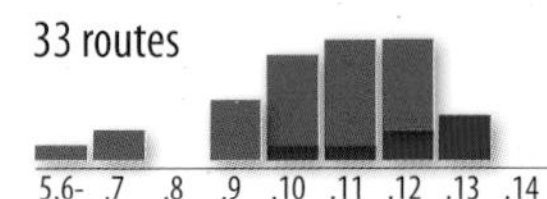

This impressive buttress sits just above Boulder Creek and hosts many exceptional climbs of varying difficulty. It's a great place to beat the heat in the summer, and the west face gets good sun during the winter.

Access: Park in a pullout on the right side of the road at 8.1 miles. Cross the road and down a short hill to the obvious log crossing. Go left a take trail angling up and left to base of the wall right below the north face of the rock. In times of high water a Tyrolean traverse just downstream from the log crossing.

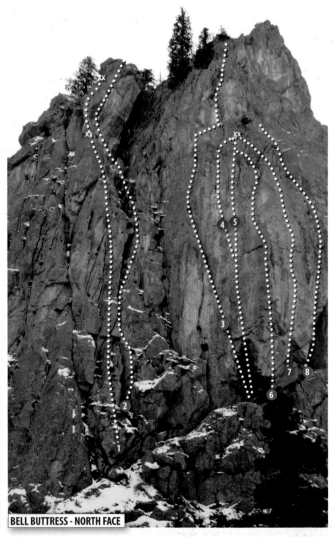

BELL BUTTRESS - NORTH FACE

❶ Bell Air 5.11b/c ★★

This 2 pitch, north-facing route starts on the left side of Bell Buttress just after you start up the ramp that leads to the main section of the cliff (about 50 feet before *Hound Dog*). Belay inside some large flakes, imbedded into the ground.

Pitch 1: 5.9. This long, mixed pitch climbs a mossy slab past 7 bolts and then crosses a corner where two natural placements can be had then up past 5 more bolts to anchor.

12 bolts, med cams.

Pitch 2: 5.11b/c. Move up and left to climb the vertical arete and face. This pitch features edges and several interesting pockets on good rock.

5 bolts.

❷ The Pitts 5.11b ★★

High up on the north face is an impressive overhanging hand crack. *The Pitts* climbs this feature.

Pitch 1: 5.7. Climb the obvious moss and dirt filled gully on the north face just right of the upper crack of *Pitts* or climb the first pitch of *Bell Air* (5.9), which get you to the base of the route in better condition.

Pitch 2: 5.11b. From the belay climb a short corner then gain the main crack and fire it to the top. Walk off to the east or rap down *Bell Air*

Gear to 3.5 inches.

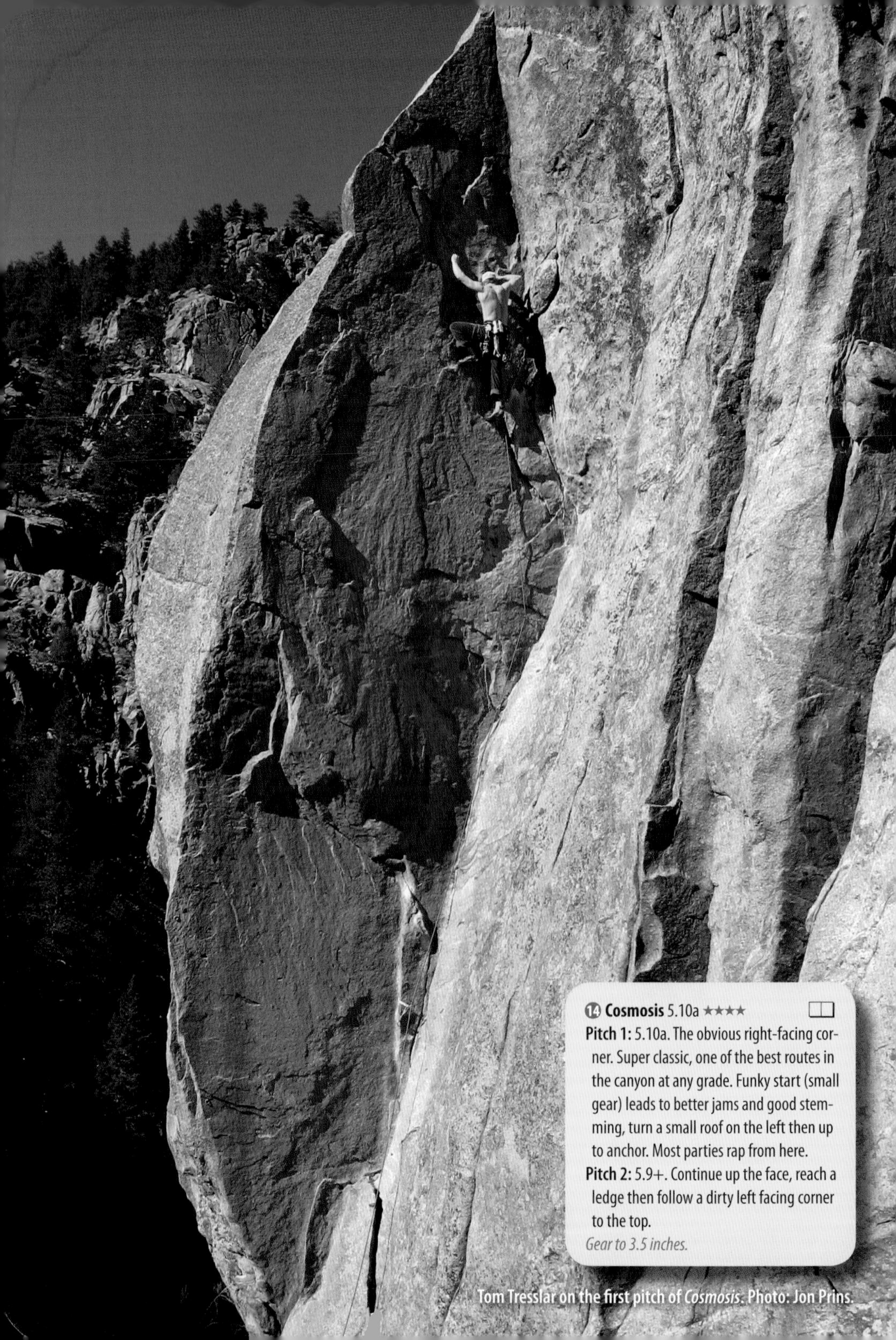

⓮ **Cosmosis** 5.10a ★★★★

Pitch 1: 5.10a. The obvious right-facing corner. Super classic, one of the best routes in the canyon at any grade. Funky start (small gear) leads to better jams and good stemming, turn a small roof on the left then up to anchor. Most parties rap from here.

Pitch 2: 5.9+. Continue up the face, reach a ledge then follow a dirty left facing corner to the top.

Gear to 3.5 inches.

Tom Tresslar on the first pitch of *Cosmosis*. Photo: Jon Prins.

❸ North Face 5.10a ★ ☐

A short distance up the trail is a tree and behind the tree a bolted face (*Hound Dog*). The climb starts here.

Pitch 1: 5.10a. Go left following brushy, right-facing corners left to a pedestal facing an alcove. Climb a thin, clean crack up and out of the alcove to a face and a second alcove. Belay on the ledge above.

Pitch 2: 5.9+. Climb a short crack and finish on the second pitch of *Cosmosis*. Walk of east or rap *Cosmosis*.

Gear to 2.5 inches.

❹ Freak on a Leash 5.13a ★★ ☐

Start as for *Hound Dog* and at bolt 8 veer left up the steep blank wall. Continuous moves from start to finish. Hard for the grade.

13 bolts.

❺ Hound Dog 11a ★★★ ☐

The obvious east facing steep wall above the tree. Climb beautiful rock up to the anchors. Classic!

10 bolts.

❻ The Grand Inquisitor 5.12a R ★★★★ ☐

Right of *Hound Dog* the wall overhangs and leans to the right, *Grand Inquisitor* climbs the left side of the wall. The bolts were placed with the aid of ladder. Fire up the face past two bolts to a small overhang, veer slightly right to get established above the roof, continue up the crack to a stance at the top. Take a deep breath and climb a steep face to a shallow corner and the anchor.

2 bolts, gear to 3.5 inches.

❼ The Purpose 5.12b ★★ ☐

Just right of the *Grand Inquisitor* is overhanging wall with thin crack/seam. The Purpose climbs the seam past 6 bolts to a anchor. The site of a nasty bolt war.

6 bolts.

❽ Gates of Eden 5.10b ★★ ☐

The daunting wide crack just left of the big slot. Climbing the overhanging handcrack to gain the wide section, fire up the easier climbing to anchor of *The Grand Inquisitor* or follow the second pitch of *Cosmosis*.

Gear to 4.5 inches.

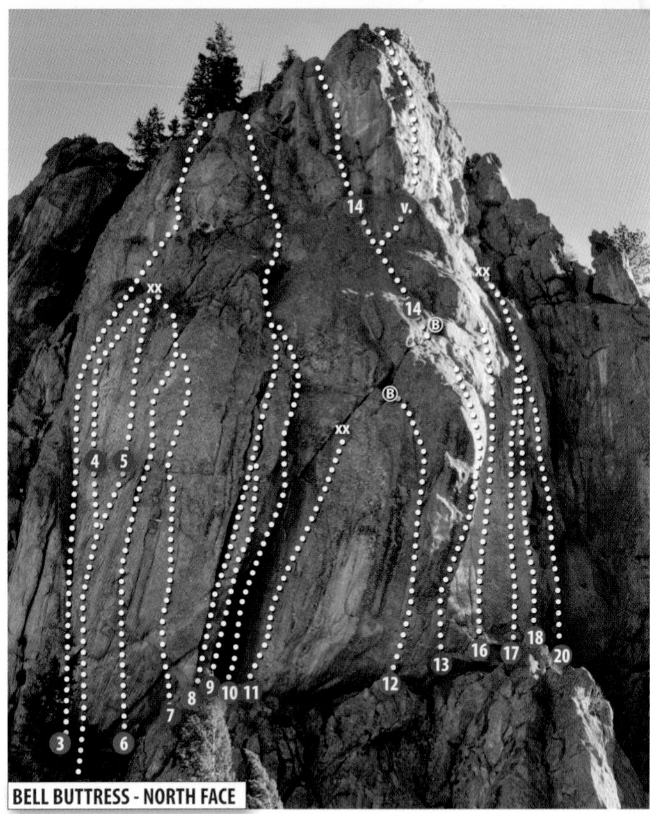

BELL BUTTRESS - NORTH FACE

❾ Tiempos de Ceguera 5.13b ★ ☐

"Times of Blindness." Start up *Gates of Eden* and move right to the technical bolted arete. You can climb *Double Jeopardy* and work the route on toprope from bolted anchors. Photo page 144.

6 bolts.

❿ Double Jeopardy 5.9 ★ ☐

Burrow back into the slot and climb the cracks and chimney up to ledge. Continue up with the second pitch of *Cosmosis*.

Gear to 3.5 inches.

⓫ Bell Buster 5.11a ★ ☐

The right side of the slot has a bolted route.

7 bolts

⓬ The Spoils 5.12b ★★★ ☐

Right of the slot is thin overhanging left-facing corner. The crux comes low and the gear is better than it looks. Great route.

Gear to 2 inches.

⓭ Verve 5.13c ★★★★ ☐

The stunning arete just left of *Cosmosis*. Christian Griffith's claim to fame and still rarely repeated. Best of the grade in the canyon. Photo page 20.

4 bolts.

⓮ Cosmosis 5.10a ★★★★ ☐

See description opposite.

Variation: The Route That Dan Missed 5.10a R ☐

Once on the ledge below the last corner climb a face just right of the arete. Runout and scary.

2 bolts and that's about it.

15 **Swerve** 5.12b
Climb about 40 up *Cosmosis* and then Swerve left to the last bolt of *Verve*.
1 bolt, gear to 2 inches.

16 **Beethoven's Fifth** 5.12d ★★★★
Climb the thin crack that splits the wall just right of *Cosmosis*, starts out hard and becomes very difficult just below a small roof. Move right to the anchor on *West Crack*.
Gear to 2 inches.

17 **West Crack** 5.10a ★★★
This route starts two cracks right of *Cosmosis*. Beautiful climbing on excellent granite.
Gear to 3.5 inches.

18 **West Face** 5.10a ★★★
The third crack right of *Cosmosis*, beautiful climbing up the crack/right facing corner, past a flake, then scamper to the anchor.
SR.

19 **Left Wall** 5.12b
A huge chimney splits the rock just past the *West Face*. This route climbs the left side of the chimney via an arete.
10 bolts.

20 **Little Man In A Boat** 5.12b R
Climb through the strange, down-pointing overlaps, which define the buttress, aiming for a crack, which splits the final roof before it trends left on easier ground to the bolt anchors atop the *Left Wall.*
SR.

21 **Epiphany** 5.11d R ★★
Pitch 1: 5.11a. The right side of the chimney forms a nice north-facing wall. Start on the left side of the wall, climb up to an old bolt, funky moves lead to the anchor.
Pitch 2: 5.11d. Face climb via a seam and reach a small ledge, trend right to another seam then up to a ledge and the anchor.

Variation: Epiphany Direct 5.12 R
From the small foot ledge veer left up the face aiming for a right facing arch leading to a roof, climb over the roof to a ledge.
SR.

22 **Arms Bazaar** 5.12a R ★★★
The obvious thin hand crack right of Epiphany. Climb the face past a bolt then veer right to the start of the crack at a small overhang, reach a good finger jam and then a good rest, fire up the crack to a bolted anchor.
Gear to 2 inches.

23 **Three Minute Hero** 5.11b/c R ★
Start just right of *Arms Bazaar* and climb past the good pocket into a small roof. Turn the roof and finger traverse right via some hard face moves. Continue up the crack to the anchor.
Gear to 2 inches.

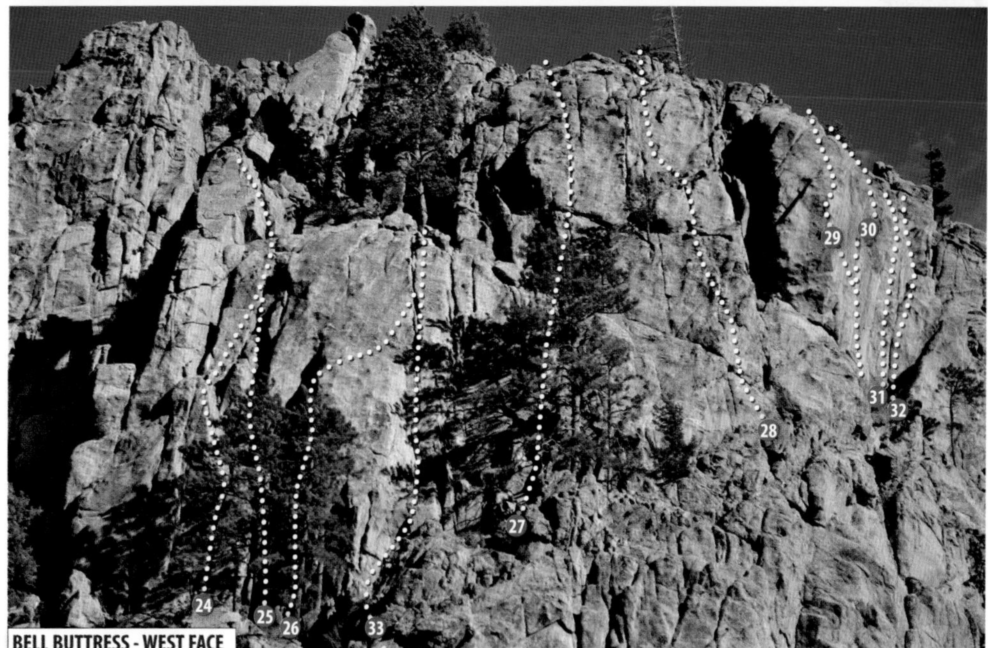

BELL BUTTRESS - WEST FACE

24 Joe Pontiac 5.7 ★ ☐

Right of *Three Minute Hero* is a boulder and then a tree. The climb starts just right of the tree. Climb over a bulge then up corners to the ledge for *Three Minute Hero*.

Gear to 2 inches.

25 Malaise 5.10c R ★ ☐

Right of *Joe Pontiac* is narrow fin of rock. Climb up the short left-facing dihedral on the left side of the fin, veer right and climb to a ledge.

Gear to 2 inches.

26 Deadalus 5.10c R ☐

Right of *Joe Pontiac* is narrow chimney. Climb the left-facing dihedral just right of the chimney over a small roof and then out right and up to a ledge.

Gear to 2 inches.

27 Wayward Puritan 5.6 ★★ ☐

Pitch 1: 5.6. Start just left of large pine in a right-facing corner. Climb the corner to a ledge.

Pitch 2: 5.5. Continue up the crack system to the top.

Gear to 2.5 inches.

28 Five-Ten-Route 5.10a ☐

The approach ramp bends right and another ramp comes in from the left, go up the ramp for a short distance to a thin crack. Climb the thin crack to a ramp and then an easier crack to top.

Gear to 2 inches.

29 Front Line 5.11b ★★ ☐

Continue up the approach ramp to the obvious clean shield of rock on the left. Climb the center of the face past two old bolts, reach a crack and then up easier rock to the top.

2 bolts, a few small and medium cams.

30 Front Line Lefthand 5.11b R ★★ ☐

After the first bolt on *Front Line* veer left to the arete then up to the top.

Gear to 2 inches.

31 Frontier 5.11b ★★ ☐

Climb the arete right of *Front Line* past two bolts to the top. Good route.

2 bolts, a few small and medium cams.

32 Tiers 5.7 ☐

The obvious corner to the right of *Frontier*.

Gear to 2.5 inches.

33 Wrinkles 5.9 ☐

Pitch 1: 5.8. Cross the creek at the log, go right below the Patio and look for a tree about 15 feet up at a good ledge. Climb the right of two cracks to the approach ramp.

Pitch 2: 5.9. Climb just left of *Malaise*. There is a right-arching flake at the bottom, Thin cracks appear and then climb a wider crack to the ledge.

Pitch 3: 5.6. Follow the crack of *Wayward Puritan* to the top.

Gear to 2.5 inches.

BEAN LIQUOR WALL 8.1 miles

Approach time: 10 - 15 minutes.
Exposure: West.

5 routes

A secluded west-facing wall on the far right side of Bell Buttress.

Access: Drive 8.1 miles up the canyon to a small pullout on the right side of the road. Drop down and cross the creek at a log, go right past the Patio along the base of the creek, and then left up a steep gully to reach the base of the wall.

BEAN LIQUOR WALL

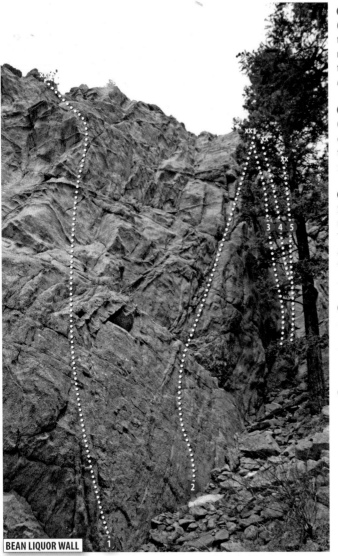

❶ Bean Banger 5.10d/11a ★★

Climb over a short bulge and then veer left to gain the arête. Make a hard move, then reach a ledge and easier climbing that leads to the anchor.

6 bolts, a couple of small to medium cams.

❷ Hambanger 5.10b ★★

Climb a short face then gain a right-facing corner. Move left to an arete at the top of the corner to reach the anchor.

9 bolts.

❸ Nice Doggie 5.12a ★

Start off a block just right of a tree. Power up the steep face with the crux down low. The upper hard move to anchor can be avoided by going left or right of bolt and then up to the anchor.

7 bolts.

❹ We Bean Jammin 5.11c/d ★

Start off the block and trend right up a right-leaning corner to a strange crux move to reach the anchor.

6 bolts.

❺ Beano Hangover 5.12a ★

The right most route on the wall. Climb to a short corner and then follow a crack with a weird move to reach the anchor.

5 bolts.

MYTH ROCK 8.2 miles

Approach time: 10 - 15 seconds.
Exposure: South.

5 routes

5.6- .7 .8 .9 .10 .11 .12 .13 .14

A short crag literaly located right on the road. You can easily belay from the car. The bottom 30 feet is part of a road cut, the upper section is good compact granite.

Access: Drive up canyon to a parking area at 8.2 miles on the right. Look right to the wall.

1 Myth of Freedom 5.10a ★
Start as for *Mjolnir* and after the second bolt, veer left up the clean face past three more bolts to the anchor.
5 bolts.

2 Mjolnir 5.10c ★★
Start on the left side of the rock, climbing into the obvious V-shaped corner.
7 bolts.

3 Excalibur 5.11b ★★
Start at a V-groove and climb past two bolts and crux to a ledge, past an optional belay, and climb the wonderful right-facing corner to the anchor.
8 bolts.

4 Thor 5.12b/c ★
Climb the center of the road cut past two bolts up to the ledge. Veer right and slap your way up the rounded arete to the anchor.
8 bolts.

5 Mithril 5.9 ★★
On the right side of the rock, climb past two bolts to the ledge and jam the obvious overhanging handcrack to a tree and the belay. Rap from the tree.
2 bolts, gear to 3 inches.

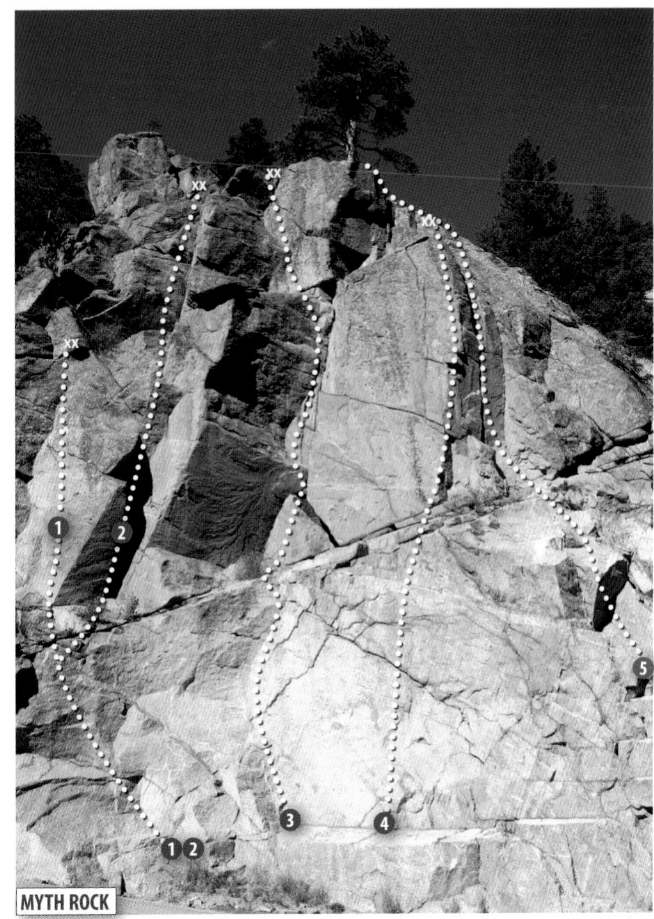

MYTH ROCK

SOLARIS 8.2 miles

Approach time: 15-20 minutes.
Exposure: North, west and northwest.

18 routes

Solaris lies just left (east) of Avalon. See overview map page 157. The crag consists of four buttresses separated by steep gullies. The main walls face west and provide morning shade or afternoon sun for climbing in cooler weather.

Access: Either park in a pullout on the right side of the road at 8.1 miles (Bell Buttress) and walk 0.1 miles upstream, or park in a large pullout on the left side of the road at 8.6 miles (Animal World) and walk 0.4 miles downstream. You can also park nearer the wall in a semi-illegal pullout on the right side of the road at 8.2 miles — however, C-Dot might ticket. From this parking area, cross the road and descend a short hill to a Tyrolean traverse. Walk downstream, passing a gully/scree slope to the lower tier.

Most of the routes are sport, but several require gear; bring a rack.

LOWER TIER

❶ Crumbs 5.8+ ★ ☐
On the left side of the wall, left of *Left Line*, is a short face leading to a crack. Climb the face then reach the crack and protection. Angle right and use the anchor for *Left Line*.
Gear to 3 inches.

❷ Left Line 5.8 ★ ☐
The obvious bolted face on the left side of the wall. The first bolt is just above a horizontal crack; a nice face leads to the anchor.
5 bolts.

❸ Right Line 5.9 ★ ☐
Start on the right side of the wall below a tree on a ledge, climb up to the tree and veer left up the face to the anchor.
5 bolts.

❹ The Right Way 5.8 ☐
Start as for *Right Line* and gain the ledge, veer left up a corner then back left to the anchor for *Right Line.*
3 bolts, gear to 2 inches.

MIDDLE TIER/MAIN WALL

To get to the Main Wall, continue up the talus and look for cairns. Go left at the cairns and follow a trail along the base of the wall. The first route you'll see is *Contact*. The other routes are several hundred feet left, just past a gully.

❺ Don't Get me Started 5.6 ☐
Climb the short face past a bolt on the left side of the wall, then climb up the bushy ramp to a steep corner. Climb the corner and the slab above to the anchors.
7 bolts.

❻ Start Me Up 5.7 ★ ☐
Climb a steep face to a blunt arete, then ramble to the anchor on easy rock. Popular.
5 bolts.

❼ The Luminosity 5.9 ★★★ ☐
Maybe the best route in the area. Start just left of the large roof and climb excellent rock with good protection to the anchor.
10 bolts.

❽ Tower of Power 5.10b ★★ ☐
Start just right of the large roof and climb to the right side. Climb the small roof then up a steep face to a ledge, then up a short headwall to the anchor.
8 bolts.

❾ My Place In the Universe 5.11a/b R ☐
Start left of *Mission to Mars*, climbing up to a slot and then a crack through a roof to the top.
Gear to 3 inches.

❿ Mission to Mars 5.10c ★ ☐
Start at a finger crack just behind a tree, plug gear in the crack, then reach a face with some bolts. Climb to the anchors.
2 bolts, two pieces to 1 inch.

⓫ Party On 5.10c ☐
Start on a spike sticking out of the ground. Plug gear in and aim for a low roof. Climb the roof up to a larger roof, over that then to the ledge.
Gear to 3 inches.

⓬ Harvest Moon 5.9 ☐
On the right side of the wall close to a tree, climb up a blunt arete to a horn, then up a crack to a tree with slings.
Gear to 2 inches.

⑬ Contact 5.9 ★★ ☐

Contact is on the far right side of the main wall.

Pitch 1: 5.7. Climb easy rock past bolts to a nice ledge and belay.

4 bolts.

Pitch 2: 5.9. Fire up past two bolts to easier rock and then onto slab that leads to the anchor.

8 bolts.

To access the next three routes, walk east to the gully separating Contact *from the Main Wall, hike up the gully to the top to a ledge and the routes will be on the right.*

⑭ Mephistophiles 5.10c ★ ☐

The finger/hand crack splitting the left side of the wall with a high bolt.

1 bolt and gear to 2 inches.

⑮ Twilight Zone 5.10a ★★ ☐

A nice route with several good moves. The bolted face just right of *Mephistophiles*.

5 bolts.

⑯ Kundalini Express 5.8 ★ ☐

Climb a left-facing corner with a finger crack that leads to a slab and then up a short headwall to the anchor.

Gear to 2 inches.

⑰ Stellar Drifter 5.9 ★★ ☐

A nice route that climbs clean rock and has great views from the belay.

Pitch 1: 5.7. Access the first pitch by climbing up the gully on the right side of the Main Wall to a ledge near a Ponderosa. Climb up short corners/hand cracks to a ledge with a large pine. Belay.

Pitch 2: 5.9. Climb the crack just left of a bolted slab to the top.

Gear to 3 inches.

⑱ Cosmic Explorer 5.11c ★ ☐

Climb the slab just right of the second pitch of *Stellar Drifter* to an anchor.

4 bolts.

AVALON 8.2 miles

Approach time: 10 - 30 minutes.
Exposure: North, west, and northwest.

Avalon is a series of multi-tiered cliffs set in the narrowest part of the canyon. It has many good sport and trad climbs in a pleasant setting. The cliffs vary in exposure and, depending on the time of year, you can chase the sun or avoid it. In the summer months, especially on the weekends, Avalon can get quite crowded; the higher you hike toward the upper tier the less crowds you'll find.

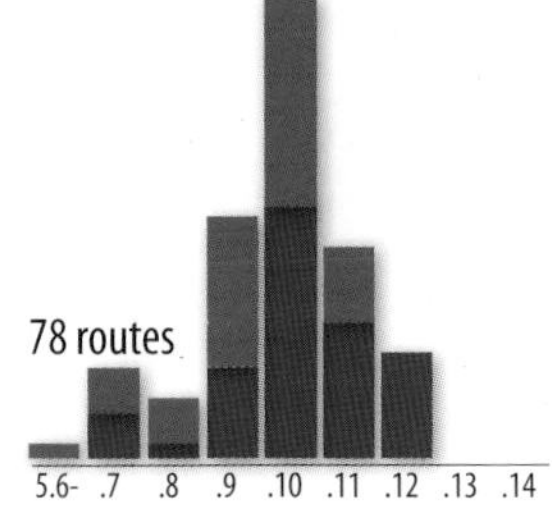

Access: Either park in a pullout on the right side of the road at 8.1 miles (Bell Buttress) and walk 0.1 miles upstream, or park in a large pullout on the left side of the road at 8.6 miles (Animal World) and walk 0.4 miles downstream. You can also park directly below the wall in a semi-illegal pullout on the right side of the road at 8.2 miles — however, C-Dot might ticket. From this parking area, cross the road and descend a short hill to a Tyrolean traverse. The trail from the traverse leads to the Lower Tier right side.

AVALON FIRST TIER

Routes are listed right to left.

❶ Catch and Release 5.12b/c ★★ ☐
Where the trail meets the Lower Tier, climb the obvious overhang leading to an arete and then up an easier face to the anchor.
9 bolts.

❷ Mists of Avalon 5.10a ★★★ ☐
Start left of *Catch and Release,* climbing blocky rock to below a roof. Fire the roof then up the easier face to the anchor.
8 bolts.

❸ Spare Rib 5.10d ★★ ☐
The obvious crack left of *Mist of Avalon*. Pitch 1: 5.10b. Climb past the first two bolts of *Mist of Avalon* and then veer left through a roof using chockstones for holds; the crack becomes easier and leads to a ledge. Most folks rap from the *Mist of Avalon* anchor. Pitch 2: 5.10d. Climb the obvious wide crack through a low roof.
2 bolts and gear to 5 inches.

❹ Sword in the Stone 5.9+ ★★ ☐
On the left side of the wall, climb over small overhangs trending left to a sharp arete. Climb the arete to the anchors.
7 bolts.

❺ Tunnel of Love 5.9 ★ ☐
Head left on the trail to the upper section of the Lower Tier. Start below the obvious chockstone high up. Climb the crack and then veer left and exit through a chockstone tunnel to an anchor.
Gear to 3 inches.

❻ Marquis de Sade 5.10c ★★ ☐
Start left of *Tunnel of Love* up a steep face to a short finger crack. Reach a roof then climb it to the anchors.
7 bolts.

❼ Body Count 5.11b ★★ ☐
Climb the steep slab up to the obvious roof. Power over the roof and reach the anchor. The crux comes low.
7 bolts.

❽ Slayer 5.10b ★★ ☐
Start near a block and then attack the face past a small overhang. Easier climbing leads to roof and then the anchors.
7 bolts.

❾ Iron Maiden 5.9+ ★★ ☐
Sweet holds lead to a roof and then a fun face to another roof. Fire the roof and follow a crack to the anchors.
8 bolts.

❿ Sex Slave 5.10c ★ ☐
Start at a short crack, stick-clip the first bolt or climb to it, pull the crux and then cruise to the top.
Gear to 2 inches and 4 bolts.

AVALON SECOND TIER

From the left side of the Lower Tier continue left on a trail that takes you to the left side of the Tarot Wall.

TAROT WALL

⓫ The Magician 5.9 ★★ ☐
Start on the very left side of the rock on the west face. Locate two bolts on a low wall, start in the corner left of the bolts in a crack, climb the corner till it ends and reach the upper wall and bolts. Cruise to the anchor. **Variation:** 5.10b. Climb the corner for a short distance and go right to the first bolt, or climb straight up past the first two bolts.
6 bolts, gear to 3 inches, and a few long runners.

⓬ Ah Ya Punter 5.11b ★ ☐
On the left side of the wall, climb the obvious corner/dihedral just left of a roof that leads to a slot. Past the slot climb easier rock/cracks to a tree.
Gear to 4 inches.

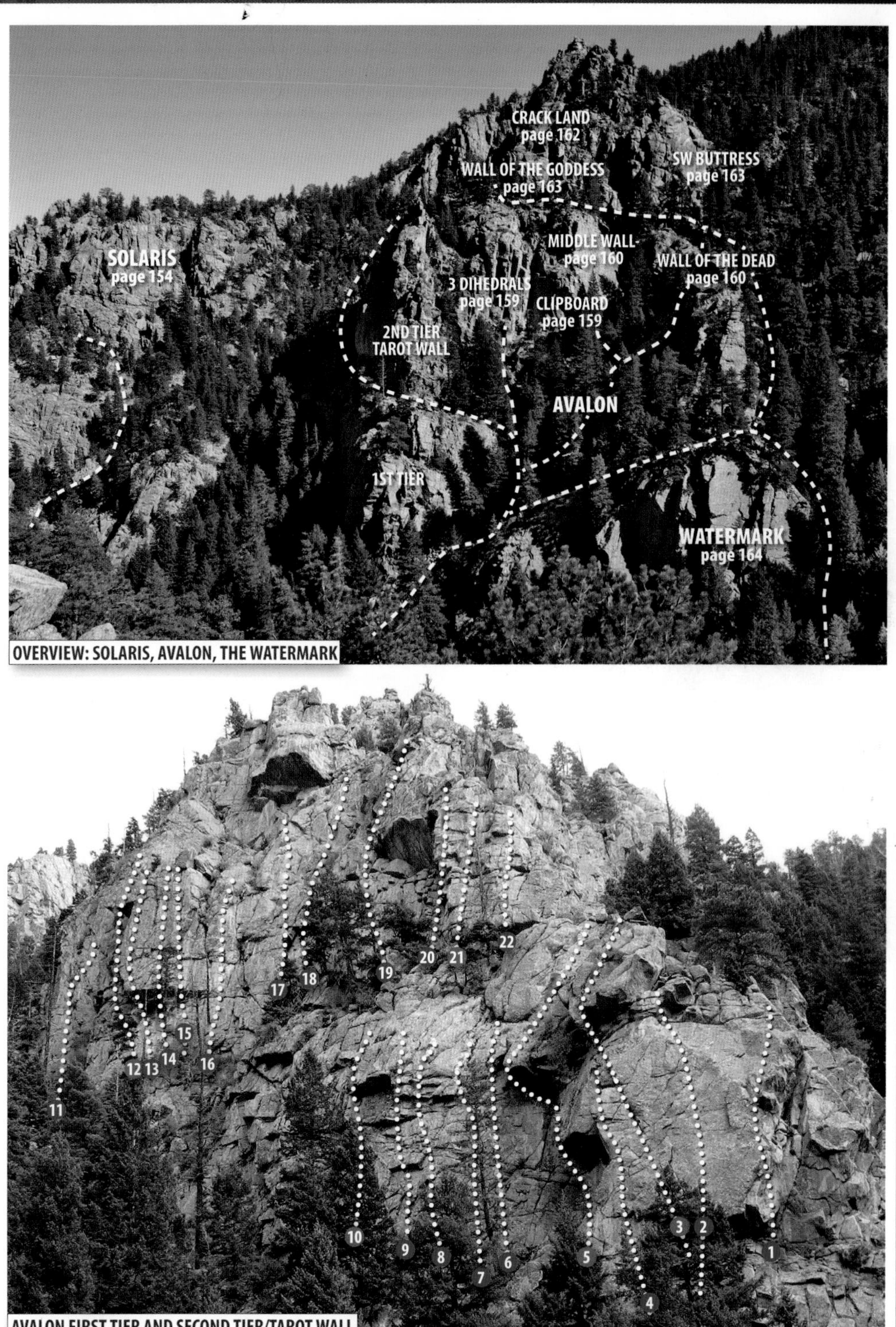

OVERVIEW: SOLARIS, AVALON, THE WATERMARK

AVALON FIRST TIER AND SECOND TIER/TAROT WALL

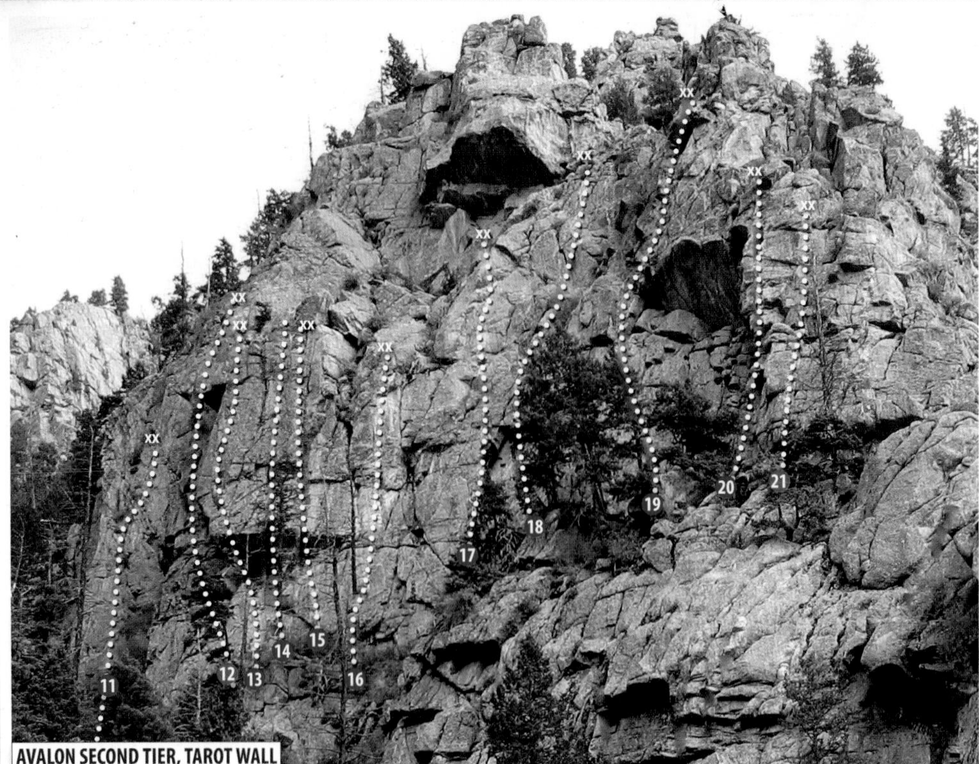

AVALON SECOND TIER, TAROT WALL

⑬ Earth Angel 5.12d ★★ ☐
Good climbing on great rock. Climb the white face to a roof, power over the roof and gain the crux arête. Continuous climbing leads to the anchor.
10 bolts.

⑭ Fapanese Direct 5.12c/d ★★★ ☐
Start right of *Earth Angel* up a short face to the business, surmount the roof then up steep and sustained climbing to the anchor.
8 bolts, long sling for below the roof.

⑮ The Constant Gardener (aka the Pursuit of Fappiness) 5.12b ★★ ☐
Start just left of *The Devil* and climb over a small roof to a steep wall, laybacking up thin seams/cracks to the anchors.
9 bolts.

⑯ The Devil 5.11d ★★★ ☐
A great route that climbs a clean panel of granite. Start at a right-facing flake and climb the steep face on the left. Reach a good horizontal crack and then fire the crux. Sustained climbing using crack and face holds leads to the anchor.
8 bolts.

⑰ Lust 5.10c ★★★★ ☐
This route offers wonderful, continuous climbing, one of the better routes in the canyon at the grade. Face moves lead to an alcove, traverse right to gain a thin crack and then go slightly left into a short, tricky corner that leads to the anchors.
12 bolts.

⑱ The Fool 5.10d ☐
The ledge becomes narrow. Start near a tree and climb up short left-facing corner bulge, outwit the crux and then up a flake system to a face and the anchor.
7 bolts.

⑲ The Tower 5.10a ★★★ ☐
A long route with excellent moves separated by good rests. You need a 60-meter rope to descend from the anchor. Start just left of low roof system. Climb up easier rock to a tricky move left, climb out the left side of a large roof, move right to a V-slot, and then blast to the anchor.
12 bolts, 60-meter rope.

⑳ Wheel of Fortune 5.10b ★★ ☐
Climb the left side of the low roof system to a shallow corner. Go up and right and then left to a short crux arete before the anchors.
7 bolts.

㉑ The Horse 5.10d ★ ☐
A crack splits the middle of the roof system. Climb the crack out a small roof past a bolt, gain a ledge and then climb the crack to the anchor.
1 bolt, gear to 2 inches.

㉒ The Hanged Man 5.11a ☐
Power out the right side of the low roof to easier rock. Climb over a small roof and then straight up to the anchor.

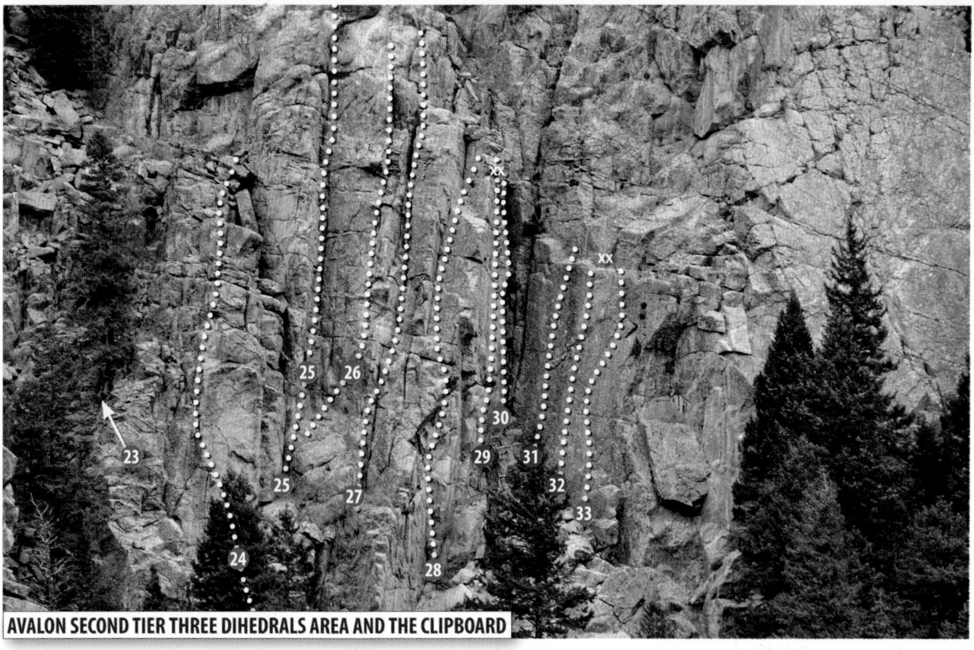

AVALON SECOND TIER THREE DIHEDRALS AREA AND THE CLIPBOARD

THREE DIHEDRALS AREA

A somewhat disjointed area up and right of the Tarot Wall. Follow the talus field uphill from the creek, staying right at a junction. You'll eventually reach a steep wall with a scooped-out face; this is the route *Strange Science* on the Middle Wall. Go left and climb up some big boulders to a flat area. The Clipboard Area is to the right, and the Dominator Wall is just left of that, at a right angle to the Clipboard Wall. Dominator Wall is rust colored, slightly overhanging and laced with cracks; it's hard to miss.

To access *Curvilinear, Dihedral One, Common Denominator,* and *Dihedral Two:* Start hiking up the hill toward the Dominator area. After 50 feet, a faint path heads off to the left. Take this to get to these routes. You'll see a low-angle slab; that's the start of *Dihedral One, Common Denominator,* and *Dihedral Two*. Go another 50' and uphill a bit to get to *Curvilinear*. See the overview topo for more orientation.

23 Curvilinear 5.10a ★ ☐
Climb the obvious curving crack to a tree.
Gear to 4.5 inches.

24 Pillar 5.7 ☐
Climb the obvious right-facing corner on the left side of the large pillar.
Gear to 2 inches.

25 Dihedral One 5.7 ★★ ☐
Climb a short ramp into the dihedral and then up the corner to the anchor.
Gear to 2 inches.

26 Common Denominator 5.9+ ★ ☐
Climb the ramp and head right toward an arete just left of *Dihedral Two*. Four bolts lead up the arete to the anchor.
5 bolts, a few cams to 2.5 inches.

27 Dihedral Two 5.8 ☐
Climb the dirty and bush-filled dihedral just right of *Common Denominator.* Not worth the effort.
Gear to 2 inches.

28 Dominatrix 5.8 ☐
Another somewhat dirty climb. Start in a left-facing corner 20 feet downhill from *Dominator*, by a large pine tree. Climb the corner past a bolt to a ledge. Step right and climb a V-dihedral with a good crack to the anchor.
1 bolt, gear to 2.5 inches.

29 Dominator 5.10c ★★ ☐
Maybe the best route in this sector. The obvious bolted crack. Climb it!
7 bolts.

30 Dom Perignon 5.9 ★ ☐
The hand crack just right of *Dominator*.
2 bolts, gear to 2.5 inches.

THE CLIPBOARD

Just right of the Dominator Wall is a flat, steep wall called The Clipboard.

31 Chairman of the Board 5.11d ★★★ ☐
Climb the left side of the beautiful flat wall on good edges and some pockets. Great route.
6 bolts.

32 The Clipboard 5.11b ★★★ ☐
Climb the center of the clean wall just left of a thin crack. Passing the small overlap is the crux.
5 bolts.

33 The Stigmata 5.10a ★ ☐
The right-angling crack on the right side of the wall. A short route with good rock and protection, but a scary flake up high.
1 bolt, gear to 4.5 inches.

AVALON MIDDLE WALL

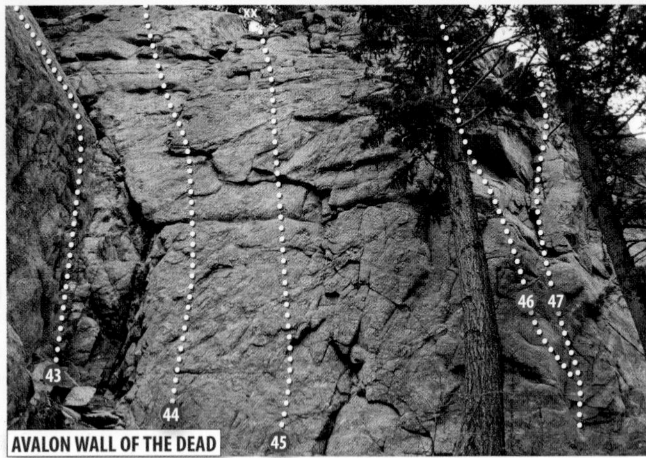

AVALON WALL OF THE DEAD

MIDDLE WALL

A clean piece of granite packed with short but quality routes. Climb up the talus field above the Tyrolean traverse. A dirt path starts at the top of the talus. Follow the path uphill until the trail splits. Continue up the hill on the right branch. You'll eventually reach a steep wall with a scooped-out face; this is the route *Strange Science*. *Free Fall* is the arete to the right. The slab routes *Disinclination* and *Incline Club* start just up the hill to the right, at a right-facing corner.

34 Supernatural 5.10d ★★ ☐
On the left side of the face. Climb nice rock to reach a short corner, step right and then up to the anchors.
7 bolts, a few small cams.

35 Strange Science 5.11d ★★★★ ☐
Classic — maybe in the Top 10 in the canyon. Really nice climbing up the scooped face leads to a testy move to gain the upper slab.
6 bolts.

36 Free Fall 5.12a ★★★ ☐
Climb a thin seam just right of *Strange Science* up to an overhanging arete, fire the crux and then easier rock to the anchor.
7 bolts.

37 Rip Cord 5.12a ★★★ ☐
Slightly harder than its neighbor to the left and little more painful. Climb steep rock out the right side of a roof using flared jams and face hold, get established over the lip and tiptoe up the slab to the anchor.
5 bolts.

38 Disinclination 5.7 ★★ ☐
Climb past the first four bolts on *Incline Club*, go left past the *Midway* crack and then angle up and left on the slab to an anchor below a short tower of rock.
8 bolts.

39 Midway 5.6 ☐
Start for *Incline Club*, climbing past the first three bolts, then follow the curving crack to the top.
3 bolts, gear to red Camalot.

40 Incline Club 5.7+ ★★ ☐
A great moderate slab climb. Right of *Rip Cord* climb the short corner to access the upper slab, following the line of bolts, angling right up the slab to the anchor.
8 bolts.

41 Flashpoint 5.11a ★ ☐
A second pitch to *Disinclination*. From the anchor of that route climb the short corner on the left side of the tower.
3 bolts.

42 Guardian Angel 5.12b ★ ☐
A lot of work for a short section hard of climbing. Climb both *Disinclination* and *Flashpoint*. From the anchor of *Flashpoint* reach right to an anchor and set a toprope.

43 Tomb of Sorrows 5.8+ ★★ ☐
A large chimney separates the Middle Wall from the Wall of the Dead. This nice route climbs the chimney then jumps left onto the clean slab, or take the direct start straight up the arete.
6 bolts.

WALL OF THE DEAD

Just right of the Middle Wall is Wall of the Dead.

44 Isle of the Dead 5.10b ★★ ☐
Climb just right of the huge chimney onto a clean face, reach a good flake and then conquer the crux to reach the anchor.
8 bolts.

45 Dead Again 5.10c ★★ ☐
Climb the center of the wall, making a dicey move past an overlap.
6 bolts.

46 The Dead Zone 5.10a ★ ☐
Climb into short right-facing corner, lean left and climb up past a bolt to a crack and a second bolt; easier climbing leads to the anchor.
2 bolts, gear to 2.5 inches.

47 Dead Can Dance 5.9+ ★★ ☐
Start as for the *Dead Zone*. Climb straight up the corner aiming for another short corner; climb a short arete, traverse left under a roof, and another corner to the anchor. Popular.
7 bolts.

Alec Sharp

I came to Boulder in 1977 after finishing college in the UK. I got my degree at the University of Wales, Bangor, and spent much of my time climbing on the cliffs in the Llanberis Pass, and on those greatest of cliffs, Clogwyn Du'r Arddu (Cloggy) and Gogarth, where I learned the excitement and exhilaration of making first ascents.

After moving to Boulder I spent time working through the Boulder classics with Chuck Fitch, climbing in the mornings then working the swing shift together at a local machine shop. I was drawn to the idea of doing new routes in the area and loved to hike around, looking at cliffs and possible lines on them, and there seemed so many untouched possibilities. My earliest explorations were in Boulder Canyon because everything was so accessible, and of these cliffs, Castle Rock was the most accessible and most magnificent. I'd already climbed *Country Club* and *Athlete's Feat* with Chuck, but how was it possible that the beautiful corners between them were unclimbed? And why was the steep crack to the left of *Athlete's Feat* untouched?

The mind plays tricks on us and once I'd decided to climb these lines they seemed so obvious that I was sure everyone else must have the same idea. I remember more than once looking up Boulder Canyon into black rain clouds, but driving up to Castle Rock anyway, hoping against hope that it was dry, worried that someone else would do these climbs before I could get there. Of course the black clouds really did mean it was raining, but eventually we had good weather and I climbed *Englishman's Home* with Bill Feiges. Back then I was still playing to a British audience and gave the climb its strange name because "An Englishman's Home is his Castle."

When I started doing new routes around Boulder there was initially some resentment that an unknown foreigner would come in, in the footsteps of giants such as Jim Erickson and Steve Wunsch, and start picking off some of these beautiful unclimbed lines. But I was driven to find and climb what I considered beautiful or interesting lines and I just kept climbing. My all time favorite in Boulder Canyon was *Never a Dull Moment* on Castle Rock, where you have to be a good all-round climber to deal with the thin face climbing on pitches 1 and 3, and the steep crack on pitch 2. Another favorite was *Grand Inquisitor*, not just for the wonderful initial moves, but also for the fun Chuck and I had carrying a ladder up to the cliff so we could place the first bolt — this was in the days when we still had to use a hammer and drill bit.

At this time I'd just started working as a software developer and I created a program to track and print out the latest new climbs in the Boulder area. In those days the Boulder Mountaineer was the main climbing store in town and I would give Dan Hare the most recent printout so climbers visiting the store could be up-to-date on the latest new route activity. As people found out what new lines were being climbed and realized that new route activity had not ended with Jim Erickson, more and more climbers started doing their own first ascents, stars such as Jeff Achey, Skip Guerin, Bob Horan, Randy Leavitt, and later, of course, Christian Griffith.

My explorations took me to new routes in Eldorado Canyon and Rocky Mountain National Park, but I've always loved the granite in Boulder Canyon, and to this day *Never a Dull Moment* remains one of my favorite climbs in the Boulder area.

UPPER TIER

To reach the Upper Tier, hike up the right side of Wall of the Dead and then angle back left — being careful not to kick off any rocks. Remote and mostly trad, the Upper Tier is a great place to get away from the crowds on busy summer days.

CRACK LAND

The upper left side of the Upper Tier hosts a number of good one-pitch crack climbs. See overview page 157.

48 **Crack Love** 5.9 ★★ ☐
The obvious V-slot on the upper left side of the wall that goes over a roof and then to the anchors.
Gear to 4 inches.

49 **Crack Love III** 5.10b ★★ ☐
Start as for *Crack Love* and tackle the roof on the right, then up the crack to the anchor.
Gear to 4 inches.

50 **Crack Love II** 5.9- ★★ ☐
Start right of *Crack Love,* following the obvious crack to the anchor.
Gear to 4 inches.

51 **The Art Of War** 5.10b ★★★ ☐
The obvious bolted arete on the upper tier of Crack Land. Great moves in a nice position.
9 bolts.

52 **The Enemy Within** 5.10a ★★ ☐
The squeeze chimney right of the *Art of War.*
2 bolts, gear to 2.5 inches.

53 **Thus Us** 5.9- ★★ ☐
Start just right of *The Enemy Within* and climb a right-facing corner/wide crack to a hand crack. Follow the good hand crack to a tree. A long pitch with great protection. You can lower from the anchors of *The Enemy Within.*
Gear to 4 inches.

54 **War Horse** 5.10c ★★ ☐
Climb the wide start of *Thus Us* and then angle right, clipping a couple of bolts to reach a right-facing corner; make a hard move past the third bolt then up a thin corner to the anchor.
3 bolts, gear to 2 inches.

The next 3 route are approached by climbing the first pitch of Ancient Light.

55 **Ancient Fright** 5.10b ★★ ☐
Nice face climbing up a clean, featured wall.
5 bolts.

56 **Resurrection** 5.9 ★ ☐
A pitch that goes to the high point of Avalon — worth the effort just to get the views from the summit. Climb *Ancient Fright* to the anchor, then climb up and left to another anchor and the start of the pitch.
2 bolts and gear to 3 inches.

57 **Ancient Sight** 5.8 PG-13 ☐
Climb *Ancient Fright* and then go up and slightly right to the summit. Somewhat dirty.
Gear to 3 inches.

58 **Ancient Light** 5.10c ★ ☐
The obvious bolted arete on the upper tier of Crack Land. Great moves in a nice position.
Pitch 1: 5.10c. Climb up a face, traverse left to an arete and continue to a big grassy ledge with a 2-bolt ring anchor on the wall above the ledge.
9 bolts.
Pitch 2: 5.10c. Work up and right past 2 bolts and pull right around the Penis Envy Pillar. Climb the right side of the pillar to a roof. Lieback through the roof, then climb straight up to a 2-bolt ring anchor on a ledge.
5 bolts gear to 3 inches.

59 **Blade** 5.10c ★★ ☐
Pitch 1: 5.10a. Climb *Ancient Light* to a big grassy ledge with a 2-bolt ring anchor on the wall above the ledge.
9 bolts.
Pitch 2: 5.10c. Start up *Ancient Light's* second pitch to the Penis Envy Pillar, go right at the base of the pillar, pull through a small roof and follow the right-angling crack to the belay for *Dragon Slayer.*
5 bolts, gear to 3 inches.

60 **Dragon Slayer** 5.10a ★★ ☐
Climb #62 or #63 to reach a ledge at the Wall of the Dragon. Climb the clean face past several bolts to an anchor. A great route in a wonderful position.
6 bolts.

61 **Dragon Fly** 5.9 ★ ☐
Climb right of *Dragon Slayer* on good holds to the first bolt; continue staying close to the bolts to the anchor.
5 bolts.

The next three climbs have a common start, about 100 feet right of Ancient Light *and just left of* Mystery Ship.

62 **Ghost Ship** 5.10a ★★ ☐
Climb easy rock and then veer left to short right-facing corner leading to an overhang. Climb up and over the overhang to a tree and lower/rap.
Gear to 3 inches.

63 **Ship of Fools** 5.10a ★★ ☐
Climb a right-facing corner to a small roof, pull right and jam a perfect hand crack to where it narrows. Continue up difficult terrain to a horizontal break. Step right and climb a flared crack to the alcove at the top of *Mystery Tour*. Climb a short crack on the left wall and gain a good ledge and the belay tree for *Dragon Slayer.*
Gear to 4 inches.

64 **Mystery Tour** 5.9 ★★ ☐
The obvious wide crack that forms a corner. Rap from a tree.
Gear to 4 inches. Double up on 2-4 inch cams.

65 **Mystery Ship** 5.10b ★ ☐
Start 10 feet right of *Mystery Tour* at a low roof. Climb over the roof then up the face to the anchors.
6 bolts.

WEST GULLY

The West Gully lies just beyond the Wall of the Goddess up a corridor of rock. It is a steep gully with no established trail. Be careful scrambling up to the wall.

66 **Merlin's Enigma** 5.11d ★ ☐
Short and to the point. Right off the trail on the left side of the wall. Climb the dihedral to an overhang, go right then back left and up to the anchor.
4 bolts.

67 Charon's Boat 5.9+ ★ ☐

Climb the face just right of the overhang, traverse left after the second bolt and climb to the anchor on *Merlin's Enigma*.

4 bolts, optional small cam.

68 Knight of Swords 5.10d ★★ ☐

Start right of a tree. Climb a steep face to the anchor. 5.11 if you start low and left.

5 bolts.

69 Dragon Direct 5.9 ★ ☐

Uphill from *Knight of Swords* is a face with two bolts; climb past the bolts then up easier rock to the top.

2 bolts, gear to 2 inches.

70 Sorcerer's Apprentice 5.7 ★ ☐

Start just left of a chockstone in the gully. Climb the short face to an anchor.

3 bolts.

AVALON UPPER TIER, CRACK LAND

WALL OF THE GODDESS

A short wall with several cracks. See overview page 157.

71 Warlock 5.10b/c R ☐

On the left side of the wall a few feet right of a shallow gully, climb a short wall to a break and crack that angles right; follow the crack.

Gear to 2 inches.

72 Yoni 5.7 ★ ☐

The left of three cracks. Climb the crack to the anchor.

Gear to 2.5 inches.

73 Amrita 5.10b ★ ☐

Climb the middle, right-angling crack to the anchor.

Gear to 4.5 inches.

74 Isis 5.9 ★ ☐

The obvious finger to hand/fist crack on the right side of the wall.

Gear to 3 inches.

SOUTHWEST BUTTRESS

The clean, west-facing buttress high above the creek and up and right of the Wall of the Goddess.

75 The Solution 5.9+ ★★ ☐

On the left side of the wall, climb a short crack that leads to a clean slab, climbing past four bolts to the anchor.

4 bolts, gear to 2 inches.

76 The Resistance 5.11a/b ★★ ☐

Start as for *The Solution* and then angle right up the slab to the anchors of *Black Tiger*.

4 bolts, gear to 2 inches.

77 Black Tiger 5.11c/d PG13 ★ ☐

In its current state you are better off toproping this route. Climb a short crack over a bulge to a slab, climb past bolts to a thin seam/finger crack and the anchor.

3 bolts, gear to 4.5 inches.

78 Jaguar 5.11b/c ★★ ☐

Start low, on the far right side of the rock. Mantel past two bolts and gain a ledge, clip a bolt and angle up and right to the arete; follow the arete to the anchor.

7 bolts, gear to 2 inches.

AVALON SOUTHWEST BUTTRESS

THE WATERMARK 8.3 miles

Approach time: 15 minutes.
Exposure: North.

9 routes

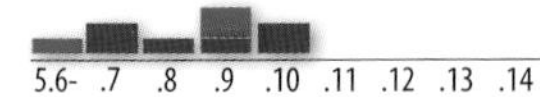

A nice little crag that sits right above the creek between Avalon and Vampire Rock. This is a great place to escape the heat and also for those who are just getting into leading sport routes.

Access: Drive 8.4 miles up the canyon to a large pullout on the left. Head down stream for a tenth of a mile and cross the creek and hike up the short hill to the crag. During high water, use the approach for Avalon (page 156) and then hike upstream via a trail.

Routes are listed from left to right.

1 Dark Tower 5.6 ☐

On the far left side of the cliff just left of a vegetated corner, climb the slab to reach a crack. Follow the crack to the top. Walk off to the east.

Gear to 2.5 inches.

2 Twin Cracks Left 5.9 ★ ☐

Climb *Twin Peaks* to the undercling and then veer up and left following the crack to the top.

Gear to 3.5 inches.

3 Twin Peaks 5.10a/b ★★ ☐

Start up the easy slab using a flake to gain the undercling, then go straight up the face on small holds to the anchor.

7 bolts.

4 Twin Cracks Right 5.9- ☐

Climb *Twin Peaks* to the undercling, then veer right up the nice finger crack to the anchors for *Glennevere*.

3 bolts, gear to 2 inches.

5 Glennevere 5.8 ★★ ☐

Start just right of *Twin Peaks*. Climbing up to a slot below a small roof, crank over the roof and then up the face to the anchors.

6 bolts.

6 The Memory of Trees 5.9 ★★★ ☐

One of the nicer routes on the wall. Climb up a short face to a blunt arete, follow the arete to below a roof. Climb the roof then up the nice slab to the anchors.

9 bolts.

7 Road to Isengard 5.7+ ★★ ☐

Start right of *The Memory of Trees*. Climb up a short face heading up and left to the slab. Follow the slab and then move up and left to the anchors.

7 bolts.

8 Minas Tirith 5.10a ★ ☐

Start as for *Road to Isengard* and then head up and right to a tricky move to reach the anchor.

6 bolts.

9 Lothlorien 5.7 ★★ ☐

Climb the nice slab on the right side of the wall.

5 bolts.

THE ZOO 8.6 miles

Approach time: 20 minutes.
Exposure: South.

4 routes

5.6- .7 .8 .9 .10 .11 .12 .13 .14

A short crag nestled in the woods with four routes in the 5.11 to 5.12 range. It lies 100 yards east of Upper Animal World and is worth a visit if you are in the area.

Access: Drive up canyon to a parking area at 8.6 miles on the left. Cross the road and then follow the trail uphill, veering right to Animal World. Skirt the cliff to the right and go to the upper east face of Animal World and then right on a faint trail to the wall.

❶ Never Was Been 5.11b ★ ☐
The route is located on the left side of the rock and is the first climb that one comes to when approaching from the Far East Buttress. Follow a line of cracks to a ledge below a large block that forms a headwall. Ascend a thin crack on the right side of the block.
5 bolts, a few small to medium cams.

❷ Living with the Apes 5.12a ★★ ☐
Start off a block in the center of the wall. Climb up to a small overhang, fire up past bolts to the anchor.
9 bolts, 0.75 micro-cam to start..

❸ Primate Studies 5.11c ★★ ☐
Climb the flaring crack just right of *Living with the Apes* to a slab and easier rock to the anchor.
9 bolts.

❹ The Monkey Wrench 5.12b/c ☐
The crux dyno comes low and then easier climbing to a hard move at the thin seam just below the anchor.
9 bolts.

THE BOULDERADO 8.6 miles

Approach time: 1 - 4 minutes.
Exposure: South and west.

9 routes

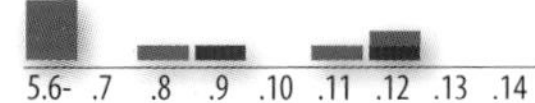

Sitting just above the road, this now popular rock is a great place for new leaders, groups, and guiding. Several of the routes have convenient anchors and during some summer weekends have top ropes hanging on them for most of the day. Routes on the right side of the wall are much higher in the difficulty scale with *Jazz On The Mezzanine* being the best of the lot.

Access: Drive 8.6 miles up the canyon and park in a large pullout on the left. Cross the road and reach the obvious wall.

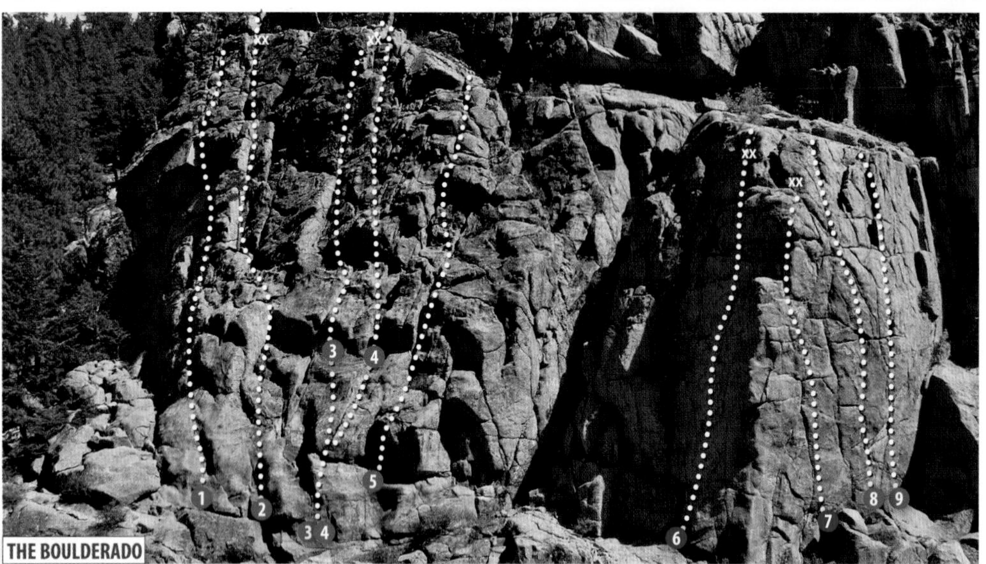

❶ Jam It 5.8 ★★ ☐
On the far left side of the crag. Climb the short face to a crack going out the roof.
SR.

❷ Ho Hum 5.4 ★ ☐
Climb the face up to a pine tree, veer left up the corner, then back right up the crack to the top.
SR.

❸ Idle Hands 5.6 ★★ ☐
Maybe the best pitch on this side of the wall. Start about 10 feet right of *Ho Hum*, climb the steep face up to a good crack and over a small bugle. Continue up to the steep headwall, step right, then up.
SR.

❹ Mons 5.5 ★ ☐
The next crack right of *Idle Hands*...pleasant face and crack climbing.
SR.

❺ Fistula 5.4 ☐
Climb the obvious wide crack on the right side of the wall.
Gear to 4 inches.

❻ Qs 5.9+ ☐
Climb the bolted southwest face on the block right of the wall. Nice moves on good rock, depending what side of the bolts you are climbing on the route can feel hard or easy for the grade.
6 bolts.

❼ Jazz On The Mezzanine 5.12b ★★★ ☐
A classic, spicy pitch. Power up the face just right of the arete, gain the arête, and then up a short crack to the anchor.
4 bolts...stick clip the first one.

❽ Hell In A Bucket 5.12d ☐
The center crack on the east face. Hard to climb and harder to protect. Top rope it.
Gear to 4.5 inches.

❾ Suite 11 5.11d ★ ☐
The crack right of *Hell in a Bucket*. Nice crack climbing leads to short crux face.
2 bolts, gear to 2 inches.

LA SPORTIVA®
innovation with passion
www.lasportiva.com
photo: Andy Mann

ANIMAL WORLD 8.6 miles

Approach time: 10 - 20 minutes.
Exposure: East, south and west.

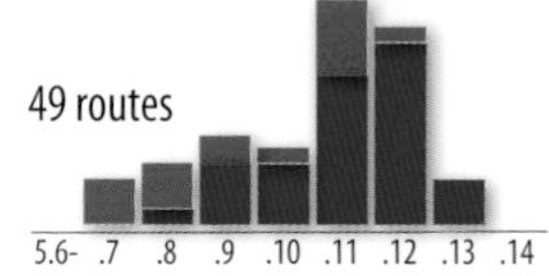

Largely ignored for years, Animal World has become one of the most popular crags in the canyon and has produced several classic routes. It has both excellent sport and trad routes, and with varying exposure you can climb in or out of the sun year round. For the sake of clarity the cliff is broken into three sectors — Lower, Middle and Upper.

Access: Park in a pullout on the left side of the road at 8.6 miles. Cross the road and follow a trail uphill that starts just left of the Boulderado. Veer right above the Boulderado where the trail splits and follow it to the west face of Lower Animal World.

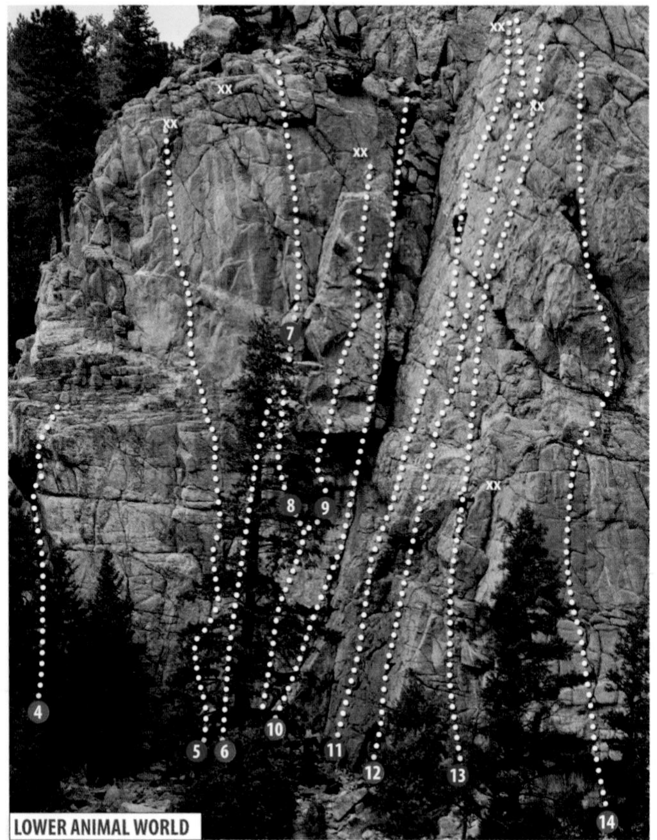

LOWER ANIMAL WORLD

LOWER ANIMAL WORLD

❶ Crack Corner 5.7 ☐
Where the trail meets the Lower Wall. Climb the obvious corner on the left. Walk off to the west.
Gear to 3.5 inches.

❷ Animal Riots Activist 5.12a ★★ ☐
Right of the corner is a steep wall with two sport routes, this is the left one. Climb a thin face and veer right on a rail, make a hard move up to get established on the upper wall. Prance to the anchors.
7 bolts.

❸ Piles of Trials 5.12b ★★★ ☐
Start just right of *Animal Riots Activist*, climb the steep face, angle to the right, reach a bulge and fire up to a good hold, then past a few bolts to the anchors. A really good route put up by long time climbing buddies Greg Hand and Bob D.
6 bolts.

❹ Automatic Choke 5.11c R ☐
The west face meets the south face at a thin seam/crack. Somewhat hard to protect and a little runout, this route is not popular.
Gear to 4.5 inches.

❺ Cannabis Sportiva 5.10d ★★ ☐
Start just left of the obvious corner on the south face. Climb with gear up the nice face to the first bolt, continue up as the difficulty increases with every clip to the crux below the anchor.
7 bolts, gear to 2 inches.

❻ Old Dihedral 5.8 ☐
Climb the obvious corner to a bolted anchor. A nice route with excellent protection.
Gear to 4 inches.

❼ Feeding The Beast 5.12a/b ★★ ☐
AKA Beast Food Right/Left. Climb *Joint Venture* to the bolt past the first anchor, step left on good holds and power up the left facing corner/crack with a hard move to gain a pod a hard one to finish when you're pumped. Staying right of the bolts in the upper corner lowers the grade a notch.
12 bolts.

❽ Joint Venture 5.11a ★★ ☐
Popular. Start below the obvious bolted face, tricky moves to gain the arete and the first anchor. Continue up, veering a little right, to the upper anchor.
9 bolts.

❾ Blockhead 5.12b ★★ ☐
Climb the first two bolts of *Joint Venture* then head up a little right into the business. Hard moves through the roof lead to nice climbing above.
12 bolts.

❿ Gull Whackers 5.7 ☐
The obvious dirty right-facing corner.
Gear to 3.5 inches.

⓫ Animation 5.8+ ★★★★ ☐
aka Jaycene's Dance
Classic climbing and good holds the whole way. One of the better routes in the canyon for the grade.
10 bolts, 60m rope critical.

LOWER ANIMAL WORLD RIGHT SIDE

⓬ Familiar Stranger 5.8+ ☐
Climb the face just right of *Animation* staying just left of the bolts of *Unfamiliar Strangers*.
Gear to 2 inches.

⓭ Unfamiliar Strangers 5.9+ ★ ☐
Begin off a boulder where the wall turns right. Cool starting moves lead to jug hauling to the anchors.
Variation 5.10: Climb past the anchor to a short corner to top.
11 bolts.

⓮ Cold Snap 5.11b R ☐
The trail goes right under an overhang to a sunny south facing wall. *Cold Snap* climbs the left side of the wall. Small gear of dubious quality and some loose rock keeps the crowds off this one.
SR, RP's.

⓯ Free Willie 5.11a ★★★ ☐
Great route with an interesting move at the finish...hence the name.
7 bolts.

⓰ Days of Future Passed 5.12a ★★★ ☐
Popular, with a quick and painless crux. Climb the seam right of *Free Willie*, step right at the top of the seam and then crank on good holds to the anchor.
8 bolts.

⓱ Threshold Of A Dream 5.11d/12a ★★★ ☐
Climb the overhang just right of *Days*, gain a face/slab and head right to the arete. Cool moves up the arete lead to a move right out the bulge and then up to the anchor. (Caution: the flake left of the upper bulge has been bolted to the wall. ***Do Not Climb On It.***)
9 bolts.

⓲ Nice To Be Here 5.11a ★ ☐
Just right of wide corner is a face with bolt, climb to the bolt and then angle right to a steep wall with a seam, climb the seam then cruise on good holds to the anchor.

⓳ Reversal Roof 5.12d ☐
The trail goes under a long roof system, this route climbs the left side of the roof. Knee bars and slopers . . . what a treat.
4 bolts.

⓴ Lovely to See You 5.12b ★★ ☐
Four routes pierce the roof, this route fires up near the center on slopers and then up a crack to a cool face and the anchors.
8 bolts, 1.5 inch cam.

㉑ Tuesday Afternoon 5.11b/c ★ ☐
The third route going through the roof. More of a variation of *Melancholy Man* to the right.
9 bolts.

㉒ Melancholy Man 5.11a/b ★★ ☐
Climb the right side of the roof and then fire up a nice face trending left near the top.
10 bolts.

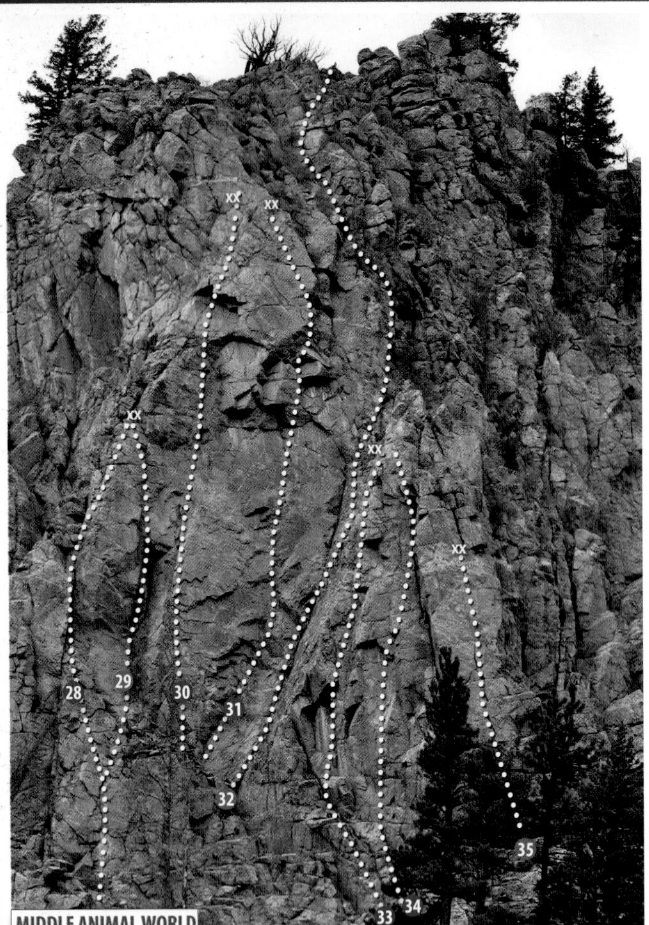

㉓ Is It Ready Yet...Moe 5.9+ ★ ☐☐
See description opposite.

㉔ We Don't Do Crack 5.9 ☐☐
Climb the corner into a slot, veer right and then to anchors of *Lazy Day* on the right.
Gear to 2.5 inches.

㉕ Lazy Day 5.9+ ★ ☐☐
The steep face right of the corner. Loose at the bottom but yields nice moves above. Good warm-up.
6 bolts.

㉖ Laurel & Hardy Meet Abbott & Costello 5.9 ★ ☐☐
Climb up a short bit to the first bolt, veer left then back right up a nice face to the anchors.
5 bolts.

㉗ Geritol Generation 5.9 ☐☐
Climb the short corner up to a face staying right of *Laurel & Hardy*.
Gear to 4.5 inches.

MIDDLE ANIMAL WORLD

Right of *Geritol Generation* is an easy 4th Class ramp system leading up and left to a large ledge and Middle Animal World.

㉘ Ride My See-Saw 5.10a ☐☐
On the far left side of the ledge is a short face with bolts just right of dead juniper tree. Climb the face and then veer left up a blunt arete, climb the arete to the anchor.

㉙ Wine & Roses 5.11a ★★ ☐☐
Climb the face as for *Ride My See-Saw* and then up the obvious crack making a hard move where it veers left. Save some juice for the top.
3 bolts, gear to 2 inches.

㉚ Talking Out of Turn 5.10a/b ★★★ ☐☐
Climb a short blocky section to a boulder just right of the *Wine & Roses* crack, clip the first bolt, then fire up the arete to a hard move gaining the upper headwall.
12 bolts.
Descent: A 60m rope is crucial – and it will only get you back to below the first bolt.

㉛ Isn't Life Strange 5.11b/c ★★★ ☐☐
Start right of *Talking Out Of Turn*, up a shallow corner. Technical moves on the face get you to below a triple-tiered roof. Power through the roof then up a face to the anchors.
14 bolts.
Descent: A 70m-rope required to lower.

㉜ POS 5.7 ☐☐
The dirty corner right of *Isn't Life Strange*. Climb the corner up to ledge and belay. From the ledge go up and left to the top.
Gear to 2.5 inches.

㉝ Strange Times 5.10d ★ ☐☐
Climb up a short section to a flake, layback the flake and step into a corner and climb to an anchor.
6 bolts and a 0.75 micro-cam.

㉞ The Balance 5.11a/b ★ ☐☐
Climb up a blocky section reaching the first bolt, make a hard move past the second bolt then climb a corner to the anchor.
7 bolts and a 2 inch cam.

㉟ Hope and Pray 5.8 ★ ☐☐
Start 20 ft right of *The Balance*. Climb up some broken ledges behind a small tree to the start of the crack. Fire up the center of the pinnacle.
3 bolts, gear to 4.5 inches.

23 Is It Ready Yet...Moe 5.9+ ★

Climb the blunt arete just left of corner. Move a little left at the fourth bolt, climb up a clean face to a corner. Move left from the corner onto a steep face, make a few moves up and clip the anchors.

8 bolts.

Climber Roxanne Raymundo. Photo Bob D'Antonio.

UPPER ANIMAL WORLD

Accessed via the trail from Lower Animal World. Walk east and then north to Upper Animal World.

36 Krakatoa 5.10c ☐
The trail soon comes to a beautiful south-facing wall, this route climbs the crack on the left side of the wall.
Pitch 1: 5.10c. Fire up the crack. Turn a roof on the right and then to a belay right of the crack. Loose.
Pitch 2: 5.9. Trend left back to the crack and follow it to the top. Walk off to the west.
Gear to 4 inches.

37 Fifth World 5.12b/c ★★ ☐
The Fifth World starts just left of *Hands of Destiny* on the east side of Animal World Rock. Climb up some short corners using gear to reach the first bolt. Make a move right and then up passing the first and second bolt to a series of technical moves up small, thin seams. Clip the third bolt and reach a good hold. Angle left and up into a V-slot. Climb out of the slot and follow a tenuous crack up a vertical wall to the anchors.
11 bolts, medium gear to reach the first bolt.

38 Hands of Destiny 5.12d ★★★★ ☐
Originally climbed as a trad route, Bob Horan returned and placed the bolts on this amazingly beautiful route.
Pitch 1: 5.12d. Climb blocky rock to gain the face, fire up the face with increasing difficulty reaching the crux moves, hang on for the hard slab moves to reach the anchors.
12 bolts.
Pitch 2: 5.10. Climb the short vertical face to anchor.
4 bolts.
Descent: Rap the route.

39 Animal Instinct 5.12c ★★★★ ☐
The striking arete just right of *Hands of Destiny*. Climb easy rock to the first bolt or clip the first two bolts of *Sun Dog*. A hard moves comes quickly before you reach a ledge and semi-rest, power up the arete trending right, the climbing eases past the last bolt. Veer right to the *Sun Dog* anchor.
8 bolts.

40 Sun Dog 5.12a ★★ ☐
Start 20 feet right of the arete up blocky rock trending up and left to a slab, reach the slab and do a hard move and then another at bolt six, tenuous moves left get you to the anchor.
9 bolts.

41 Evolution Revolution 5.12b ★★ ☐
The big roof just right of *Sun Dog*. Fire the lower slab to a good rest before tackling the roof. Several sequential moves get you to the lip and jugs. Climb easier rock to the anchor.
9 bolts.

42 Global Gorilla 5.12c ★★★★ ☐
Pitch one is extremely popular 11b in its own right. The route can be done in one very long classic pitch.
Pitch 1: 5.11b. Climb a left-facing dihedral and step right to the arete, make a hard move right then climb to another cruxy move, up the arete to good holds and the anchor. This pitch is extremely popular and often done by itself.
11 bolts.
Pitch 2: 5.12b. Climb a steep face with hard moves getting past the third bolt.
5 bolts.
Pitch 3: 5.12c. Trend right toward the arete and power past the second bolt (crux) and then up the arete to a testy move before the anchor.
6 bolts.
Descent: Rap the route.

43 Animal Magnetism 5.11c ★★★★ ☐
Classic. Start right of *Global Gorilla* on a ledge that gains a clean face. Climb the face past the first crux to a ledge and then up lower angle rock to a bugle and the upper crux...race your arms to the anchor.
13 bolts.

44 Closer To God 5.13c ★★ ☐
Chipped. Climb *Animal Magnetism* to bolt eight, veer right to a large roof, traverse left under the roof and then up to the anchor.
16 bolts.

45 Cujo Tranquilizer 5.12b ★★★ ☐
Start right of *Animal Magnetism* up a steep face that leads to a ledge (crux), fire up and right along the long slab moving right to the arete then up to the anchor.
16 bolts.
Variation: Cujo Magnetism 5.12b ☐
Climb to the fourth bolt and the ledge, veer left and past three bolts meeting *Animal Magnetism* at its eight bolt, continue up to the anchor.
13 bolts.

46 Wandervogel 5.11b R ★★ ☐
Pitch 1: 5.11b. Start 75 right of *Global Gorilla* climbing left to gain a left-facing dihedral. Fire up the dihedral to a belay at 85 feet below a roof.
SR.
Pitch 2: 5.11a. Turn the roof on the left, follow the dihedral to a crack on the right, finish with the crack.
SR.

47 Pit Bull Browser 5.13a ★★ ☐
Pitch 1: 5.11b. Start right of *Wandervogel* at a large pine tree. A short crux down low leads to pleasant climbing up past a shallow groove to the anchor.
16 bolts.
Pitch 2: 5.13a. Climb the steep face with a hard move at the first bolt, make a big move past the third bolt and hang on to the anchor.
4 bolts.

48 New Beginnings 5.11c ★ ☐
Start right of *Wandervogel* near the right edge of the wall. Climb up the face past several bolts to a thin layback, crank a mantel to a good edge, follow bolts to the anchor.
8 bolts.

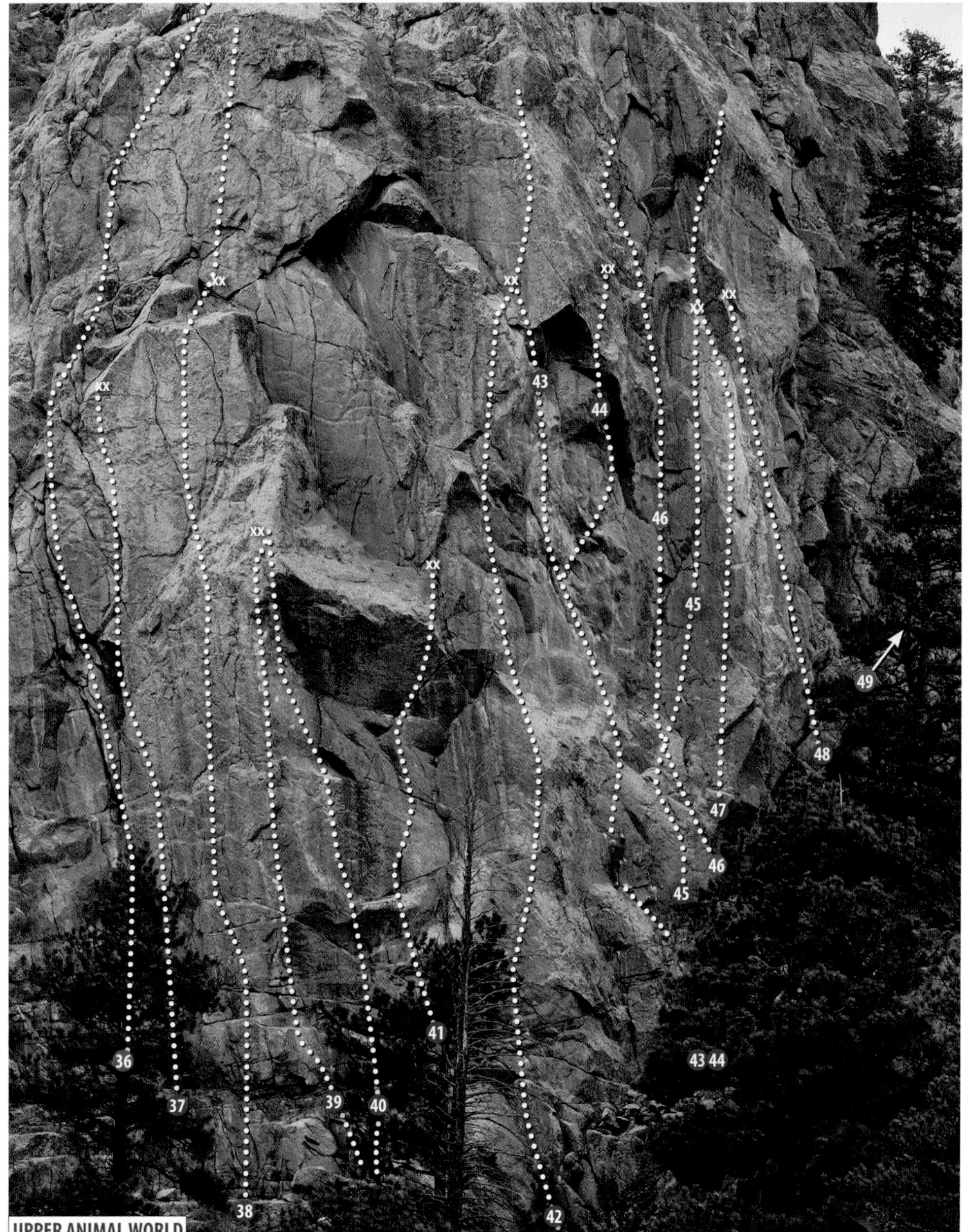

49 Rush Of Blood To The Head 5.11d ★☐
This route begins on the far east side of Animal World. The first pitch is a sport route, the second requires some gear. Follow the trail around the rock to the far east side of the cliff. Locate two bolts on a short steep face.

Pitch 1: 5.11c. Climb past the bolts with hard, tricky moves on devious holds.
4 bolts.

Pitch 2: 5.11b/c. Climb a shallow corner past bolts, trending to the left at the top of the corner. Place some gear and gain a ledge below a blank-looking, blunt arete. Crank up the arete on small, insecure holds (crux) climbing to the anchor.
6 bolts, plus some small-to-medium gear.

THE MINE HOLE 8.6 miles

Approach time: 10 - 15 minutes.
Exposure: South and west.

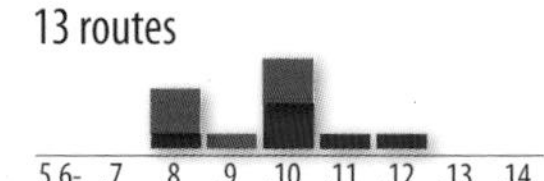

This 60-foot wall lies above the Animal World Crag and has several sport and mixed routes in a pleasant setting close to an old mine hole.

Access: Travel 8.6 miles up the canyon to a pullout/parking area on the left side of the road for Animal World. Cross the road and follow the trail skirting the left side of the Boulderado uphill till a fork in the trail. Animal World takes the right fork; continue straight uphill on the trail to the Mine Hole Crag on the right.

1 Firing Squad 5.8 ★ ☐
Left of the mine hole climb a dirty face leading up to a crack through a roof. Be careful of loose rock down low.
Gear to 2.5 inches.

2 The Hot Donut 5.8 ☐
Start above the mine hole in a shallow corridor, climbing somewhat suspect rock to a crack, and then right to the anchor for *Sofa Kingdom*.
Gear to 3.5 inches.

3 Couch Potato 5.10a ★ ☐
Begin as for *Sofa Kingdom* and find the first bolt near the pine tree on the left. After the 2nd bolt, place red and green Aliens to protect a hard move past the flake. Easy climbing leads to two more bolts on the arete and then right to the *Sofa Kingdom* anchors.
4 bolts, cams to 2 inches.

4 Sofa Kingdom 5.10a ★★ ☐
Scramble to the ledge and start just right of a pine tree. Climb the nice face/slab past seven bolts to the anchor.
7 bolts.

5 Ruff Roof 5.12a ★ ☐
Climb a short face up through a roof using a thin seam and flakes to the upper easier face and the anchor.
10 bolts.

6 Just Another Cow's Climb 5.10a/b ★ ☐
Climb up to the ledge right of the roof clipping a bolt. Follow the right-angling flake to another bolt and then up a right-leaning crack to the anchor for *Just Moo It*.
4 bolt, gear to 2 inches.

7 Just Moo It 5.10c/d ★ ☐
Climb a ramp past two bolts to a ledge, follow a right-facing corner to another corner, then make hard moves over the roof to the anchor.
4 bolts, gear to 2 inches.

8 Get Your Dieck Off My Barnyard Animals 5.9 ★ ☐
Climb a short corner/face over a small roof and then up the nice rock to the anchor.
4 bolts, one 2 inch piece.

9 Little Stevie's Favorite Heifer 5.10d ★★ ☐
Follow the line of bolts up the obvious dyke using laybacks and flakes to a stiff move getting to the anchor. This is one of the better routes on the wall.
6 bolts.

10 Bull Fight 5.12a ★ ☐
Start right of the dyke and crank through a bulge to easier climbing to the anchor on the left.
6 bolts.

11 Don't Pull on the Udder 5.8+ ★ ☐
Start right of *Bull Fight*, climbing up and left into a slot/crack to the anchor.
3 bolts, couple of small cams.

12 Salisbury Steak Crack 5.8 ★★ ☐
Climb the right-leaning hand crack up to a ledge, past a tree, and then easier climbing leads to the anchor.
Gear to 2 inches.

13 Cow Patty Crack 5.9 ★★ ☐
Climb a short corner on the far right side of the wall. Go left at a small roof and then up a nice face to the anchor.
Gear to 3 inches.

MINE HOLE CRAG LEFT

MINE HOLE CRAG CENTER

MINE HOLE CRAG RIGHT

VAMPIRE ROCK 8.6 miles

Approach time: 10 - 20 minutes.
Exposure: North and northwest.

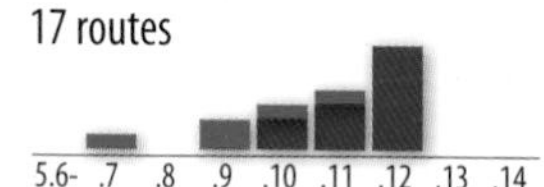

This large, solemn-looking north-facing rock has several good routes both trad and sport. It is a great place to beat the heat in the summer months. It's unclimbable in the winter except on really warm days.

Access: Park in a pullout on the left side of the road at 8.6 miles. Walk down stream on the inside of the guard and cross the creek at the rock. A Tyrolean traverse is usually set up year-round. Take a nice path up the hill and then go left to the rock.

❶ Climb Eye Knight 5.12c ★★ ☐
On the far left side of the cliff on the east face is a large right-facing corner. The route starts here.
Pitch 1: 5.10c/d. Climb the face and corners to an overhang. Make nice moves past the overhang and climb the tricky face above. Work right to a short finger crack and continue up to the anchor.
Pitch 2: 5.12c. Continue up the crack to face, crank the hard moves and reach a belay.
Pitch 3: 5.11d. Climb the gold headwall up to a small roof and then up a beautiful face to anchors. Rap the route.
15 quickdraws and few small cams.

❷ The Bureau 5.12b/c ★★ ☐
Pitch 1: 5.11d. Start on the left side of the white wall, follow bolts up a steep wall just right of a roof to the anchors.
Pitch 2: 5.12b/c. Climb out a the reachy roof then up to a second roof with a fixed wire and a block chained to the wall (hard/weird), and then to the belay.
Pitch 3: 5.11d. Climb the gold headwall up to a small roof and then up a beautiful face to anchors.
12 quickdraws.
Descent: Rap the route.

❸ Wanker 5.12a/b ★★ ☐
Start just right of *The Bureau* and head up a white face and meet with the first anchor of that route.
5 bolts.

❹ Monkey's Uncle/Sister 5.10c/d ★★ ☐
These two routes and a common start and diverge at the small roof. Start right of *Wanker* up blocky rock to a small roof (*Monkey's Uncle* continues straight up from here) climb over the roof and step right onto the slab (*Monkey's Sister*) climbs up staying right of upper roof then back left to the anchors.
10 bolts.
Variation: A.C.E. 5.12a ☐
From the third bolt go left over the small roof then up to the anchors.
8 bolts.

❺ Red Sonja 5.7 ★ ☐
Pitch 1: 5.7. Climb a left-leaning corner to a stance, go slightly left to a right-facing corner and climb it to just below an overhang and belay from gear.
Pitch 2: 5.7. Skirt the roof on the right and head up a left-leaning trough to the top.
SR.

❻ Transylverlina 5.12b ★★ ☐
Continuous climbing with several short, hard sections.
Pitch 1: 5.10b. Start to the left of a blunt arete and then veer up and right to the anchor.
8 bolts.
Pitch 2: 5.12b PG-13. Trend right up and over a small roof following bolts up a steep face to the anchor.
11 bolts.
Pitch 3: 5.12a. Trend right and up over a small bugle to a nice face leading to an arête. Climb the short arete to the anchor.
9 bolts.
Pitch 4: 5.12b. Climb the roof above the belay to the top.
4 bolts.
Descent: Rap the route or walk off.

❼ Heart of the Narrows 5.12b ★★★ ☐
Great route that climbs some great sections of rock with good protection. One of the better routes on the wall.
Pitch 1: 5.10a. Climb up the right-facing corner going right through a small overhang to the belay.
6 bolts.
Pitch 2: 5.12b. Move slightly right then up the steep wall with a hard move to reach the anchor.
5 bolts.
Pitch 3: 5.7. Up easier rock to a ramp, climb the ramp to a belay.
2 bolts.
Pitch 4: 5.12b. Continue up the ramp to the obvious arete. Climb the slightly overhanging arete to a small roof, crank the roof, then go straight up to the anchor.
5 bolts.
Descent: Rap the route.

❽ That's Weak 5.10a ★★★ ☐
A great warm up on good holds just left of a mossy crack (*Vampire* start). Climb the face with the crux coming low, continue up and then a little left to the anchor.
8 bolts.

❾ The Good, The Bad, and The Jacked 5.12a ★★★ ☐
Nice climb with beautiful moves up a gold-colored wall. Climb the first pitch of *That's*

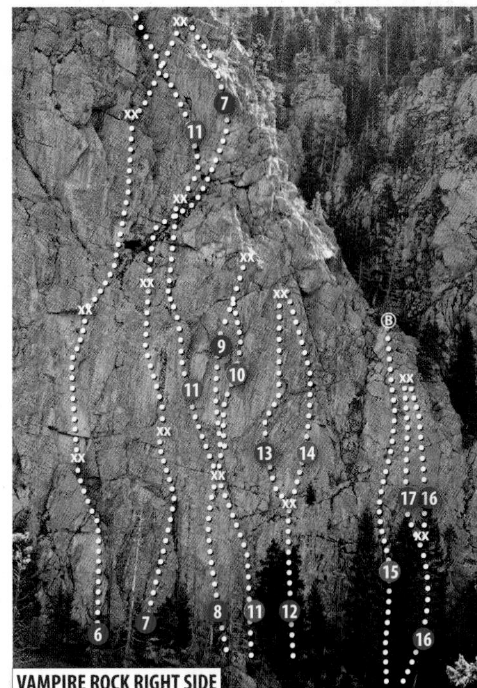

Weak. Continue straight from the belay, then angle right and up a steep, featured wall to the anchor.
9 bolts.

⑩ Crack of Desperation 5.10a ★ ☐
Climb the first pitch of *That's Weak*. From the anchor, climb up and right to the obvious wide crack. Follow the crack over a roof and then to a horizontal crack, go right and climb past three bolts to an anchor.
10 bolts and gear to 4 inches.

⑪ The Vampire 5.9 ★ ☐
The route and the climbing get better the higher you go.
Pitch 1: 5.7. Climb the obvious crack right of *That's Weak* to the anchor of *That's Weak*.
Pitch 2: 5.9. Clip a bolt then head left to an obvious corner into a slot and then over a roof on the right and up to a belay on a slab.
Pitch 3: 5.8. Work up and left under the big roof. Go left around the roof and then up to a belay at chains.
Pitch 4: 5.9. Climb the ramp and then up and left into a left-facing corner that leads to a handcrack to a slab and the top.
SR.

⑫ Pin Cushion 5.11c ★★ ☐
A nice short pitch. Somewhat of a pump with widely spaced bolts. Climb the face 30 feet right of *That's Weak* to the anchor.
4 bolts.

⑬ Blood Doll 5.12b ★★★ ☐
Climb *Pin Cushion* to the belay. Fire up and a little right past a weird ramp. Gain a ledge and then climb to a steep headwall, crank the crux, and then reach the anchor.
9 bolts.

⑭ Stage Fright 5.11a ★ ☐
Climb *Pin Cushion* to the bolted anchor or *The Vampire* first pitch to a bolted belay below two right-angling cracks. Climb up to the cracks and then follow them to a small roof, go left and then back right to another crack, make a hard move, then up to the anchor.
8 quickdraws and SR.

⑮ One Withered Arm 5.9+ ☐
Climb the obvious left-facing corner just left of the *Le Stat*. Dirty rock mars the start. Rap off from the upper pitch of *Le Stat* or top out and walk off to the west.
SR.

⑯ Le Stat 5.12a ★★★ ☐
Maybe the best route on the rock.
Pitch 1: 5.12a. On the right side of the wall, start below a small roof and climb up and right to a left angling seam/crack. Veer left and then fire for a horn. Another hard move gets you to the anchor.
8 bolts.
Pitch 2: 5.11c. Head straight up the steep headwall on nice crimps.
8 bolts.

⑰ Fear of Sunlight 5.11c ★★ ☐
Climb the first pitch of *Le Stat*. From the anchor take the bolted line on the left. Climb the rounded arete to a ledge, then fire up the steep headwall to the anchor.
8 bolts.

BLACK WIDOW SLAB 8.6 miles

Approach time: 10 - 20 minutes.
Exposure: North, east, and northwest.

16 routes

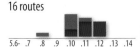

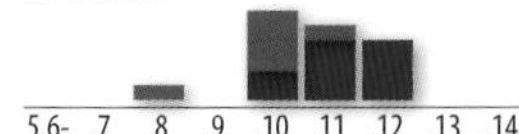

Lying just right of Vampire Rock and separated by a large gully is Black Widow Slab, another large east and north facing rock with several nice slab routes and a few worthwhile trad routes.

Access: Park in a pullout on the left side of the road at 8.6 miles. Walk down stream in the inside of the guard and cross the creek at the rock. A Tyrolean traverse is set up during high water. Take a nice path up the hill and then go right to the rock.

1 Left Side 5.9

Pitch 1: 5.9 Start left of *Kate Moss* and follow indistinct cracks up to a large ledge below a gold roof.

Pitch 2: 5.9 Climb the roof on the right and then easier terrain to the top.

Gear to 3.5 inches.

2 Kate Moss 5.10b ★★

This route lies on the left-side of the rock, just left of *Consilence*. This is a long pitch and a 60-meter rope will not get you to the ground. Climb the long slab veering left past several short corners to the anchor.

15 bolts.

Descent: A 70-meter rope is required to lower.

3 Consilence 5.11c ★★★

Exceptional slab climbing. Climb up to the first bolt with caution or just stick-clip it. Reach a small crack and the first of several technical moves. Fire straight up on good holds and reach a small ledge. Climb up through a small bulge and get ready for 40 feet of great, near vertical slab climbing. The crux is getting to the ledge just below the overhang. Reach the ledge, climb right out the overhang on good edges and cruise up to the anchor

15 bolts

Descent: a 60-meter rope barely makes it to the ground.

4 Center 5.10a

Pitch 1: 5.10a. Start in the obvious corner above a dead tree. Climb the corner to a small roof and step right and then up cracks to large ledge.

Pitch 2: 5.7. Traverse right to a large ledge to a dirty left-facing corner.

Pitch 3: 5.7. Follow the corner and then up blocky rock to the top. Walk off to the west.

SR.

5 Gyromancy 5.11a ★★

The blunt bolted arete just right of *Left Side*.

6 bolts.

5a Project 5.14a?

The bolted arete left of *Dracula*. Photo page 1.

6 Dracula 5.12b ★★

Start on a slab down and right of *Gyromancy*, climb the slab and then into a steep section onto an arete, make several hard moves up the arete then go right and up a slab to the anchor. Photo page 181.

12 bolts.

6a Project 5.13+?

Roofs and face right of *Dracula* to same finish.

7 Specter 5.10d ★★

Start right of *Dracula* below the left side of a large roof. Climb to the roof/slot and follow good jams out the roof into a left leaning corner, climb the corner to a face then up to the anchor.

SR.

8 SMERSH 5.11c ★★

Start as for *Specter* and climb to the roof/slot, go right out the roof up a crack and then right to another crack, follow the crack and then left to the anchor for *Specter*. Somewhat of a wandering line.

SR, couple of 3 inch pieces.

9 Resonator 5.12d ★★

Powerful. Climb the bolted stepped roof just right of *Specter* making a hard move onto a slab, run it out to the anchor.

6 bolts.

10 Bong Session 5.10a ★★★

A nice crack climb that takes the crack system just right of *Resonator*, power through the roof and then up to a continuous crack to a wide hand crack on the right, follow the crack to a bolted anchor.

SR and few larger 4 inch pieces.

11 Pipe Dreams 5.12b ★★★

A cool route with very different crux moves. Climb the bolted face just right of *Bong Session* making a hard mantel to a rest, climb up the featured face past an anchor to a crack on the left, climb the crack and then move up and right to anchor.

12 bolts.

12 Fuck You 5.11c ★★

Stand on a boulder and make a hard move to the first bolt (stick clip), tenuous moves lead to a good ledge, from the ledge fire up the arete/face to a hard move, climb a short crack to the anchors.

12 bolts.

13 Band of Gold 5.11d ★★

Start just right of *Fuck You* climbing into a dihedral, climb the corner to a ledge, reach a short headwall and then a crack to anchors.

10 bolts.

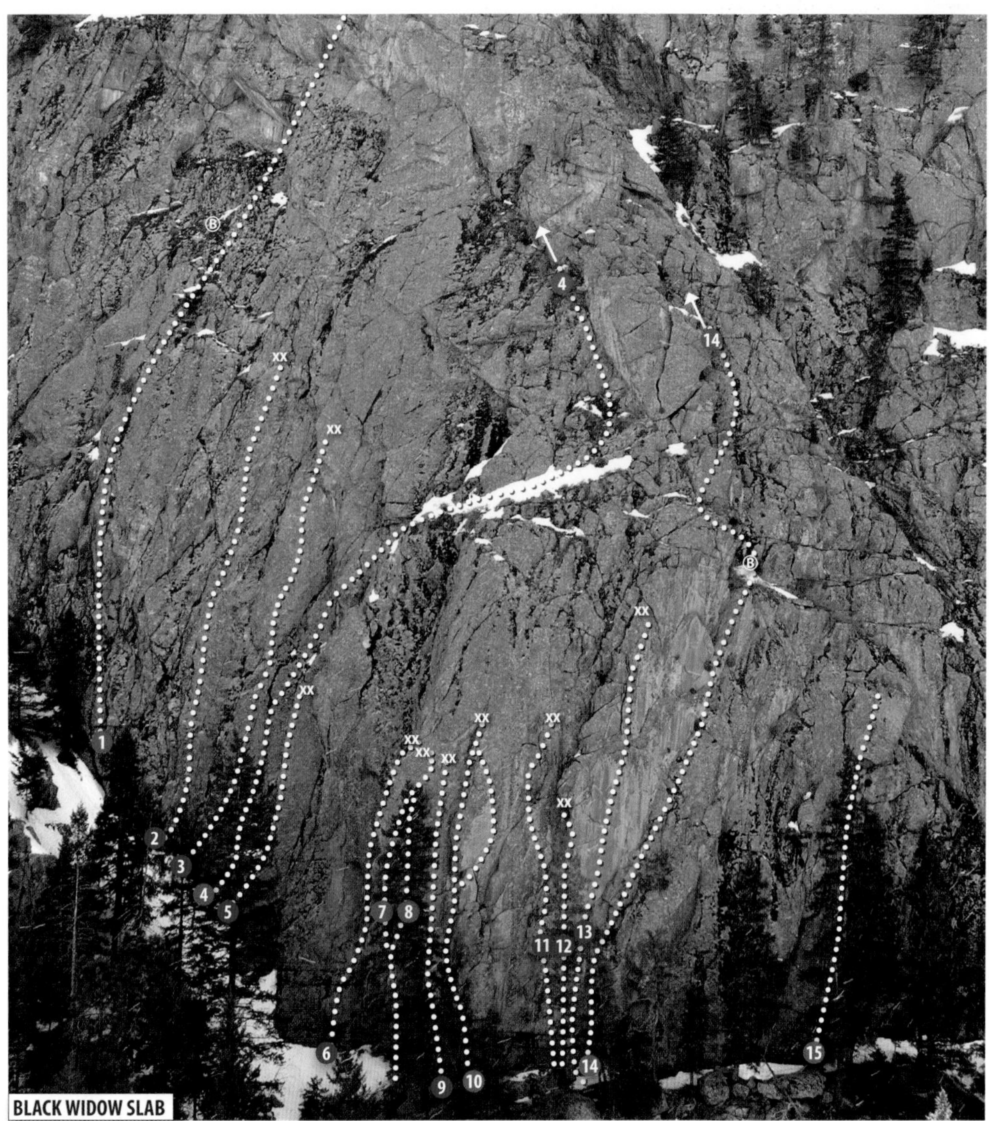

⓮ **Wired** 5.8 ★ ☐☐

Pitch 1: 5.8. Climb the obvious corner just right of *Band of Gold* to ledge.

Pitch 2&3: 5.8. Continue up non-descript rock for two pitches to the top.

SR.

⓯ **Right Side** 5.10b/c R ☐☐

On the right side of the rock is a right-leaning crack/corner leading to a roof, climb up to the roof making a scary move to gain the roof. After the roof climb a nice crack and face to the anchor of *Smoke Down*.

SR, RP's.

⓰ **Smoke Down** 5.11a ★★ ☐☐

Climb up a short face to a blunt arete aiming for a roof; turn the roof on the right then up to the anchor.

5 bolts.

⓱ **Caught in the Web** 5.12c ☐☐

On the far right side of Black Widow Slab is a leaning-overhanging face/corner that faces north. Climb up a short slab to a ledge. Make some hard moves past a thin crack to reach a small ledge. Power up on small holds into a short-overhanging corner making tenuous moves up to a jug. Follow good holds to the anchor.

8 bolts.

TROUT ROCK 8.6 miles

Approach time: 2 - 5 minutes.
Exposure: North.

4 routes

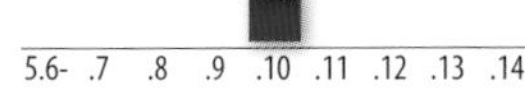

A small, easy to access, rock that sits directly across the creek from the Animal World parking lot. Good routes on nice granite. Shaded in the early morning during the summer months. Bring a few small pieces to supplement the bolts on the sport climbs.

Access: Park in the Animal World (page 168) lot at 8.6 miles and cross the creek to the obvious short, north facing rock.

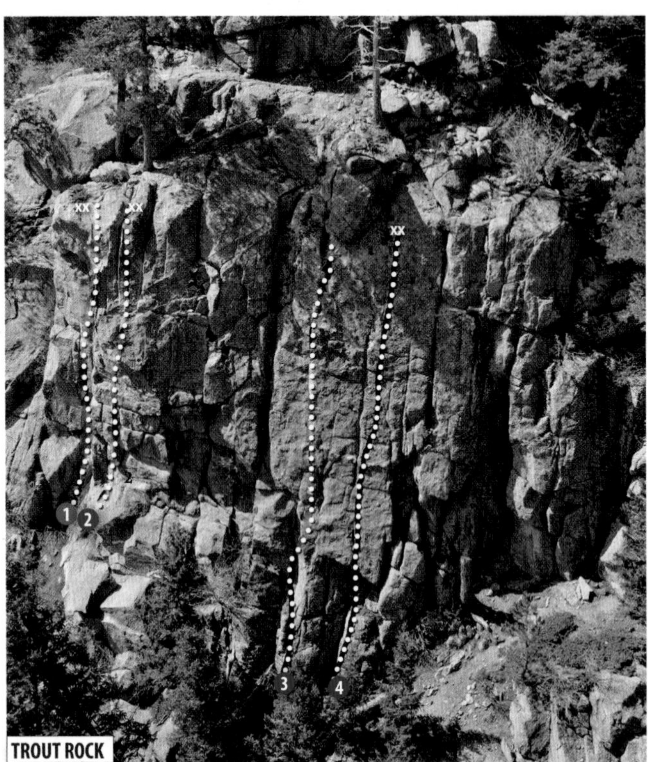

❶ **Where's Vaino?** 5.10a ★
Climb the obvious steep left-facing corner on the left side of the rock.
Gear to 2 inches.

❷ **Griffon** 5.10a ★★
Just right of *Where's Vaino* is this short, steep face.
4 bolts.

❸ **Greenback** 5.10a ★
Climb the bolted line that shoots up the center of the slab.
5 bolts, 0.5 inch micro-cam..

❹ **Cutthroat** 5.10a ★★
Climb the nice slab on the right side of the rock.
5 bolts, 0.5 inch micro-cam.

Darek Krol stakes out *Dracula* 5.12b, Black Widow Slab, page 178. Photo: Darek Krol collection.

SLEEPING BEAUTY 8.6 miles

Approach time: 15 - 20 minutes.
Exposure: Northwest.

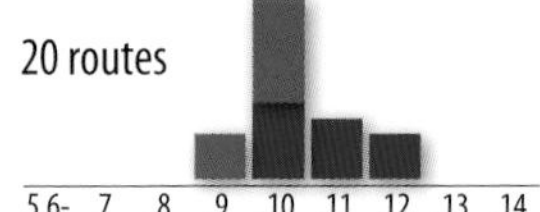

Sleeping Beauty is an impressive piece of black granite perched high on a hillside above Boulder Creek. Excellent routes in all grades, sport and trad.

Access: Park in a pullout on the left side of the road at 8.6 miles. Cross the creek using a Tyrolean traverse or hop rocks in low water. Head up towards the Beer Can but head left on the obvious trail that skirts the bottom of the crag. Follow the trail to the left side of the cliff and up to a large ledge system.

1 Jungle of Stone 5.9 ☐
On the far left side of the wall. Follow the trail up to the main ledge, traverse on the main ledge for 100 feet to a shelf. On the left side of the shelf is a hand crack. Climb up mossy rock gaining a good crack system. Follow the crack and then traverse to the upper bolts on *Black Rain*.
3 bolts, gear to 3.5 inches.

2 Black Rain 5.10b ★★★ ☐
Just right of *Jungle of Stone* is this beautiful streaked wall.
12 bolts.
Descent: You need a 70-meter rope to rap this route.

3 Water Spirit 5.10a ☐
The obvious overhanging black crack just right of *Black Rain*.
Gear to 2.5 inches.

4 Prince Charmer 5.9+ ★ ☐
The obvious corner right of *Black Rain*.
7 bolts and gear to 2 inches.

5 Aerial Boundaries 5.12a/b ★★★ ☐
Beautiful and classic slab/face climbing. One of the better routes on the wall. Start right of *Prince Charmer* and climb past three bolts to a small roof. Trend a little left over the roof (crux) and then fire up the easier slab to the anchor.
11 bolts.

6 Lightspeed 5.11a ☐
Start at the left side of the main ledge. Climb the roof protected by bolts. Continue up the nice featured face to the anchors.
8 bolts.

7 Kama Sutra 5.10b/c ★★★ ☐
The best crack climb on the cliff. Start left of the tree.
Pitch 1: 5.10b/c. Power through a roof climbing a perfect hand crack. Continue to where the crack goes wide. Jam the wide crack and gain a ledge with a small tree and belay.
Pitch 2: 5.9. Follow a crack of varying width to near the top of the wall, then veer left and belay from the anchors on *Aerial Boundaries*.
Gear to 3 inches.

8 Sleeping Beauty 5.10 ★ ☐
Pull over a roof at a black knob and follow thin cracks to a bulge, then go right to another crack and gain a ledge. Follow a hand crack for about 30 feet then go up and right along a flake and join *Wings Of Desire*.
Gear to 3.5 inches.

9 Wings of Desire 5.11b ★★★ ☐
A really good and really long slab pitch. Start just right of the tree. Power up the first moves then go slightly right (dicey) and then up the beautiful slab with the crux coming around bolt 12.
16 bolts, use long slings on the first four.

10 MLK 5.12a ★★★ ☐
Start right of the tree. Climb up a short crack and then up a black wall to a flake. Continue up to a steep face below a small roof, crank the roof (crux) and continue up to the anchor. This route was named after one of my personal heroes: Martin Luther King.
11 bolts and medium gear for the start.

11 Walk on the Wide Side 5.9 ★★ ☐
Pitch 1: 5.9. Start as for *MLK*, then go right at the first bolt (don't clip) to a flake, gain a wide crack and continue for 90 feet to a belay on a ledge with a ring anchor. Rap only with a 70-meter rope.
Gear to 3.5 inches. Double up on the bigger size of cams.
Pitch 2: 5.7. Sport pitch. Move right from the anchor and clip the first bolt, continue up easier ground to the two bolt belay (no rings), traverse right to the anchor for *Immaculate Deception* to rappel.
5 bolts.

12 Immaculate Deception 5.10c ★★ ☐
Pitch 1: 5.10c. Start about 15 feet right of *MLK* on a slab on the right side of a roof. Climb the slab to an anchor below the upper roof. **Direct Start:** 5.11c/d. Climb the obvious bolted seam/crack over a roof to the belay.
Pitch 2: 5.8. Step left and then reach a ledge, clip a bolt and then climb the crack to a large ledge.
Gear to 4.5 inches.

13 Crack of Dawn 5.10a ★ ☐
Pitch 1: 5.10a. Start right of roofs at the obvious crack. Climb the crack and then left on the face past a roof. Continue up the wide crack to belay at a ring anchor.
Pitch 2: 5.8. Climb the bolted face to an anchor.
Gear to 4.5 inches and 10 quickdraws.
Descent: Rap the route

⓮ **Mystic Mile** 5.10b ★★★ ☐

Pitch 1: 5.10b. Start right of *Crack of Dawn* and just left of a small pine tree. Climb over a roof and then up to another roof; tackle this and then up the slab to anchor.
10 bolts.

Pitch 2: 5.9+. Continue up the slab to an anchor.
8 bolts.

Variation: The Wave 5.12b ☐

From the top of pitch1, head right and then up a steep headwall to the anchor.
6 bolts.

⓯ **The Spell** 5.10a ★ ☐

Pitch 1: 5.9. Climb a mossy crack left of *Mind Bender* and belay beneath a huge left-facing dihedral.

Pitch 2: 5.10a. Continue up the dihedral turn a roof (crux) and continue to the top of the wall.
Gear to 4.5 inches.

⓰ **Eight Miles High** 5.10a ★★ ☐

Pitch 1: 5.10a. Climb through the first 6 bolts of *Mind Bender*, then veer left to an arete, climb the arete to the anchor.
9 bolts.

Pitch 2: 5.6. Climb the easy slab to the top of the wall and an anchor.
3 bolts.

⓱ **Mind Bender** 5.11c/d ★★★ ☐

One of the nicer pitches on the wall. Fire up the steep wall and into a short corner, climb the corner then reach the anchor.
10 bolts.

⓲ **Sunlight Makes Me Paranoid** 5.10c ★★★ ☐

Start just right of *Mind Bender* at a single bolt belay on a large ledge. Climb straight up from the anchor and follow a line of bolts to a small overhang. Veer right under the overhang, reach for good holds and fire straight up to a good stance. Continue up on good holds to a short corner then swing right and then straight up to the anchor. Good route with good protection and holds. Photo page 184.
11 bolts.

⓳ **Arcanum** 5.10a ★★★ ☐

Begin near a large pine, a few feet left of a big flake that leans against the wall.

Pitch 1: 5.10a. Climb a slab, then climb a steep finger and hand crack through a roof. Continue up the crack system until it fades, then climb past another bolt and gain a 2-bolt anchor at a narrow stance.

Pitch 2: 5.8. Climb a sloping shelf to a short headwall and gain a 2-bolt anchor on a nice flat area.
Gear to 2 inches and 12 quickdraws.

⓴ **Lost Highway** 5.10c ★★★ ☐

Traverse the ledge and then drop down and right to a rap anchor. Rap to a nice ledge and walk right to the start of this route.

Pitch 1: 5.10a. Climb over some bulges on positive holds into a small right-facing corner. Easier rock leads to a small ledge and the anchors.
6 bolts.

Pitch 2: 5.7. Pull over the headwall. Climb up a white quartz dike to a vegetated ledge below a left-facing corner. Move right around the arête and climb nice slab moves to a good ledge and the anchors.
5 bolts.

Pitch 3: 5.10c. Climb a short headwall to the base of a right-facing corner. Climb the corner making some hard moves near the top. Go left then up to the anchor.
9 bolts.

㉑ **Orgasmatron** 5.11b ★★ ☐

Climb the first two pitches of *Lost Highway*. From the second belay climb up going left before the corner, reach an exposed arete and climb to the top of the wall.
10 bolts.

Descent: Rap *Lost Highway*.

Brenda Leach on *Sunlight Makes Me Paranoid* 5.10c, Sleeping Beauty, page 182. Photo Ron Olsen.

THE BEER CAN 8.6 miles

Approach time: 10 minutes.
Exposure: East and north.

4 routes

5.6- .7 .8 .9 .10 .11 .12 .13 .14

The Beer Can sits just above the Animal World parking area and has easy access and great early morning sun.

Access: Park in a pullout on the left side of the road at 8.6 miles. Cross the creek using a Tyrolean traverse or hop rocks in low water. Head up the obvious trail to the rock.

❶ **Beer Belly** 5.9+ ☐
On the far left side of the wall. Belay from a two bolt anchor. Climb the obvious wide crack via face moves on the right.
2 bolts, gear to 5 inches.

All three sport routes share a common anchor.

❷ **Hydraulic Sandwich** 5.10b ★★ ☐
Belay from a two-bolt anchor below the wall. This is the left most of three bolted routes. Start with some easy climbing up and right, then trend left towards the left side of the huge roof. Clip a bolt under the roof and move out right and then up the clean face to the anchor. The crux comes just before reaching the anchor.
12 bolts.

❸ **Icy Paralyzer** 5.11a ★★ ☐
From the top of the approach trail to the Beer Can, scramble up to a small ledge with a two-bolt belay anchor. Continue 20 feet right to another 2-bolt belay anchor; start here. Climb up and right, clipping the first 7 bolts of *Drink to Puke*. Head left over the roof and climb a thin face and corner past 3 more bolts to the anchor.
16 bolts and a 60 meter rope.

❹ **Drink to Puke** 5.10c ★ ☐
From the top of the approach trail to the Beer Can, scramble up to a small ledge with a two-bolt belay anchor. Continue 20 feet right to another 2-bolt belay anchor; start here. Climb up toward the right side of the roof, onto a ramp, then chimney and stem around the roof. Continue up a slab/corner and angle left to the anchor.
14 bolts.

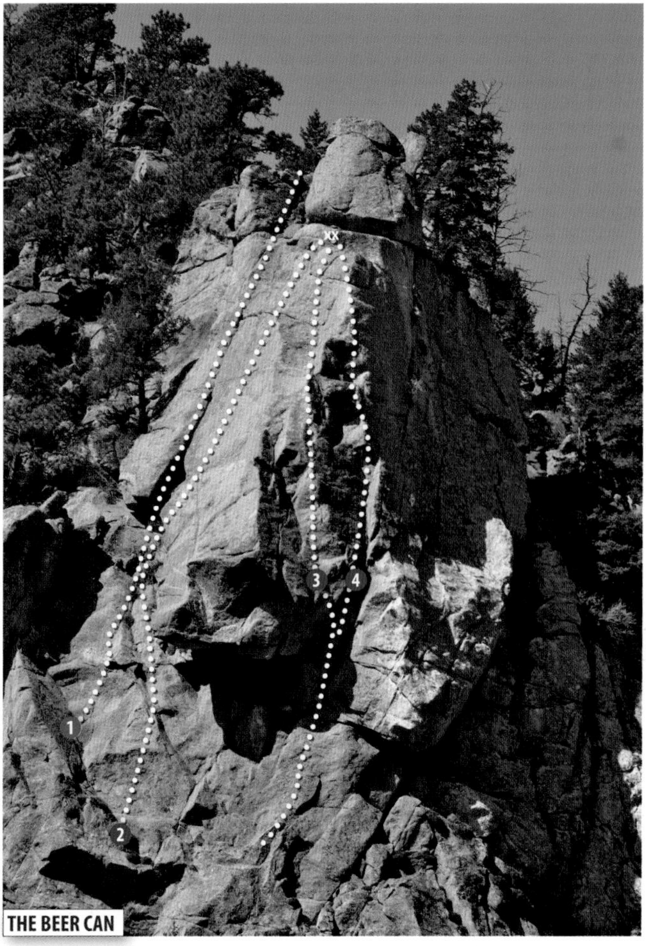

THE BEER CAN

LOST ROCK 8.8 miles

Approach time: 10 - 15 minutes.
Exposure: West.

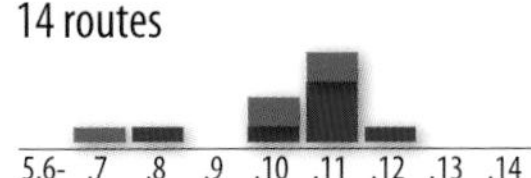

Lost Rock faces west allowing for good afternoon sun and early morning shade. The climbs are in a nice setting in the woods and along the creek. Bring gear as several of the routes require some and there are a few pure trad climbs on the wall. Currently, climbs are located in four areas: Left Side, Upper Left, Upper Center, Upper Right.

Access: Drive 8.8 miles up the canyon to a pullout on the left about a quarter of mile past Animal World parking lot. Cross the creek at a large boulder and then follow directions for each rock.

LEFT SIDE

The farthest area left down near the river level.

❶ Fearless Leader 5.11a ★★ ☐☐
Just off the trail, locate bolts on a clean arête. Sustained steep climbing leads to a rest midway.
6 bolts.

❷ Gomer Pyle 5.7 R ☐☐
Locate a clean looking slab a few hundred feet right of *Fearless Leader* at a talus field. Start in the crack on the left then head straight up the center of the face. Walk off right after 60 feet, or any of several second pitches can be discovered.
Gear to 2 inches.

UPPER LEFT

Follow a gully right of *Gomer Pyle* to access the upper tier of rock. This will put you on the same ledge as the second pitch of *Gomer Pyle*.

❸ Good Vibrations 5.10a ★ ☐☐
About 70 feet left of two oddly located brown hangers in a low overhang behind two pine trees.
5 bolts and light rack to 2 inches.

❹ Blood Donor 5.11c ★
Just right of *Good Vibrations* follow a slightly overhanging crack/flake to a bolted anchor.
Gear to 2 inches.

❺ Misanthrope 5.10b ★ ☐☐
Locate two oddly located brown hangers in a low overhang behind two pine trees. Climb the overhang and up a slab a short ways to anchors.
2 bolts and gear to 2 inches.

❻ Lost Souls 5.8 ★ ☐☐
15 feet right of #5. Minor cruxes at most bolts. After 7th bolts follow either groove (left or right) to anchors. Good climbing is interrupted by many ledges.
7 bolts and few small pieces.

UPPER CENTER

Cross the river at the parking area (if possible), hike about 100 feet down river and then contour uphill and left towards a notch. Continue up some moss covered ledges to a featured clean wall.

❼ No How, No Way 5.12a ★ ☐☐
Begin left of the dead tree. Technical moves getting over the small roof, then cool stemming up the corner, swing left at the top of the corner and make a hard slab move to reach the anchor.
8 bolts.

❽ The Escapist 5.11a ★ ☐☐
Begin just right of the dead tree and traverse behind it. The crux is getting over the bulge on flaring jams. Once over the bulge go straight up and then right into a short corner and head straight up the face and join the *Knob* route at the last bolt.
Gear to 2 inches.

❾ Safety In Numbers 5.10c ★ ☐☐
Start just left of the knobby wall at a thin crack. Climb the crack and then make an awkward move to reach a small ledge. Stack gear in flakes and then move into a short corner. Climb the corner and then a face stemming on two knobs. Clip the last bolt on the knob route and then reach the anchors.
Gear to 2 inches.

❿ My ... Nice Knobs You Have 5.10c ★★★ ☐☐
Climb the obvious knob-covered wall past two bolts to a small ledge. Use a hold on the rounded arete and reach left to a flake, crank a hard move, passing two bolts and then reach another ledge. Angle up and a little left past the fifth bolt to the anchor.
5 bolts and a 5.5 inch cam.

⓫ Don't Panic 5.11a R ★ ☐☐
The crux is insecure laybacking right off the ground with hard to place gear. The R-rating comes from this ...blowing any of the first couple of placements and you are on the ground.
Gear to 2 inches.

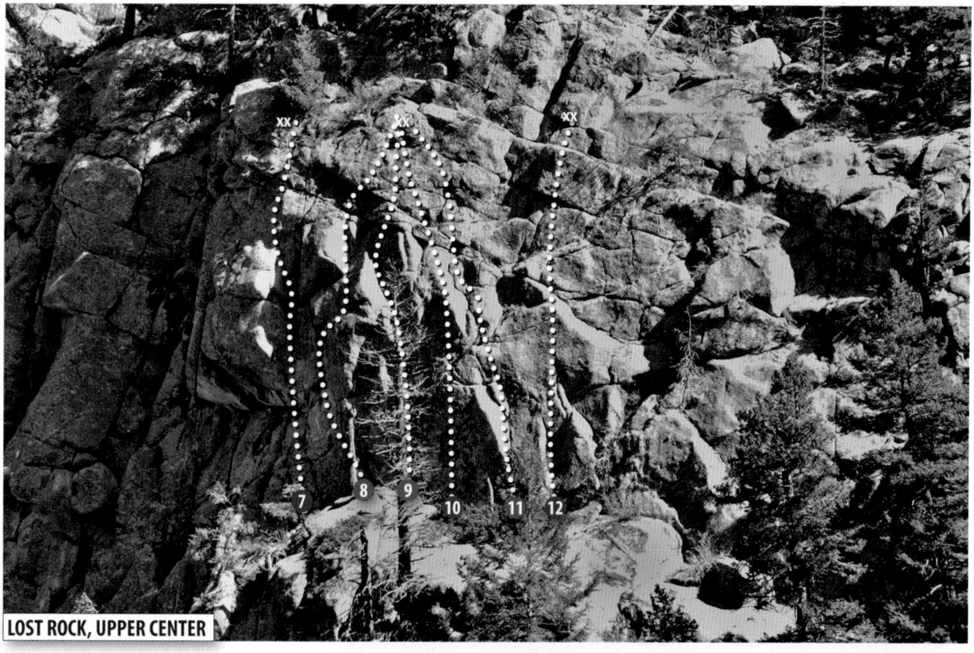

LOST ROCK, UPPER CENTER

⑫ Clocks 5.11b/c ★★ ☐☐

The crux is getting past the second bolt. I lunge. Cool moves that will be harder for those folks under 5'8".

3 bolts, a 2 inch cam and 0.5 inch micro-cam.

UPPER RIGHT

Cross the river at the parking area (if possible), hike straight uphill then slightly left until a boulder problem (easy 5th Class) puts you on a ledge. Walk 50 feet right to the climbs.

⑬ Joe the Lunger 5.11b ★ ☐☐

Getting past the first bolt is the crux....lunge it! Start at a large pine and climb beautiful featured granite to the anchor.

3 bolts and 3.5 inch cam.

⑭ Lost In A Lost World 5.11a ★★ ☐☐

Begin just left of a large pine tree near the rock. Follow obvious line for 5 bolts to a rest near some bushes. Then move right to a rest below a slab. A hard slab move gains a big rail below the roof. Pull the roof to the anchor. Great varied climbing.

8 bolts.

LOST ROCK, UPPER RIGHT

EASTER ROCK 9.0 miles

Approach time: 5 - 10 minutes.
Exposure: North and east.

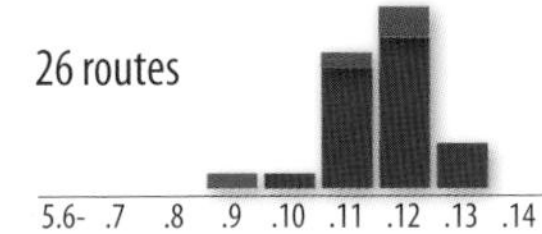

Easter Rock is a large, steep north-facing chunk of granite with many excellent sport routes in a pleasant setting just off the road. The rock is popular in the summer months and offers relief from the heat and sun. The bulk of the routes are on the north face and a handful are located on the east face. The original route on the rock (*East Face*) was done by Layton Kor in the early 1960s.

Access: Drive 9.0 miles up the canyon to a small pullout on the right side of the road. A small cairn and trail leads uphill to the north face. If the parking area is full, use a large parking area on the left at 8.8 miles and walk up the road to the cliff.

EASTER ROCK EAST WALL

EAST WALL

The gray and somewhat dark east face has several routes that breach the large overhangs in the middle of the wall. There is also a good warm-up to do before jumping on the harder overhanging walls.

❶ East Face 5.9 ★ ☐

Pitch 1: 5.9. Start on the lower east face and climb an easy ramp to below a large roof, bypass the roof on the right and then gain a dihedral and belay.

Pitch 2: 5.9. Continue up the broken corner to a slab and then easier rock and the top.

SR.

❷ Chickenshit Armchair Environmentalist 5.12c/d ★ ☐

Start on the left side of the wall on a ledge with a two-bolt anchor at the last switchback on the trail to the main face. Climb to below a huge roof, where optional anchors exist, then fire out the roof reaching a good holds at the lip.

12 bolts.

❸ Trustafarian Panhandler 5.12c/d ★ ☐

Start right of *Chickenshit* at a two-bolt belay on a ledge. Climb slightly left from the belay over a bulge to easier climbing. Continue up below a large overhang and fire through the overhang via a thin crack below the anchors.

12 bolts.

❹ Surrounded By Reality 5.12c ★ ☐

Look for a belay bolt right off the trail at the last switchback. Climb the short wall and reach a short corner below a roof. Climb the roof on the right side, then go up easier rock to a larger, easier roof to the anchors.

13 bolts.

❺ Knappweed Herbacide 5.10b ★ ☐

A good warm up that starts on the right side of the east face where the trail turns to meet the main wall. Fire up the blocky corner to belay below a roof.

5 bolts.

Variation: 5.13a ★ ☐

Continue past the anchor making powerful moves on manufactured holds over a series of small, tiered roofs.

11 bolts.

❻ Barbarians 5.12a/b ★★ ☐

Start just left of the arete that splits the east and north faces, climbing pleasant rock to sloping moves at the arete that leads to the anchor.

9 bolts.

NORTH FACE

The north face is defined by the wall right of the arete that splits the two walls. Excellent sport climbing with a few hard trad routes to keep the crowds honest.

7 Empire of the Fenceless 5.12a ★★★★ ☐
Classic. Top 10 in the canyon. Climb the bolted route on the right side of the arete. Continuous and excellent climbing all the way to the anchor.
7 bolts.

8 Tell-Tale Heart 5.12b ★★★★ ☐
Another classic route that fires up the obvious corner right of the arete through small roofs. Take a rest before the roof... you'll need it.
8 bolts.

Variation: Nevermore 5.13a ★★★ ☐
Climb through the crux roof of *Tell-Tale Heart* (7 bolts) and move up right up past two bolts and slopers to the anchor.
9 bolts.

9 Elanor 5.11c/d ★★★ ☐
Climb the obvious steep left-facing corner up to a good stance above the middle section of the route, milk the rest then fire the crux to the anchor. Great route.
8 bolts.

Variation: Evermore 5.12d ★★★ ☐
Climb *Elanor* to the rest; then head left past a couple of dyno's to the anchor.
8 bolts.

10 Thunderdome 5.12a ★★★ ☐
Climb the overhanging, right-angling, thin crack past a roof and then up to the anchor for *The Riddler*.
Gear to 3 inches.

11 Dark Knight 5.11d ★★ ☐
A wandering line. Start right of *Thunderdome* and climb a short face past two bolts then veer left, passing over *Thunderdome*, to an undercling and then up to the anchors for *Elanor*.
6 bolts.

EASTER ROCK NORTH FACE

12 The Riddler 5.11c ★★ ☐
Start for *Dark Knight* and then veer right past the second bolt to tricky moves to gain a short corner. Climb the corner to the anchor.
6 bolts.

13 The Joker 5.11c ★★★ ☐
Start right of *The Riddler* making hard moves to gain a corner. Climb the corner and avoid the tree to the anchor.
7 bolts.

Variation: Mr. Two-Faced 5.11d ★★ ☐
Start as for *The Joker*, then move left after the third bolt into the corner for *The Riddler*, climbing it to the anchor.
7 bolts.

14 The Penguin 5.12c ★ ☐
Start right of a short, thin crack. Climb a face just right of the tree to hard moves getting to bolt five. Move past the tree to the anchor on the right.
5 bolts.

Variation: Catwoman 5.12d ★★ ☐
Climb the thin crack just left of the normal start. Stick clip the first bolt.
5 bolts.

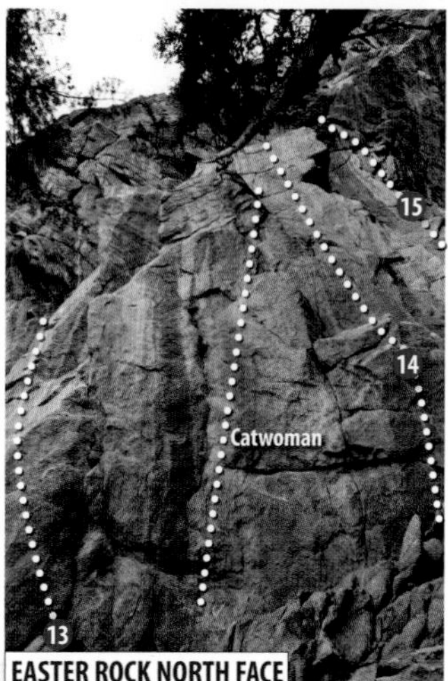

EASTER ROCK NORTH FACE

15 Willard 5.11c ★★ ☐
Climb the cool right-facing corner. Stemming up a bizarre finish gains the anchor.
6 bolts.

⑯ White Men Can't Jump Left 5.12a/b ★★ ☐
Climb a short face, then head up a corner to a good ledge below a roof. Jump past the roof to gain good holds and then the anchor.
6 bolts.

⑰ Dynamic Duel 5.13b ★ ☐
Start just right of *White Men* on causal climbing to a series of hard moves to the crux at the overhang. Climb the overhang via a thin seam to the anchor.
7 bolts.

⑱ Pterodactyl Traverse 5.12d ★★ ☐
Climb past the obvious flake on the right side of the wall using surgical gloves (tons of bat shit). Climb left up the severely overhanging wall to the crux to gain the anchor.
7 bolts.

⑲ The Flying Beast 5.13a ★★★ ☐
See description opposite.
7 bolts.

⑳ Rain Shadow 5.12b ★★ ☐
The obvious crack line right of *the Flying Beast*. The roof is the crux.
Gear to 2.5 inches.

㉑ Wagging the Nub 5.11d ★ ☐
Traverse a narrow ledge on the far right side of the wall to a two-bolt anchor and the start.
Pitch 1: 5.11a. Climb a steep face past bolts to a ledge.
Pitch 2: 5.11d. Climb the overhanging left-facing corner using a fist crack to reach the anchor.
8 quickdraws and a light rack to 4 inches.

㉒ New Test Of Men 5.11d ★★ ☐
This is the second to last route on the far right (uphill) of the north face.
Pitch 1: 5.11b/c. Climb past a hard 5.11 start followed by a nice corner to the anchor.
Pitch 2: 5.11d. Move up left through a bulge and the crux. Reach a rest, then one final hard move to the anchor.
11 quickdraws.

㉓ Road To Emmaus 5.11a/b ★★★ ☐
Last route on the far side of the wall near the top of the hill.
Pitch 1: 5.11b. Climb over the low roof making a hard move and then up the wall above with another hard move to reach the anchor.
Pitch 2: 5.11a/b. Climb right from the belay through a roof and then to a second roof. Easier climbing leads to the anchor.
11 quickdraws.

⑲ The Flying Beast 5.13a ★★★
Climb the corner/seam just right of the flake to the roof and then the anchor.
7 bolts.

Climber Dan Levison. Photo Adam Brink.

HIGH ENERGY CRAG 9.1 miles

Approach time: 10 - 15 minutes.
Exposure: North and west.

9 routes

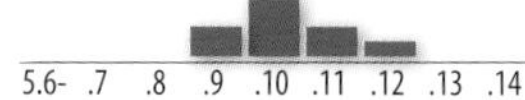

This short, compact piece of granite offers several good, short, overhanging crack climbs in a nice setting right above Boulder Creek. The crag gets good afternoon sun and stays shaded in the morning.

Access: Travel 9.1 miles up the canyon to a pullout on the right side of the road (same as for Easter Rock). Cross the road and creek via rocks or wading and then up the short hill to the crag.

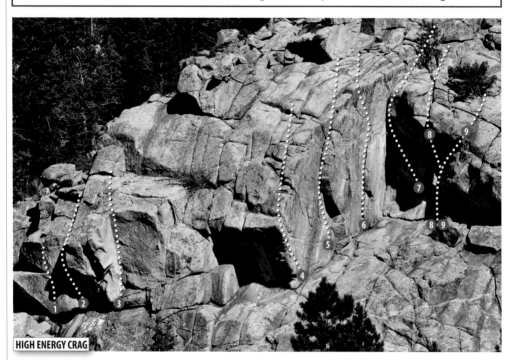

HIGH ENERGY CRAG

1 Eugenics Wars 5.12a ☐
On the far left side of the rock, climb a short steep face to a large ledge.
Gear to 2 inches.

2 No Preservatives 5.10b ★ ☐
Climb the short left-facing corner on the left side of the rock.
Gear to 4.5 inches.

3 Star Span 5.11b/c ★★★ ☐
The overhanging right-facing corner on the left side of the rock. Hard!
Gear to 2 inches.

4 Golden Bull 5.10a ☐
On the left side of the west face is a shallow thin crack on an arete.
Gear to 4.5 inches.

5 Proton 5.9 ☐
The least difficult climb on the cliff. Just right of *Golden Bull* is a left-leaning corner.
Gear to 2 inches.

6 Neutron Star 5.10b R ☐
Another short left-facing corner crack. Start right of *Proton*. Difficult gear.
Gear to 4.5 inches.

7 Diet of Worms 5.10a ★★ ☐
The obvious corner/crack. Great little route.
Gear to 2 inches.

8 Imp-Passable Crack 5.11b/c ★★ ☐
Climb the obvious fist and hand crack jutting trough a roof. Hard.
Gear to 3.5 inches.

9 Next to Imp-Passible 5.9 ★ ☐
Climb the first roof of *Imp-Passable Crack* then veer right under-clinging the roof.
Gear to 3.5 inches.

HIGHER ENERGY CRAG 9.1 miles

Approach time: 20 - 30 minutes.
Exposure: West.

5 routes

5.6- .7 .8 .9 .10 .11 .12 .13 .14

A crag set in a nice place high above the creek and canyon. Worth a trip if just for the setting. Like High Energy Crag, the routes are short.

Access: Travel 9.1 miles up the canyon to a pullout on the right side of the road (same as for Easter Rock). Cross the road, then the creek, and head up the short hill to High Energy Crag. Skirt the crag on the left then head straight up the steep hill to the Higher Energy Crag.

1 Twisted Chopper 5.9-
On the left side of the cliff. The crux is near the top under-clinging a shallow flake.
Gear to 2 inches

2 Blood Whine 5.11a ★
The crux is getting over the roof at the start. Start as for *Red Bull*, clip a bolt over the roof, and make a series of hard moves getting established over the roof. Clip the third bolt and then reach a ledge. Place the cams and then fire up the cool arete past two more bolts to the anchor.
5 bolts, 0.75 micro-cam, 3.5 inch cam.

3 Red Bull 5.11a/b ★★
The obvious route up the center of the crag. Cool moves down low then nice face climbing to the anchor.
4 bolts, 0.75 micro-cam.

4 Mike's Short Route 5.10b
The wide crack splitting the wall.
Gear to 5 inches.

5 Full Throttle 5.11d ★★
The best route on the crag. Short, overhanging, and powerful.
4 bolts, 0.75 micro-cam.

CONEY ISLAND 9.2 miles

Approach time: 5 - 10 minutes.
Exposure: South, east and west.

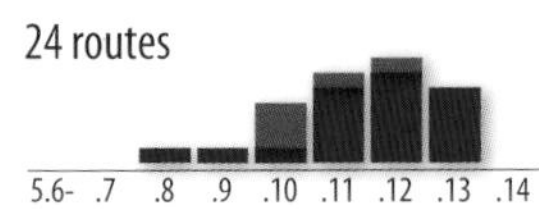

Coney Island is a two-tier rock with several hard sport routes in a sunny setting just minutes from the road. The upper tier offers many good routes on excellent granite while the lower tier has a number of short powerful routes that suit the strong boulderer.

Access: Travel 9.2 miles up the canyon to a pullout on the left side of the road just past the rock and near a guardrail. There is a bigger, more spacious pullout just a little farther up the canyon. Cross the road and follow the trail to the lower tier, to access the upper tier just continue past the lower and make a left up the hill — be careful not to knock rocks into the road.

1-7. LOWER CONEY ISLAND LEFT

❶ The Bait 5.11a ★★ ☐
Maybe the best route on the lower wall. The obvious corner splitting the left side of the wall. Start directly below the corner or to left on a gold wall with two bolts.
6 bolts, couple of mid-size stoppers.

❷ Twist and Shout 5.13c ★★ ☐
Powerful. Climb the blunt arete on the right side of the corner, power past a fixed draw to good stance and then up to the anchor. Photo next page.
3 bolts, small cams for the crack.

❸ Fly Trap 5.12a ★★ ☐
Climb the steep face right of the arete.
5 bolts.

❹ Flies in the Soup 5.11c ★ ☐
Start just right of *Flies in the Soup*, climb up to the first bolt then power up the short, black face.
3 bolts.

❺ Prong 5.12d ★ ☐
Powerful climbing just left of the arete on the right side of the wall. Short and technical.
4 bolts.

❻ Fly Swatter 5.10b/c ☐
Climb the right side of the arete using good edges and flakes. Nice warm-up.
3 bolts.

❼ New Fanatic 5.12a ★★ ☐
Start as for *Fly Swatter* clipping the first bolt. Move right then up the steep slab.
5 bolts.

❽ Work It On Out 5.12d ★★ ☐
Right and down of *Fly Swatter* is a short, severely overhanging, black wall. *Work it On Out* climbs the left side of the wall on powerful slopers, underlings and edges.
3 bolts.

❾ Dampened Enthusiasm 5.12a ★ ☐
Climbs the center of the short black wall. Nice short route.
3 bolts.

❿ Red Badger 5.11d ★ ☐
Climb the right side of the black wall trending left to the third bolt on *Dampened Enthusiasm*.
3 bolts.

Variation: Overenthusiasm 5.13c ☐
Low traverse from *Red Badger* into *Work it Out.*

⑪ The Badger Traverse 5.13a ★★ ☐

Start 15 feet right of *Red Badger* traversing all the way to the crux of *Work It On Out* and then to anchor.

6 bolts.

CONEY ISLAND UPPER TIER

⑫ Feeding the Beast 5.12b ★ ☐

On the upper left side of the upper tier is a fin of rock, climb the fin via strenuous moves and weird clips.

4 bolts.

⑬ Joy Ride 5.12b ★★★ ☐

If you are climbing at this grade, it will be a joy ride. Excellent route that climbs the left side of the clean south face with continuous climbing to the anchor.

9 bolts.

⑭ Der Letzte Zug 5.12c ★★★★ ☐

Climb the beautiful face right of *Joy Ride*. Engage the crux low down and reach a nice ledge. Continue straight up with excellent continuous climbing to the anchor.

7 bolts.

⑮ Die Reeperbahn 5.13b ★★ ☐

Excellent route that starts 25 feet right of *Joy Ride*. Climb up a short slab to corner/arete, trend left climbing the face/arete to a stopper move near the top.

8 bolts.

⑯ Loading Zone 5.10d/11a R ★ ☐

The obvious right facing corner just right of *Die Reeperbahn*. Start for *Die Reeperbahn*, clipping the first two bolts, then stem your way up the stepped dihedral veering left at the top. Reach a crack and then climb it to the top.

2 bolts, gear to 2 inches, RP's.

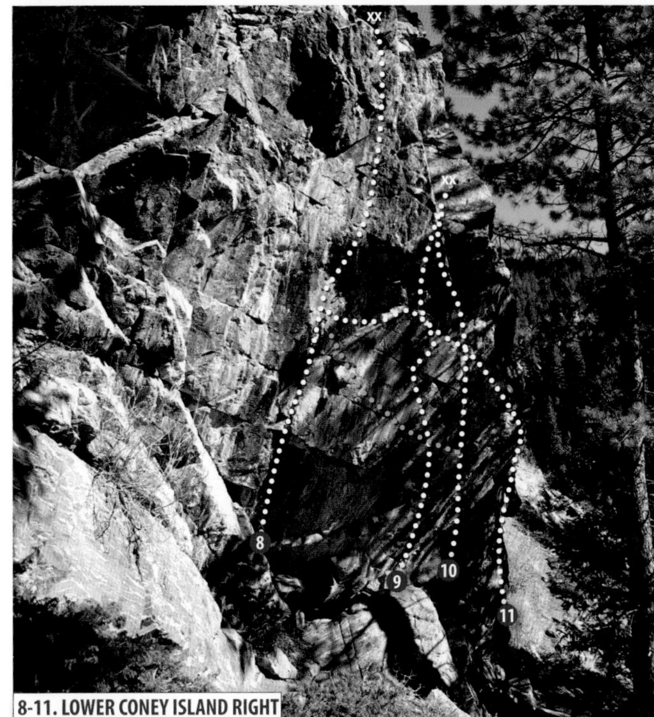

8-11. LOWER CONEY ISLAND RIGHT

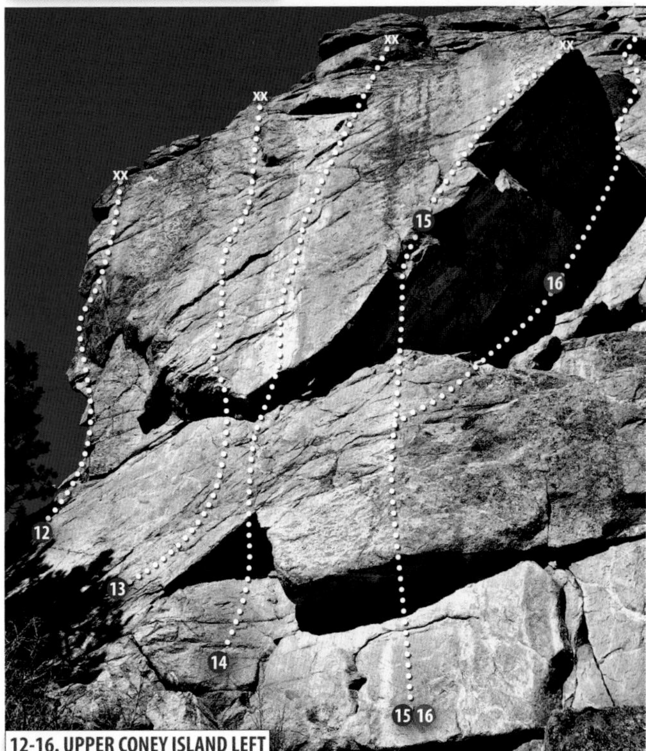

12-16. UPPER CONEY ISLAND LEFT

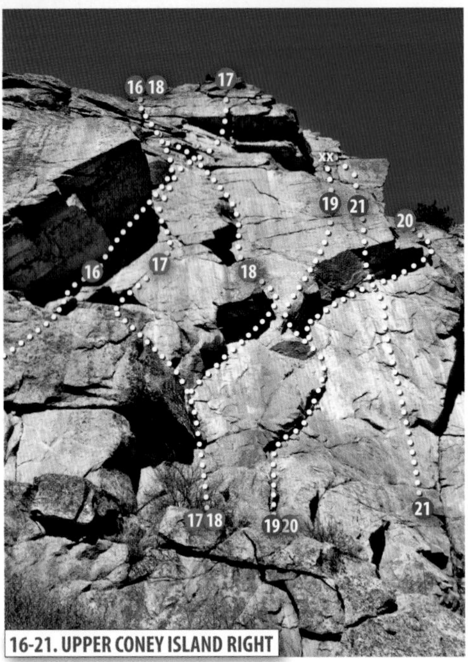

16-21. UPPER CONEY ISLAND RIGHT

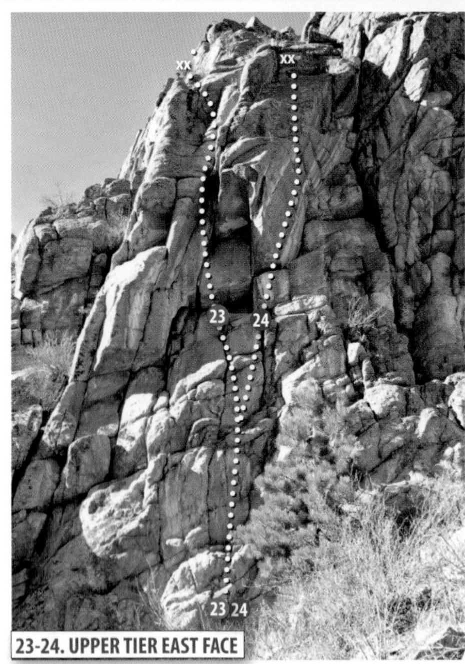

23-24. UPPER TIER EAST FACE

⑰ Psyclone 5.11d ★ ☐

Climb blocky corner right of *Loading Zone* trending left and reach a ledge just right of the corner of *Loading Zone*. Fire up the thin crack and then go left to the easy crack of *Loading Zone*, climb the crack and veer right up and over a roof via a fist crack to the top.

Variation 1: 5.10c. After the easy crack trend further right and climb a wide crack up a right facing corner to the top. Gear to four inches.

Variation 2: 5.10d. Traverse a ledge system way right to the base overhanging fist crack that faces east. Dirty and hard.

SR.

⑱ Quintet 5.10d ★★ ☐

Climb the multi-tier roof system just right of *Psyclone*. A cool route with excellent climbing. Can be done in one really long pitch.

Gear to 4 inches.

⑲ Give the Dog a Bone 5.13a ★★★ ☐

A classic pitch that climb a steep wall just left of *Coney Island Baby*. A ledge breaks the climb in half and also makes for a great rest before sending the upper crux moves.

7 bolts, gear to 2 inches for the start.

⑳ Coney Island Baby 5.12a ★★ ☐

Climb the right arching corner system with tricky protection and moves to the anchor for *Gagger* on the left.

Gear to 2.5 inches.

㉑ Gagger 5.13d ★★ ☐

Start right of *Coney Island Baby* and climb a streaked wall (hard) up to a roof, crank the roof (crux) and then fire up the steep and difficult slab.

8 bolts.

㉒ Runaway 5.8 ★★★ ☐

Down and right of *Give the Dog a Bone* is a large blocky wall that is inset somewhat. *Runaway* climbs the right side of the wall in one long pitch to the upper anchor. Good thoughtful climbing and a great route for the 5.8 leader. There is an anchor at 60 feet that is used for rapping back to the ground.

11 bolts and few small cams and stoppers.

UPPER TIER EAST FACE

The best approach is to veer right from just above the Lower Tier cutting across the hillside to the East Face.

㉓ Pri-Moe 5.10d ☐

Locate three bolts up a steep, blocky face. Climb past the bolts trending left into a chimney/flared slot. Clip a bolt and make a long reach into a finger crack. Climb up steep rock on good jams to a good rest. Crank up past the last bolt making a dicey move to the anchor.

4 bolts, gear to 2 inches.

㉔ Lucky Strikes Again 5.9 ★★★ ☐

Great route. Start as for *Pri-Moe*. Climb scaly but okay rock past 4 bolts, and step right onto a big shelf. Gaze at the steep and intimidating headwall, then cast off on subtle but amazing jugs and swarm to the top.

6 bolts.

Ian Spencer Green on *Twist and Shout* 5.13c (page 194). Photo Stewart Green.

NIP AND TUCK CRAGS 10.5 miles

Approach time: 1 - 2 minutes.
Exposure: South and southwest.

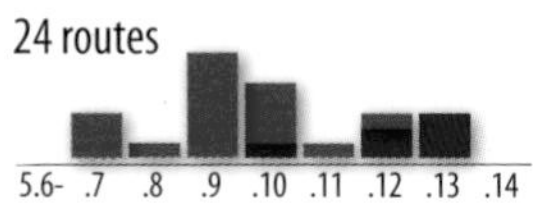

These two crags are located right off the road and offer easy access for a quick workout on quality granite. There are several desperate routes, along with nice moderates, and some excellent bouldering (see page 256).

Access: Travel 10.5 miles up the canyon to a pullout/parking area on the right side of the road. This will put you at the far right side of Tuck Crag. Walk up canyon to the obvious wall set back in the trees to reach Nip Crag. Take care with both parking and pulling out as the cliff is on a bend.

NIP CRAG

1 Ebb Tide 5.10a ★★ ☐
Climb the strenuous crack on the left side of the wall just left of a large overhang and orange lichen streak. Short but good.
Gear to 2 inches.

2 Night Train 5.9+ R ★ ☐
Climb the short corner up to the left side of the roof. Go left under the flake and then up the short corner to the top.
Gear to 3 inches.

3 Heart Throb 5.10d ★★ ☐
Climb the first part of *Night Train* up to the roof, veer right, then clip an old bolt above the roof and then up an easier slab to the top.
Gear to 3 inches.

4 Lethal Dose 5.10b R ★ ☐
Climb the obvious thin corner on the right side of the roof up to a steep face and runout climbing. Tricky placements and some questionable rock add to the excitement.
Gear to 2 inches.

5 Small Dose 5.12a ★★ ☐
Start 10 feet right of the corner. Climb over a small roof to a ramp and then a horn. Sling the horn and climb the face up and right to the finish for *Beguiled*.
Gear to 2 inches.

6 Beguiled 5.11a R ★ ☐
Climb a short left-facing corner right of *Small Dose* to right-facing flakes and then up the slab/face to a dirty right-facing corner and the top.
Gear to 2 inches.

7 Borrowed Time 5.10b R ★ ☐
Climb a short thin flake to a slab and then angle right up to the finish for *Left-Angling Crack*.
Gear to 2 inches.

8 Left-Angling Crack 5.9 ★ ☐
Near a cluster of small aspens, climb a short left-facing flake to a small roof and then up to a thin left-leaning crack. Climb the crack into a large corner to the top.
Gear to 2 inches.

9 Doc's Route 5.7 ★★ ☐
The obvious bolted route just left of a large corner. A medium stopper calms the nerves to the first bolt.
5 bolts, medium stopper or small cam.

10 Bock 5.7 ★ ☐
Climb the face/corner just left of the *Arete*. Veer right near the top for the anchor on *Arete*.
Gear to 3 inches.

11 Arete 5.10b ★★ ☐
Climb the nice looking arete on the left side of a block, passing five bolts to the anchor.
5 bolts.

⑫ Antagonism 5.12a/b ★★ ☐
Climb the clean face just right of the arete, pulling a hard move over a small roof near the top. Foot intensive.
4 bolts.

⑬ Finger Crack 5.9 ★★★ ☐
Classic. Climb the nice finger crack on the right side of the block. Strenuous with flaring locks.
Gear to 2 inches.

TUCK CRAG

Go right from *Finger Crack*, past a gully, to the start of Tuck Crag.

⑭ Surprising Slab 5.8 R ★ ☐
Climb the left of two thin seams with sparse gear up a nice slab about 15 feet left of the obvious corner.
Gear to 2 inches.

⑮ Hare Balls 5.7 ★ ☐
Climb the slab/thin seams with little protection five feet left of the corner.
Gear to 1 inch.

⑯ Dan-D-Line 5.7 ★★ ☐
Climb the slab right of the corner up to a slab, then through a small roof to a face and the top.
Gear to 2 inches.

⑰ Hypotenuse 5.9+ ★★ ☐
Climb the attractive left-facing dihedral up past a short roof.
Gear to 1 inch.

⑱ Spread Eagles Dhare 5.9 R ★ ☐
Start for *Hypotenuse*, climbing past the first roof. Veer right (dicey) to gain the arête. Climb the arete/crack and then move left near the top to finish.
Gear to 2 inches.

⑲ Constrictor 5.9 ★ ☐
Start right of the arete up a flaring slot/corner to a ledge and a thin crack. Follow the crack and then the broken face to the top.
Gear to 2 inches.

⑳ Boiling Point 5.9+ ★★ ☐
Climb a corner/ramp that leads to a vertical crack through a roof and then up a short face.
Gear to 2 inches

㉑ Argus 5.13c ☐
A series of burly moves (sloping/bear hugs) off the ground leads to much easier climbing up a steep face to the anchor. The route has been bouldered to the ledge 25 feet up, and in this form is known as *Caddis v9/10 (see page 261)*.
5 bolts.

㉒ Gyro Captain 5.12b/c ★★ ☐
Start on the right side of the severely overhanging east face. Make a mantel move to gain a ledge, veer left from the ledge, and power over the lip to the anchor. Short and powerful.
4 bolts.

㉓ Mr. Spiffy 5.13a ★★ ☐
Start as for *Gyro Captain* to the ledge. Climb slightly right and then straight up using power side pulls to a hard lip encounter. Whimper over the lip and then up to the anchor.
5 bolts.

㉔ Mr. Stiffie 5.13d ★★ ☐
Start as for *Gyro Captain* to the ledge, move up and right following the right angling crack/seam past four bolts to the anchor.
6 bolts.
Variation: **Low Left Start** 5.14a ★★ ☐

STEPPING STONES 10.8 miles

Approach time: 5 - 8 minutes.
Exposure: Southwest.

A nice compact piece of stone set on a forested hillside back in the woods. The west-facing wall receives great late-afternoon sun. The wall has seen a number of good routes put up in the last year and is popular with the pad people for its long bouldering traverse (The Barrio) in a slot on its southwest face. For more on The Barrio see "Bouldering in Boulder Canyon," page 256.

Access: Park at a large pullout on the left side of the road 10.8 miles up the canyon. Hike back down canyon for 100 yards and cross the road to a guardrail. Follow the trail that leads up and left to the wall.

❶ Contortionist's Pleasure 5.9+ ☐
On the left side of the wall is a great warm-up that climbs a short dihedral which leads left to a short hand crack.
Variation: 5.9. Climb in from the right (bolts) and join *Contortionist's Pleasure* at the third bolt.
4 bolts and a 1.5 inch cam.

❷ Bruno 5.10a ★ ☐
The third bolted line on the left side of the wall. Shares anchors with *Contortionist's Pleasure*.
5 bolts.

❸ Turkey Neck Direct 5.11d ★★ ☐
The fourth route from the left. Climb a white corner to stepped roofs to the anchor.
7 bolts.

❹ El Gallito 5.11b/c ★ ☐
The second route left of the black streak (*Magie Noire*). Good, short, and little runout to the anchor.
4 bolts.

❺ Pinche Guey 5.12b ★★★ ☐
Start by *Magie Noire* and head up and left to clip the first bolt. Continue up to the roof were the business begins, climb the roof, and race your arms to the anchor.
6 bolts.

❻ Magie Noire 5.11b/c ★★ ☐
Cool climbing up a black-streaked wall leads to crux moves at the fourth and fifth bolts.
6 bolts.

❼ Warlock Pinchers 5.12a ★★ ☐
A direct start to *Magie Noire* that has bouldery moves on nice, featured black granite. Join *Magie Norie* at the fourth bolt.
7 bolts.

❽ Québec Connection 5.11a ☐
The overhanging dihedral on the right side of the wall. Bouldery moves past the first two bolts lead to easier climbing above. Nice route.
4 bolts and cams 2-4 inches.

Around the corner to the right is a long traversing wall, filled with chalk and a fair amount of glue. The Barrio offers a good pump on now solid rock. The traverse is rated 5.13b and is worth the effort and pump to attempt. See the Bouldering Section page 256.

❾ Steeping Stone 5.8 ☐
Start on the far right side of the *Barrio Traverse*; ascend a featured wall with good climbing on somewhat dirty rock.
SR.

❿ Cruisin' For Neo's 5.10b ★ ☐
A separate pillar with a wide crack faces west about 20 feet right of the traverse. Start right of the crack and fire into a thin dihedral to a finger and handcrack at the top.
Gear to 4.5 inches

⓫ Barney Rubble Pile 5.11a/b ☐
A large roof juts out of the south face. This route climbs up to and through the roof.
TR.

CASTLE ROCK, THEN AND NOW

Royal Robbins Athlete's Feat

I have always thought Boulder Canyon is a marvelous resource. There is so much there and it is all granite. Of course, the main rock is Castle Rock, and it is a delicious hunk of rock with many fine routes on which to use up one's excess energy. Most of the routes have good protection and Boulder Canyon and Castle Rock are close to Boulder, where there are many climbers and where I spent a lot of time. I remember Boulder Canyon as a place where the climbs were all challenging testpieces and where one had to be quite physically fit.

What I remember about *Athlete's Feat* is the difficult, scary beginning. As I remember, you do a difficult mantel onto a sort of white flake. I was having a good day then as it was rather unprotected. Then there were crack pitches above, the third one off the ground requiring aid at the time. It was hard, strenuous jamming up there, and you had to thrash around and jam the feet and hands, but at least there were cracks where you could get protection. Ultimately, what sticks in my mind after all of these years is the risky first pitch and the strenuous jams above. I was glad to have Pat with me. I knew I could rely on him.

Matt Wilder **Viceroy**

Castle Rock was the very first place I climbed in Boulder Canyon. From the beginning the cliff struck me with its unique setting and position. As I became familiar with some of the routes, I began looking at the wall with a more inquisitive eye: is that a climb there, what about that feature, I wonder if there is any gear up there on that face? It seemed that much of the cliff had been developed but one blunt arête feature stood out. It loomed above a striking existing crack climb that ended in the middle of the face. From the ground, the arête looked possible and it appeared as if there might be enough gear. Having gleaned as much info as I could from the ground, I decided to rap the route to check out the upper section. Upon closer inspection, I realized that the climb was completely possible.

Inspired by the beauty and feasibility of the line, I quickly began working it on toprope. As I started making bigger links, I began thinking about the style I wanted to climb the route. It quickly became evident to me that I wanted to redpoint the route using only traditional gear even though the lower section was equipped with bolts and the upper section also had one bolt. The lower part of the route is a crack that takes good gear and the upper section has a perfect gear pod in the middle of it. I felt as if the wall should never have been bolted and decided to establish the extension without using the bolts. Because of its difficulty and danger, I decided to rehearse the moves on toprope before committing to the full lead. Eventually I felt confident on the moves and my endurance was also up to the challenge. I sent the route on my first redpoint attempt not counting the attempts I had made the previous season when I was far from ready to send. I named the route *Viceroy* because the upper section of the route looks to me like the *Star Wars* character Nute Gunray when viewed in profile.

NURSING HOME 10.8 miles

Approach time: 5 minutes.
Exposure: South and west.

10 routes

A convenient crag that has a few good routes and some excellent bouldering (see page 256) on its south-facing walls.

Access: Park at the large pullout on the left side of the road 10.8 miles up the canyon. Cross the road and climb the short hill to the lower tier.

bouldering (page 256)

bouldering (page 256)

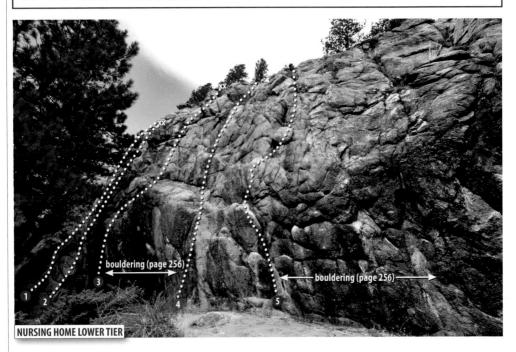

NURSING HOME LOWER TIER

LOWER TIER

❶ Sundowning 5.9+ ☐

The left route on the lower tier.

4 bolts.

❷ Grampa's Day Out 5.9 ★ ☐

Just right of *Sundowning*. Short but with several nice moves.

4 bolts.

❸ Aricept 5.11a/b ★★ ☐

Start below the obvious black streak. Easier if you use the block. Climb the black overhanging flare making hard moves past the first bolt. Clip the second bolt then continue straight up on good holds passing two more bolts getting to the anchor.

4 bolts.

❹ Lost Dentures 5.9+ ☐

Start at an obvious flake in the center of the rock. Climb the flake (or climb the thin crack on the left, 5.10). Veer left, then straight up thin seams/cracks to the anchor.

1 bolt and small to medium gear.

❺ Hip Replacement 5.10d ★★ ☐

Start on the same flake for *Lost Dentures*. Stick clip the first bolt and reach right to a small layaway. Crank to a good bucket and then follow the bolts to the anchor.

3 bolts.

Really good bouldering exists on this wall, with several problems in the V0 to V11 range.

UPPER TIER

Reach the Upper Tier by skirting the Lower Tier on the left.

6 Elder Abuse 5.11a R ☐☐

Climb a short slab to a bolt, then corner crack on the left. Follow the handcrack to the top.

1 bolt, gear to 2.5 inches

7 Sponge Bath 5.9+ ☐☐

Sponge Bath climbs the slab and then the handcrack on the left up a steep face past two bolts.

2 bolts, couple of 2 inch cams

8 Depends 5.7- ☐☐

Start as for *Sponge Bath*. Climb the slab, clip the first bolt and then climb straight up to a short corner past a bolt to the anchor.

2 bolts, small to medium wires.

9 Devil in Disguise 5.10a ★★ ☐☐

The short bolted corner on the upper tier.

3 bolts.

10 Angel of Mercy 5.11a ★★ ☐☐

Maybe the best route on the rock. The overhanging face just right of *Devil in Disguise*.

4 bolts.

NURSING HOME UPPER TIER

NURSING HOME UPPER TIER

RETIREMENT CRAG 10.8 miles

Approach time: 10 - 15 minutes.
Exposure: West.

5 routes

5.6- .7 .8 .9 .10 .11 .12 .13 .14

A very nice west-facing crag that gets great afternoon sun in the winter.

Access: Park at the large pullout on the left side of the road 10.8 miles up the canyon. Cross the creek and then angle slightly up and right (west) to the crag. There is a faint trail but be aware of sticker bushes.

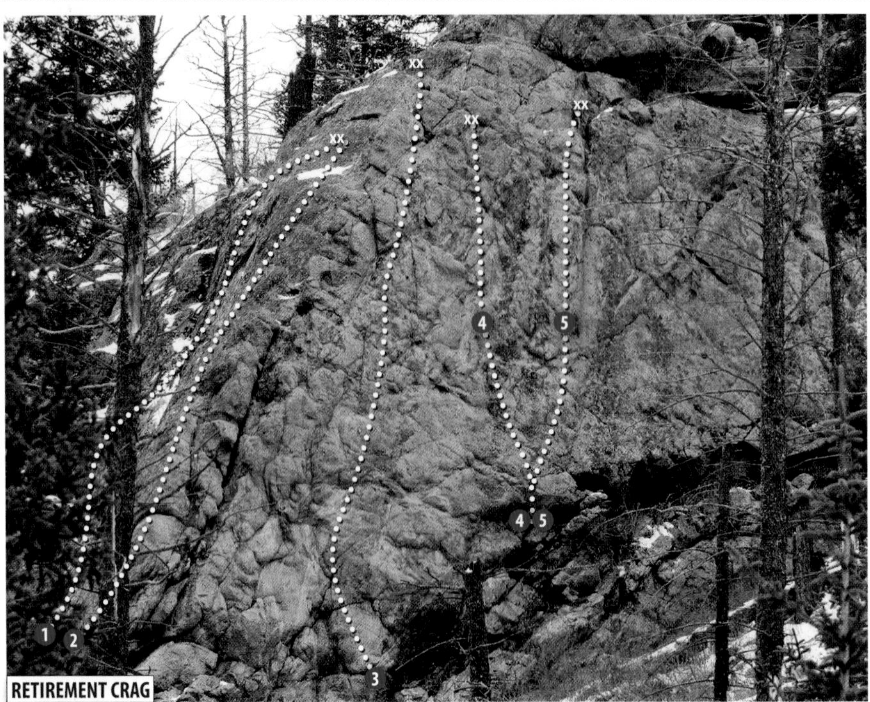

RETIREMENT CRAG

1 Second Career 5.8
A short safe lead on the north-facing slab on the far left side of the rock.
5 bolts.

2 Senior Discount 5.8 ★
Climb the right side of the slab with some nice moves. Use as an access route to hang draws or set top ropes for routes on the west face.
5 bolts.

3 Let the Daylight In 5.12b ★★
Start just right of the arete on the west face. Make a hard move left past the first bolt. Several hard moves get you to a dish and bad holds. Crank the crux moves and power up and left to the arete. Follow the bolts to the anchor.
7 bolts.

4 Early Bird Special 5.11a ★★
On the west face, start 15 feet right of the arete. Climb up the steep face on small holds to a two-bolt anchor on a ledge. A good route that gives a forearm pump.
6 bolts.

5 Fixed Income 5.11a
The start is the same as *Early Bird Special*. Climb up to the first bolt on *Early Bird Special* then move right to the second bolt. Fire straight up on fairly good holds to the crux around the fourth bolt. Power past the fifth bolt and reach a two-bolt anchor. Good route and wonderful face climbing. Should clean up with more ascents.
6 bolts.

COUCH FIRE CRAG 11.6 miles

Approach time: 5 - 10 minutes.
Exposure: South.

2 routes

5.6- .7 .8 .9 .10 .11 .12 .13 .14

A short wall located on the north side of the road, just downstream from Castle Rock.

Access: Drive 11.6 miles up the canyon to a small pullout on the right side of the road. Angle up and right to reach the base of the wall.

1 Recliner 5.10b ★
On the left side of the crag climb a short face up to a roof, crank the roof and reach the anchors.
3 bolts.

2 Sofa Mart 5.11a ★
Climb the blunt arête to good holds, continue straight up to the anchors.
4 bolts.

3 Loveseat 5.12b ★
Fire up the short face and gain the corner and then the anchor.
4 bolts.

4 Couch Fire 5.12d ★★
Climb the steep face via cracks/ seams to the anchor.
4 bolts.

5 Open Project 5.13?
Hard crack.
Bolt anchors.

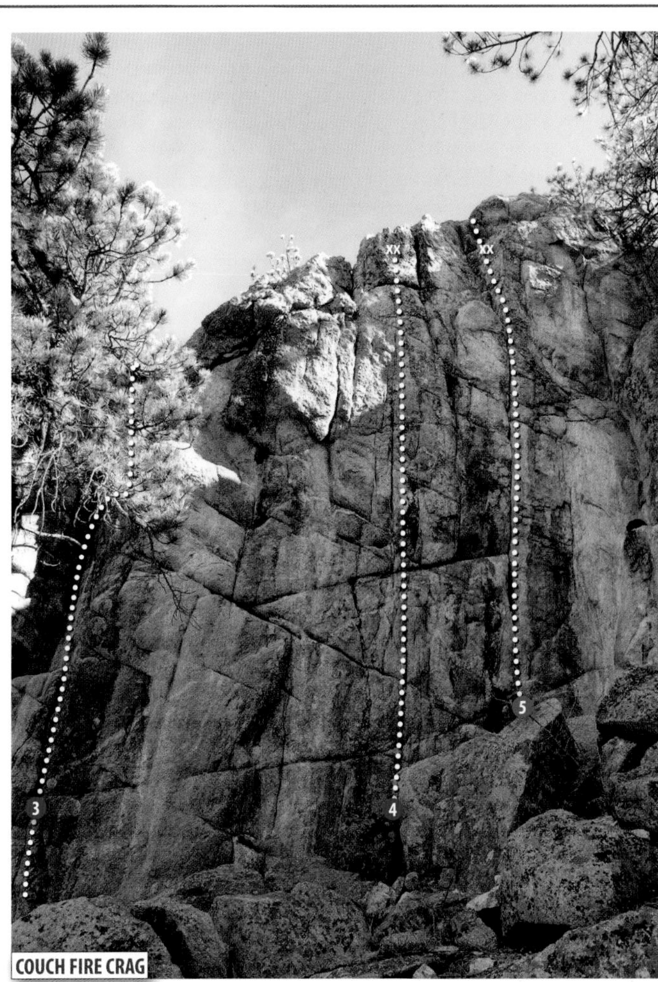

COUCH FIRE CRAG

CASTLE ROCK 12.0 miles

Exposure: East, south and west.
Approach time: 30 seconds to two minutes.

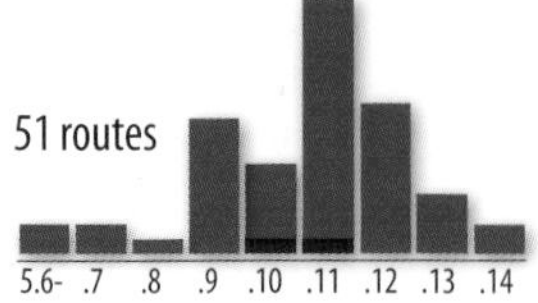

This impressive crag sits just off the highway and offers the best selection of trad routes in the canyon. A road circles the rock and offers easy access with approaches taking seconds...not minutes. Castle Rock is also the most historic crag in the canyon and was the site of the hardest multi-pitch route in America in the early 60's. Classic routes and test pieces abound. The scenic Boulder Creek runs by the rock and offers a serene setting and cool water on hot summer days.

Access: Travel 11.8 miles up the canyon to a turnoff on the left for Castle Rock. Turn onto a dirt road that runs along the base of the wall. Find a parking space on the right by the creek.

Descent: Most of the popular routes can be rappel back to the base. The walk off is down the north face of the wall and is somewhat confusing for the first time user. Trees can be used to rappel off the descent route.

1 North Face 3rd Class to 5.4 ★ ☐
The descent route on the north face follows a series of ramps and ledges up or down the north face. If descending, one can rappel from trees back down to the base of the wall.
Gear to 2 inches.

2 West Face 5.6 ★ ☐
Pitch 1: 5.6. Climb a face and cracks just left of a wide crack on the left of the wall to an anchor below a tree about 80 feet up. One can also ascend the wide crack directly to the anchor.
Pitch 2: 5.5. Continue up and slightly right in a chimney and crack system behind the left side of a short tower of rock, aiming for the summit.
Variation: Big Deal Pinnacle 5.9 ☐
From the first belay, climb up to the tower/pinnacle, then climb the steep slab and reach a handcrack on the right that leads to top. Popular with the guiding crowd.
SR.

3 Polyester Leisure Suit 5.11a ★ ☐
Locate bolts just right of the wide crack. Climb a short face up and over a small roof. Power through the roof and climb the steep face up to a tree. Rap the route.
3 bolts, light rack to 2 inches.

4 Times Past 5.9 R ☐
Climb a shallow flare/groove just right of *Polyester Leisure Suit*. Climb through a small roof and then up and slightly left to a tree/anchor.
Gear to 3.5 inches.

5 Another Roadside Attraction 5.10c R ★ ☐
Climb a short face that leads to a thin angling crack over a small and then up the steep face. Reach a ledge at 70 feet and go left to the tree to rappel.
Gear to 2 inches.

6 Skunk Crack 5.9+ ★★ ☐
Climb a crack that leads into a slot. Struggle into and out of the slot and then angle right and up to a rap anchor.
Gear to 3 inches.

7 Comeback Crack 5.10b ★★★ ☐
Start just right of *Skunk Crack*. Hard moves off the ground lead to better jams. Climb over a small bugle and gain a ledge following thin cracks to the anchor.
Gear to 1.5 inches.

8 Storming the Castle 5.11b/c ★★ ☐
This route starts as for *Curving Crack* and then goes left to gain the smooth arete. Cool moves up the arete get you to a rap station.
5 bolts.

9 Curving Crack 5.9+ ★★ ☐
The obvious curving crack on the right side of the west face. Classic, and the grade depends on the humidity level.
Gear to 2 inches. Rap from the anchor.

10 Invisible Idiot 5.9 R ★ ☐
Start right of *Curving Crack* up shallow cracks to a hanging corner. Climb the corner and veer left up a short arete to the anchor for *Curving Crack*.
Gear to 3 inches.

11 Bailey's Overhang 5.8 ★★ ☐
Climb the obvious right-facing corner that leads to a roof to a cable anchor on the left. Rap to the ground.
Gear to 4 inches.

12 Final Exam 5.11a ★★★ ☐
Tricky. Climb a bulge with a thin crack running through it just right of *Bailey's Overhang*. Reach a good horn/hold and then follow cracks to below a roof, go left to the anchor for *Bailey's Overhang*.

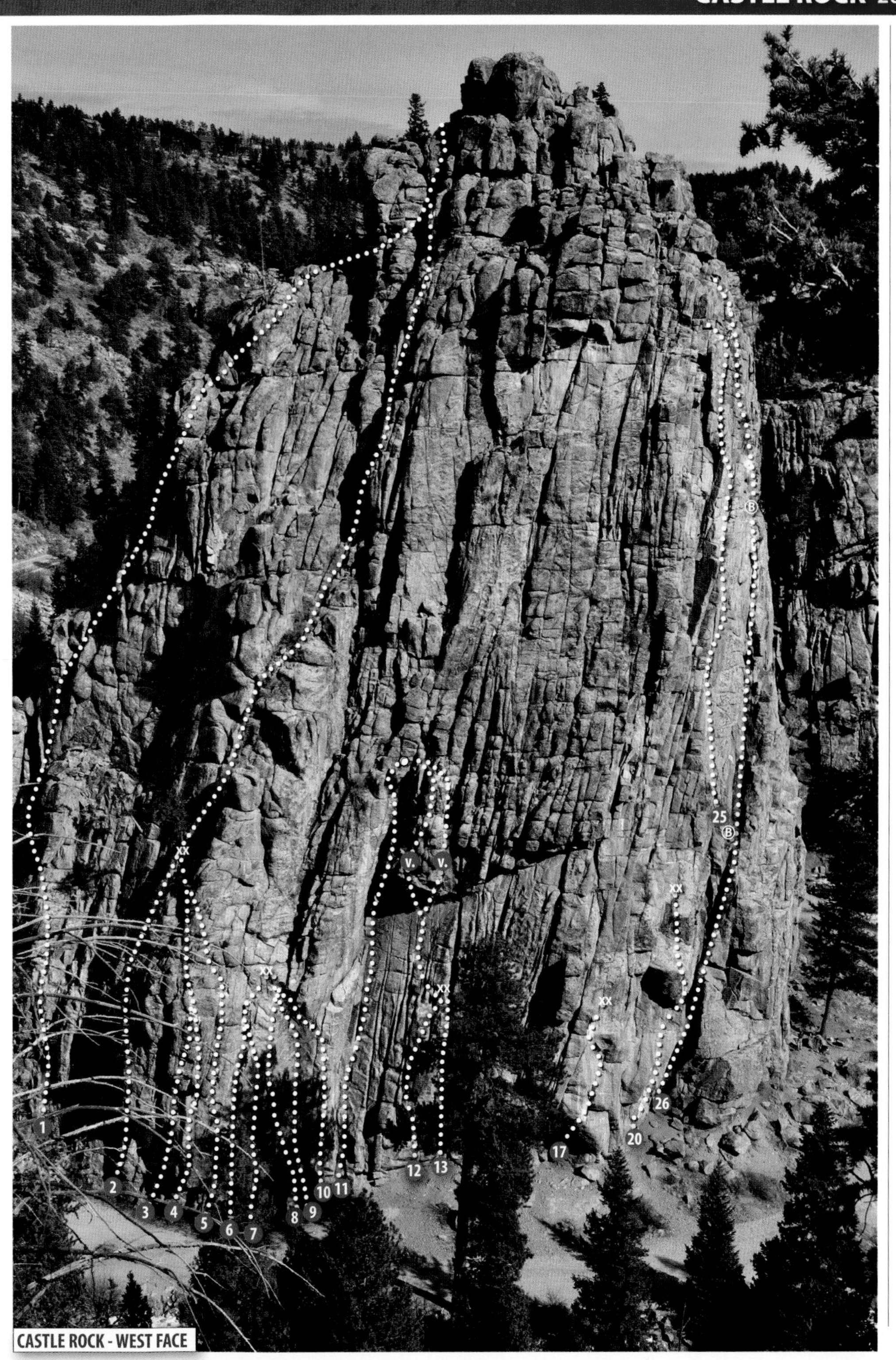

CASTLE ROCK - WEST FACE

Variation: Pass/Fail Option 5.11c ★★★ ☐

Instead of traversing left, continue up and over the large roof to a belay. Continue up easier rock or rappel from anchors.

Variation: Dropout Option 5.12b ★★ ☐

Climb the roof system six feet right of *Pass/Fail Option*.

Gear to 2.5 inches.

⑬ Coffin Crack 5.10b ★★ ☐

Climb the obvious wide crack just right of *Final Exam*. The business comes low and easier climbing leads to the belay. Rap from a station slightly down and right.

Gear to 5 inches.

⑭ By Gully 5.9+ ★★ ☐

Climb the large wide crack/slot just left of the large roof system to a ledge. Rap or continue up the easier crack to the top.

Gear to 5 inches.

⑮ Headline Project ☐

This impressive route tackles the large roof just right of *By Gully*. It follows the old *Practice Aid Roof* (C2) and has seen lots of free climbing attention, though no free ascent as of publication.

Gear to 2 inches.

⑯ Deadline 5.13d ★★ ☐

Climb the right side of the large roof out a black crack to the lip passing two bolts and pins.

2 bolts, gear to 1.5 inches.

⑰ The Campaigner 5.12d ★★ ☐

Climb the obvious flaring crack on the right side of the roof. The crux comes quickly, once over the bulge rap from a fixed anchor.

Gear to 2 inches.

⑱ Rebellion 5.12b ★★ ☐

Climb the left-facing dihedral just right of *the Campaigner*. Make a hard move at a bolt to reach the slab and then angle left to *the Campaigner* and rap/lower.

1 bolt, gear to 1 inch.

⑲ Victim of Circumstance 5.13b ★★ ☐

Climb a short face that leads to a smooth left-facing corner. Decipher technical moves through the corner and then go left to the *Campaigner*. Grossly underrated by the FA party at 5.12b.

Gear to 1 inch.

⑳ Viceroy 5.14a/b ★★★ ☐

See description opposite.

㉑ Nuclear Winter 5.12b ★ ☐

A large gully (*Jackson's Wall*) splits the west face from the south face. This route starts near a cave in the gully. Follow a line of bolts then veer left across the wall to the anchor for *Viceroy*.

7 bolts.

㉒ Cussin' Crack 5.7 ★★★ ☐

Pitch 1: 5.7. Climb the face right of the chimney. Place small gear and continue up and traverse straight left to a ledge with an old bolt. Make a tricky move past the bolt and gain a ledge.

Pitch 2: 5.7. Move the belay to a higher ledge at the start of the V-slot. Climb the slot to a belay on a good ledge at the top of the V-slot.

Pitch 3: 5.7. Continue up to a corner and roof, pass it on the left, and enjoy easier climbing up to a good ledge about 30 feet below the summit. Belay here. Scramble to the top and walk off to the north.

SR.

㉓ Cadaver Crack 5.11a ★ ☐

Pitch 1: 5.7. Climb the first pitch of *Cussin' Crack* to a belay at the V-slot.

Pitch 2: 5.11a. Move left from the belay and then climb a steep handcrack to a ledge and the anchor.

Gear to 2.5 inches.

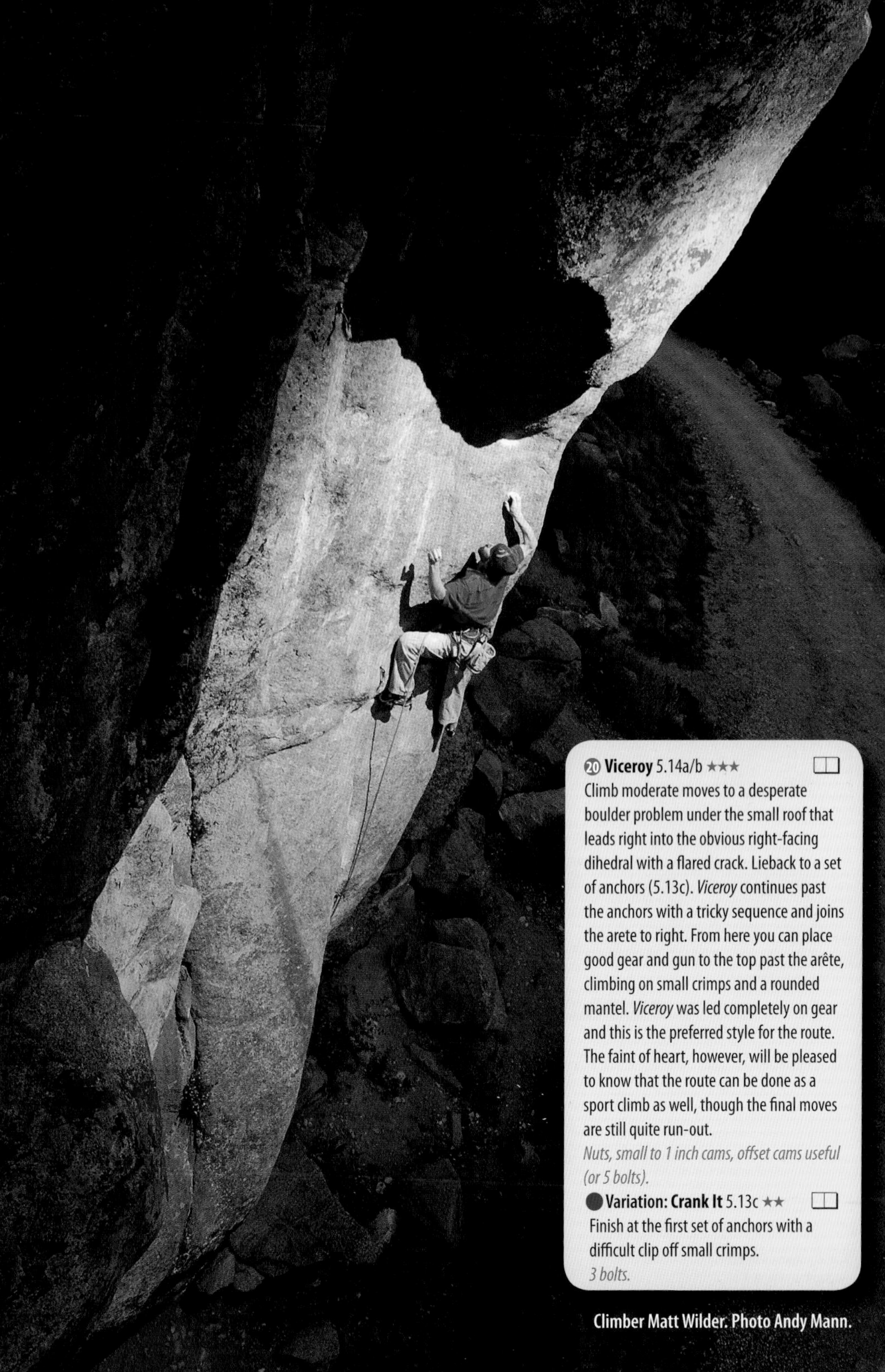

⑳ Viceroy 5.14a/b ★★★ ☐

Climb moderate moves to a desperate boulder problem under the small roof that leads right into the obvious right-facing dihedral with a flared crack. Lieback to a set of anchors (5.13c). *Viceroy* continues past the anchors with a tricky sequence and joins the arete to right. From here you can place good gear and gun to the top past the arête, climbing on small crimps and a rounded mantel. *Viceroy* was led completely on gear and this is the preferred style for the route. The faint of heart, however, will be pleased to know that the route can be done as a sport climb as well, though the final moves are still quite run-out.

Nuts, small to 1 inch cams, offset cams useful (or 5 bolts).

● **Variation: Crank It** 5.13c ★★ ☐

Finish at the first set of anchors with a difficult clip off small crimps.

3 bolts.

Climber Matt Wilder. Photo Andy Mann.

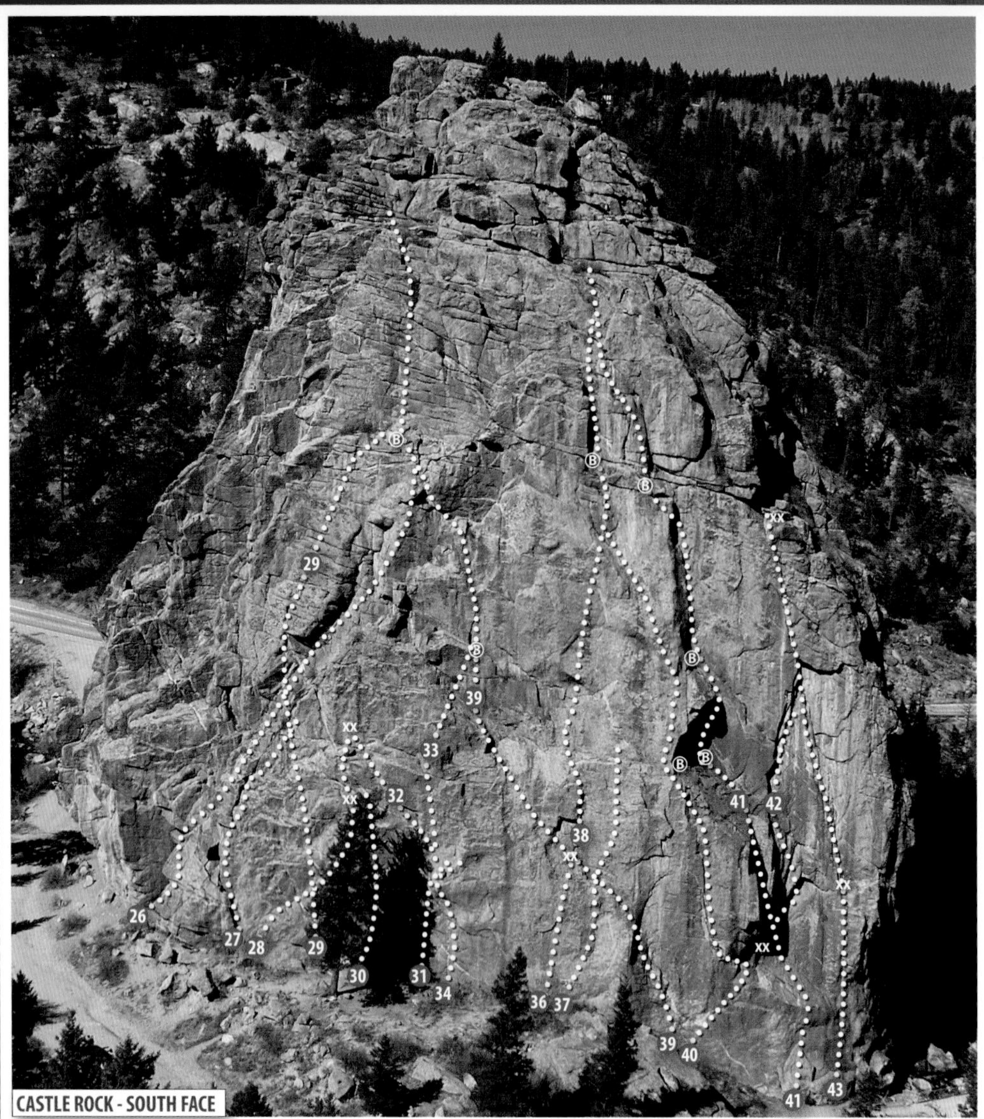

CASTLE ROCK - SOUTH FACE

24 Sticky Fingers 5.10c/d ★★ ☐

Pitch 1: 5.7. Climb the first pitch of *Cussin' Crack* to the V-slot.

Pitch 2: 5.10c/d. Step right from the belay and climb a thin crack to the belay pitch below the third pitch of *Cussin Crack*.

SR.

25 Western Pleasure 5.11a ★★ ☐

Pitch 1: 5.11a. Climb the chimney/face start of *Jackson's Wall* for 90 feet to a shallow dihedral on the left. Climb the dihedral past pins, over a small roof to gain a steep face (bolts) to a belay left of *Jackson's Wall*.

Pitch 2: 5.10a. Climb the steep face above the belay to a finger crack; climb the crack then up to the summit. Walk off to the north.

2 bolts, pins, gear to 3 inches.

26 Jackson's Wall 5.7 ★★ ☐

Pitch 1: 5.6. Climb the chimney or the face to the right to easy climbing trending right to a ledge with an anchor at 150 feet.

Pitch 2: 5.6. Move slightly right then up to gain a crack/ramp that leads to summit.

SR.

27 Circadian Rhythms 5.9+ ★★ ☐

Right of *Jackson's Wall*, a chimney meets a sloping right-angling ramp. Climb the squeeze chimney to a thin crack, follow the crack to its end and then go right to the anchor for *Tongo*.

Gear to 2 inches. Rap from the anchor.

28 Tongo 5.11a R ★★★ ☐

Pitch 1: 5.10b. Climb the ramp/crack right of the squeeze chimney to a belay below a small roof. One can also climb a short face on the right (start of *After Forever*) to gain the ramp.

Pitch 2: 5.11a. Fire the roof using face holds on the left up the anchor. Rappel. Classic!

Gear to 2 inches.

29 After Forever 5.11c ★★ ☐

A wandering line that packs a lot of climbing into one pitch. Start right of *Tongo* at a pine tree. Climb up a short face to gain the ramp, continue past two bolts to *Jackson's Wall*, traverse left toward *Cussin' Crack* and climb right of *Sticky Fingers* past a roof to a thin crack. Follow the crack to the belay for *Western Pleasure*.

3 bolts, gear to 3 inches.

30 Atlas Shrugged 5.11d ★★★ ☐

Right of *Tongo* is a right-leaning ramp just left of a fire pit. Climb the steep ramp/face (RP's) past two bolts to a left-leaning crack. Fire out the crack and then to the anchor for the first pitch of *Tongo*.

Gear to 2 inches.

31 Black Crack 5.9+ ★ ☐

Climb the right-leaning crack right of the fire pit over a small roof to anchors.

Gear to 2.5 inches.

32 The Sting 5.11c R ★ ☐

Start with *Black Crack* and climb to the anchor. Head left on the face to a reach a shallow dihedral moving right to the anchors on *Tongo*.

Gear to 2.5 inches.

33 Stingray 5.12a ★ ☐

Climb to the anchor for *Black Crack*. Climb left on *The Sting* and then over a small roof and up short face to a ledge. Go right to anchor for *South Face*. Rappel.

Gear to 2 inches.

34 The Gill Crack 5.12a ★★★ ☐

Climb the obvious thin finger crack, stepping left to *Black Crack* after 25 feet. Follow *Black Crack* to the anchor or down climb *Black Crack* below the roof. Three stars for historical merit — John Gill soloed the route on the FFA (also see the bouldering section, page 256).

Gear to 1 inch.

35 Alien Sex Toy 5.13b ★★★ ☐

Right of the *Gill Crack* is an arching roof/flake down low. Climb over the roof, then up the steep face past several bolts to the anchor for the *South Face*. I don't know of anyone who has repeated this route.

5 bolts, pins and micro-cams.

36 Close to the Edge 5.12b/c ★★ ☐

Right of *Alien Sex Toy* is a smooth, steep slab/face. Climb the face past three bolts with the crux clipping and climbing past the third bolt. Move right to the anchor for the *South Face*.

2 bolts, gear to 1.5 inches.

37 The Boot Lead 5.12a R ★★ ☐

Pitch 1: 5.12a R. Climb a short face to a right leaning flake/shallow corner. Make hard moves up the shallow corner past a fixed head to the *South Face* anchor.

Pitch 2: 5.11a. From the anchor, step right and climb the steep face past two bolts to a fixed anchor.

Gear to 1 inch.

Descent: Rap the route.

38 Corinthian Vine 5.12c/d ★★ ☐

Pitch 1: 5.9+. Climb the first pitch of the *South Face* to the anchor.

Pitch 2: 5.10b R. Climb up a short corner going right out a small roof and then straight up to a belay.

Pitch 3: 5.12c/d. Climb up a ramp to the right of the belay past bolts leading to a roof. Crank the roof (crux) and then up a ramp to a ledge and the belay.

Pitch 4: 5.9. Climb the obvious right-facing corner to the summit.

SR, plus extra quickdraws.

39 South Face 5.9+ ★★★ ☐

A true classic that weaves a great line up the south face of *Castle Rock*.

Pitch 1: 5.9-. Climb a short face leading to a right-facing corner. Climb the corner for 15 feet then go left, passing an anchor. Climb left past the anchor on a smooth slab and then up to a ledge with a fixed pins.

Pitch 2: 5.9+. Climb up and then slightly right onto a ramp. Follow the ramp, stepping left at the top. Make a dicey move to another ramp/crack with a fixed pin. Climb up to a good ledge and belay.

Pitch 3: 5.6. Follow the upper pitch of *Jackson's Wall* to the summit.

SR.

40 Never a Dull Moment 5.12a/b ★★★ ☐

Pitch 1: 5.12a. Climb a smooth slab traversing right to the anchor for *Athlete's Feat* and belay.

Variation: 5.12a/b. Locate a lone bolt left of the normal start that leads directly to the second crack pitch of *Never a Dull Moment*.

Pitch 2: 5.12a/b. Move left from the belay and then fire up the crack with hard moves to reach the belay ledge.

Pitch 3: 5.11b. Move left and climb a shallow corner past two bolts, reach a third bolt on the arete, go left and up a ramp climbing easier rock to a ledge.

Pitch 4: 5.8. Climb the nice corner to the summit.

SR.

41 Athlete's Feat 5.11a ★★★★ ☐

Mega classic and one of the finest routes in the canyon. This route may have been one of the longest and hardest free climbs in the world when Royal Robbins and Pat Ament climbed it free in 1964.

Pitch 1: 5.11a. Climb a short pointed boulder then up a short face past past two bolts and then left across the slab to the anchor.

Pitch 2: 5.10d. Climb the obvious strenuous flaring corner/crack to a good ledge and the belay.

Pitch 3: 5.10b/c. Climb another layback crack/corner to a good ledge and belay.

Pitch 4: 5.10b/c. The difficulties continue up the flaring crack/corner that leads to a good ledge.

Pitch 5: 5.9+. A short right-facing corner leads to the summit.

SR.

Descent: Walk off to the north.

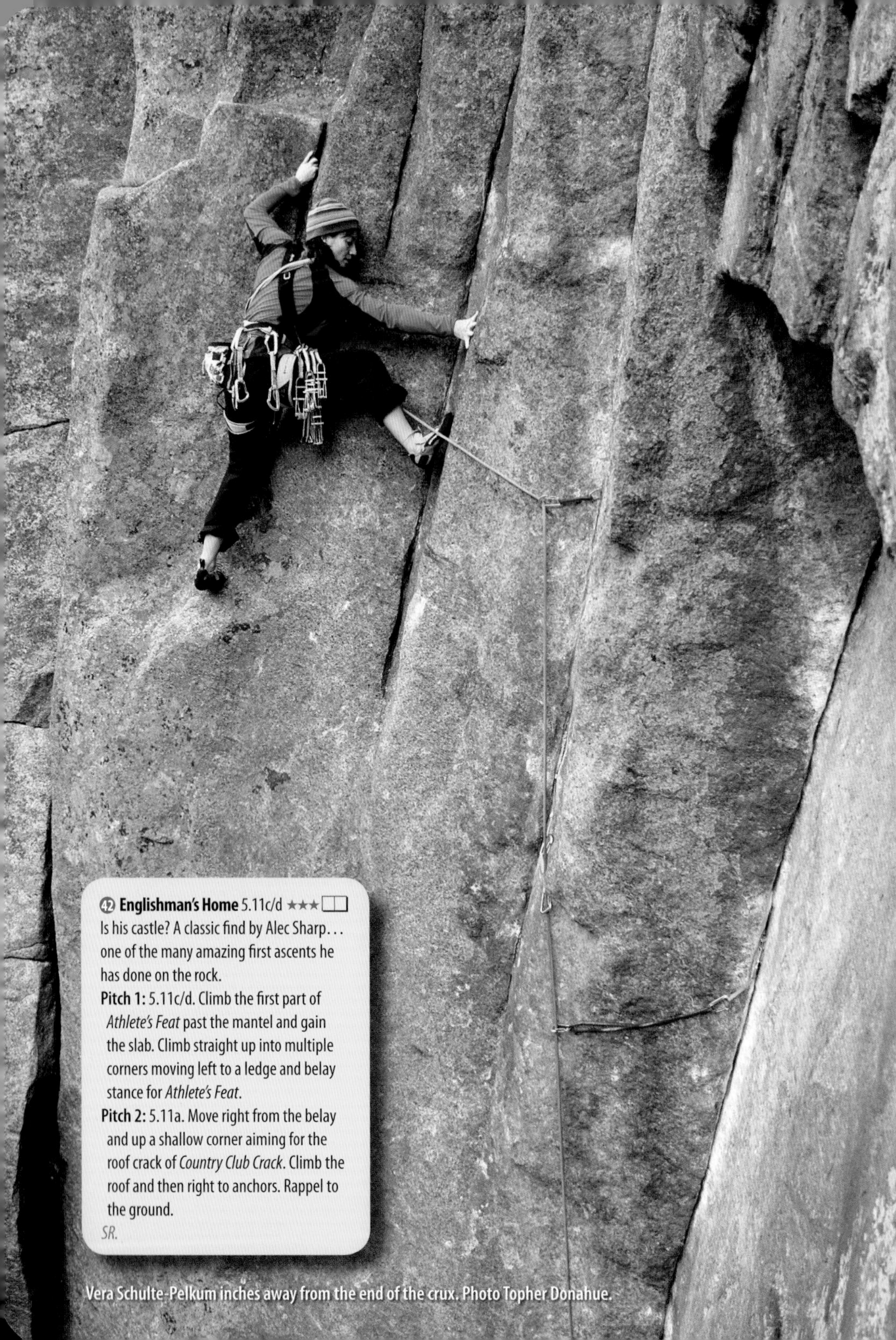

42 Englishman's Home 5.11c/d ★★★ ☐☐
Is his castle? A classic find by Alec Sharp... one of the many amazing first ascents he has done on the rock.

Pitch 1: 5.11c/d. Climb the first part of *Athlete's Feat* past the mantel and gain the slab. Climb straight up into multiple corners moving left to a ledge and belay stance for *Athlete's Feat*.

Pitch 2: 5.11a. Move right from the belay and up a shallow corner aiming for the roof crack of *Country Club Crack*. Climb the roof and then right to anchors. Rappel to the ground.

SR.

Vera Schulte-Pelkum inches away from the end of the crux. Photo Topher Donahue.

42 Englishman's Home 5.11c/d ★★★ ☐
Description opposite.

43 Country Club Crack 5.11c ★★★★ ☐
Classic and historical. For years this was *the* testpiece in Boulder Canyon.
Pitch 1: 5.11c. Climb a short flake to a blank face. Crank past two bolts and gain a ledge, follow the crack up to spacious belay ledge.
Pitch 2: 5.11a. Continue up the crack with increasing difficulty to below the roof. A kneebar gains a slight rest. Fire the roof and then thin finger jamming with fading feet will get you to the anchor on the right.
Variation: Spin Off 5.11c ☐
After the bottom face moves on pitch 1 go left to a thin right-facing corner, climb the corner (vegetated) moving right at the top to the belay.
Variation: Nobody's Home 5.12d ☐
Undercling right halfway out the roof on pitch 2 and gain a sloping rail/holds that lead to the anchor.
SR to 3.5 inches.

44 Tourist Extravagance 5.13a ★★ ☐
Start right of *Country Club Crack* near the water. A steep slab past two bolts gains a flake and then a good stance. Climb a thin crack and then move right to the anchor for *Radio Andromeda*.
SR to 2 inches.

45 Radio Andromeda 5.11b/c ★★ ☐
Burly climbing on somewhat polished rock.
Pitch 1: 5.11a/b. Climb up a wide flaring crack to below a small roof/overlap on the left. Traverse left under the roof and belay below an overhanging fist crack.
Pitch 2: 5.11b/c. Tackle the hand/fist crack past hard jams to a wider section, cruise to the ledge. Follow corners to the top. Walk off to the north.
SR to 4 inches.

46 First Movement 5.11a ★ ☐
Start as for *Radio Andromeda* but continue straight up into a wide vegetated slot to a good belay ledge. Climb easy rock to the summit. Walk off to the north. Can be done in one long pitch.
SR to 4 inches.

CASTLE ROCK EAST FACE

47 Water World 5.11a/b ★★ ☐
Step left off the boulder onto the main wall and over to the wide slot that is the start of *First Movement*. Climb a short way up the slot, past an old pin, and work right to a small stance. Place pro in a good finger crack, then step onto the right wall, and make a slippery move up and right to a good edge. Continue up steep cracks to the top of the headwall. Clip the first bolt and make a difficult high-step mantel move onto the slab. Continue up the slab past three more bolts to the anchor.
4 bolts, light rack to 1.5 inches.

48 Route 66 5.9 ★ ☐
Climb the wide crack right of *Water World* gaining a wide slot. Continue up the slot and then easy rock to the top. Can be done in one long pitch or belay at the base of the slot.
SR to 4 inches.

49 Subterranean Homesick Blues 5.12a ★★ ☐
Pitch 1: 5.11b/c. Climb up and over a small roof (gear) and make a weird move to the first bolt. Crank up a seam past several bolts with dicey moves. At the sixth bolt, make a hard move straight up, and then continue straight up (gear & bolts) the cool slab to a two-bolt anchor.
Pitch 2: 5.12a. Crank up a flake and seam past two bolts, make a very hard slab move clipping and moving past the third bolt. Cool climbing past five more bolts leads to a two-bolt anchor. Rap the route.
14 quickdraws and #4 RP, 0.75 and 1 inch micro-cams.

50 Water Hazard 5.10a/b ★★ ☐
Pitch 1: 5.10b. Climb up shallow cracks to a good layback hold/crack. Step up and right on steep climbing (crux) past two bolts following the thin seams and cracks to a two-bolt anchor.
Pitch 2: 5.8. Follow cracks straight up from the belay to a ledge and two bolt anchor.
Eight quickdraws and gear to 3.5 inches.

51 The Big Splash 5.10b ★★ ☐
Pitch 1: 5.10b. The right-most route on the east face. Climb a nice slab up to a short steep headwall, crank through the headwall and then reach the anchor.
Pitch 2: 5.10b. Begin just left of the anchor. Climb the nice slab to the crux headwall. A red Alien may be placed before the 5th bolt.
8 quickdraws and 1 inch micro-cam.

BROKEN ROCK 12.0 miles

Approach time: 1 - 3 minutes.
Exposure: North and southwest.

14 routes

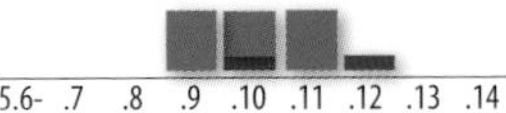

Right next to one of the most popular cliffs in Boulder Canyon, Broken Rock doesn't seem to garner much interest or attention. A great little crag with some very nice crack and face climbs.

Access: Travel 12.4 miles up the canyon to a turnoff on the left for Castle Rock, go to the bridge and park on the right just past the bridge. The rock is on the right.

Descent: Walk off to the west.

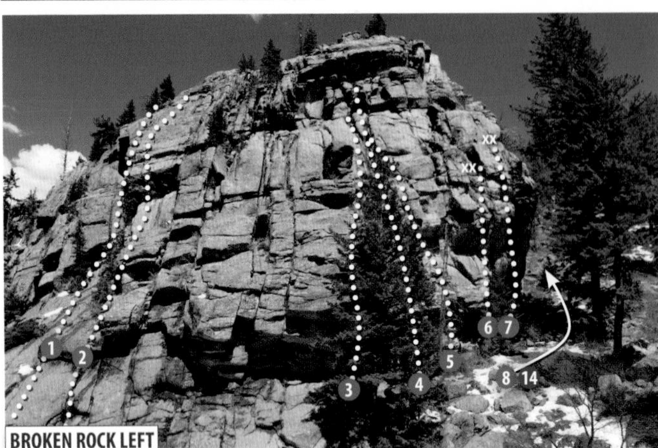

1 Undercling 5.9 ★ ☐
Pitch 1: 5.9. On the far left side of the rock, climb a slab to the obvious right-facing corner that faces northwest, then out a roof to a ledge.
Pitch 2: 5.7. Climb easier rock to the top.
Gear to 3 inches.

2 Whimsey 5.11b/c ★★ ☐
Pitch 1: 5.11b/c. Climb a short slab just left of the bridge aiming for a shallow crack below a square cut roof. Fire up and over the roof via bad and flaring jams. Belay on a good ledge.
Pitch 2: 5.8. Climb slabbier rock to the top.
Gear to 3 inches.

3 Cosmic Whimp-Out 5.11a/b ★ ☐
From the low point of the rock near the bridge, fire up a hand crack through a roof.
Gear to 3 inches.

4 Tree Trimmer 5.11c ★ ☐
Climb the obvious tiered overhang up and right of *Cosmic Whimp-Out*.
2 bolts, gear to 2 inches.

5 Hung Jury 5.9+ ★ ☐
Finding this route is the crux. Find a roof with a handcrack going out it 40 feet left of *Momentum Operator Crack*.
Gear to 3 inches.

6 Out to Pasture 5.10c/d ★★ ☐
Climb past two bolts and gain parallel cracks over a roof.
2 bolts, gear to 3 inches.

7 Momentum Operator Crack 5.11b ★★★ ☐
Climb the overhanging finger crack/slot to the roof, struggle past the roof, and gain a ledge.
Gear to 3 inches. Rap.

8 White Trash 5.11b ★★ ☐
Climb a crack up for 20 feet, step left and gain a blunt arete, then follow bolts to the anchor.
3 bolts, gear to 2 inches.

9 Crack Up 5.9 ★★ ☐
Climb the overhanging hand and fist crack in the corner up to a good ledge and the anchor.
Gear to 3 inches.

10 Eulogy 5.9+ ☐
Climb the left-facing corner just right of #9.
Gear to 3 inches.

11 Sue Song 5.10c/d ★ ☐
Climb the obvious flake moving left into a wide crack.
Gear to 3 inches.

12 South Beach 5.10a/b ★★ ☐
Start up a small overhang to reach a block, climb the left side, then go left and up the face/arete to the anchor.
6 bolts, a few small cams.

13 Fit for Life 5.12a ★★★ ☐
On the right side of the wall behind a large pine tree, climb steep rock up laybacks and crimps to a short crack and then the anchors. Technical and devious.
6 bolts and few small cams.

14 Muad'Dib 5.10b ★★ ☐
A cool slab climb located 50 feet up and right of *Fit for Life*. The crux comes low, with some cool moves to the anchor.
6 bolts.

Chris Carithers on *Tongo* 5.11a R, Castle Rock, page 206. Photo Adam Brink.

THE OVERLOOK 12.0 miles

Approach time: 10 minutes.
Exposure: North and west.

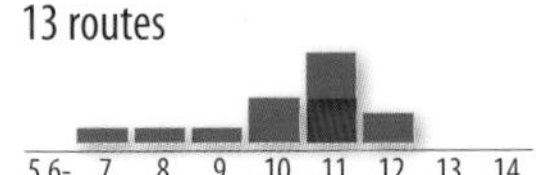

Sitting high above Castle Rock, The Overlook offers a few nice trad and sport routes with great views and seclusion.

Access: Drive 12.4 miles to Castle Rock, parking just past the bridge on the Castle Rock Road near the creek at the base of Broken Rock. Skirt Broken Rock on the right and hike five minutes uphill to trail that leads hard left once above Broken Rock. Contour left on this, along a big bench, to the crag.

1 Transylvania 5.11a ☐
On the very left side of the crag. Drop down past the overhanging section of the cliff to a cave and a large pine tree. The route starts at the pine tree and climbs up 20 feet to the steep face and the first bolt.
2 bolts and gear to 3.5 inches.

2 Yosemite Sam 5.10d ★★ ☐
Start 15 feet left of *Louisville Slugger* at the obvious overhanging crack. At the top, traverse right to the anchors of *Louisville Slugger* or walk off to the west.
Gear to 2.5 inches

3 Louisville Slugger 5.11b/c ★★ ☐
Start ten feet left of *Straight Out of Compton* and five feet left of *Golden Child* on the left side of the cliff. Cool moves to start.
5 bolts and a 1 inch micro-cam.

4 Golden Child 5.11c ★★ ☐
Power overhanging moves on good holds to start lead to easier climbing above. Tricky at the start and easier climbing up the crack to the anchor.
4 bolts, 1.5 inch and 2.5 inch cams.

5 Straight Out of Compton 5.8- ☐
The obvious right-facing corner.
Gear to 3.5 inches.

6 Denver Nugget 5.7+ ☐
The crack/corner right of *Straight Out of Compton*.
Gear to 3.5 inches.

7 Minnesota Fats 5.10a ★★★ ☐
Start ten feet right of *Denver Nugget*. Climb a short face to seams/crack. Really good route on excellent rock.
Gear to 2.5 inches

8 Lobo 5.10c ★ ☐
Climb the steep somewhat dirty crack just right of *Minnesota Fats*. At the top of the crack veer up and left to the anchor for *Minnesota Fats*.
Gear to 2.5 inches.

9 Greenfield 5.11b/c ★ ☐
Start just right of *Lobo*. Place an RP, make a hard move and then clip a bolt. Technical moves get you to a finger crack. Climb the crack to a large flake on the right. Move right into another corner and climb that to the top. You can also traverse at the top to the anchors for *Philadelphia Flyer* and lower from there. Great route with bouldery moves at the start.
2 bolts, gear to 2 inches.

10 Obscurity Risk 5.12a ★ ☐
Climb the steep wall/arete right of *Greenfield* past several pins and fixed wires.
Pins, fixed wires, bring small gear.

11 Philadelphia Flyer 5.11b/c ★★★ ☐
The route starts just left of *Jersey Devil*. Crank up on a good holds to clip the first bolt. Better yet, stick-clip it. Fire off a series of technical moves to a small corner and the second bolt. Make a hard move past the second bolt and reach a good flake. Place several good pieces and then reach a small stance below an overhanging handcrack. Fire up the crack (strenuous) to a weird move and then climb 20 feet to the anchor.
2 bolts, gear to 2.5 inches

12 Jersey Devil 5.9- ★★ ☐
Climb the obvious right-facing flake on the right side of the wall. A good route with the crux down low.
3 bolts, 1.5 inch cam.

13 The Probe 5.11b/c ☐
The first bolted route on the right side of the crag out a roof feature.
4 bolts, 1.5 inch cam.

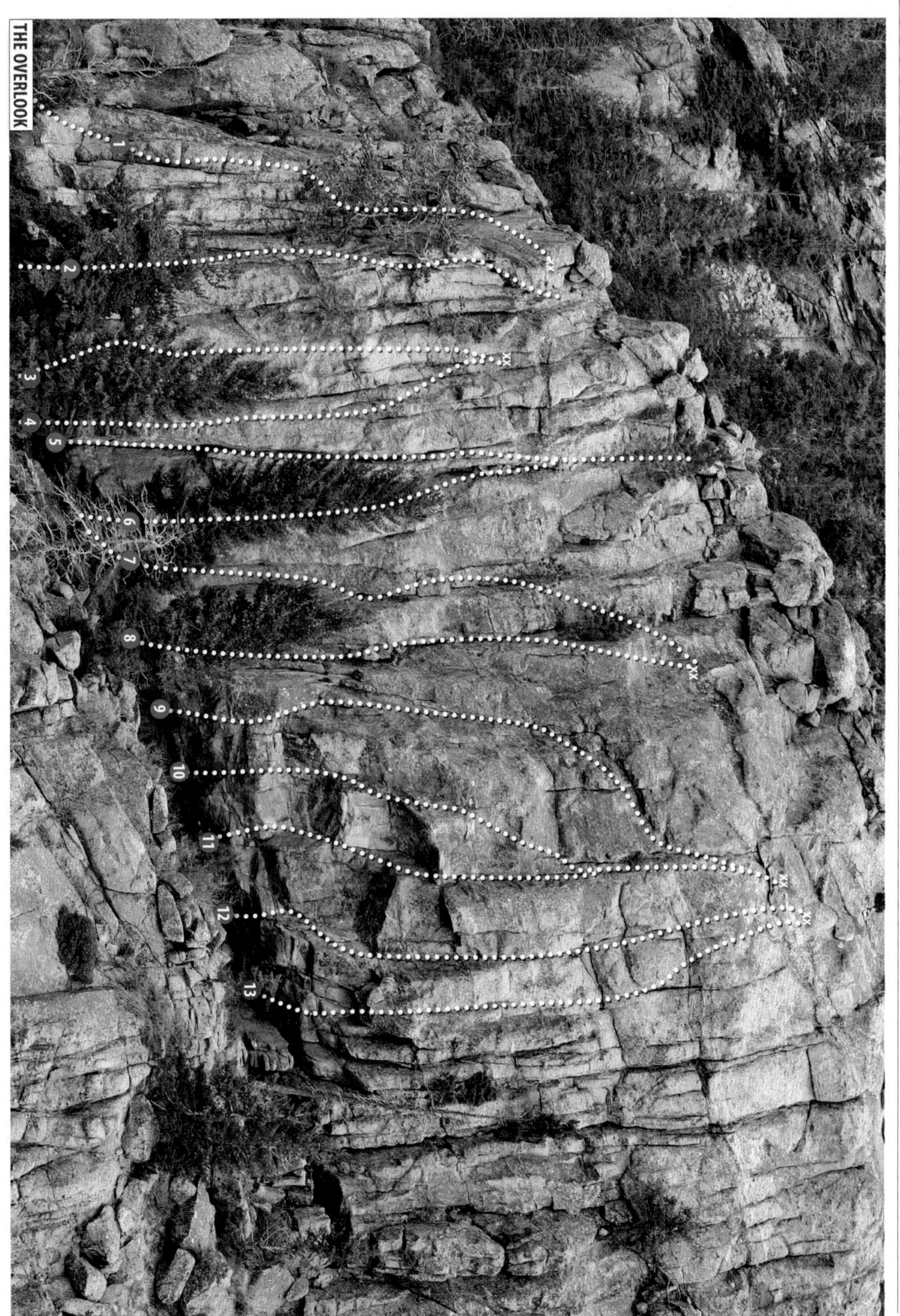
THE OVERLOOK
1
2
3
4
5
6
7
8
9
10
11
12
13
XX
XX
XX
XX
XX

MOUNTAIN ROSE/ FRISKY CLIFF AREA 12.0 miles

Approach time: 10 - 15 minutes.
Exposure: North and southwest.

20 routes

These two crags sit high above Castle Rock and Boulder Creek in a nice setting along the Aqueduct Trail. The rock on Mountain Rose is good in some sections and friable in others. Frisky Cliff has fairly solid rock but is of limited interest to the masses due to the extreme difficulty of most of its routes.

Access: Travel 12.4 miles up the canyon to a turnoff on the left for Castle Rock, follow the dirt road that circles the rock and park just past the bridge at a pullout on the right at the base of Broken Rock. Skirt the west side of Broken Rock and follow a trail up past the Overlook to the obvious Aqueduct Trail. Go right for a couple hundred feet on the Aqueduct Trail to reach the first routes on the Mountain Rose Crags. Frisky Cliff is ¼ mile west on the Aqueduct Trail and is easily recognized by the enormous roof system and huge hole/aqueduct at the base of the wall.

LEFT MOUNTAIN ROSE CRAG

Climbs listed from left to right.

1 Mountain Rose 5.10a ★ ☐
Climb a short right-facing corner on the left side of the wall up to bolt. Follow the face/cracks up to a short roof and then the top.
Gear to 2 inches.
Descent: Walk off to the east.

2 Golden Rose 5.12a ★★ ☐
Locate a bolted face just left of the shallow left-facing corner about 30 feet right of *Mountain Rose*. Climb the steep face up to a bulge and the crux. Easier climbing leads to the anchor.
5 bolts.

3 Yellow Tail 5.11d ★ ☐
Locate a bolted face 20 feet right of *Golden Rose*. Stiff moves off the ground lead to easier climbing.
6 bolts.

4 Steel Pulse 5.11c ★ ☐
This is the third bolted route on the wall and it climbs through the angling white dyke to the anchor.
6 bolts.

5 Big Tuna 5.11a ★ ☐
Start right of *Steel Pulse* and pull through a roof and then up easier ground to the anchor.
Bolts.

6 Time Lords 5.7 R ☐
Start just left of the large corner on the right side of the wall. Climb a short slab that leads to a left-facing corner. Climb the corner to the top. Walk off to the east.
Gear to 2 inches. Better to top rope it.

7 The Ancient of Days 5.9 ★ ☐
Climb the slab just left of the large corner aiming for small roof and short corner above the roof. Climb through the roof and then straight up to a ledge and large pine tree.
5 bolts.

8 Hummingbird 5.5 ★★ ☐
Climb the obvious corner up through a small roof and then slightly right to the top. Walk off to the east.
Gear to 3 inches.

9 War Drums 5.9 ★ ☐
Start right of the corner, climbing a nice face past three old bolts. Veer right to a tree near the top. Rap from the tree.
Gear to 1.5 inches.

10 Sick Puppy 5.12a ★★★ ☐
Start uphill from *War Drums* on a slab leading to a rounded arete. Make a hard move to gain the arête, then climb past several bolts up the arête. Go left at the top and rap from tree near *War Drums*. No anchors
4 bolts.

RIGHT MOUNTAIN ROSE CRAG

A gully separates the right from left Mountain Rose Crags. The following three routes start about 40-50 feet right of a large hole in the aqueduct.

11 Short Sport 5.11b/c ☐
Climb the short face over a small roof on the left side of the wall.
4 bolts.

12 Heatwave 5.10c ★ ☐
Start just left of the right-facing corner, climbing over a short roof and past several bolts up the face/arete.
3 bolts, gear to 1.5 inches.

13 Short but Sweet 5.8 ☐
What's in a name?? This route is horrible. Climb the corner, scratching your way over a roof to the top.
Gear to 2 inches.

14 Around the Corner 5.8 ☐
Climb the short wall on the right side of the face to anchors.
4 bolts.

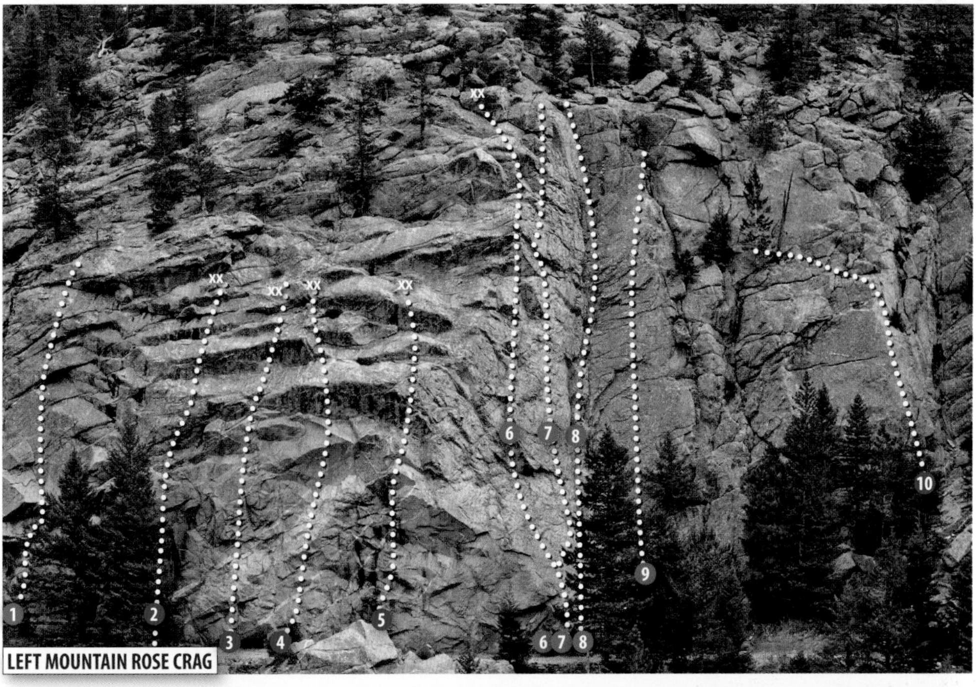

LEFT MOUNTAIN ROSE CRAG

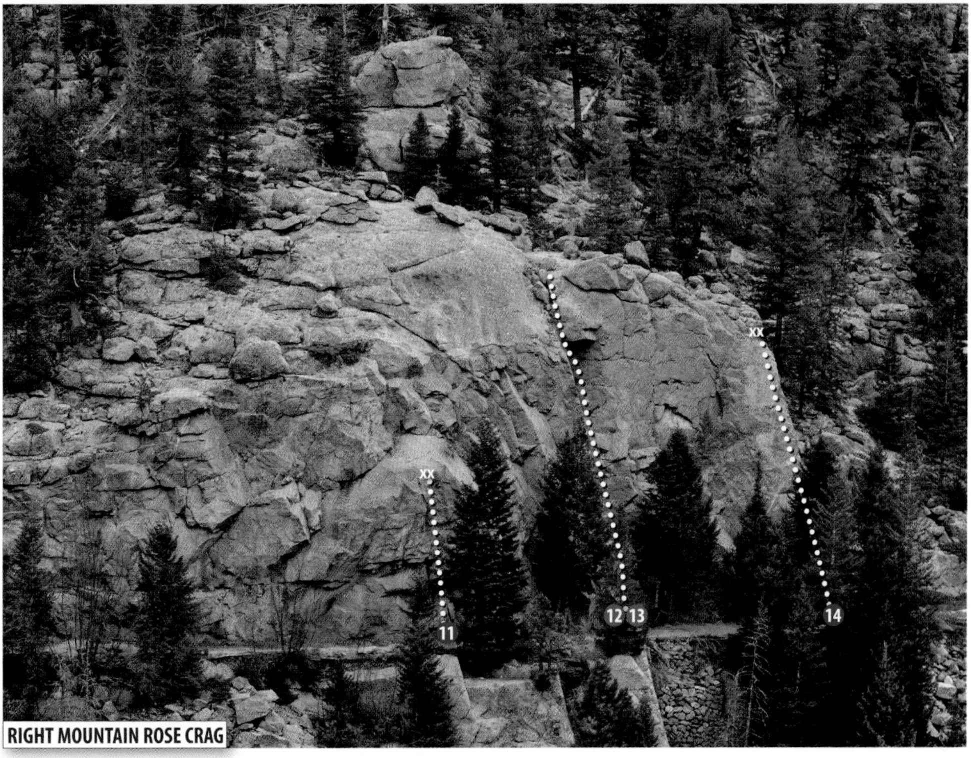

RIGHT MOUNTAIN ROSE CRAG

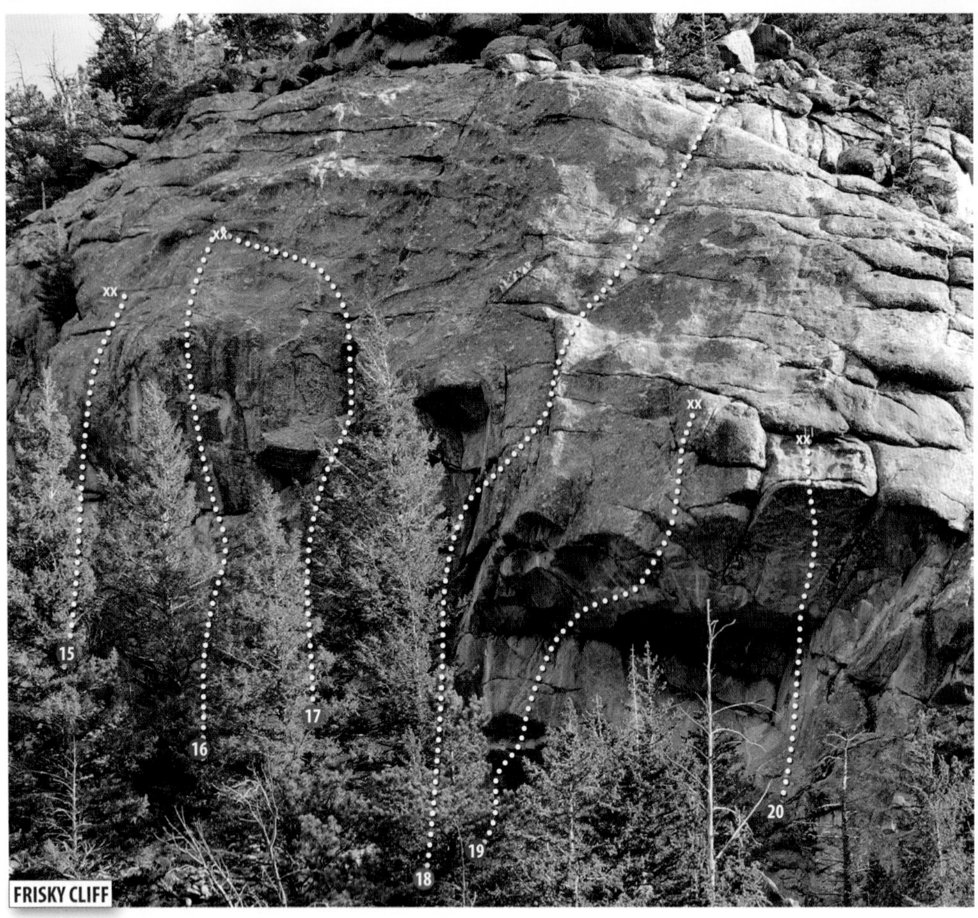

FRISKY CLIFF

Located about a ¼ mile west of Mountain Rose Crag, Frisky Cliff is the home of several outstanding and difficult routes.

⑮ The Orb 5.13b ★★ ☐

Start on the far left side of the wall below a short roof and short shallow corners. Power up through the initial roof and move right via power laybacks using a thin seam on the right. Clip the third bolt and hang on for dear life to the anchor.

5 bolts.

⑯ Sinopia 5.13a ★★ ☐

Looks like an easy 5.10. Start down and right of *The Orb*. Climb a short corner past bolts to a good ledge. Veer left and engage the crux over a bulge, then continue up to a left-facing corner and several hard moves to the anchor.

8 bolts.

⑰ Last Tango 5.10c ★★ ☐

Start right of *Sinopia*. Climb a left-leaning crack up to large left-facing dihedral. Climb the dihedral and go left at the top to the anchor for *Sinopia*.

Gear to 3 inches.

⑱ Frisky 5.10a ★★ ☐

Start left of the large overhang and follow a corner to below a square roof. Climb the roof on the right and then head up discontinuous cracks to the top.

Gear to 3 inches.

⑲ The Borg 5.13c ★★★ ☐

This obvious route climbs out the massive roof on the right side of the wall. Classic… if you climb at this grade.

6 bolts.

⑳ Rumors of Glory 5.13b ★★ ☐

The obvious route on the right side of the wall. Climb past three bolts with a wild throw at the lip of the roof. Gain the slab and then the anchor.

3 bolts.

CENOTAPH CRAG 12.5 miles

Approach time: 5 minutes.
Exposure: South and west.

9 routes

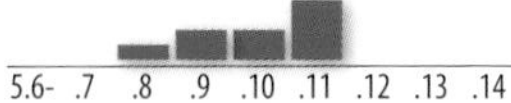

This steep, 40-foot high, wall is located just west of Castle Rock on the north side of the road. The rock is hidden and is hard to locate if you're driving up the canyon. It may be best to drive to the Sport Park at 12.5 miles, turn around, and then locate the cliff. You can park just before double no parking signs on the creek side of the road.

Access: Travel 12.5 miles up the canyon to a pullout/parking area on the left side of the road just past two no parking signs. Cross the road and then hike uphill to the crag.

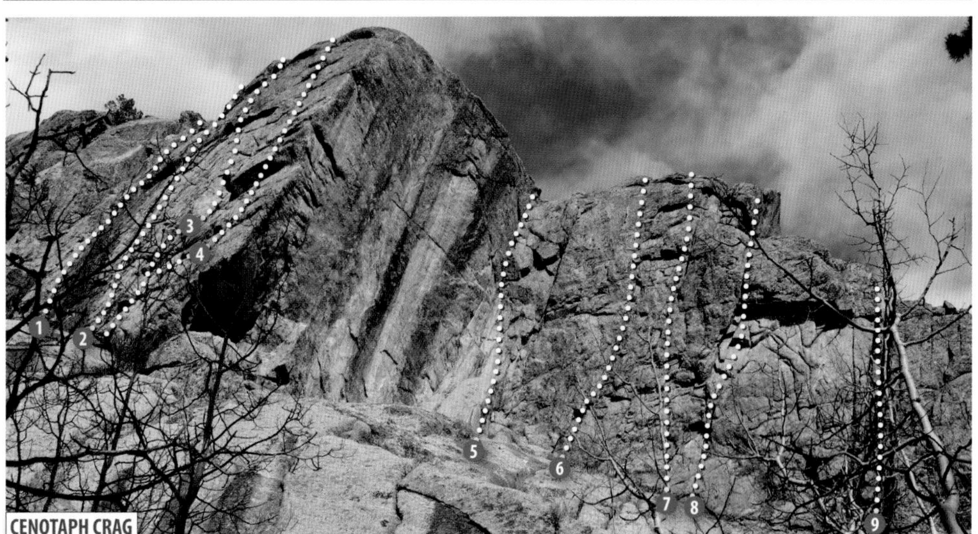

1 Going Down on It 5.9 ★ ☐
Climb a thin crack/seam on the far left of the wall going up a black streak.
Gear to 1 inch.
Descent: Walk off to the north.

2 Ethereal 5.9 ★ ☐
Climb the short crack just right of the black streak.
Descent: Walk off to the north.

3 Apparition 5.11a ★ ☐
Start left of the obvious arete up double cracks. Veer right up the steep face over a small roof following fixed gear to the anchor.
2 bolts, pin, gear to 2 inches.

4 Phantasm 5.11c ★★ ☐
Start for *Apparition* and then go right, aiming for the arête, climbing past bolts to the anchor.
4 bolts, light rack for the start.

5 Right to Life 5.10a ★ ☐
Climb the obvious corner up the center of the wall.
Gear to 2 inches.

6 Phaedra 5.11c ★ ☐
Locate a lone bolt right of the corner and climb up the steep face to a right-slanting crack and the top. Bolts are missing on the route and it may be best to top-rope it.
1 bolt, gear to 2 inches.

7 Euphoria 5.11c ★ ☐
Start just right of *Phaedra*, climbing the steep face past one bolt (two are missing) and then left to the crack finish of *Phaedra*. Toprope it.
1 bolt, gear to 2 inches.

8 Up Above It 5.10d ★ ☐
Climb the nice thin crack on the right side of the wall past a short roof near the top.
1 bolt, gear to 2 inches.

9 Five Eight Crack 5.8 ☐
The short wide crack on the far right side of the wall.
Gear to 3 inches.

THE SPORT PARK 12.5 miles

Approach time: 5 - 10 minutes.
Exposure: South and west

Once a seldom-visited area with a few bold traditional climbs, The Sport Park has been transformed into one of the most popular areas in the canyon. Easy access, lots of sunshine, and many well-protected sport routes make for a friendly gym-style atmosphere. The style employed to establish some of the climbs has provided fodder for heated debate. Regardless, many of these climbs see lots of traffic.

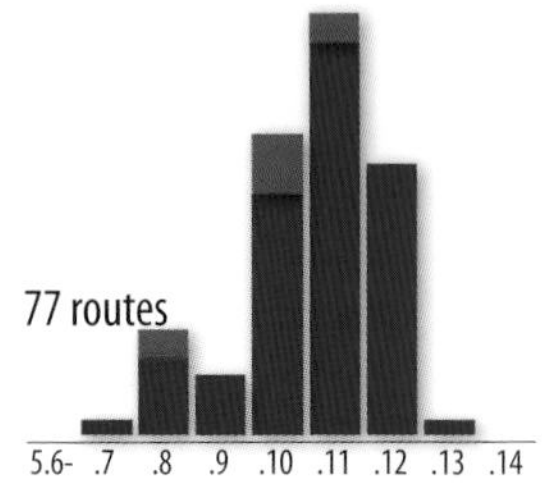

Access: Travel 12.5 miles up the canyon to a pullout/parking area on the right side of the road. Walk back down canyon for 50 yards and cross the creek at a guardrail. To reach the Overhung Wall go left downstream along the creek to the obvious wall on the right. To access the other areas follow the obvious trail up the hill.

Routes are listed left to right.

OVERHUNG WALL

This steep 50-foot-high south-facing wall is located near the creek just down and east from the south face of Surprising Crag. It has several good sport routes in a pleasant setting. This wall has no photograph.

❶ Build a Dam, Boys 5.12b ★ ☐
Climb the steep face on the left side of the wall past hard moves at the third bolt. Easier climbing leads to the anchor.
7 bolts.

❷ Whipping Post 5.12a/b ★★ ☐
Climb a slab up to a short corner, then power through the roof to easier climbing and the anchor.
5 bolts.

Variation: Whipping Factor 5.12b ☐
Climb through the first three bolts on *Whipping Post* and then head left, climbing the crux moves of *Warf Factor* to the anchor.

❸ Warf Factor 5.12a ★★ ☐
Start up a short slab and then veer left, powering past the roof on good holds to the upper slab and the anchor. Maybe the best route on the wall.
6 bolts.

❹ Warf Post 5.11a ★★ ☐
The best warm up on the wall. Climb through the first four bolts on *Warf Factor* and then veer left and finish on *Whipping Post.*
6 bolts.

❺ Hard Warm Up 5.11c ★★ ☐
Climb the steep wall just left of *Invisible Touch* past a hard move over a bugle then up to the anchor.
5 bolts.

❻ Invisible Touch 5.12b/c ★★ ☐
The furthest route on the right side of the wall. Engage a hard move past the first bolt and a harder one higher up before the anchor.
5 bolts.

SURPRISING CRAG

This great west-facing crag has some good routes on excellent granite in a nice setting with views above Boulder Creek. There are several dicey trad climbs and several well protected sport climbs. For the trad routes bring small gear (RP's, Aliens, cams and maybe double ropes), as most of them are hard to protect and require tricky placements.

The South Face (right side of the wall) features several controversial but popular bolted cracks.

❼ Wise Crack 5.8 ☐
The obvious bolted hand and fist crack on the far left side of the wall.
6 bolts.

❽ Pocket Fisherman 5.11b ★★ ☐
Climb over a short roof on the left side of the wall gaining a short corner then up easy rock to the anchor.
7 bolts.

❾ Curve of Binding Energy 5.12a/b ★★ ☐
Climb the devious overhang just left of a small tree about 15 feet off the ground. Easier climbing leads to the anchor.
7 bolts.

❿ Entrapment 5.10d R ★ ☐
Boulder up (no gear) and through the short overhang, sling the tree and then veer left up a thin crack to the top.
Gear to 2.5 inches.

⓫ Heart like a Wheel 5.10a R ★ ☐
Start for *Entrapment* and climb to the tree, climb right up the thin crack to the top.
Gear to 2.5 inches.

⓬ Space Goats 5.11d ★ ☐
Climb past the roof on good holds to a tricky move past the third bolt. Climb easier rock to the anchor.
10 bolts.

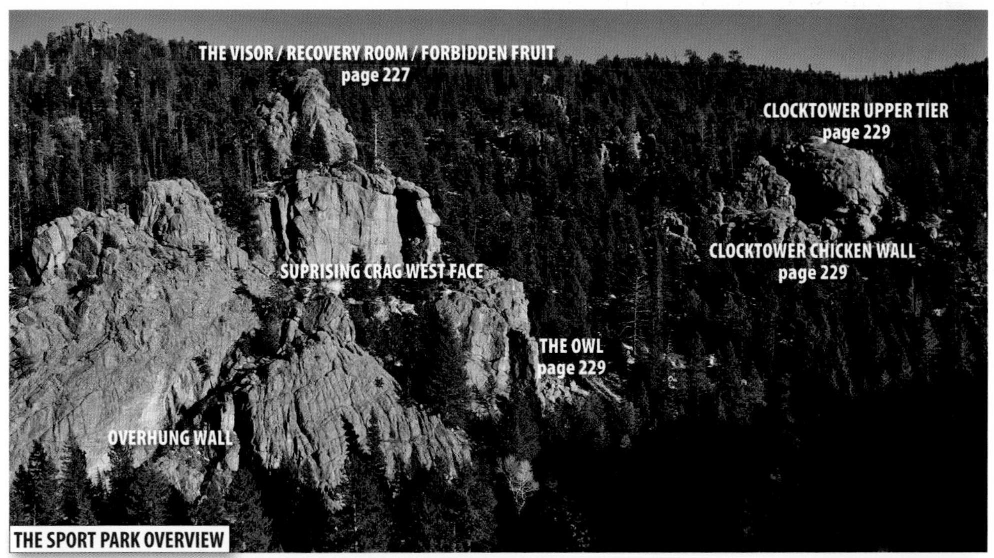

THE SPORT PARK OVERVIEW

SURPRISING CRAG WEST FACE

⑬ Furious Howard Brown 5.12a/b ★★☐
Hard moves over the roof lead to another crux gaining a short corner. Climb up to another hard move, which can be avoided by stepping left, and then up to the anchor.
10 bolts.

⑭ Buried Alive 5.10 R ★ ☐
Start in a short corner near the center of the wall, climb left to a thin crack and then up the left-facing corner to the top.
Gear to 2 inches.

⑮ Power Line 5.11c/d ★★ ☐
Climb the appealing thin yellow cracks near the center of the wall to a horizontal crack, veer left then up easier rock to the top.
Variation: 5.10d. At the horizontal crack go right up the thin crack to the top.
Gear to 2 inches.

21 Choss Temple Pilots 5.8 ★

Climb blocky rock on the left side of the wall to the anchor.

6 bolts.

Climber: John Grayson. Photo: Ron Olsen.

⑯ American Beauty 5.12c ★★★ ☐
The best sport climb on the wall. Start just right of the yellow cracks and climb thin seams to a baffling move near the top.
7 bolts.

⑰ Amber 5.11d ★ ☐
Climb discontinuous seams past two bolts to the top. Hard moves at the bolts and tricky gear in between.
2 bolts, gear to 2 inches.

⑱ Mercy Drilling 5.12a ★★★ ☐
Climb the obvious seam just left of the wide crack/corner to a hard move near the top. Great route on bullet granite.
6 bolts.

⑲ North Crack 5.8 ★ ☐
Climb the dark obvious corner crack on the right side of the wall.
Gear to 4 inches.

⑳ The Other One 5.11a ★★ ☐
Climb the nice prow on the far right side of the wall past several small roofs to the anchor.
7 bolts.

㉑ Choss Temple Pilots 5.8 ★ ☐
See description opposite.

㉒ Killer Fish Taco 5.10d/11a ★ ☐
Start for *Choss Temple Pilots* climbing past the second bolt and then right up to a huge flake/roof. Pull the roof and then up the face to the anchor.
6 bolts.

㉓ The Fix 5.11a ★★ ☐
Climb the right side of the flake/overhang and then up the steep face to the anchor.
7 bolts.

㉔ South Crack 5.8 ★★ ☐
Climb the wide crack up the steep corner.
Gear to 4 inches.

SURPRISING CRAG SOUTH FACE

The next five routes are on the short west-facing wall on the south face. All are bolted cracks and are extremely well protected.

㉕ Chasing Sticks 5.9 ★ ☐
Climb the blocky face up through the layback crack to the anchors.
5 bolts.

㉖ Vitamin V 5.9+ ★★ ☐
Climb easy rock up to small bulge spilt by thin cracks, layback and jam your way to the anchor.
5 bolts.

㉗ Wavy Gravy 5.10a ☐
Climb the crack through a small bulge jamming your way to the anchor.
5 bolts.

㉘ Dutch Oven 5.9 ★★ ☐
Start just right of *Wavy Gravy* and climb the hand crack past several bolts to the anchor.
5 bolts.

㉙ Monkey Bob 5.8 ★ ☐
Climb blocky rock over a small roof and then up the blunt arete to the anchors.
4 bolts.

㉚ Hood Surfing in Socks 5.11c ★★ ☐
A nice slab route just right of *Monkey Bob*, the crux is getting to the anchor. Tricky.
6 bolts.

㉛ Platinum Curl 5.11b/c ★★ ☐
Climb over a short roof using the obvious layback into a short corner.
6 bolts.

㉜ The Touch 5.8 ★ ☐
Climb the obvious corner crack making a tricky move past the second bolt.
5 bolts.

㉝ Dirty Dave's Dumpster Dive 5.10a ★ ☐
Climb a bolted thin crack just right of short corner up to ledge, face climb to the anchors.
6 bolts.

㉞ Double Down 5.10a ☐
Climb a thin face on the right side of the rock just left of a corner crack.
6 bolts.

㉟ Frictionary 5.7 ★ ☐
A nice slab and great beginner lead on the right side of the rock.
6 bolts.

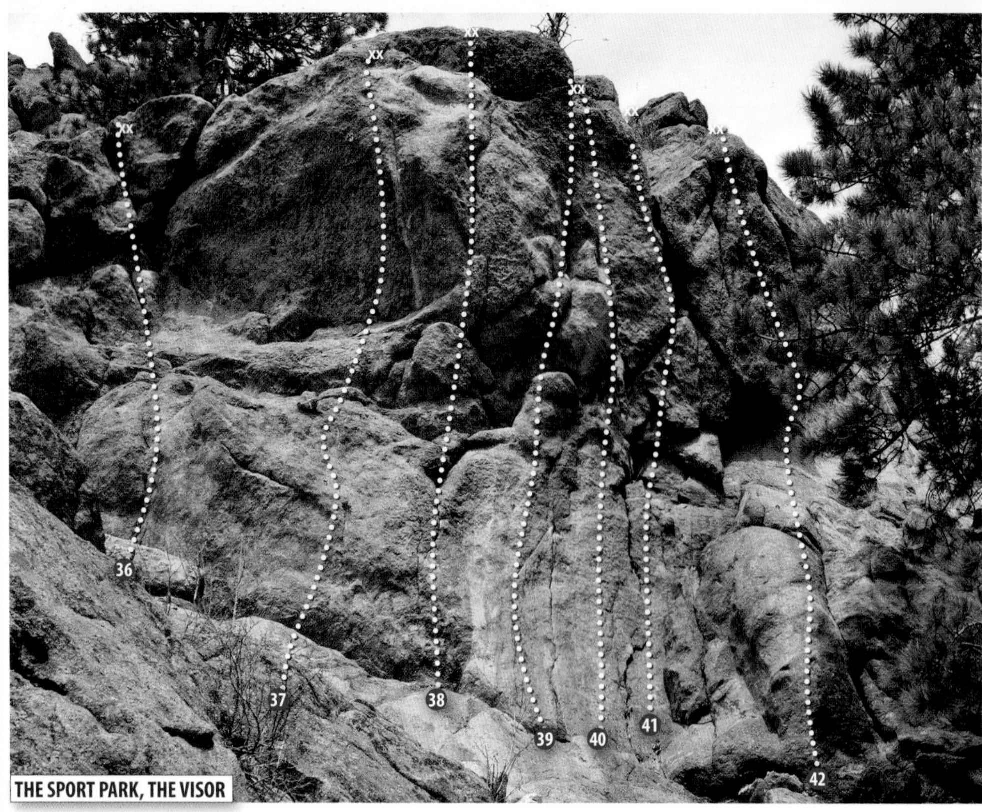

THE SPORT PARK, THE VISOR

THE VISOR

A 40-foot-high wall located just east (uphill) from the south face of Surprising Crag. Some routes are chipped.

36 Absolute Boulder Canyon 5.11a ★ ☐
On the far left side of The Visor, climb hard moves off the ground and then a stiff move to the anchor.
7 bolts.

37 Dyno Monkey 5.11d ★ ☐
Climb the steep face on the left side of the Visor using some very unusual holds (chipped) to a big move before the anchors.
4 bolts.

38 Rubberneck 5.12a ★★ ☐
Climb up the steep face to a pillar, launch off the pillar, then make a big move to the anchor.
5 bolts.

39 Flying Machines 5.11a ★ ☐
Climb a short slab up to a left-facing dihedral on overhanging jugs to the anchor.
5 bolts.

40 Bone Hone 5.10c/d ★ ☐
Climb the handcrack up to the obvious wide crack.
5 bolts.

41 Welcome Wagon 5.10c ☐
Climb up a short face up to the chipped arete and then to the anchor.
5 bolts.

42 Hair of the Dog 5.10a ★ ☐
Climb a short steep face to a small roof and the up to anchor.
6 bolts.

43 Geek in the Creek 5.8 ★ ☐
On the far right side of the Visor, climb blocky rock to a short corner, then up to the anchor.
5 bolts.

RECOVERY ROOM

This short wall is located directly above the Visor. Take the trail on the left side of the Visor uphill and then slightly right to the wall.

44 Stryker 5.10a ★ ☐
Climb the short arete on the left side of the wall. Left of the arete is 5.10a, right of the arete is 5.11b/c.
3 bolts.

45 Jaws 5.11a/b ★ ☐
Climb the obvious layback flake up to the anchor.
3 bolts.

46 Blackout 5.12a ★ ☐
Climb the obvious chipped face up the center of the rock.
4 bolts.

47 Coffee Pot Crack 5.10d ★ ☐
The chipped route on the right side of the wall.
4 bolts.

FORBIDDEN FRUIT CRAG

This wall is located directly above the Recovery Room. Follow the trail on the left side of the Recovery Room up hill to the crag.

48 Percocet Arete 5.10c/d ★ ☐
Climb the short arete on the left side of the wall to easier climbing above.
4 bolts.

49 King of the Highway 5.11a/b ★★ ☐
Climb a short corner just left of the obvious crack up to a steep face and then the anchors.
6 bolts.

50 Forbidden Fruit 5.10b ★★ ☐
Climb the fist crack to thin fingers and stemming moves to anchor on *King of the Highway*. Somewhat dirty.
Gear to 3 inches.

51 Knocking on Heaven's Door 5.11c ★ ☐
A stiff move down low leads to another one near the fourth bolt.
5 bolts.

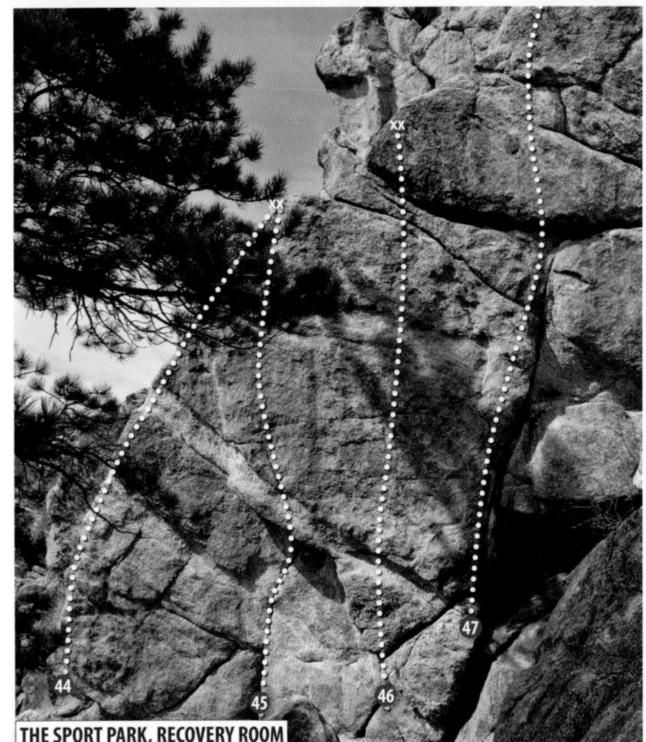

THE SPORT PARK, RECOVERY ROOM

THE SPORT PARK, FORBIDDEN FRUIT

53 **Owl on the Prow** 5.11b ★★★

The best route on the wall, start left of the tunnel and climb the steep wall via face moves, laybacking and some jamming. *7 bolts.*

Climber: Gabe Neely. Photo: Ben Ingman.

THE OWL

A 40-foot-high south-facing wall located just west (downhill) from the south face of Surprising Crag. Some routes are chipped.

52 Owl Juju 5.11a ★ ☐

On the far left side of the Owl, climb hard moves off the ground and gain a short corner leading to a crack and the anchors.

6 bolts.

53 Owl on the Prow 5.11b ★★★ ☐

See description opposite.

54 Linking Logs 5.11d ★★ ☐

Start just left of the tunnel, climbing a steep face up to below a shit infested horizontal. Traverse right avoiding the crap and then up the steep wall to the anchor.

7 bolts.

55 Ground Zero 5.11b ★ ☐

Start just right of the tunnel with hard moves off the ground. Climb the steep face to the anchor.

5 bolts.

THE SPORT PARK, THE OWL

THE CLOCK TOWER

This fun west-facing rock has some of the best routes at the Sport Park, despite some chipped holds. All the routes are sport and require only draws and a rope. A great spot for a workout or to break into higher grades.

THE SPORT PARK, THE CLOCK TOWER, CHICKEN WALL

LOWER LEFT SIDE/CHICKEN WALL

56 Chicken Delight 5.10a/b ★★ ☐

The obvious bolted face on the far left side of the wall.

7 bolts.

57 Rubber Chicken 5.10c ★★ ☐

Climb the nice face just right of *Chicken Delight*.

7 bolts.

58 Chicken Lips 5.11b ★★ ☐

Climb the face just right of the corner/arete on the left side of the wall.

5 bolts.

59 Alfa Chick 5.11d ★ ☐

Climb a clean slab, make a hard move up to short corner, and then go straight up to the anchor.

6 bolts.

60 Chicken Hawk 5.9 ★★ ☐

A nice warm up near the center of the wall.

6 bolts.

61 Daddy Blocker 5.11a ★★ ☐

Climb the steep face where the trail meets the rock on the right side of the wall.

7 bolts.

62 Mommy Blocker 5.10a ★ ☐

Climb a short face over a small roof to the anchor.

5 bolts.

63 Weasel in the Chicken Coup 5.10a R ★ ☐

The last route on the right side of the lower wall and right off the trail.

5 bolts.

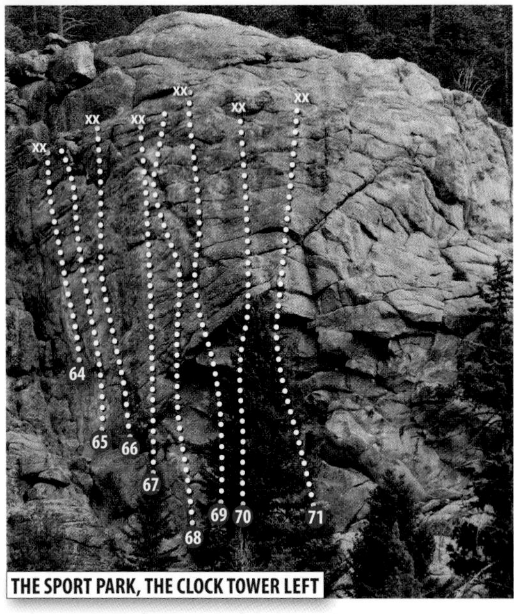

THE UPPER WALL

From the lower wall follow the trail right/west to the upper wall.

64 Ditch Witch 5.12a ☐

On the far left side of the wall climb a face just right of the gully. The crux is trying not to use holds on *Hee Haw*.

7 bolts.

65 Hee Haw 5.11a ★ ☐

Nice jug haul on the left side of the wall.

7 bolts.

66 Leave it to Beaver 5.11c ★ ☐

Climb the obvious short left-facing corner on the left side of the wall.

6 bolts.

Variation: Beaver Fever 5.12b ☐

Climb the thin seam just right of the normal start to the fourth bolt on *Leave it to Beaver*.

67 Mutant Overload 5.12c ★★ ☐

Climb the obvious steep face up the black streak.

7 bolts.

68 Butt Lucious 5.11d ★ ☐

Climb the left side of the large roof system then up the steep face on jugs to the anchor.

8 bolts.

Variation: Go Dog Go 5.12a ★ ☐

Climb the steep gold wall just right of the normal start.

10 bolts.

69 Jolly Jug 5.12a ★ ☐

Creative (chipped) holds get you over the roof and then jugs to the anchor.

10 bolts.

70 Hair Shirt 5.12b ★★ ☐

Tackle the largest part of the roof system via a lunge/chipped holds (or step left to *Jolly Jug*) and then up the easier face to the anchor.

9 bolts.

71 No Doze 5.12b ★★ ☐

Maybe the best route chipped on the wall. Near the right side of the roof at a tree. Fire up through the roof to easier climbing.

10 bolts.

72 The Big Dipper 5.11a ★★★ ☐

Maybe the best non-chipped route on the wall. Climb the steep wall just right of the tree over a small roof then up the slab to the anchor.

9 bolts.

73 Pump Truck 5.12c ★ ☐

Start just right of *The Big Dipper*, climbing through the roof and face to easier moves to the anchor.

6 bolts.

74 Salad Shooter 5.12d ★ ☐

Steep crimping face moves lead to hard moves at the roof. Easier climbing past the roof gets you to the anchor.

7 bolts.

75 Three Little Pigs 5.11a ★★ ☐

The third route on the left side of the wall, crux moves are separated by ledges.

8 bolts.

76 Mother Goose 5.10a ☐

Climb past a low bolt to a weird clip at the third bolt, then enjoy jugs to the anchor.

8 bolts.

77 Infra-Red Riding Hood 5.10a ★ ☐

Climb the bolted crack on the far right side of the wall.

8 bolts.

Dan Hare

My favorite route that I was involved in establishing in the Boulder area was my first new route in Boulder Canyon. Perhaps it's just nostalgia, but I like multi-pitch routes that have varied pitches. *Where Eagles Dare* on Blob Rock fills the bill. The early 1970s were a time of change in American climbing. Aid climbing big walls was beginning to lose a tiny bit of its luster as the ultimate goal and free climbing was coming into its own. Royal Robbins himself had helped stir the pot in Boulder with hard free ascents (with Pat Ament) on Castle Rock back in the mid-1960s. After a brief lull, people like Jim Erickson, Duncan Ferguson, Pat Ament and Rodger Briggs picked up where he had left off. There was a lot of rock to be had near Boulder, much of it still untouched. Ament's 1970 edition *High Over Boulder* encompassed the entire area, including Eldorado, in just over 300 pages of small-format book. Boulder Canyon got 40 of those pages with a total of less than 70 routes.

My partners in climb on Blob Rock were Brad Gilbert and Scott Woodruff. We were sort of the out-of-town gang as the three of us had been living in Fort Collins and going to school at CSU. But we had done a lot of climbing in the Boulder region and were beginning to find the gaps in the matrix. In my mind Brad was the ringleader, as he was an extremely talented natural climber with a positive mindset — the kind of guy who could get you into and out of a tough situation. Scott was rock-steady and a bit more willing to go for it than me. I would get called from the bullpen when things looked strenuous and called for someone would could hang out and put in pro.

On a beautiful winter day we scoped the obvious upper crack and looked for a way to get up there. For the uninitiated, Blob Rock is not a straightforward read. In fact, at first look it appears to be a pile, very much reminding me of photos of some of the "classic" British cliffs that used to horrify me. But by coming in from the left on the first pitch of the *Center Direct* route we sneaked up to the comfortable ledge just below the wild hand traverse of the third pitch. Sensing it would be a bit strenuous, Brad and Scott sent me out onto this wildly exposed traverse and then hunkered down while I battled the superb final headwall crack. As the shadows crept up the hillside we traversed off from the big ledge at the end of the route all the while knowing that we had to come back.

A few weeks later we were standing at the base again. This time we were armed with the latest technology. Our friend Tim had sent us the secret weapon from Australia, a few tiny brass nuts made by an Aussie named Roland Pauligk. All three of us were extremely dubious about these little units and their funky construction but Tim assured us they would hold falls. Our more direct start this time had some thin cracks and immediately the "RPs" were put to use. Above this section Brad led the very spooky second pitch up to the comfy ledge we had been on before and we know we had it.

UPPER DREAM CANYON

Wild, rugged, scenic and peaceful, Upper Dream Canyon is a rare gem, providing seemingly remote climbing less than 45 minutes from downtown Boulder. Some of the longest climbs in the area are found on its soaring granite walls. The canyon has a good mix of sport and traditional routes, good moderate routes and some of the hardest climbs in the area. The canyon has long been a refuge for those seeking solitude and alterative lifestyles and to this day remains a haven for nude swimmers, sunbathers and the gay community around Boulder. Be respectful and realize that others also love and enjoy this beautiful area.

The cliffs in Upper Dream Canyon face in multiple directions. Due to its higher elevation Upper Dream Canyon can be cooler than the main canyon and a good venue in the summer months.

Access: See maps at front of book and on next page. Drive 3.9 miles up Boulder Canyon to Sugarloaf Rd, turn right and travel 3.1 miles to Lost Angel Road, turn left and continue for 1.5 miles on Lost Angel Road (staying straight ahead at a branch after 1 mile, and right shortly thereafter to avoid private property) to a parking area on the left. Keep in mind that the area surrounding the canyon is private property and show respect by not speeding, littering, or parking along the road or in private areas and driveways.

West Trail: This is the main trail that leads to all of the rocks and the most straightforward approach for the first time visitor. From the parking area walk west down the road for 150 feet to a well-marked trail on the left leading downhill along a fence line. Follow the trail to the creek passing Thunder Point and The Icon to the creek. Go downstream to the to reach the Oceanic Wall, and the cliffs beyond.

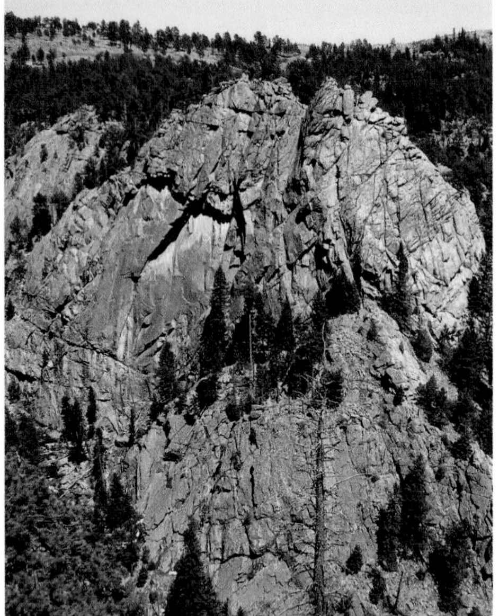

Lost Angel Cliff, Upper Dream Canyon. Photo: Bob Horan.

South Trail: This trail provides a faster approach to right side of Lost Angel, Midnight Rock and Vanishing Point. It can be confusing and potentially dangerous for first-time users.

From the parking area follow the trail/old mining road southwest, after a hundred yards a trail goes right toward Dream Dome. To reach Lost Angel and Midnight Rock continue on the main trail downhill for another hundred yards to a trail that leads right to a notch, drop down the through the notch and cut right across a slab/ledge to a steep gully near a large ponderosa pine at the base of the Wake-Up Wall (on the east side of the Lost Angel cliff). To reach the central section of Lost Angel continue west/right along a rugged trail just below the Wake Up Wall. Hug the trail along the wall and then go up a steep gully to a notch, drop down through the notch and continue beneath the main wall to the creek.

To reach Midnight Rock and Vanishing Point continue down the gully at the east side of Wake Up Wall for 100 feet and then go left near a small pine across a slab to Midnight Rock.

Dream Dome Trail: Access this trail by following the South Trail for 100 yards and then going right through trees on a narrow path that leads down between the west side of Lost Angel and the east side of Dream Dome. You can access rappel anchors on the top of the Zen Garden Wall (left side of Lost Angel cliff) from this trail.

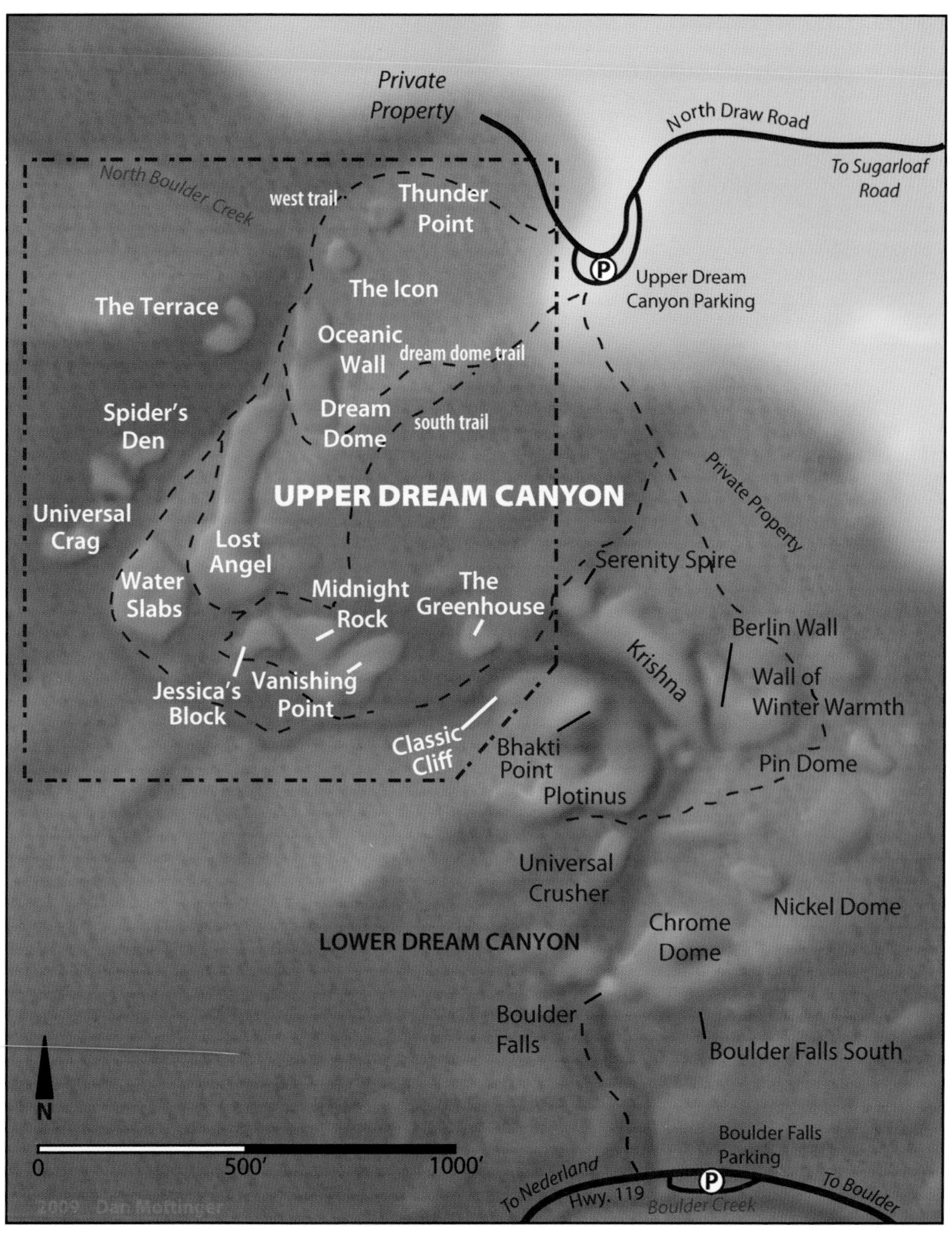
Private Property
North Draw Road
To Sugarloaf Road
North Boulder Creek
west trail
Thunder Point
Upper Dream Canyon Parking
The Icon
The Terrace
Oceanic Wall
dream dome trail
Spider's Den
Dream Dome
south trail
UPPER DREAM CANYON
Private Property
Universal Crag
Lost Angel
Serenity Spire
Water Slabs
Midnight Rock
The Greenhouse
Berlin Wall
Krishna
Wall of Winter Warmth
Jessica's Block
Vanishing Point
Classic Cliff
Bhakti Point
Pin Dome
Plotinus
Universal Crusher
Nickel Dome
Chrome Dome
LOWER DREAM CANYON
Boulder Falls
Boulder Falls South
N
0
500'
1000'
Boulder Falls Parking
To Nederland
Hwy. 119
Boulder Creek
To Boulder

THUNDER POINT UDC

Approach time: 10 - 15 minutes.
Exposure: Southwest.

4 routes

5.6- .7 .8 .9 .10 .11 .12 .13 .14

Located right off the Fence Approach trail, this piece of rock has two routes of different difficulty and quality.

Access: From the parking area follow the West Trail down towards the Oceanic Wall (page 236). Thunder Point will be the first rock you come to before the creek.

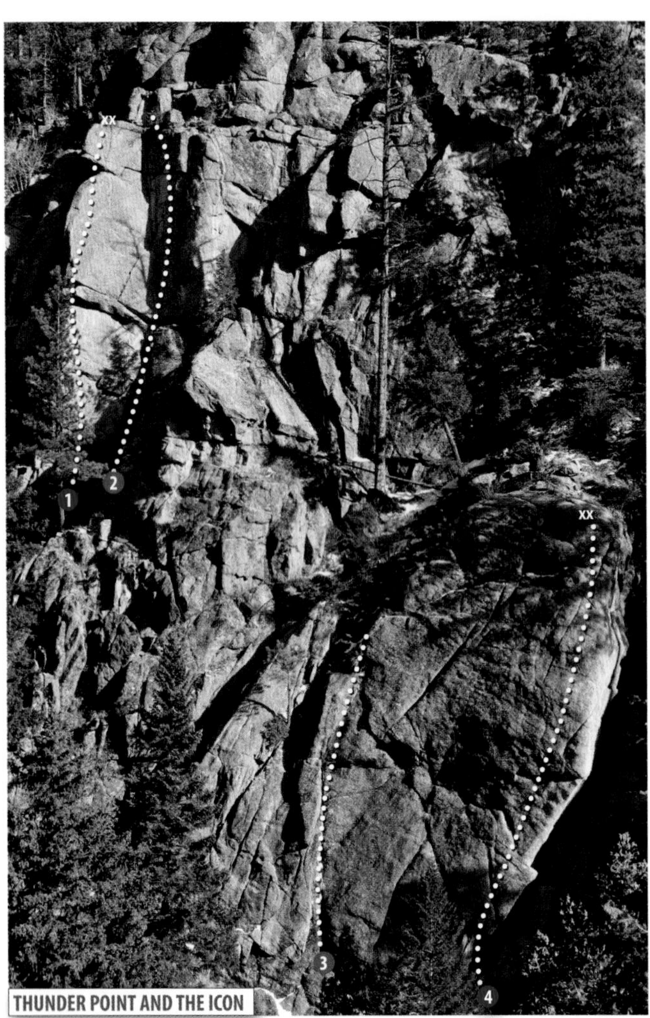

THUNDER POINT AND THE ICON

❶ **Sunset Arete** 5.11d ★★ ☐
Climb the obvious short face leading to the arête. Climb the arete on the left then up to the anchor.
9 bolts.

❷ **Center Tap Corner** 5.7 ★ ☐
Climb dirty rock up a short gully leading to a corner to the top.
Gear to 3 inches.

THE ICON

This short piece of rock is located right off the trail less than 100 feet from the Oceanic Wall.

❸ **Buddhist Pest** 5.9 ★★★ ☐
Climb the right-facing dihedral on the left side of the rock.
Gear to 4 inches.

❹ **Mantra** 5.11a/b ★★ ☐
Climb up a short corner to the first bolt and then up the face on the left side of the arete.
7 bolts.

CLIMBERS, the **ENVIRONMENT** and **ACCESS** are all interconnected
Know how you fit in. ››

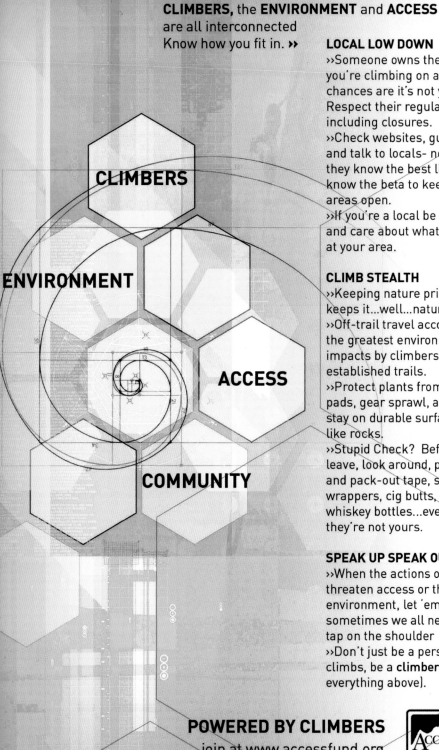

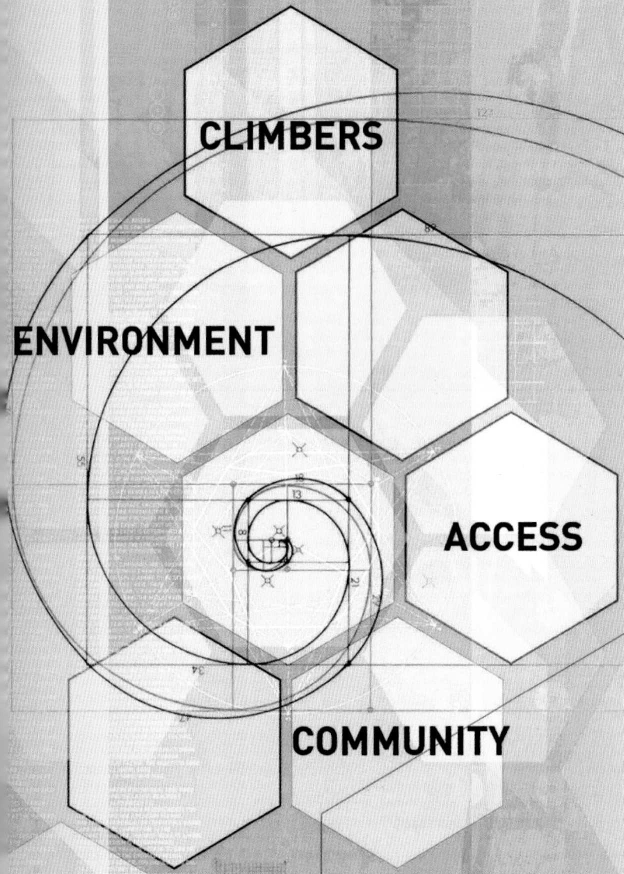

CLIMBERS

ENVIRONMENT

ACCESS

COMMUNITY

LOCAL LOW DOWN

››Someone owns the land that you're climbing on and chances are it's not you. Respect their regulations, including closures.

››Check websites, guidebooks, and talk to locals- not only do they know the best lines, they know the beta to keep the areas open.

››If you're a local be informed and care about what happens at your area.

CLIMB STEALTH

››Keeping nature pristine keeps it...well...natural.

››Off-trail travel accounts for the greatest environmental impacts by climbers - stay on established trails.

››Protect plants from packs, pads, gear sprawl, and feet; stay on durable surfaces - uh, like rocks.

››Stupid Check? Before you leave, look around, pick-up and pack-out tape, spilt chalk, wrappers, cig butts, whiskey bottles...even if they're not yours.

SPEAK UP SPEAK OUT

››When the actions of others threaten access or the environment, let 'em know- sometimes we all need a little tap on the shoulder

››Don't just be a person who climbs, be a **climber** (psst...see everything above).

POWERED BY CLIMBERS

join at www.accessfund.org

Approach time: 10 - 15 minutes.
Exposure: East, south and southwest.

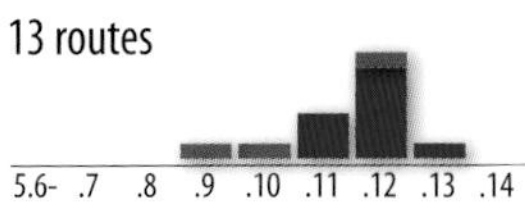

A beautiful piece of granite located right beside Boulder Creek. Quality routes, seclusion, and a great place to just hang.

Access: See directions for Upper Dream Canyon (page 232).

❶ In Your Dreams 5.11a ★★ ☐
On the far left side of the wall, start below an apex roof. Climb up and over the roof following a crack and then up and right to the anchors for *The Deep*.
11 bolts, a few small cams.

❷ The Deep 5.11c ★★ ☐
Start right of *In Your Dreams*, making a mantel move off the ground. Angle right and then back left climb over a small roof, gain a ledge, and then go up the nice face to the anchors.
10 bolts.

❸ Sargasso Sea 5.12a ★★★★ ☐
Climb up to short right-facing corner making hard moves to gain a ledge. Move left then up the thin seam/slab and then straight up to the anchor.
9 bolts.

❹ Challenges of Leisure 5.13a ★★★ ☐
Start up a right-facing corner, making a hard move to gain the face. Steep slab climbing leads to the crux going left using a horizontal crack. Get established above the crack and you're home free.
13 bolts.

❺ Leviathan 5.11d ★★★ ☐
Climb a steep face past three bolts, go left up the steep face to a hard move to gain the anchor.
8 bolts.

Variation: Dream On 5.11c ★★ ☐
Climb *Leviathan* to the fifth bolt then head up right, climbing a shallow crack to the anchor.
8 bolts.

❻ Mudshark 5.11d ★★ ☐
Start as for *Leviathan*, climbing to the lower anchor/ fourth bolt of *Leviathan*. Trend right up a flaring crack. At the top of the crack move up and right, making a hard move onto a slab, then straight up to the anchor.
7 bolts.

❼ Creature from the Black Lagoon 5.11d ★★★ ☐
A great route with technical moves up a black arching crack. Maybe the best route on the wall.
10 bolts, pin, and couple of medium cams for the start.

❽ Twisting by the Pool 5.10c ★ ☐
Start as for *Creature from the Black Lagoon* and then angle right to a corner and then back left following the line of weakness up to a big ledge.
7 quickdraws and gear to 3 inches.

❾ Sheik YerBouti 5.11d ★★ ☐
On the right side of the wall, boulder over a small roof and then up the corner. Veer left at the top and then up the steep face to the anchor.
5 bolts, pins and micro-cams to 1.5 inches.

❿ Permanent Restraining Order 5.11a ★ ☐
Start right of *Skeik YerBouti*, climbing just left of a black streak and meeting *Shiny Toys* near the top.
2 bolts and gear to 2 inches.

⓫ Shiny Toys 5.9+ ★★ ☐
On the right side of the wall, climb up the black streak on featured rock to the anchor.
2 bolts, pin and gear to two inches.

⓬ Dream Come True 5.12a/b ★★ ☐
This and the next route start on the upper ledge of the Dream Dome. Access by climbing one of the routes on the main wall or climb the gully which separates Oceanic Wall from Dream Dome. Traverse the ledge to a two bolt belay below a large roof, fire up the left side of the roof and then the steep face to hard move before the anchor.
5 bolts.

⓭ Nightmare Come True 5.12a/b ★ ☐
Start as for *Dream Come True* and climb to the third bolt, move right and follow the thin crack to the anchor.
3 bolts, gear to 1.5 inches.

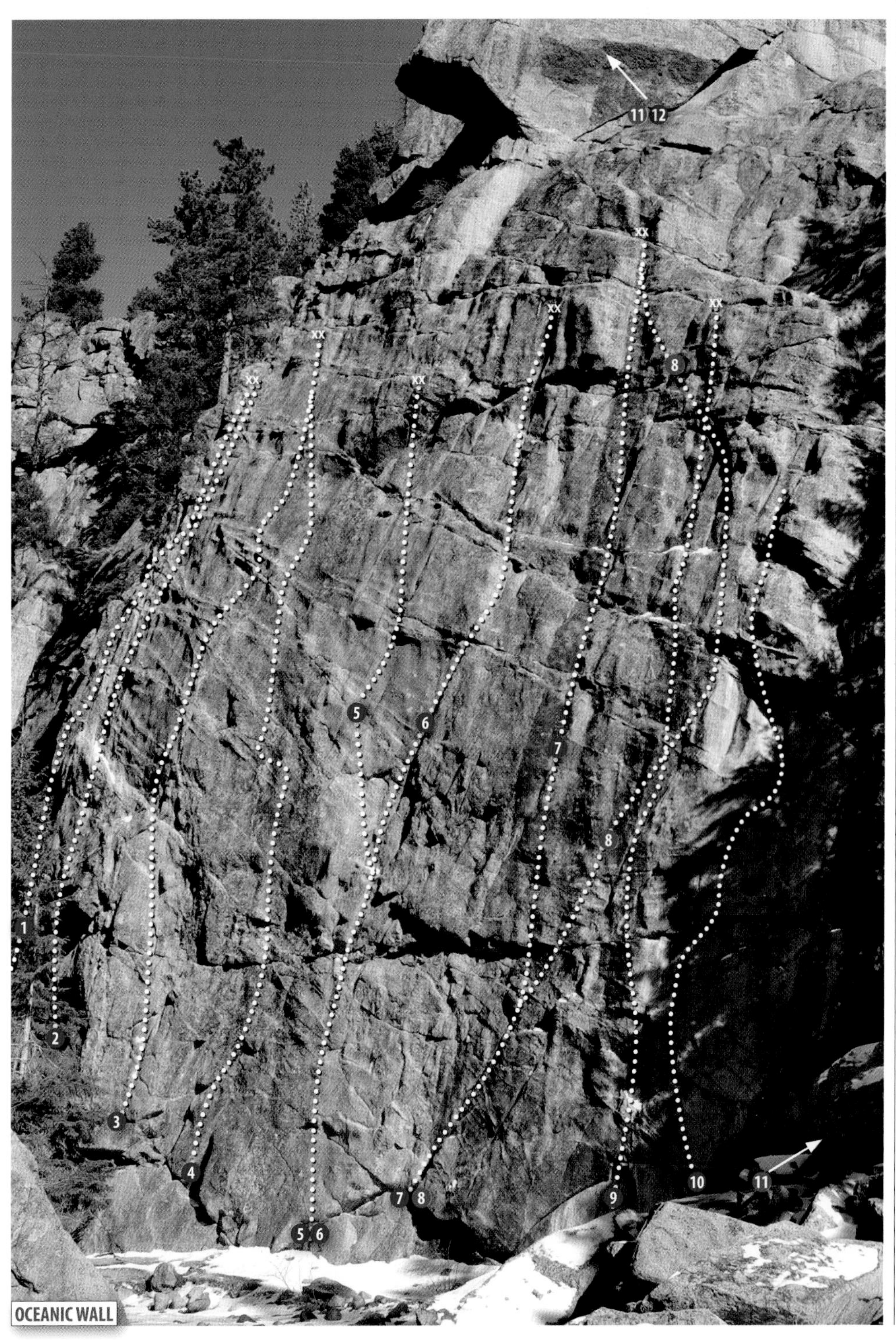
xx
xx
xx
xx
xx
xx
8
11 12
1
2
3
4
5
6
7
8
5 6
7 8
9
10
11
OCEANIC WALL

DREAM DOME UDC

Approach time: 10 - 15 minutes.
Exposure: Southwest.

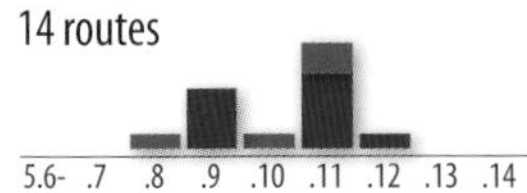

Another beautiful piece of granite located right beside Boulder Creek and just right of the Oceanic Wall. Quality routes, seclusion and a great place to just hang.

Access: See direction for Upper Dream Canyon (page 232). To reach Dream Wall just walk slightly right of Oceanic Wall to a gully that separates the two walls. This puts you at *Wrinkles in Time* on Dream Dome. To access the routes 1 to 6 on the upper left side of the wall you have to climb a short 5.7 section with gear (to 2.5 inches).

1 Dreamscape 5.8 ★★ ☐
On the far left side of the cliff and about seventy feet up the gully, climb a slab up to a corner past four bolts, trend right and finish on the last two bolts of *Sea of Dreams*.
6 bolts, gear to 2.5 inches.
Descent: Rap from a tree or walk off.

2 Sea of Dreams 5.11b ★★ ☐
Climb a nice dihedral/arete system up to a lower-angled slab. Rap from a tree or walk off.
8 bolts and medium cams for the belay.

3 Flying Vee 5.10b R ★ ☐
Climb the V-shaped corner with scarce gear up to the anchor on *Soul on Ice*.
1 bolt, gear to 2 inches.

4 Soul on Ice 5.11a ★★★ ☐
Pitch 1: 5.11a. A good route that climbs the face/arete just right of *Flying Vee*. Continuous moves on excellent granite. One of the better pitches on the rock.
Pitch 2: 5.9. An easy short pitch leads to the top.
13 bolts, gear if you belay at the base of the climb.

5 Dry Ice 5.11a/b ★★ ☐
Climb past a bolt and then into a short corner that leads to a flake going left. Make a difficult move past the flake and then up to the anchor for *Soul on Ice*.
9 bolts a few small cams.

6 Stained Glass 5.11b ★★★ ☐
Pitch 1: 5.11a/b. Start about 20 feet up the gully and climb a short overhang to a ledge, angle right and follow the line bolts to the anchor.
9 bolts.
Pitch 2: 5.11c. Climb the short corner/slab and then up a short headwall to the anchor on the left.
13 quickdraws.

7 Wrinkles in Time 5.9 ★★★★ ☐
Pitch 1: 5.9 Start at the obvious flake/crack just right of the gully. Gain a finger crack and then climb the beautiful featured rock to the anchor.
Pitch 2: 5.8 Continue to anchors at the top.
Can be done in a single 60-meter pitch with lots of quickdraws.
Lots of bolts and few small to medium cams.

8 Phantasmagoria 5.11a ★ ☐
Pitch 1: 5.11a. Climb a short face past a bolt, then up past overlaps and a small roof and then to the belay.
Pitch 2: 5.10b/c. Climb the clean slab with a thin crack to the anchor. Rappel the route.
7 quickdraws and gear to 2.5 inches.

9 Tales of Power 5.11b ★★★ ☐
Pitch 1: 5.11b. Climb up right to a small roof and pull it on the right. Layback up to a right-facing corner and then left out a small roof and the anchor.
Pitch 2: 5.11b. Climb the slab/groove to the upper anchor. Rappel the route.
Variation: Journey to Ixtlan 5.11a ☐
Clip the first bolt on the second pitch then veer right up the slab.
12 quickdraws.

10 Red Limit 5.12d ★★★ ☐
Begin 30 feet right from *Tales of Power* at a left-facing corner. Climb up easy rock past three bolts, then difficult moves into a shallow dihedral. Thin liebacks lead up the dihedral to the anchor.
9 bolts.

11 A Brief History of Time 5.9 ★★ ☐
Climb the obvious right-facing crack/flake on the right side of the wall to a nice face to a finger crack that leads to the anchors.
2 bolts and gear to 3 inches.

12 Timeless 5.9+ ★★ ☐
Start just right of *A Brief History of Time* on a scooped face that leads to a nice slab and the anchor.
10 bolts.

13 Gully Washer 5.9+ ★★ ☐
Climb featured rock on the far right side of the wall. Nice warm-up.
6 bolts.

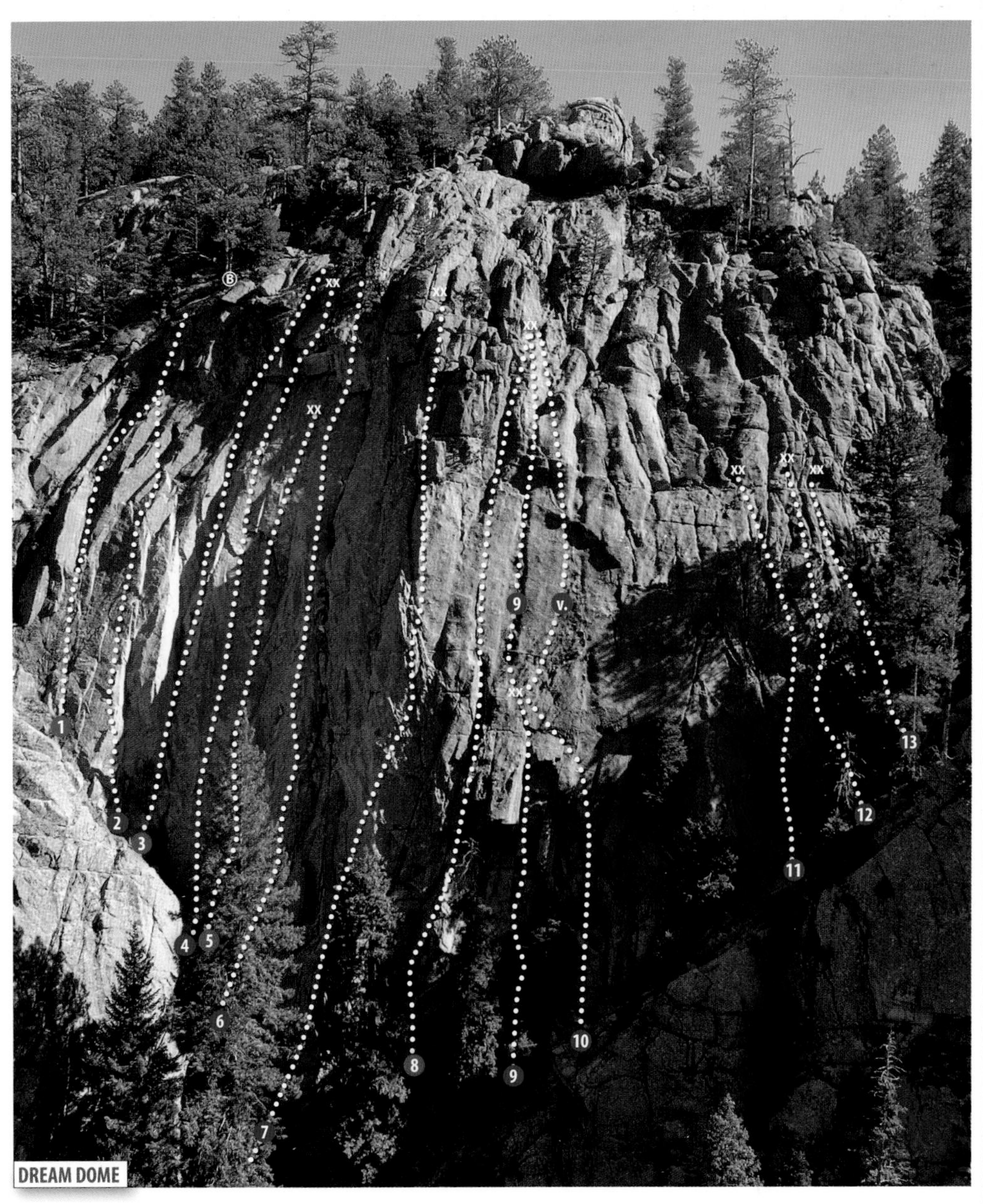
DREAM DOME
1
2
3
4
5
6
7
8
9
9
10
11
12
13
V.
B
XX

THE TERRACE UDC

Approach time: 5 minutes.
Exposure: South and east.

2 routes

5.6- .7 .8 .9 .10 .11 .12 .13 .14

A short wall located just downstream from the Oceanic Wall.

Access: See page 232. From the Oceanic Wall, cross the stream and walk downhill for 50 yards. Head right up the hill to the base of the wall.

Climbs listed from left to right.

❶ Arete 5.9 ★
Cimb the slab on the left side of the arete to reach the arete proper.
4 bolts.

❷ Dream Scene 5.11b ★★
Climb a short face on the right side of the arete to gain a ledge. Move up and left from the ledge to the arête, then on to the anchor.
8 bolts.

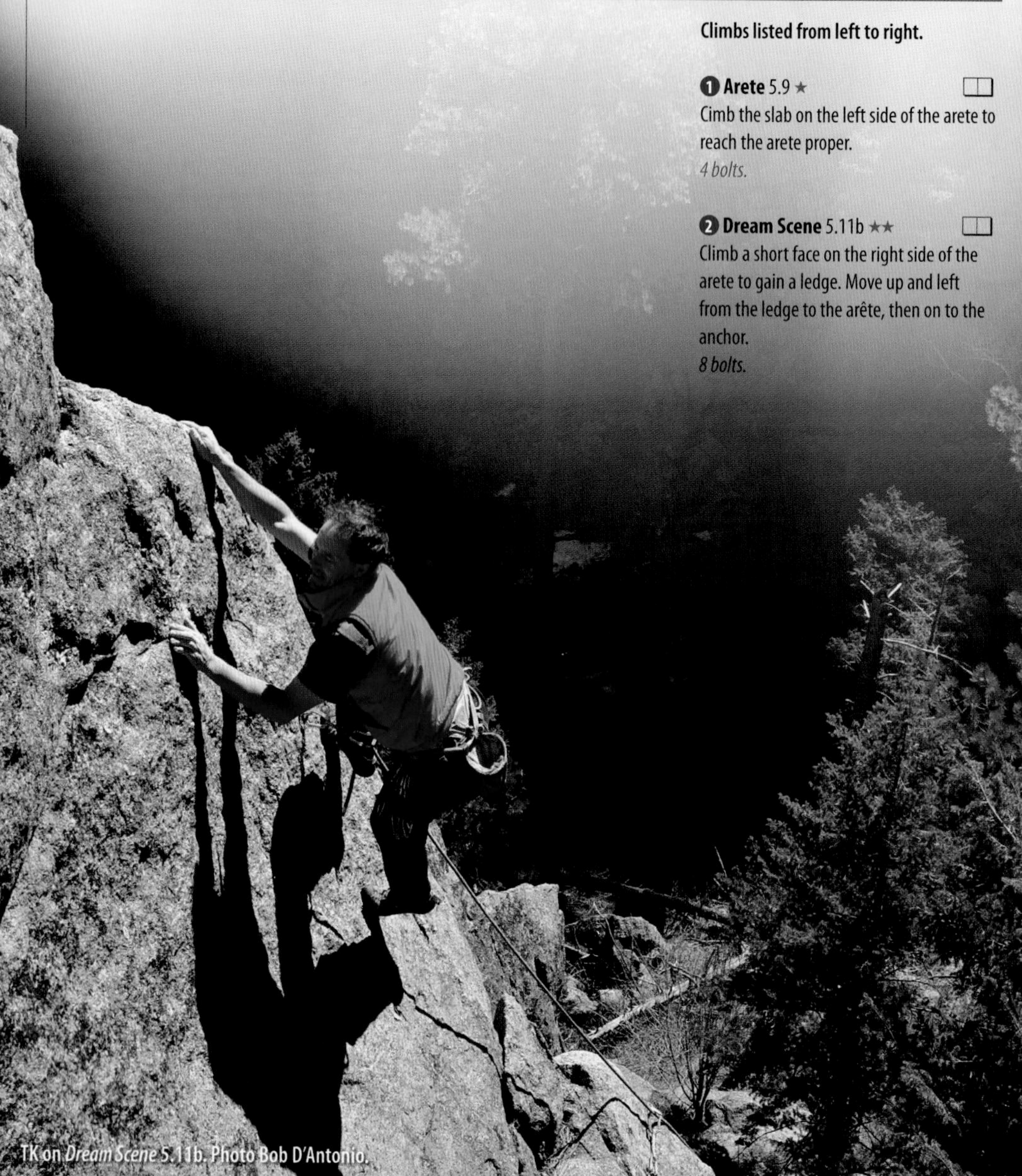

TK on *Dream Scene* 5.11b. Photo Bob D'Antonio.

UNIVERSAL CRAG/SPIDER'S DEN UDC

Approach time: 5 minutes.
Exposure: North.

9 routes

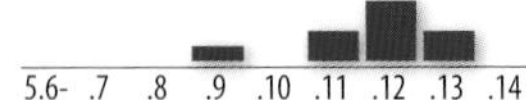

An extremely overhanging granite block located slightly downstream and across the creek from Lost Angel.

Access: See directions for Upper Dream Canyon (page 232). From the base of the Lost Angel, walk downhill and cross the creek at a log crossing. Follow a trail down along the creek for 200 yards to the obvious rock on the right.

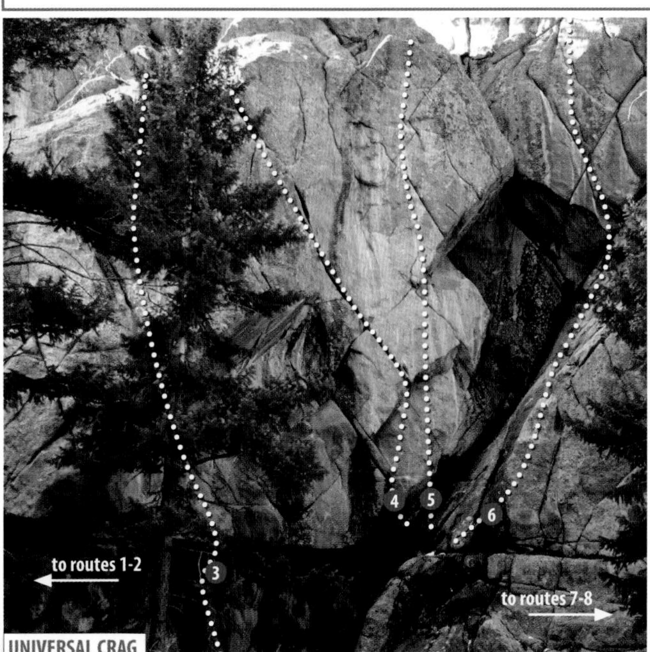

9

THE SPIDER'S DEN

❶ Palm Pilot 5.13d ★★★ ☐
Powerful climbing through a series of roofs to a severely overhanging arete.
8 bolts.

❷ Fighting Irish 5.12d ★★★ ☐
Climb the whitish overhanging dihedral on the left side of the wall.
5 bolts.

❸ Dream Machine 5.12c ★★ ☐
Climb a short face to an overhang, power out the roof, then up the face to a hard move to reach the anchor.
9 bolts.

❹ Equator 5.11c ★★★ ☐
Climb the overhung crack system just right of the roof. Great route. Good warm-up.
7 bolts.

❺ Magna Headwall 5.13a ★★ ☐
Climb the steep wall just right of *Equator*.
7 bolts.

❻ Cum Laude Overhang 5.12c/d ★★ ☐
Short and powerful, possible sandbag. Climb the slab to a belay bolt, then swing left up the steep face using cracks to gain slab and the anchor.
4 bolts.

❼ Cognitive Ability 5.12b ★ ☐
Climb a short right-facing corner with a thin crack to gain the arête. Move right on the arete with a hard move to gain the anchors.
7 bolts.

❽ Temptress 5.9 ★ ☐
On the right side of the wall is short finger crack. Climb it.
Gear to 1.5 inches.

THE SPIDER'S DEN

From the log crossing, go right, upstream, for a hundred feet to the wall on the left. A lone bolted route shoots up the steep face.

❾ Spider's and Snakes 5.11c/d ★★ ☐
Climb the obvious steep face and race the pump factor to the anchor. Good route in a nice setting.
8 bolts.

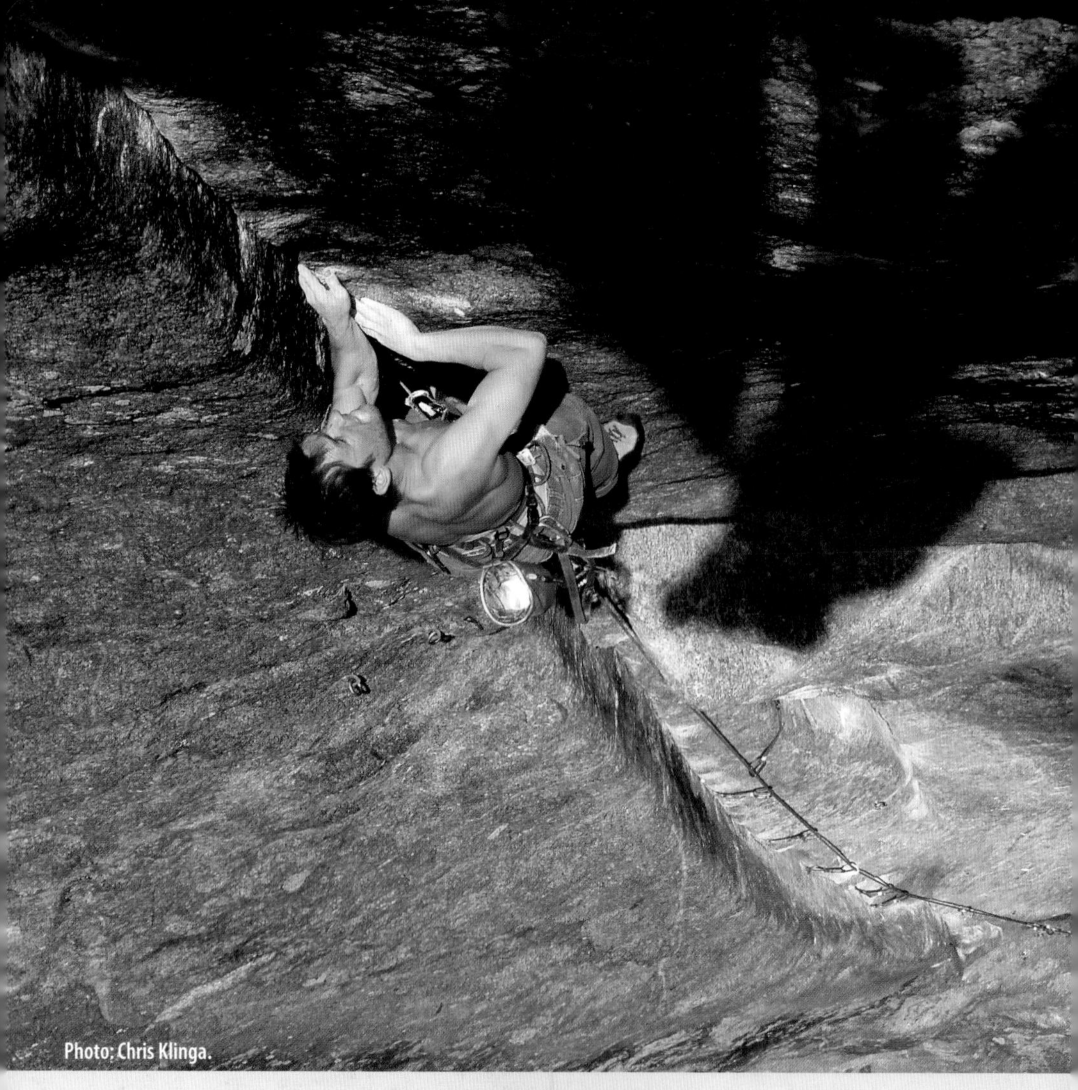

Photo: Chris Klinga.

Mike Patz, **China Doll**

"Like a lot of obsessive climbers I am always looking for the coolest hardest routes that I can fathom attempting. *China Doll* is one of the few routes that has left me with some lasting satiation. In the spring of 2007 I had medical school on the East Coast scheduled to start in the coming months, so I was looking for something that would represent the culmination of my life as a 'Colorado climber.' The unclimbed full pitch of *China Doll* was the obvious line, but the thought of placing gear on the sketchy lower section and then falling repeatedly in the last 30 feet and then having to climb to the top to clean the gear for each burn just made it seem like too much of a bitch. Fortunately, I had found a motivated partner to try it with, Brian Kimball, so I really had no choice.

"Taking the bolts out on the original 13c lower section has been debated but to date they remain. For those seeking the trad experience they can easily be ignored. Whether the bolts are chopped or not, I hope that people will make an effort to leave *China Doll* free of further change (leftover protection or new pin scars) that would detract from the next free ascent. Enjoy!"

LOST ANGEL WALL UDC

Approach time: 10 - 15 minutes.
Exposure: East, south and southwest.

41 routes

5.6- .7 .8 .9 .10 .11 .12 .13 .14

Lost Angel Wall is the largest piece of granite in the Boulder area and host to a number of really good routes on excellent granite. Several multi-pitch routes grace the wall, as do many single pitch routes of high quality. The routes vary in length from one to five pitches and most routes are equipped with rappel anchors.

Access: See directions for Upper Dream Canyon (page 232).

THE ZEN GARDEN WALL

This nice wall is on the far left side of the Lost Angel Wall and has a handful of nice routes up less than vertical rock. Rap from a two-bolt anchor located just left (climber's left) of the gully to reach a ledge where all the routes start.

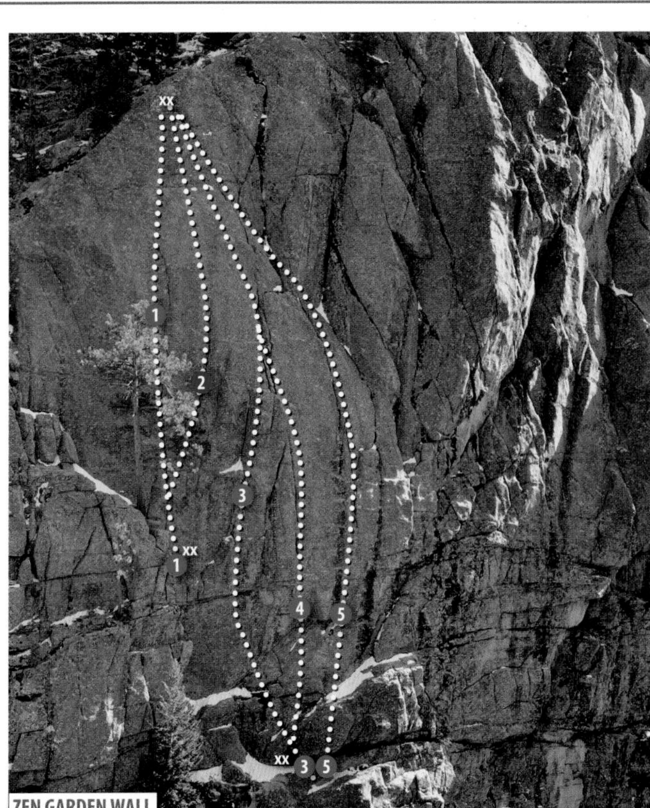

ZEN GARDEN WALL

❶ Time Traveler 5.9 ★★ ☐

This route is the farthest left route on Zen Garden Wall. Scramble down the gully to a large tree and locate a two-bolt anchor. Climb up the perfect hand/finger crack as it gets smaller and turns to a seam...then to blank face with two bolts until you reach the anchor.

2 bolts, light rack to 2 inches.

❷ Shape Shifters 5.9- ★★ ☐

Climb the first 20 feet of *Time Traveler* and then move right to the *Shape Shifters* crack. Follow the crack to slab and past two bolts to the anchor.

10 bolts.

❸ Be Here Now 5.8 ★ ☐

Start right of *Shape Shifters* and climb a face leading to a corner/crack system. Jam the crack and then veer left past bolts to the anchor for *Time Traveler*.

5 bolts, light rack to 1 inch.

❹ Knowoneness 5.9 ★ ☐

Climb a short roof past three bolts then into a wide fist crack. Veer left at the top and join *Be Here Now* and follow it to the anchor.

6 bolts, light rack to 4 inches.

❺ Crazy Wisdom 5.11a ★★ ☐

Climb the short roof on the right side of the wall, gain a finger crack, and then go left to *Be Here Now* and to up to the anchors.

5 bolts, gear to 1 inch.

The next routes start from the bottom of the wall by the creek.

❻ Raise the Titanic 5.11a ★★ ☐

This route starts from the creek on the far left side of the wall. Climb up a nice slab to a roof. Fire the roof to reach a two bolt anchor.

5 bolts.

7 Strange Cargo 5.11a ★★★ ☐

Pitch 1: 5.11a. Climb the obvious roof just right of *Raise the Titanic* to a bolted belay.

Pitch 2: 5.10a. Follow a line of bolts up the vertical face.

Pitch 3: 5.10b. Climb up to a tree and then gain the arête. Follow the arete past several bolts to the anchor. Walk off to the left and down the gully.

12 quickdraws and gear to 1.5 inches.

8 Autumn 5.11a/b ★★★ ☐

Great route and climbing.

Pitch 1: 5.10c. Climb a steep face past two bolts to easier ground and then up vertical ground to the anchor.

Pitch 2: 5.10b. Up steep terrain past bolts to a belay at the base of a corner.

Pitch 3: 5.11a/b. Follow bolts left of the belay up a steep face just right of wide crack to the anchors. Rap the route or walk off to the west.

14 quickdraws and gear to 3 inches.

9 Hunky Monkey 5.11a/b ★★★ ☐

Classic.

Pitch 1: 5.10b/c. Climb the obvious, large, right-facing corner to a good belay on the left.

Pitch 2: 5.10a/b. Step right and up past bolts to a roof. Veer right past the roof and then gain a corner leading to a sloping ledge and the anchor.

Pitch 3: 5.11a/b. Climb up the slab and then left up a steep wall to gain another slab. Follow the steep slab to good ledge and the anchor.

Pitch 4: 5.10b/c. Climb the slab past a ledge and then up to a small roof. Climb the roof and then reach the anchor. Rap the route or walk off to the west.

14 quickdraws.

10 Divination 5.11b ★★★ ☐

Classic.

Pitch 1: 5.11b. Climb up just right of the water line from a ledge, going left to gain a steep face. Climb the face past several bolts and two small roofs to gain the belay.

Pitch 2: 5.10c. Climb the obvious corner till it ends, go left and gain another corner and follow that to the anchor.

Pitch 3: 5.10a. Climb the ramp to a small roof. Climb the roof and then reach the anchor.

Variation: 5.11d. Climb a short face starting at the waterline gaining the start of the first pitch.

15 quickdraws.

11 Dynamometer 5.13a ★★ ☐

Pitch 1: 5.13a. Climb the steep face just right of *Divination* via side-pulls, sloping holds, and weird laybacks, ending on same belay ledge as *Divination*.

Pitch 2: 5.11d. Climb up to a ramp and then gain a short arete that leads to the anchor. Rap the route. A hard onsight.

15 quickdraws.

12 Earth Voyage 5.12a ★★★★ ☐

Pitch 1: 5.12a. Start left of *China Doll*, up easy rock to the first bolt. Veer left and then mantel to gain a short crack. Climb it to reach a hanging belay.

Pitch 2: 5.12a. Climb up the steep face gaining a ramp; follow the ramp up to the anchors. Tricky and sustained.

Pitch 3: 5.11d. Climb the tricky slab to a good ledge and anchor.

Pitch 4: 5.10b. Continue up the slab to a roof, fire the roof and then reach the anchors. Rap the route or walk off to the west.

15 quickdraws.

⑬ China Doll 5.14a R ★★★★ ☐

An incredible route with an interesting convoluted history. It was first climbed as a multi-pitch aid route. Bob Horan then freed the lower part of the main dihedral on toprope, later leading it after adding bolts and a belay anchor at a hand jam. Adam Stack later freed the pitch, rated 5.13b/c, using only traditional gear. His ascent used a foothold, which had been previously reinforced with glue and necessitated a rightward traverse midway. The foothold has since fallen off, and the dihedral can be climbed directly at 5.13c R. The dihedral continues beyond Horan's anchor, and this extension was pink-pointed by Mike Patz, and redpointed shortly thereafter by Stack at 5.13d R. However, Patz and buddy Brian Kimball did not see the route as complete, hoping it would go in a single monster pitch. It starts with Horan's bolted .13c linking into an overhanging, right leaning, 30-foot corner, protected by only 2 small wires. In 2007 Patz freed the route in a single, 130-foot traditionally protected pitch from the ground at 5.14a R. This pitch stands as one of the best and hardest traditional routes in the country. The original aid route continues for a couple more pitches of easy but chossy climbing.

● The bolts are still in place and Horan's ☐ original line can be led as a 5.13c sport climb.

Rack to 1.5 inches.

⑭ Beauty and the Bolts 5.11d ★★ ☐

This route can easily be reached by rapping from the top of the rock.

Pitch 1: 5.10b. Start from the top of the free version of *China Doll* and climb a nice face past six bolts to anchors.

Pitch 2: 5.11d. Fire up the steep face to a small roof and then easier rock to top. Walk off to the west.

12 quickdraws and gear to 2.5 inches.

⑮ Archangel 5.12 A0 ☐

Pitch 1: 5.9. Climb a short face just right of a black streak to a ledge and anchor.

Pitch 2: 5.12 A0 The obvious right-facing corner, may not yet be fully equipped or freed.

3 bolts and gear to 1.5 inches.

⑯ Digital Dilemma 5.12a ★★ ☐

The second route right of *China Doll*. Climb over a short roof to gain a steep face and then climb a small corner to reach the anchor.

8 bolts.

⑰ Dyno Arete 5.11b ★ ☐

A strange one-move wonder. Climb as for *Freedom* and then go left to the arête. Continue up the arete to the anchors.

7 bolts.

⑱ Freedom 5.9+ ★ ☐

Climb a short face to gain a right-facing corner. Climb the corner, then traverse right for 30 feet to the anchor for *Rock Odyssey*.

8 bolts and maybe a few finger size pieces.

⑲ Rock Odyssey 5.12c ★★ ☐

Pitch 1: 5.11c. Start about 35 feet right of Freedom and climb a nice face/slab to the anchor.

Pitch 2: 5.11d. Traverse left across the face, following bolts, to gain a short corner/crack that leads to the anchor.

Pitch 3: 5.10a. Traverse left and gain a ledge just left of *China Doll*.

Pitch 4: 5.11d. Go left from the belay and then up a slab on the left side of the arete to a belay.

Pitch 5: 5.12c. Veer left from the belay and then up and left to a roof, passing a loose block. Fire the roof and then up the face to the woods.

Variation:

Tripendicular Wildman 5.12c ★★ ☐

From the start of pitch five on *Rock Odyssey*, trend right and up over the obvious tiered roof and then a steep face to a belay. Climb a steep face past bolts to gain the top. Walk off to the west.

16 quickdraws and few long slings.

⑳ Awakenings 5.12a ★★ ☐

Pitch 1: 5.11a/b. Start as for *Rock Odyssey*. Climb past the second bolt and then up and right up a steep slab to the belay.

Pitch 2: 5.12a. Clip a bolt on the right and then head up a thin flake/crack to a right-facing corner. Climb the corner and then over a small roof to a ledge. Follow the thin seam past hard moves to gain the anchor.

Pitch 3: 5.9. Follow cracks in the steep face to the top.

14 quickdraws and light rack to 1.5 inches.

㉑ Naked Lunch 5.11d ★★★ ☐

Pitch 1: 5.10d. Climb easy rock up and right to the obvious right-leaning corner. Climb the corner then step left up the face to anchors. Step left on the ledge past the anchor and reach the anchor for *Rock Odyssey*.

Pitch 2: 5.10b. Go up and right from the belay gaining a short corner, step left out the corner then up the face on the right side of the arete to the belay.

Pitch 3: 5.11d. Go right to gain a ramp/corner. Climb up a thin seam, gaining the arete, then the anchor.

Pitch 4: 5.10b. Step left to gain a chimney, climb over a small roof and then gain the anchor. Rap the route.

14 quickdraws.

㉒ Zentropa 5.11c ★★ ☐

Great route and climbing.

Pitch 1: 5.11c. Locate a bolt just of left of a handcrack. Climb past the bolt to reach a finger crack. Climb the crack to a steep face past three bolts and then head right on a ramp to the anchors.

Pitch 2: 5.8. Climb the obvious corner to a two-bolt belay at 50 feet on the right.

Pitch 3: 5.10c/d. Climb a short face to gain a beautiful finger crack, then follow the bolts to the top.

10 quickdraws and light rack to 1.5 inches.

㉓ Sighs of Life 5.11a ★★ ☐

Just left of *Long Dong Dihedral*. Go over a small roof past a bolt to another roof, making a hard move to gain the face. Climb the face to a corner, then reach an arete that leads to the anchor.

11 bolts.

㉔ Long Dong Dihedral 5.8 ★★ ☐

This route climbs the obvious right-facing dihedral system that splits the right side of the wall in three pitches.

SR.

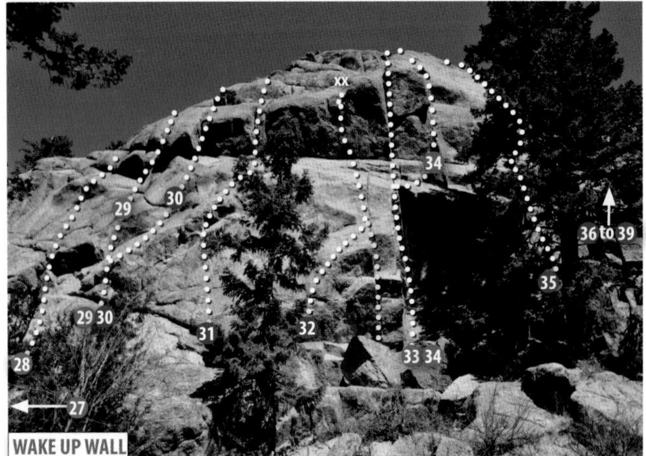

25 Disneyland 5.11d ★★ ☐

Pitch 1: 5.11d. Start right of *Long Dong Dihedral*. Climb a ramp that leads up to a steep face and then into a short corner system, climbing over a roof to the belay/ anchor.

Pitch 2: 5.11a. Head left up the slab and then into a corner. Angle left from the corner and then up the face to the anchor.

13 quickdraws.

26 Weenie Roast 5.9 ★ ☐

Pitch 1: 5.9. Start on the right side of the wall climbing through a V-shaped dihedral to a good belay ledge.

Pitch 2: 5.9. Follow steep cracks to a flaring hand crack. Follow the crack to the top.

SR.

WAKE UP WALL

This excellent section of the Lost Angel Wall is located just right of the approach gully and has several good one-pitch routes.

27 Life on Mars 5.10a/b ★★ ☐

This is the left-most route on the wall and is gained by walking across the low angle slab to a left-facing corner. Climb the corner, moving right past a roof, and then up a thin crack to the top.

Gear to 2 inches.

28 Killing in the Name 5.9 ★ ☐

Climb a short face past a bolt to gain a crack. Climb the crack then go right to the anchors for *Take the Power Back*.

Gear to 2 inches.

29 Take the Power Back 5.9 ★★ ☐

Climb a short face past a bolt and then left into a corner/crack system that leads to the anchor.

1 bolt, gear to two inches.

30 Rush 5.11b/c ★★ ☐

Start with *Take the Power Back* and go right past the first bolt over a bulge and then a strenuous overhang. Veer left to the anchors for *Take the Power Back*.

5 bolts.

31 Rage Against the Machine 5.11a/b ★★ ☐

Climb a short slab, then over a small roof up to a roof with a splitter crack. Fire the roof and then gain an easy crack that leads to the anchor.

6 bolts.

32 The Host 5.12a ★ ☐

Start just left of the obvious right-facing corner. Climb a short slab to reach a thin seam, follow the seam and then go left over the roof to the anchor.

Variation: The Vaino Step 5.12a ☐

Start just left of the corner using an arete to gain the thin seam.

8 bolts.

33 Jungle Blues from Jupiter 5.11a/b ★★ ☐

This route climbs the obvious overhanging right-facing corner over a series of roofs to easy climbing to the top and the anchor.

Gear to 3 inches.

34 Spiders from Mars 5.11b/c ★★ ☐

Start for *Jungle Blues*. Climb over the first roof, traverse right to gain a right-facing corner, climb the steep corner, and then head back left to the last section of *Jungle Blues*.

Gear to 3 inches.

35 The Caterer 5.12b ★★ ☐

Climb up easy rock just right of *Jungle Blues* to gain a short right-facing corner with gear. Angle right up a steep face past several bolts to the anchor.

9 bolts, few small pieces for the corner.

36 Drop Zone 5.10b/c ★ ☐

Start at a tree. Climb the face past several bulges to the upper face/slab that leads to the anchor.

8 bolts.

37 AA Arete 5.10b ★★ ☐

A nice route that climbs the obvious arete right of *Drop Zone* and left of *Boy's World*.

8 bolts.

38 Technical Remote Viewing 5.11a ★★ ☐

Start next to a large pine near the rock, about 30 feet right of *AAArete*. Climb up to, and then follow, a left-angling small roof. Step over the roof and follow a slab to the anchors.

7 bolts.

39 Standard Route 5.6 ☐

Start from a shelf about 15 feet right of *Technical Remote Viewing*, at the far right side of the Wake Up Wall, and near the top of the trail/gully. Follow bolts up the nice slab, trending left near the top to reach the last bolt of *Technical Remote Viewing* or continue up to a crack.

6 bolts.

JESSICA'S BLOCK UDC

Approach time: 10 - 15 minutes.
Exposure: Southwest and west.

3 routes

5.6- .7 .8 .9 .10 .11 .12 .13 .14

A nice, short, compact block of granite located just west of Midnight Rock.

Access: See page 232. From the Wake Up Wall (Lost Angel), continue straight down the gully for 300 feet, then go left across easy slabs and look left and up to the wall located 150 feet before Midnight Rock.

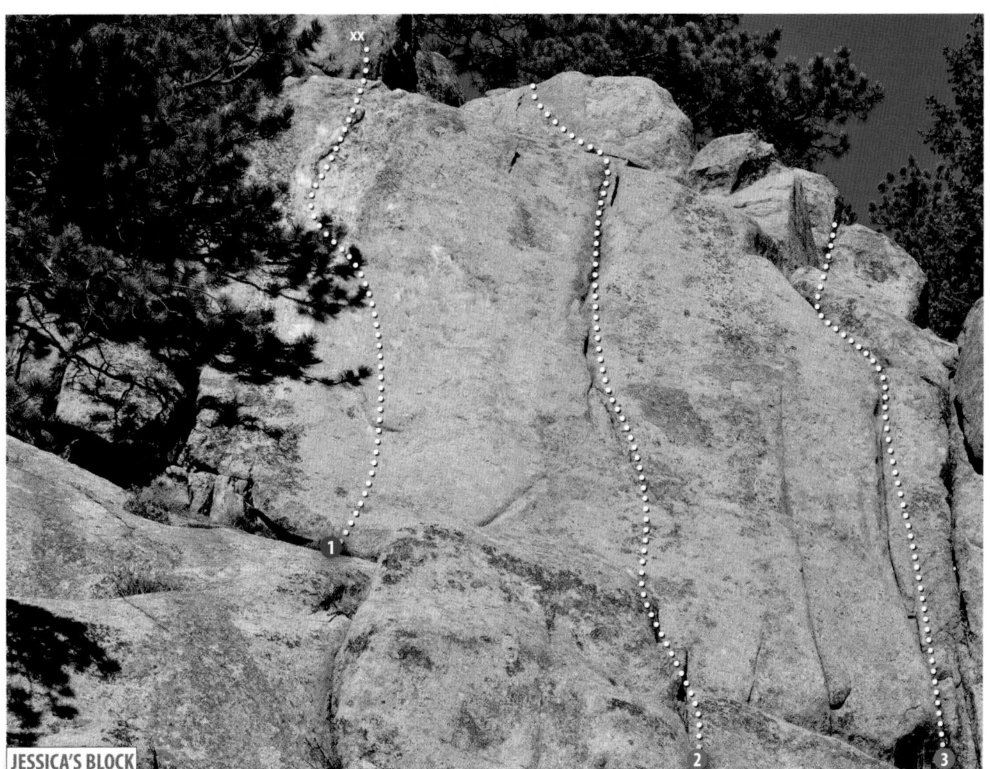

1 Sister Sweetly 5.12a ★
The clean, short face on the left side of the rock.
4 bolts.

2 Jessica's Route 5.9 ★
The short crack that splits the wall.
Gear to 2 inches.

3 Kids Line 5.10b ★★★
The nice crack on the right side of the wall. Short and sweet.
Gear to 3 inches.

MIDNIGHT ROCK UDC

Approach time: 10 - 15 minutes.
Exposure: Southwest and west.

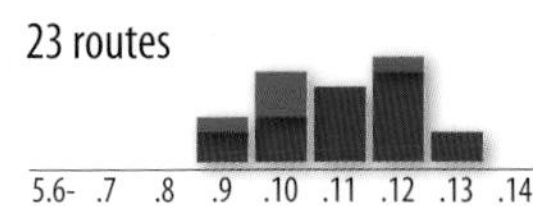

A nice compact cliff with several good trad and sport climbs located on two separate tiers. The cliff has nice exposure and can be climbed year round.

Access: See page 232. From the Wake Up Wall (Lost Angel) continue straight down the gully for 300 feet, then go left across easy slabs to the base of Midnight Rock.

1 The Cage 5.9+ R ★ ☐
On the far left side of the wall, start below a roof leading to a flake. Climb to the flake, then angle left up thin cracks to a ledge. Walk off to the north.
Gear to 2 inches.

2 Birds of Prey 5.10b/c ★ ☐
Climb a shallow corner/crack on the left side of the wall, climbing over a roof then up a thin crack angling slightly left to the anchors.
Gear to 2 inches.

3 Cirque Du Soleil 5.12c ★★★ ☐
Climb the short face up past bolts to the left-leaning arete and then up to the anchors. Devious and technical.
7 bolts.

4 Hammer Down 5.11d ★★★ ☐
Climb a short right-facing corner over a roof and then tenuous moves lead up a slab to the crux roof and the anchors.
9 bolts.

5 Union with Earth 5.10d ★ ☐
Climb the obvious roof crack just right of *Cirque Du Soleil.*
3 bolts, gear to 2 inches.

6 Around Midnight 5.13? ☐
Climb the face up to the large roof, tackle the roof (A0) and then up and left to finish for *Hammer Down*.
10 bolts, 1 pin.

7 Flake Roof 5.12c ★★ ☐
Climb the slab just left of the large chimney up to a roof. Power over the roof and into a left-facing corner leading to the anchors.
10 bolts.

8 Melt Down 5.10d ★★ ☐
Start as for *Flake Roof* but go right at the roof up a ramp and steep face leading to a thin crack and anchor.
10 quickdraws and gear to 3 inches.

The next two routes start on the ledge right above the anchor for Melt Down *and use a common anchor to belay from.*

9 The Engine 5.10d ★★ ☐
Climb a thin crack on the left side of the ledge that leads up a steep bolted face and the anchor.
5 bolts, and gear to 1 inch.

10 The Caboose 5.11c ★★ ☐
Climb the wide crack up to a thin seam and the anchor.
6 bolts.

11 Pirate Radar 5.12a ★★ ☐
Start on the face below the obvious large roof. Climb through the roof via laybacks and jams and then up to the anchor.
6 bolts and one 2 inch piece.

12 The Jet Stream 5.12a ★★ ☐
Just right of a large roof, climb a dihedral up to slab, go left and then up a right-angling crack to the anchor.
5 bolts, gear to 2.5 inches.

13 Midnight Cowboy 5.12a/b ★★ ☐
Climb the *Jet Stream* to the slab. Fire up the short right-facing corner to a ramp. A hard move and thin seam get you to the anchors.
9 bolts and few finger size pieces.

14 Midnight Express 5.10d ★★ ☐
Climb the right of two corners up to easy rock and then a clean face to the anchors.
Variation: After Midnight 5.11c ☐
At bolt 6 go left and finish for *Jet Stream*.
9 bolts.

15 Karma Kamelian 5.11c ★★ ☐
This route starts on a ledge above *Midnight Express*. Climb a short pitch past the anchor for *Midnight Express* and belay at an anchor below the route. The route climbs three clean faces broken by ledges.
12 bolts and one 2 inch piece.

16 The Stoke of Midnight 5.10d ★★ ☐
Climb over a short roof to a slab and then to a shallow corner and crack.
9 bolts.

17 Weather Report 5.9 ★ ☐
Climb a short face/slab and then up an arete past several bolts, then up a short corner to the anchor.
9 bolts.

18 Crack a Smile 5.11c ★★ ☐
Climb the obvious right-facing corner on the right side of the rock to a thin crack and hard moves past bolt four. Continue up the face on the right of the arete to the anchor.
9 bolts and couple of small stoppers.

MIDNIGHT ROCK
XX
XX
XX
XX
XX
XX
XX
XX
1
2
3
4
4
5
5
6
7
8
7
8
9
10
11
12
13
14

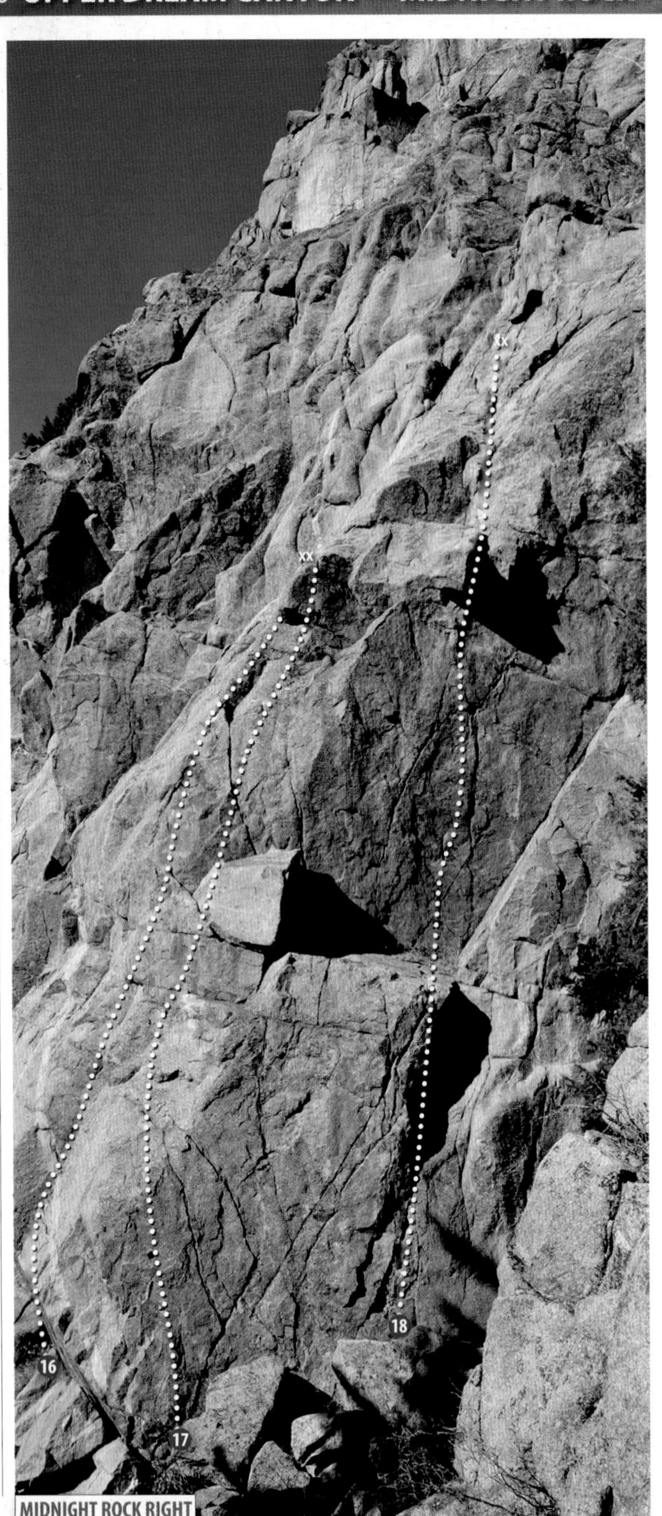

⑲ Grande Finale 5.12c/d ★★ ☐

Climb the overhanging face right of *Crack a Smile* to a right-facing corner and the anchor.

7 bolts.

⑳ Viola 5.12b ★ ☐

The right-most route on the lower wall. Climb a steep face past several bolts and hard moves up to easier rock.

11 bolts.

The next three routes are located on the upper right side of Midnight Rock just above Weather Report. *The best way to access the climbs is by climbing* Weather Report *or from the top of Midnight Rock via a gully that leads to the base of the climbs.*

㉑ Geminae Cracks 5.13a ★★ ☐

Climb the bolted flaring cracks on the left side of the upper ledge/wall. Hard and technical.

5 bolts.

㉒ Deus Ex Machina 5.11c ★★ ☐

The route climbs the left side of an overhanging face through a small overhang.

5 bolts.

㉓ Dyno Mart 5.12b ★★ ☐

Climb a short left-facing corner up to a roof to reach the anchors.

5 bolts.

Sarah Fritz on The Vanishing 5.11c/d, Vanishing Point, next page. Photo Dan Hare.

VANISHING POINT UDC

Approach time: 10 - 15 minutes.
Exposure: Southwest.

10 routes

5.6-	.7	.8	.9	.10	.11	.12	.13	.14

Another beautiful piece of granite located right beside Boulder Creek and just right of the Oceanic Wall. Quality routes, seclusion, and a great place to just hang.

Access: See page 232. Follow the main trail to the upper right side of Lost Angel Wall (Wake Up Wall, pg. 246). From the Wake Up Wall, continue straight down the gully for 300 feet then go left across easy slabs to the base of Midnight Rock. From Midnight Rock continue downhill to the rock on the left. The wall is split in two…the Left Side and the lower Right Side.

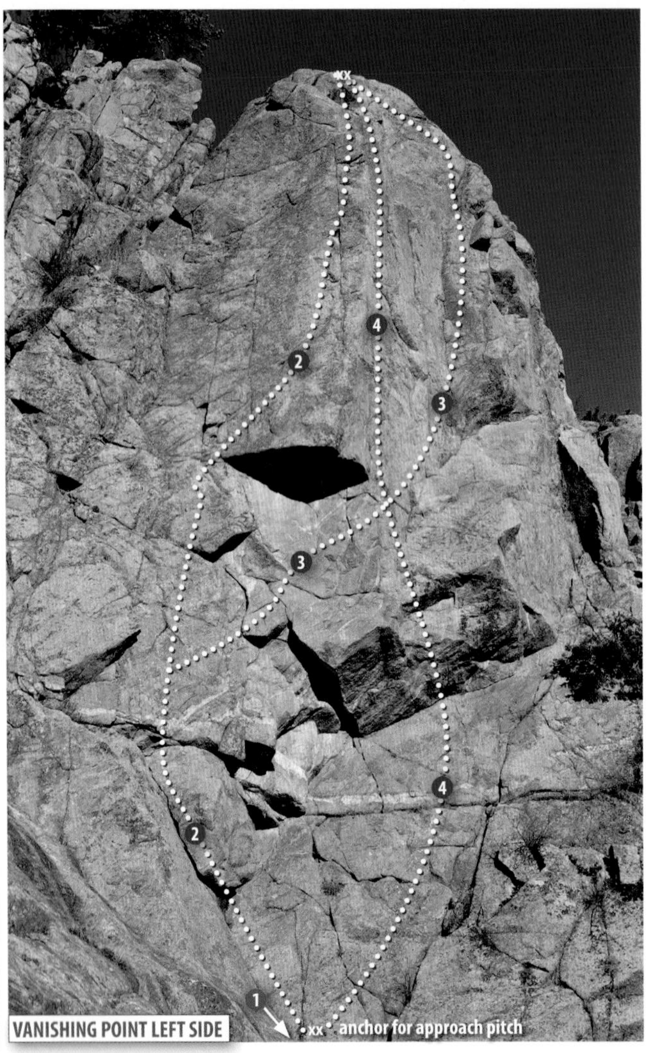

VANISHING POINT LEFT SIDE

THE LEFT SIDE

❶ Approach Pitch 5.6 ★ ☐
To access the climbs on the Left Side you must climb this pitch to a semi-hanging belay.
Gear to 2 inches.

❷ The Vanishing 5.11c/d ★★ ☐
Climb the *Approach Pitch* and climb up left, passing a roof to gain the left side of an arete. Fire the arete to the anchors. Photo page 251.
12 bolts.

❸ Phantom Bridge 5.10b/c ★★ ☐
Climb the *Approach Pitch* and then clip the first four bolts on *The Vanishing*. Veer right under a roof and then up the obvious dihedral to the anchor.
12 bolts.

❹ Vanishing Ink 5.12b ★★ ☐
Climb the *Approach Pitch* and then climb slightly right to a high bolt below the roof. Fire the roof and veer left and climb the right side of the arete to the anchor.
12 bolts.

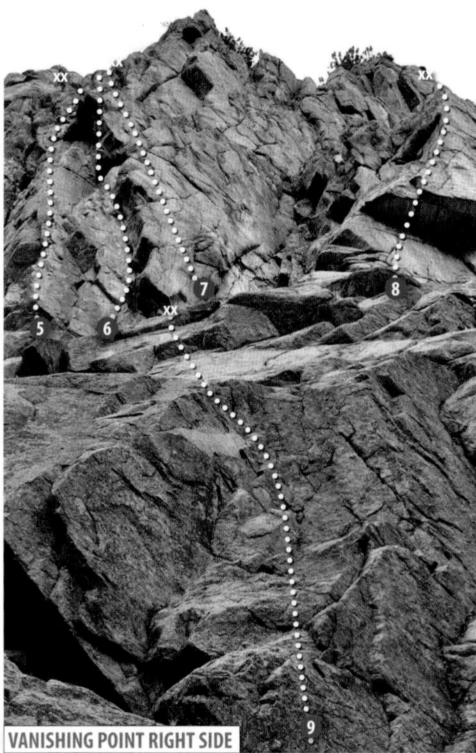

VANISHING POINT RIGHT SIDE

VANISHING POINT RIGHT SIDE

THE RIGHT SIDE

To reach the Right Side, scramble down a steep gully to the obvious, large, right-facing corner.

5 Stand Back 5.11a/b ★ ☐

Climb blocky rock to the first bolt and then climb up the arete with care, passing a few tenuous clips and a loose block around bolt seven.

9 bolts.

6 The Producers 5.11d/12a ★★ ☐

Climb up the gully past the start of *Stand Back* to a two-bolt anchor. Climb the left-facing dihedral via stems to an anchor.

9 bolts.

7 Dreamer's Dream 5.11b/c ★★ ☐

Start from the belay of *The Producers* and then climb the steep face just right of the arete to the anchor.

6 bolts.

8 Didgeridoo 5.11d ★ ☐

Approach from the belay of *Dreamer's Dream* and traverse 50 right on an exposed ledge to the start of the climb. Climb up a steep face through a roof and then the arete to the anchor.

8 bolts.

9 Alpine Moe 5.8 ★ ☐

Climb the obvious slab at the low point of the rock near the trail. Rap from the anchors of *Dreamer's Dream*.

6 bolts and a few small to medium pieces.

10 Werner's Legacy 5.8 ★★★ ☐

The right-most route on the wall and one of the best. Climb the obvious face/arete to the anchor.

7 bolts.

11 Roc Doc 5.10a/b ★★ ☐

Start right of *Werner's Legacy*. Climb the right side of the arete to a steep finish.

4 bolts and gear to 1.5 inches.

12 Orion 5.11b ★★★ ☐

An excellent route that climbs the crack just right of *Roc Doc* through a crux roof.

Gear to 2.5 inches.

THE GREENHOUSE & CLASSIC CLIFF UDC

Approach time: 20 - 25 minutes.
Exposure: North (Classic Cliff), and Southwest (Greenhouse).

6 routes

5.6- .7 .8 .9 .10 .11 .12 .13 .14

These two short cliffs are located on the far southern end of Upper Dream Canyon. They offer short, hard routes away from the crowds in a nice setting. Classic Cliff is somewhat appealing and all of the climbs start right by the creek.

Access: See page 232. Follow the creek downstream, past the last mine pit, then angle slightly south down a narrow trail and gully to the Greenhouse cliff which is located on the right of the trail about 100 feet above the creek. Follow the trail down to the creek for Classic Cliff, which is located directly across from where the trail meets the creek.

3-4. CLASSIC CLIFF LEFT

5.6. CLASSIC CLIFF RIGHT

GREENHOUSE

Routes are listed from left to right.

1 IR 5.11b/c ★
Climb the thin, right-leaning finger crack with tenuous gear to the anchor.
Gear to 1 inch, mostly RP's.

2 UV 5.11a/b ★
Climb the flaring, leaning crack just right of *IR* to the same anchor.
Gear to one inch.

CLASSIC CLIFF

3 Grace Poole 5.11d ★★
Climb the left-most route on the wall starting out of the creek. Clip a high bolt then fire up strenuous laybacks trending right to the anchor.
6 bolts.

4 Jane Eyre 5.11b ★★
Climb the left-leaning black crack up power laybacks to the anchor.
6 bolts.

5 Heathcliff 5.11a ★★
Start 20 feet right of *Jane Eyre*. Climb up a featured face through the obvious overhang to the anchor.
7 bolts.

6 Far From The Madding Crowd 5.11c ★★
Start right of *Jane Eyre*, powering up laybacks to reach a fin and then up the slab to the anchor.
7 bolts.

BOULDERING IN BOULDER CANYON

By Peter Beal. Photos: Andy Mann.

Sadly the reality of bouldering in Boulder Canyon does not equal the promise of its name. However in recent years a small number of very high quality problems and areas have been developed. The rock is very compact granite with an interesting mix of slopers, edges, very small crimps and often very small footholds. The best season to try many of the problems is winter but shade and cooling breezes can be found year-round, depending on the location. Try early evening or morning for the best conditions outside of winter.

This section presents a selection of the highest quality and most accessible problems, none of which are more than a short walk from the car. That said, some are on the far side of Boulder Creek and require some maneuvering to get to — especially if you bring a few pads. Speaking of pads, some of the landings are fairly dangerous without a good pile of pads protecting the base of the problem. There are few true highballs, but hard, uneven talus landings often threaten ankles, backs, and heads. When in doubt, pad thoroughly and bring a spotter or two.

For more Boulder Canyon bouldering beta and videos visit: bouldercanyonbouldering.blogspot.com/

Daniel Woods working the famous and still unclimbed *Cob Rock Roof Project*, a potential v15 (next page). Photo Andy Mann.

EAGLE ROCK

6.2 miles – page 43

Park as for Eagle Rock. *ABD* lies on the south side of the river just upstream from the Eagle Rock Sport Climbing crossing.

Access: See page 43.

AUTHENTIC BATTLE DAMAGE

DAVEY JONES' FOOTLOCKER

❶ Authentic Battle Damage v13 ☐

SDS as low as you can go on gut-busting slopers and battle your way via compression to the finish. There's a v8 stand start from the undercling. A campusy warm-up climbs the underside of the roof left.

❷ Davey Jones' Footlocker v8 ☐

Found 20 yards upstream from *Authentic Battle Damage*. This classic problem climbs the stellar overhanging face to a committing crux move out left that will soak you and your spotters if blown.

Chris Shulte making the first ascent of *Authentic Battle Damage* v13 (opposite). Photo Andy Mann.

COB ROCK 6.6 miles – page 48

A landmark is the famous Cob Rock Roof Project, a massive cave front and center in the talus below the north face of the obvious pinnacle-shaped crag. The bulk of the bouldering is found just east (downstream) of the Roof Project. Another important formation is the Sleepy Hollow Boulder which is found on the west edge of Cob Rock, at the base of the cliff. Descriptions start with that boulder.

Access: Park in a pullout on the left side of the road at 6.6 miles. Locate the Tyrolean traverse just down stream, cross the creek on rock, or wade during low water.

SLEEPY HOLLOW BOULDER

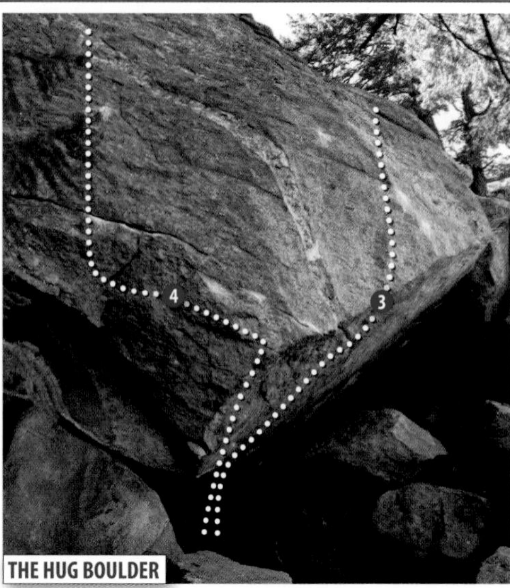

THE HUG BOULDER

Sleepy Hollow Boulder

Head up the talus to the northwest corner of Cob and locate a stunning pillar leaning against the wall.

❶ Sleepy Hollow v9 ☐

Start very low on the pillar and work your way up and left to an obvious jug. Rest up and attack the headwall on thin crimps to a cool two-finger pocket. More like a route than a problem. The landing is complicated and the falls could be serious. Bring multiple pads and a spotter or two.

❷ Headless Horseman v10 ☐

Same start as *Sleepy Hollow* but head out right to the sloping arete and finish up that. Same landing issues as *Sleepy Hollow.*

East Side Boulders

Head east a few dozen yards along the path past the roof project. *The Hug* is just at the edge of the trees. There are a number of problems here at moderate grades (v3-v7) with fairly bad landings. Most boulderers come here to try *The Hug.*

The Hug Boulder

This boulder is uphill and east of the Cob Roof Boulder. It is easily distinguished by a steep undercut base and an obvious flat hold at the lip.

❸ The Hug v11 ☐

Start very low with RH on a good sidepull and LH on the arete. Throw to the lip and work out a very strenuous, technical sequence going right to a spicy final slab. Very uneven landing, so bring lots of pads.

❹ Left Hug v9 ☐

Use the same start as *The Hug* but move left from the lip along the obvious cracks to finish. Same landing issues.

❺ The Roof Project v15

The big overhang at the base of the talus. By any standard, the most obvious Last Great Problem on the Front Range. Many have worked on this behemoth, all have walked away empty handed. Big, steep, with terrible holds and a bad landing. There is said to be a stand-start version of v10 or v11 difficulty. Photo previous page.

THE GRAHAM BOULDER 7.0 miles

Just east of Boulder Falls, a small, isolated boulder on the south side of the stream packs a lot of punch. With at least one v11, a v10 and a v9/10, the Graham Boulder has a lot to offer strong climbers. You'll find good landings and a pleasant atmosphere here.

Access: At about seven miles up-canyon, just across from the "Boulder Falls 1000 feet" sign, locate a pullout on the south side of the creek. Depending on the water level, it is best to cross in the vicinity of the pullout. Expect cold fast water. The trail is a bit difficult to find at first but trend right and it soon gains talus and goes beneath a cliff band. The boulder is about 100 yards downstream. Depending on the water and bushwhacking, expect to take 5 to 10 minutes.

Problems listed from east to west.

1 Left Graham Arete v11 ☐
Sit-start matched on the obvious undercling on the far left side of the north face. The beta varies, but ultimately you are aiming for a poor crimp at the lip for your right hand using an undercling with your left. Go left to a better crimp and then up and right. The stand start is a good v4/5 by itself. Very sharp holds and terrible feet. An alternate finish goes left on good edges behind the tree.

2 North Face Traverse v2/3 ☐
Start at a big jug above head height and traverse across the break, moving up and right to the top. Starting from the LGA undercling is v8, probably harder if you can't dyno for the jug.

3 The Fields Problem v6 or v7/8 ☐
Start on two head-height crimps about 4 feet right of the ramp. Go straight up on small crimps to the rail. The easier version (v6) does a quick pop off the starting holds to a LH intermediate sharp edge and a go-again to the rail. The harder slightly more direct version moves off the LH sharp edge to a bad RH edge straight up, then to the rail.

4 The Capps Problem v10 (or harder) ☐
Right again in a shallow-scoop feature is a likely v10+ problem that starts on two very thin edges and moves to very poor higher edges. Go from these to the rail above. There is some uncertainty as to whether this has in fact been done.

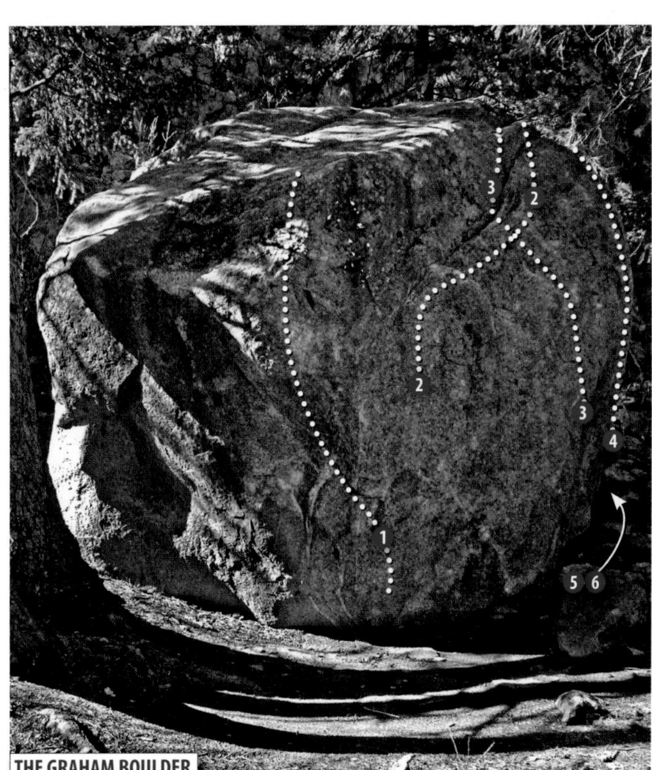

THE GRAHAM BOULDER

5 Right Graham Arete v9/10 ☐
aka The Little Sloper That Could
Start with a poor LH fin-like hold and a sloper just right of the arete. Pop left to a bad sloper and then catch a small crimp RH. Go right again to a better edge and grab the rail on the left. Tiny tiny footholds. This has been called v8 by those who should know better. It's not. A v9 rating might apply in crisp conditions.

6 Warm-Up Corner v4 ☐
This is a difficult warm-up but a classic line. Sit start at the base of the obvious dihedral. Painful climbing follows.

LDC – THE FREEDOM BOULDER 7.6 miles

This boulder is located in Lower Dream Canyon just north of Boulder Falls. It has some high quality problems in a beautiful setting.

Access: See page 92.

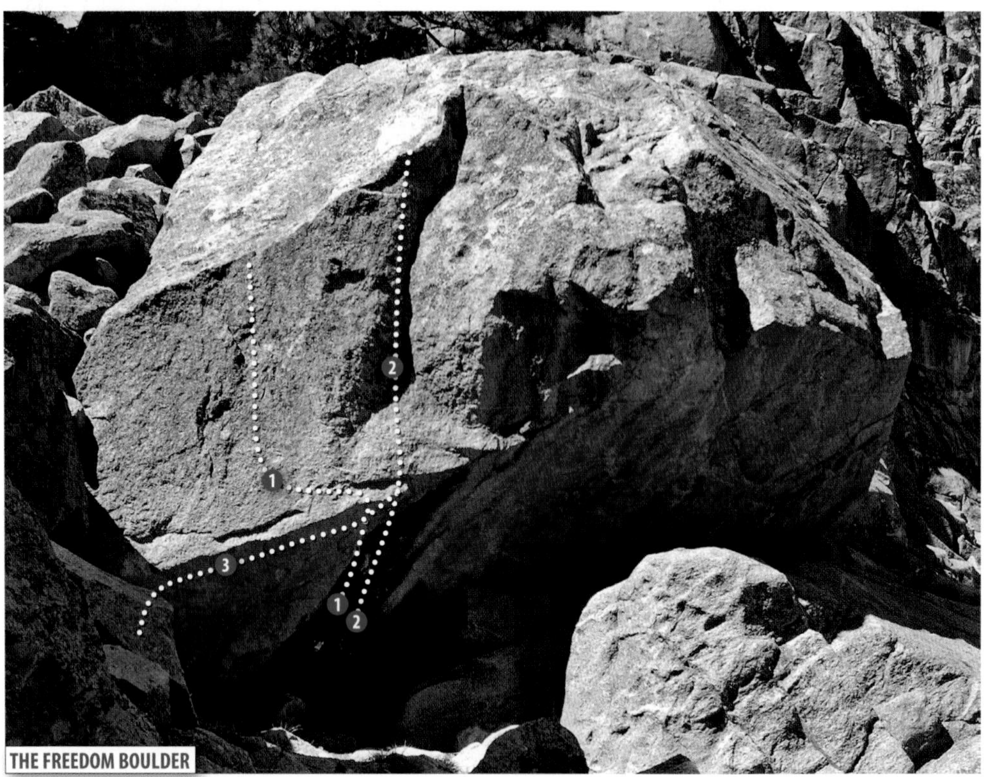

THE FREEDOM BOULDER

1 Freedom v9/10 ☐

This attractive problem tackles the obvious roof on the Freedom Boulder. Start matched on a bad set of crimps in the middle of the roof and throw for the lip. Hold the swing, rock over and deal with the worrying slab going left. The v9 is for starting with a foot already out on the lip. The stand start is around v7. The landing is uneven so come prepared.

2 Freedom Direct v10 ☐

Instead of heading left, maneuver up the narrow groove on the right. Taller, scarier and harder than the regular problem.

3 The Amendment v11 ☐

A left sit-start leads across the lip and joins either of the above options. Very sloping holds.

NIP AND TUCK CRAGS

10.5 miles - page 198

These cliffs have easy roadside access. *Caddis* v9/10 gained a measure of fame as the first 5.13c ever soloed — fame that didn't last owing to its low crux.

Access: Travel 10.5 miles up the canyon to a pullout/parking area on the right side of the road. This will put you at the far right side of Tuck Crag. Walk up canyon to the obvious wall set back in the trees to reach Nip Crag. **NB: Take care with both parking and pulling out as the cliff is on a bend.**

Tuck Bouldering

The first feature on Tuck is an obvious east-facing overhung panel with a crack. This is the location for routes such as *Gyro Captain, Mr. Spiffy,* and *Mr. Stiffy,* as well as the problem *Caddis*. Miscellaneous low problems can be devised on the short wall/ slab right of the east-facing overhang.

TUCK BOULDERING

❶ Mr Spiffy Direct Start v9 ☐

Start up the obvious vertical crack at the base of the overhanging panel. The crux is getting established with your feet above the horizontal crack. After achieving this head up for death or glory on *Gyro Captain* or *Mr Spiffy,* 12b/c and 13a (toprope practice advised), or jump, or move right to the ledge.

❷ Caddis v9/10 ☐

This well-known problem starts on the left arete of the striking overhanging panel, just a few yards from the road. Start standing and execute hard crimpy moves to a break and better holds. Decision time. Most will jump or otherwise bail. The bold will continue up the flake to the easier climbing above and a retreat down a crack on the left. You can also rope up for this and finish direct at 13b/c (*Argus*, page 199), though the crux is still the boulder problem.

Nip Bouldering

The next problems are found about 100 yards west, upstream, near the left end of Nip, the left of the two roadside crags.

❸ Sloping Arete v5 ☐

Start sitting on the underclings and work your way up the arete. It appears that you can step left and down-climb the ramp on the side.

❹ Ulysses' Journey v9/10? ☐

Left of the sloping arete is a tall overhanging wall. Follow a left trending seam to the lip. This is a serious and tall problem with no known repeats. The grade is likely to be in the v9 or 10 range at least. Plan your escape off the top in advance.

❺ The Dihedral Problem v? ☐

A serious and steep undertaking out the overhanging dihedral left of *Ulysses' Journey.*

NIP BOULDERING

STEPPING STONES / THE BARRIO

10.8 miles – page 200

This cliff has long been a favorite of local climbers, not least because of roadside access to a steep, lengthy traverse, *The Barrio.*

Access: Park at a large pullout on the left side of the road 10.8 miles up the canyon. Hike back down canyon for 100 yards and cross the road to a guardrail. Follow the trail that leads up and left to the wall. You can also reach this area by hiking west around the corner from Nip Crag.

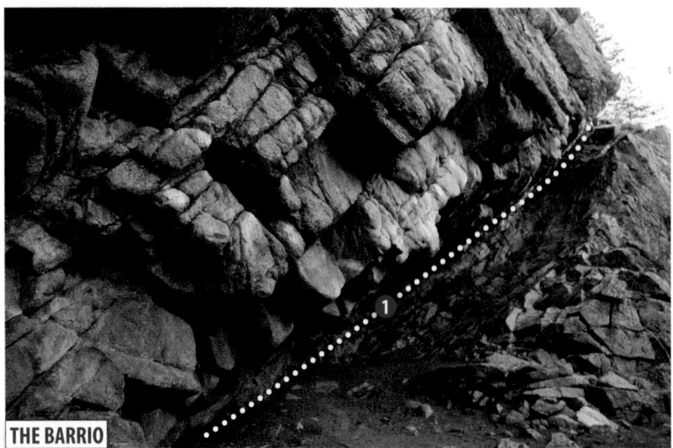

THE BARRIO

1 The Barrio Traverse v9/5.13b ☐☐

This is found at the right end of the crag, in a low diagonaling slot that runs 50 feet or more from left to right. This area required a lot of reconstructive work to be solid and climbable but is now one of the area's most popular outdoor training "gyms." The full traverse is in the v9/5.13b range with harder variations possible. Problems that go directly through the slot have also been done — but be aware that there is a 40 foot drop behind you at the top of the slot.

THE NURSING HOME

10.8 miles – page 202

The Nursing Home is a low cliff-band, about a quarter of a mile west of *The Barrio*. Look for a steep dark wall running along its base. This wall is primarily famous for a problem commonly known as *Freak Brothers*, a steep clean line on the left. However several more moderate problems exist farther right, as well as a long, potentially difficult traverse. Topping out is problematic owing to the extensive low-angle slab above, judicious retreat options include down-climbing adjacent features or jumping.

Access: Park at the large pullout on the left side of the road 10.8 miles up the canyon. Cross the road and climb the short hill to the wall.

THE NURSING HOME

1 Where the Monkey Sleeps v10/11 ☐☐
aka Freak Brothers

After he did it, Jay Droeger estimated this striking thin seam at v8. Tyler Landman flashed it, thinking it was new, and graded it v11, naming it *Freak Brothers II* after a problem in Switzerland. Taller climbers may find it v10, shorter people more like v11. Find a striking black wall just right of where the approach trail meets the cliff band. Start at the obvious poor break and stretch left to a terrible crimp in the seam. Reach right to a bad crimp and then move left, aiming for a jug. Jump or climb up, across and down to the right. A decent landing but a spotter is advised due to the slope below the problem.

2 Freak Accident v12 ☐☐

Tyler Landman added a start coming in from the right, starting on the obvious vertical crack 5 feet right of the regular start. Lousy feet and small awkward grips lead to the previous problem.

CASTLE ROCK AREA

11.8 miles – page 206

There are lots of bouldering opportunities in the vicinity of Castle Rock. This area has been transformed into one of the centers of hard bouldering on the Front Range, with ease of access and quality problems, such as *Midnight Express* and *Cage Free*, making it a popular destination.

Access: Travel 11.8 miles up the canyon to a turnoff on the left for Castle Rock. Turn onto a dirt road that runs along the base of the wall. Park on the right by the creek, at the west end to access *Hardboiled* and farther east for the *Citadel* and other problems. The bridge just below *Country Club Crack* is a useful landmark.

THE CITADEL BOULDER

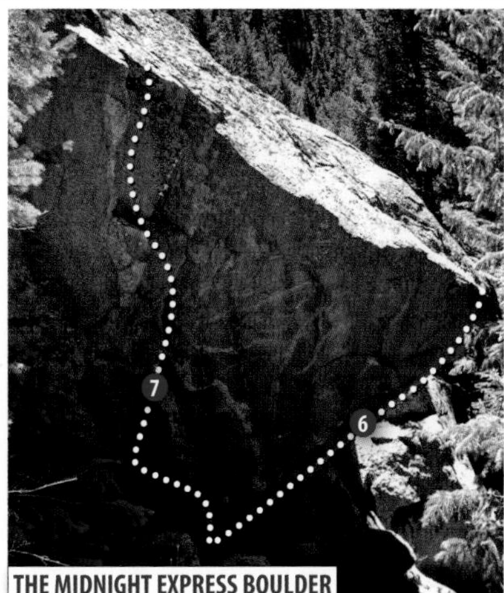

THE MIDNIGHT EXPRESS BOULDER

The Citadel Boulder

This is the obvious large boulder on the north bank of the creek, just east of the bridge below *Country Club Crack*. It holds a number of difficult testpieces, including the namesake v8, *Surface Tension* v10, and *Cage Free* v13.

Access: It can be approached from just east of Castle Rock, just before the guard rail starts, by heading down a steep slope to the creek. During low water, the creek can also be crossed easily from the road just past *Country Club Crack*.

❶ Standard Bulge v5 ☐

On the west face of the boulder, start on chest-high sidepulls, and make hard moves to the lip. Bring pads for the prominent boulder at the base

❷ The Citadel v8 ☐

From a low start, climb the southwest arete on crimpy slopers. Technical and slippery.

❸ Free Range v13 ☐

Sit-start low on the arete, move to a crimp with the right hand and traverse right into *Cage Free*. Very technical and powerful.

❹ Cage Free v11 ☐

Just right of the tree, find a terrible sidepull for the LH. Pull on a bit down and to the right on an OK undercling, reach left for the sidepull and throw for the flat lip with the RH. One move but it's a long one.

❺ Surface Tension v10 ☐

Start low on the southeast arete, over the creek, on an obvious flake. Move up to the arete (heelhook on the left) and finish. Best to wait for low water on this one. v7 for the stand start.

The Midnight Express Boulder

This is a large boulder/outcropping just south of Castle Rock, uphill from the bridge. *Midnight Express* (v14) starts low on the right and goes out the obvious flake. The crack to the left is *Trainspotting* (v12).

❻ Midnight Express v14 ☐

One of the hardest problems close to Boulder, *Midnight Express* offers very powerful climbing low and bold moves at the top. Start low on a flake LH and a poor pinch RH. Do a powerful cross to a sharp undercling LH. Reach right along the flake to an OK pinch, catch a thin crimp LH and go very big to the shelf. From here the problem gets much easier but a huge drop presents itself as you approach the lip. There's a toprope anchor to ease working the topout. Bring many pads and spotters.

❼ Trainspotting v12 ☐

Start low and right and work into the striking vertical crack. A committing problem.

Castle Rock

A number of problems exist on the main formation of Castle Rock. The two most notable ones are from the legendary founder of modern bouldering, John Gill.

8 Acrobat's Overhang v5 ☐

Start right of *Jackson's Wall* (#26, page 210), the obvious leaning ramp/gully on the south side of the formation. A horizontal seam under an overlap is the start. Head left and up on increasingly serious terrain. Photo opposite.

ACROBAT'S OVERHANG

9 The Gill Crack 5.12a or v5/6 ☐

Route #34, page 211. Farther right is an obvious 20-foot finger crack just right of a black streaked crack called *Black Crack*. Climb the finger crack, with or without a rope. Tall and serious — especially in hiking boots and no crashpad as Gill did it.

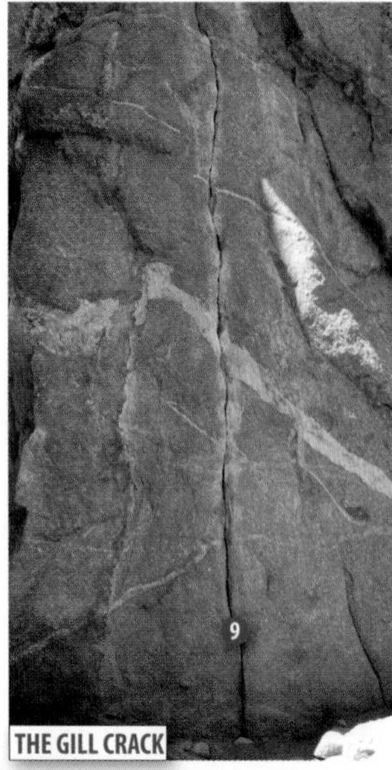

THE GILL CRACK

THE EGG

The Egg

This boulder is small but desirable, holding a very popular v11. Though not very tall, the landing area is very rocky — bring as many pads as possible.

Access: Head west along the road about 200 yards from Castle Rock and look for a fallen log that allows a stream crossing. From the crossing, move up the slope and trend west across talus beneath several popular ice climbs. Just west of the talus is The Egg, invisible until you go around and see it from the west.

10 Hardboiled v11 ☐

A Boulder Canyon classic, though dismissed by some as scrunchy and weird. Start low in the obvious cave at a fin feature for the LH and gun for the lip. A potentially heartbreaking slab section awaits.

11 Softboiled v7/8 ☐

Start with your RH on the edge just above the lip and your LH on the good edge below it. Finish as for HB.

12 Replacement Killers v11 ☐

Start as for *Hardboiled* but move left up the arete. Heel hooks and slopers are the theme.

13 Southwest Arete vB ☐

From the obvious incut ledge, do a surprisingly tricky mantel to the top.

14 The South Face v3 ☐

Start just right of the arete on two small holds on the South Face. Reach right to a sharp crimp and make a dicey reach to a poor crimp up and left. Only two moves but miserable feet.

15 Nintendo v4 ☐

Climbs the striking but short double arete on the boulder above The Egg. Sit start. Watch out as a fall to the left as it could be very dangerous. Manteling direct would be harder and scary, otherwise traverse off right.

16 The North Slab v0 ☐

Nice edges on the slab just north of The Egg. Tree branches make topping out difficult.

John Gill

I never thought of Boulder Canyon — in particular, Castle Rock, with its long leads — as an attractive destination. In the early and mid 1960s I was drifting away from roped climbing and reaching for my roots as a Third-Class climber ... more concerned with the tactics of motion on rock than the strategies of lengthy pitches with their logistics and complexities. My guidelines were simple: hard things low down, complemented by easier days in airy exposure.

Early in the decade I had discovered the small outcrop that I called *Acrobat's Overhang*. I liked long athletic reaches and recall — here my memory is a bit fuzzy — avoiding a small intermediate hold on the problem. Crash pads were a quarter of a century away, and I never used a toprope on any of the things I did at Castle Rock, instead, moving up and down in a slow progressive fashion, guaranteeing a retreat under my own power ... hopefully! But *Acrobat's* topped out conveniently and, thankfully, I didn't need to reverse my sequence of moves.

This was not the case with several other divertissements. Dave Rearick had mentioned climbing something called Coffin Crack, and said he thought I might be interested in bouldering the bottom section. And I learned that Royal Robbins had done a severe route nearby, humorously labeled *Final Exam* by a passing motorist. Apparently, both these climbs had their cruxes in the first twenty feet, so they could be considered bouldering excursions, using an incremental up-and-down strategy I had practised on the *Thimble* in 1961.

However, after squeezing myself into the lower smooth and overhanging folds of *Coffin Crack*, and contemplating the struggle from there, I elected to decline Dave's tongue-in-cheek invitation and move to something less confining! Off to the right, if my memory serves, I spied a fairly short, thin finger crack that had a virginal and seductive aura about it [*The Gill Crack*]. So, up and down I went, a little higher — and a little more painful — each cycle, until I had had my way with the temptress and downclimbed to the base. For the time being, that was enough of chimneys and cracks — terrain I never cared for, being anatomically proportioned for better things!

On one visit in the mid 1960s, intrigued by an athletic testpiece with an academic moniker, I had an hour or so of focused entertainment on the *Final Exam*. The same simple but effective strategy — up and down, a little higher each time — until I felt I had completed the pitch, then I reversed the now familiar sequence and descended to the base. I never ventured on the rock above any of these short projects, embellishing my reputation as a most peculiar climber!

John Gill tackles *Acrobat's Overhang* in the 1960s. Photo Gill collection.

ICE CLIMBING IN BOULDER CANYON

By Jack Roberts

Will Gadd on an iced up ascent of *Stage Fright* 5.11a on Vampire Rock during the winter of 1997 when, for one season, Boulder Canyon had the best ice park in the country. Photo: Topher Donahue.

People have been climbing ice in Boulder Canyon since the early 1960s. Bob Culp, owner of one of the first climbing stores in Boulder, recalls that "only a few people could climb vertical ice back then." He remembers ice climbing taking place as early as 1962. Gary Neptune, owner of Boulder's Neptune Mountaineering climbing shop, remembers that these ice flows had become established destinations and were frequently visited as early as 1970.

Many of Boulder's best climbers and alpinists have cut their teeth on the various ice and mixed climbs in the canyon, sometimes honing their skills on toprope and thereby pushing the existing limits of the sport. Prominent climbers such as Duncan Ferguson, Jeff Lowe, Bob Culp, David Breashears, Art Higbee, Paul Sibley, Charlie Fowler, and Mark Wilford were all instrumental in the development of climbing technique and equipment technology. And that all happened in Boulder Canyon. Lowe Alpine Systems ice climbing gear and clothing were developed on these ice climbs. Axes were bent and reforged in Paul Sibley's garage and then tested on the rock and ice of the canyon.

About ten years ago ice farming was used to create new and exciting multi-pitch routes on some of the canyon's crags. Black Widow and Vampire Rocks were iced over and for a time offered the best ice and mixed climbing in Colorado. Unfortunately, the farming operation was done illegally and the authorities shut it down after just one season. Since that time the City of Boulder has slowly and methodically plugged most of the leaks in the aquaduct that supplies the water for the ice flows and so currently we have less ice to climb on than ever before. Whether or not this changes in the future no one can tell. Maybe with enough climber support we can yet again have lots of ice climbing to recreate on.

There are two ice-climbing areas in Boulder Canyon. The easternmost, just above Castle Rock, is referred to as The Lower Falls Area. The westernmost, approximately 0.5 miles above Castle Rock, is referred to as The Upper Area. Both the Lower and Upper Areas are situated entirely on Boulder Canyon Open Space. Retaining ice climbing in these areas has been approved as part of the Boulder County Platt Rogers Open Space Management Plan (adopted by the Board of Commissioners Nov. 2000).

THE LOWER FALLS AREA 11.8 miles

The Lower Falls Area is about 150 yards west of Castle Rock and about 50 yards directly south of the Boulder Canyon highway, across Boulder Creek. The area consists of three reliable ice climbs of approximately 200 feet in length separated by rock buttresses. In addition to these climbs, less reliable climbs sometimes form both to the left and right of the regular climbs.

Access: Travel 11.8 miles up the canyon to a turnoff on the left for Castle Rock. Turn onto a dirt road that runs along the base of the wall and park. Hike upstream (west) and cross the creek to the Lower Falls Area.

Descent: A trodden path behind the climbs descends to the east.

THE UPPER AREA 12.3 miles

The Upper Area is about 0.5 miles above Castle Rock, and again about 50 yards from the highway. This area is narrower and shorter than the Lower Area. There are four distinct routes that are usually steeper than anything at the Lower Area. While these climbs vary considerably from year to year, when formed they are considered the steepest and most challenging in the canyon. Currently, the water level varies yearly and so it is difficult to predict how the ice will form from year to year.

Access: Park in a pullout with room for about 8 cars, across the highway and slightly down-canyon from The Upper Area. You can also walk to The Upper Area from Castle Rock.

Descent: Descent: Typically slings around trees are used as toprope anchors for all the routes in this area. Some slings are fixed for this purpose. If you don't lower from the anchors, you must climb above them to a dirt path where it is safe to untie. The path leads back down to the base of the climbing. Be very careful when climbing above the anchors since some moderate but icy scrambling through trees and loose, rocky terrain is necessary to reach the dirt path.

GRADED LIST OF SPORT CLIMBS

5.14a

Route	Stars	Page
☐ The Agony and Ecstasy	★★	74
☐ Mr. Stiffie Left Start	★★	199

5.13d

Route	Stars	Page
☐ Palm Pilot	★★★	241
☐ Gagger	★★	196
☐ Mr. Stiffie	★★	199

5.13c

Route	Stars	Page
☐ Verve	★★★★	149
☐ China Doll (bolted first pitch)	★★★★	245
☐ The Borg	★★★	220
☐ Closer To God	★★	172
☐ Twist and Shout	★★	194
☐ Crank It	★★	209
☐ Overenthusiasm		194
☐ Argus		199

5.13b

Route	Stars	Page
☐ The Lorax	★★★★	56
☐ Eastern Promises	★★★	108
☐ The Enlightment	★★	67
☐ Die Reeperbahn	★★	195
☐ The Orb	★★	220
☐ Rumors of Glory	★★	220
☐ Eagle Warrior	★	44
☐ Heart of Darkness	★	136
☐ Tiempos de Ceguera	★	149
☐ Dynamic Duel	★	190

5.13a

Route	Stars	Page
☐ Buddha Belly	★★★★	44
☐ Vasodilator	★★★★	64
☐ Nevermore	★★★	189
☐ The Flying Beast	★★★	190
☐ Give the Dog a Bone	★★★	196
☐ Challenges of Leisure	★★★	236
☐ War on Freedom	★★	99
☐ La Lune	★★	123
☐ Freak on a Leash	★★	149
☐ Pit Bull Browser	★★	172
☐ The Badger Traverse	★★	195
☐ Mr. Spiffy	★★	199
☐ Sinopia	★★	220
☐ Magna Headwall	★★	241
☐ Dynamometer	★★	244
☐ Geminae Cracks	★★	250
☐ Knappweed Herb Variation	★	188

5.13

Route	Stars	Page
☐ Around Midnight		248

5.12d

Route	Stars	Page
☐ Lucid Dreaming	★★★★	100
☐ Hands of Destiny	★★★★	172
☐ The Buzz	★★★	56
☐ The Juice	★★★	73
☐ Ecstasy of the People	★★★	74
☐ Central Insecurity	★★★	74
☐ East Germany	★★★	108
☐ Evermore	★★★	189
☐ Red Limit	★★★	238
☐ Fighting Irish	★★★	241
☐ Earth Angel	★★	158
☐ Resonator	★★	178
☐ Catwoman	★★	189
☐ Pterodactyl Traverse	★★	190
☐ Work It On Out	★★	194
☐ Couch Fire	★★	205
☐ Tears of a Clown	★	60
☐ Wind Walker	★	60
☐ Prong	★	194
☐ Salad Shooter	★	230
☐ Reversal Roof		169

5.12c/d

Route	Stars	Page
☐ Big Sky Corner	★★★★	103
☐ Fapanese Direct	★★★	158
☐ Cum Laude Overhang	★★	241
☐ Grande Finale	★★	250
☐ Chickenshit .. Environmentalist	★	188
☐ Trustafarian Panhandler	★	188

5.12c

Route	Stars	Page
☐ Interrogation	★★★★	108
☐ Animal Instinct	★★★★	172
☐ Global Gorilla	★★★★	172
☐ Der Letzte Zug	★★★★	195
☐ Amazing Face	★★★	134
☐ American Beauty	★★★	225
☐ Cirque Du Soleil	★★★	248
☐ The Jitters	★★	56
☐ Hot Wire	★★	73
☐ Super Bon Bon	★★	134
☐ Climb Eye Knight	★★	176
☐ Mutant Overload	★★	230
☐ Dream Machine	★★	241
☐ Tripendicular Wildman	★★	245
☐ Rock Odyssey	★★	245
☐ Flake Roof	★★	248
☐ Shiny Dog	★	134
☐ Surrounded By Reality	★	188
☐ The Penguin	★	189
☐ Pump Truck	★	230
☐ Caught in the Web		179

5.12b/c

Route	Stars	Page
☐ Porch Monkey	★★★	52
☐ Waterboarding	★★★	108
☐ Fly Off The Handle	★★	97
☐ Catch and Release	★★	156
☐ Fifth World	★★	172
☐ The Bureau	★★	176
☐ Gyro Captain	★★	199
☐ Invisible Touch	★★	222
☐ Cave Traverse	★	111
☐ Poolside	★	145
☐ Thor	★	153
☐ Pariah		86
☐ The Monkey Wrench		165

5.12b

Route	Stars	Page
☐ Plan B	★★★★	73
☐ Tell-Tale Heart	★★★★	189
☐ Teenage Terrorists	★★★	76
☐ Lucky Strikes	★★★	99
☐ Fall of the Wall	★★★	108
☐ Jazz On The Mezzanine	★★★	166
☐ Piles of Trials	★★★	168
☐ Cujo Tranquilizer	★★★	172
☐ Heart of the Narrows	★★★	176
☐ Blood Doll	★★★	177
☐ Pipe Dreams	★★★	178
☐ Joy Ride	★★★	195
☐ Pinche Guey	★★★	200
☐ Hypertension	★★	65
☐ Prince Of Thieves	★★	79
☐ The Art of Dreaming	★★	99
☐ Full Circle	★★	110
☐ Next to Nothing	★★	134
☐ The Purpose	★★	149
☐ The Constant Gardener	★★	158
☐ Blockhead	★★	169
☐ Evolution Revolution	★★	172
☐ Transylverlina	★★	176
☐ Dracula	★★	178
☐ Let the Daylight In	★★	204
☐ Hair Shirt	★★	230
☐ No Doze	★★	230
☐ The Caterer	★★	246
☐ Dyno Mart	★★	250
☐ Vanishing Ink	★★	252
☐ Avalon Rising	★	30
☐ True Comedian	★	60
☐ Eldo of the People	★	74

Route	Stars	Page
Guardian Angel	★	160
Feeding the Beast	★	195
Loveseat	★	205
Build a Dam, Boys	★	222
Cognitive Ability	★	241
Viola	★	250
Left Wall		150
Cujo Magnetism		172
The Wave		183
Whipping Factor		222
Beaver Fever		230

5.12a/b

Route	Stars	Page
Return To Sender	★★★	55
Tipskin Jihad	★★★	76
Meteor Roadblock	★★★	134
Aerial Boundaries	★★★	182
Voodoo Child	★★	52
Neuromuscular Toxin	★★	136
Feeding The Beast	★★	168
Wanker	★★	176
Barbarians	★★	188
White Men Can't Jump Left	★★	190
Antagonism	★★	199
Whipping Post	★★	222
Curve of Binding Energy	★★	222
Furious Howard Brown	★★	223
Dream Come True	★★	236
Midnight Cowboy	★★	248
Welcome Home	★	54
Edge of Reality	★	84

5.12a

Route	Stars	Page
Jolt Cola	★★★★	64
The Ticket	★★★★	67
Angle of Repose	★★★★	106
Empire of the Fenceless	★★★★	189
Sargasso Sea	★★★★	236
Earth Voyage	★★★★	244
Rise and Shine	★★★	56
Hot Flyer	★★★	73
Panic Attack	★★★	76
The Illusionist	★★★	80
Boulder Quartz System	★★★	100
Big Sky Arete	★★★	103
War on Peace	★★★	145
Free Fall	★★★	160
Rip Cord	★★★	160
Days of Future Passed	★★★	169
The Good ... and The Jacked	★★★	176
Le Stat	★★★	177
MLK	★★★	182
Fit for Life	★★★	214
Sick Puppy	★★★	218
Mercy Drilling	★★★	225
Eagle Eyes	★★	44
Contender	★★	46
Lost and Found	★★	60
Take Five	★★	60
Ginseng Rush	★★	64
I Reckon	★★	88
Edge-a-macation	★★	89
English Immersion	★★	102
Alpha-Bob	★★	104
On The Bough	★★	106
Midnight Dari	★★	115
Babylon Is Burning	★★	124
A Tall Cool One	★★	133
Living with the Apes	★★	165
Animal Riots Activist	★★	168
Sun Dog	★★	172
Fly Trap	★★	194
New Fanatic	★★	194
Warlock Pinchers	★★	2000
Golden Rose	★★	218
Warf Factor	★★	222
Rubberneck	★★	226
Digital Dilemma	★★	245
Awakenings	★★	245
Pirate Radar	★★	248
Eagle Tricks	★	44
Scratch	★	48
Just a Little Insecure	★	73
Enema of the People	★	74
The Law Comes Down	★	130
Clyde's Big Adventure	★	145
Nice Doggie	★	152
Beano Hangover	★	152
Ruff Roof	★	174
Bull Fight	★	174
No How, No Way	★	186
Dampened Enthusiasm	★	194
Blackout	★	227
Jolly Jug	★	230
The Host	★	246
Sister Sweetly	★	247
A.C.E		176
Ditch Witch		230
The Viano Step		246

5.11d/12a

Route	Stars	Page
Vishnu	★★★	111
The Future Of Life	★★★	142
Huck Finn	★★★	142
Threshold Of A Dream	★★★	169
Respite	★★	64
The Producers	★★	253

5.11d

Route	Stars	Page
Strange Science	★★★★	160
Russian Bride	★★★	47
Erki Nool	★★★	65
Sands of Iwo Jima	★★★	86
The Bobsled	★★★	99
Prodigal Summer	★★★	115
Tall Talking Midget	★★★	131
The Devil	★★★	158
Chairman of the Board	★★★	159
Leviathan	★★★	236
Creature from .. Black Lagoon	★★★	236
Naked Lunch	★★★	245
Hammer Down	★★★	248
Suffering Succotash	★★	52
The Far Side	★★	60
Blood Diamond	★★	84
Centennial	★★	133
Band of Gold	★★	178
Dark Knight	★★	189
Mr. Two-Faced	★★	189
New Test Of Men	★★	190
Full Throttle	★★	193
Turkey Neck Direct	★★	200
Linking Logs	★★	229
Sunset Arete	★★	234
Mudshark	★★	236
Sheik YerBouti	★★	236
Beauty and the Bolts	★★	245
Disneyland	★★	246
Grace Poole	★★	254
Sucker Punch	★	46
Turmoil	★	72
Excalibur	★	80
Just Like Nebraska	★	133
Repo Man	★	138
Lichen Has Feelings Too!	★	142
Merlin's Enigma	★	162
Red Badger	★	194
Yellow Tail	★	218
Space Goats	★	222
Dyno Monkey	★	226
Alfa Chick	★	229
Butt Lucious	★	230
Didgeridoo	★	253

5.11c/d

Route	Stars	Page
Mind Bender	★★★	183
Elanor	★★★	189
Golden Eagle	★★	44
Standing Eight Count	★★	46
Contender Direct	★★	46
Topiary	★★	80
Schizophrenia	★★	129
Spider's and Snakes	★★	241
The Vanishing	★★	252
Two Minute Warning	★	60
Trouble with the Law	★	130
Underbelly	★	145
We Bean Jammin	★	152

5.11c

Route	Stars	Page
Animal Magnetism	★★★★	172
Robbin' The Hood	★★★	78
Consilence	★★★	178
The Joker	★★★	189
Equator	★★★	241
Orange Crush	★★	64
A Hike For Y2K	★★	65
Crash Test Blondes	★★	73
Sheriff's Tariff	★★	79
The Vortex	★★	86

Route	Stars	Page
Flight of the Bumbly	★★	102
Black Pool	★★	110
Take the Termites Bowling	★★	134
Primate Studies	★★	165
Pin Cushion	★★	177
Fear of Sunlight	★★	177
Fuck You	★★	178
The Riddler	★★	189
Willard	★★	189
Golden Child	★★	216
Hard Warm Up	★★	222
Hood Surfing in Socks	★★	225
The Deep	★★	236
Dream On	★★	236
The Caboose	★★	248
Karma Kamelian	★★	248
Crack a Smile	★★	248
Deus Ex Machina	★★	250
Far From The Madding Crowd	★★	254
Iggle	★	43
Iggle Direct	★	43
Boy Howdy	★	88
King Slopers	★	96
Engineering Marvel	★	96
Dari Design	★	114
Hard Times	★	117
Carrying Futons	★	145
Cosmic Explorer	★	155
Flies in the Soup	★	194
Steel Pulse	★	218
Knocking on Heaven's Door	★	227
Leave it to Beaver	★	230
Shiva the Destroyer		111
New Beginnings		172
After Midnight		248

5.11b/c

Route	Stars	Page
Eagle Hardware	★★★	44
War is Love	★★★	76
Isn't Life Strange	★★★	170
Shady Deal	★★	132
Nowhere Man	★★	142
Bell Air	★★	146
Clocks	★★	187
Magie Noire	★★	200
Storming the Castle	★★	206
Louisville Slugger	★★	216
Platinum Curl	★★	225
Rush	★★	246
Dreamer's Dream	★★	253
Ziggurat	★	124
Midge Squadron	★	134
Bad Girls Get Spanked	★	134
Tuesday Afternoon	★	169
El Gallito	★	200
The Probe		216
Short Sport		218

5.11b

Route	Stars	Page
The Clipboard	★★★	159
Wings of Desire	★★★	182
Owl on the Prow	★★★	229
Stained Glass	★★★	238
Tales of Power	★★★	238
Divination	★★★	244
Wounded Knee	★★	61
Silver Glide	★★	81
By Cracky	★★	89
Sleepless in Boulder	★★	99
Walpurgisnacht	★★	108
Higher Rites	★★	111
Mental Imbalance	★★	129
Excalibur	★★	153
Body Count	★★	156
Orgasmatron	★★	183
Pocket Fisherman	★★	222
Chicken Lips	★★	229
Sea of Dreams	★★	238
Dream Scene	★★	240
Jane Eyre	★★	254
Evolution	★	72
Cracking the Code	★	73
Sacrificial Virgin	★	90
Lucky Strike	★	134
Frothing Green	★	134
Never Was Been	★	165
Joe the Lunger	★	187
Ground Zero	★	229
Dyno Arete	★	245
Pesky Varmints		89

5.11a/b

Route	Stars	Page
Road To Emmaus	★★★	190
Autumn	★★★	244
Hunky Monkey	★★★	244
No Direction Home	★★	76
The Alter	★★	90
Father Figure	★★	132
Melancholy Man	★★	169
Red Bull	★★	193
Aricept	★★	202
Mantra	★★	234
Rage Against the Machine	★★	246
Sport Crystal	★	102
The Balance	★	170
Jaws	★	227
Stand Back	★	253
I Looked at That		127
Bottom Feeder		145
For Whom the Bell Tolls		145
King of the Highway		227

5.11a

Route	Stars	Page
Fearless Leader	★★	186
The Hanged Man		158
The Scientist	★★★★	99
Miss Mantel	★★★	36
Sea Breeze	★★★	81
Hound Dog	★★★	149
Free Willie	★★★	169
The Big Dipper	★★★	230
Soul on Ice	★★★	238
Strange Cargo	★★★	244
No Man Is An Island	★★	36
Wild Cat	★★	61
Merry Men	★★	78
Can't Please Everyone	★★	80
Heavy Cipherin'	★★	89
Tooth Fairy	★★	99
The Twilight Kid	★★	118
Family Guy	★★	123
Aqua Regia	★★	126
Bell Bottom Blues	★★	145
Joint Venture	★★	169
Gyromancy	★★	178
Smoke Down	★★	179
Icy Paralyzer	★★	185
Lost In A Lost World	★★	187
The Bait	★★	194
Angel of Mercy	★★	203
Early Bird Special	★★	204
Warf Post	★★	222
The Other One	★★	225
The Fix	★★	225
Daddy Blocker	★★	229
Three Little Pigs	★★	230
In Your Dreams	★★	236
Raise the Titanic	★★	243
Sighs of Life	★★	245
Technical Remote Viewing	★★	246
Heathcliff	★★	254
Lily and the Jack of Hearts	★	38
Comedy Works	★	60
Cold Shot	★	72
Led Astray	★	73
The Minstrel	★	81
Leave No Trace	★	83
Flesh Eating Flies	★	86
Bob the Builder	★	96
Universal Crusher	★	97
Generous Donation	★	116
Oil Pan Service	★	134
Victory in De Feet	★	138
Bell Buster	★	149
Flashpoint	★	160
Nice To Be Here	★	169
Blood Whine	★	193
Sofa Mart	★	205
Big Tuna	★	218
Absolute Boulder Canyon	★	226
Flying Machines	★	226
Owl Juju	★	229
Hee Haw	★	230
Permanent Restraining Order	★	236
Wonky		83
Moonshine		89
Unknown		90
Lightspeed		182
Québec Connection		200
Fixed Income		204

Route	Stars	Page
☐ Journey to Ixtlan		238

5.10d/11a

Route	Stars	Page
☐ Bean Banger	★★	152
☐ Killer Fish Taco	★	225
☐ Ruins		90

5.10d

Route	Stars	Page
☐ Sidekick	★★★	117
☐ Eagle Snacks	★★	44
☐ Dagnabitol	★★	89
☐ Book Learnin'	★★	89
☐ The Daily Grind	★★	99
☐ Adam's Arete	★★	112
☐ Tag Team	★★	116
☐ Supernatural	★★	160
☐ Knight of Swords	★★	163
☐ Cannabis Sportiva	★★	168
☐ Little Stevie's Favorite Heifer	★★	174
☐ Hip Replacement	★★	202
☐ Melt Down	★★	248
☐ Midnight Express	★★	248
☐ The Stoke of Midnight	★★	248
☐ Eagle Chicks	★	44
☐ Jethro	★	89
☐ Ellie May	★	89
☐ Checkpoint Bravo	★	108
☐ The Coug	★	111
☐ Bobby's Back	★	117
☐ Strange Times	★	170
☐ Coffee Pot Crack	★	227
☐ Fin		133
☐ The Fool		158

5.10c/d

Route	Stars	Page
☐ Oh Boy	★★	84
☐ Assault on the Earth	★★	138
☐ Monkey's Uncle/Sister	★★	176
☐ Bone Hone	★	226
☐ Percocet Arete	★	227

5.10c

Route	Stars	Page
☐ Lust	★★★★	158
☐ Chore Boy	★★★	99
☐ Sunlight Makes Me Paranoid	★★★	183
☐ Lost Highway	★★★	183
☐ My ... Nice Knobs You Have	★★★	186
☐ Tuckered And Fried	★★	79
☐ Tony Bubb's Little Stick	★★	79
☐ Bobby's Wall	★★	112
☐ Mjolnir	★★	153
☐ Marquis de Sade	★★	156
☐ Dominator	★★	159
☐ Dead Again	★★	160
☐ Rubber Chicken	★★	229
☐ First Round	★	46
☐ Mission to Mars	★	154
☐ Ancient Light	★	162
☐ Drink to Puke	★	185
☐ My Buddy		98

Route	Stars	Page
☐ Welcome Wagon		226

5.10b/c

Route	Stars	Page
☐ Men In Tights	★★★	79
☐ Drop Zone	★	246
☐ Fly Swatter		194

5.10b

Route	Stars	Page
☐ Rhodian Shores	★★★	84
☐ Flags of Our Fathers	★★★	86
☐ The Art Of War	★★★	162
☐ Black Rain	★★★	182
☐ Mystic Mile	★★★	183
☐ Lease Agreement	★★	80
☐ Toe The Line	★★	116
☐ Sunlight Arete	★★	123
☐ The Good Book	★★	138
☐ Roadrash	★★	140
☐ Hambanger	★★	152
☐ Tower of Power	★★	154
☐ Slayer	★★	156
☐ Wheel of Fortune	★★	158
☐ Isle of the Dead	★★	160
☐ Ancient Fright	★★	162
☐ Kate Moss	★★	178
☐ Hydraulic Sandwich	★★	185
☐ Arete	★★	198
☐ The Big Splash	★★	213
☐ Muad' Dib	★★	214
☐ AA Arete	★★	246
☐ Like Water for Bob	★	88
☐ I'll be Dipped	★	88
☐ Square Dance	★	88
☐ Hankerin' in the Midsection	★	89
☐ Bedtime Story	★	98
☐ Mystery Ship	★	162
☐ Misanthrope	★	186
☐ Knappweed Herbacide	★	188
☐ Recliner	★	205

5.10a/b

Route	Stars	Page
☐ Wake Up Call	★★★★	99
☐ Snooze Button	★★★	99
☐ Talking Out of Turn	★★★	170
☐ Twin Peaks	★★	164
☐ Chicken Delight	★★	229
☐ Happy Ending	★	132
☐ Weasel in the Chicken Coup	★	229

5.10a

Route	Stars	Page
☐ Tese	★★★	76
☐ Napster	★★★	99
☐ Mr. Sandman	★★★	99
☐ Stayin' Alive	★★★	117
☐ Mists of Avalon	★★★	156
☐ The Tower	★★★	158
☐ That's Weak	★★★	176
☐ New Lease on Life	★★	80
☐ Le Nouveau Riche	★★	81
☐ Puff Daddy	★★	84
☐ Smell the Coffee	★★	99
☐ Mine all Mine	★★	103
☐ Total Eclipse	★★	117
☐ Ground Swell	★★	126
☐ Splitting Hares	★★	132
☐ Curb Service	★★	133
☐ Twilight Zone	★★	155
☐ Dragon Slayer	★★	162
☐ Sofa Kingdom	★★	174
☐ Griffon	★★	180
☐ Cutthroat	★★	180
☐ Eight Miles High	★★	183
☐ Devil in Disguise	★★	203
☐ Boyz From The Hood	★	78
☐ The Prince and the Pauper	★	78
☐ Birthday Suit	★	81
☐ Beer Dog	★	83
☐ Canine Corner	★	83
☐ A Fly in the Ointment	★	84
☐ Before The Deluge	★	118
☐ Myth of Freedom	★	153
☐ Minas Tirith	★	164
☐ Greenback	★	180
☐ Bruno	★	200
☐ Dirty Dave's Dumpster Dive	★	225
☐ Hair of the Dog	★	226
☐ Stryker	★	226
☐ Mommy Blocker	★	229
☐ Infra-Red Riding Hood	★	230
☐ Ride My See-Saw		170
☐ Wavy Gravy		225
☐ Double Down		225
☐ Mother Goose		230

5.9+

Route	Stars	Page
☐ The Young and the Rackless	★★★	67
☐ Bolt Cola	★★	62
☐ Pup	★★	73
☐ High Hard One	★★	84
☐ Twilight Time	★★	117
☐ Sword in the Stone	★★	156
☐ Iron Maiden	★★	156
☐ Dead Can Dance	★★	160
☐ Vitamin V	★★	225
☐ Timeless	★★	238
☐ Gully Washer	★★	238
☐ DH 1	★	67
☐ Bowling Ball and Chain	★	134
☐ Charon's Boat	★	163
☐ Unfamiliar Strangers	★	169
☐ Is It Ready Yet...Moe	★	170
☐ Lazy Day	★	170
☐ Freedom	★	245
☐ Qs		166
☐ Contortionist's Pleasure		200
☐ Sundowning		202

5.9

Route	Stars	Page
☐ Wrinkles in Time	★★★★	238
☐ Mosquito Burrito	★★★	134

Route	Stars	Page
The Luminosity	★★★	154
The Memory of Trees	★★★	164
Lucky Strikes Again	★★★	196
Diamonds and Rust	★★	84
Hold The Line	★★	84
Brand New Bosch	★★	122
Contact	★★	155
The Magician	★★	156
Dutch Oven	★★	225
Chicken Hawk	★★	229
A Brief History of Time	★★	238
Romancing the Stone	★	76
Bosch Blanket Bingo	★	81
Dry Run	★	132
The Forgiven	★	138
Right Line	★	154
Dragon Fly	★	162
Laurel & Hardy Meet ...	★	170
Get Your Dieck Off My	★	174
Grampa's Day Out	★	202
Chasing Sticks	★	225
Arete	★	240
Temptress	★	241
Weather Report	★	248
Maid Marian		79
Like a Wonk		83
The Unknown		83
Bell Bottom		145

5.9-

Route	Stars	Page
Shape Shifters	★★	243

5.8+

Route	Stars	Page
Animation	★★★★	169
Tool King	★★	84
It's Time for Change	★★	84
Buried Treasure	★★	117
Tomb of Sorrows	★★	160
Don't Pull on the Udder	★	174
Tree Line		117

5.8

Route	Stars	Page
Runaway	★★★	196
Werner's Legacy	★★★	253
Topless Etiquette	★★	81
Group Therapy	★★	84
Dan's Line	★★	84
Trick or Treat	★★	84
Edges and Ledges	★★	122
The Mustard Seed	★★	138
Glennevere	★★	164
Where's Ray?	★	86
Hoo-doggy	★	88
Left Line	★	154
Lost Souls	★	186
Senior Discount	★	204
Choss Temple Pilots	★	225
Monkey Bob	★	225
The Touch	★	225
Geek in the Creek	★	226
Alpine Moe	★	253
Abandonment		81
Second Career		204
Around the Corner		218
Wise Crack		222

5.7+

Route	Stars	Page
Incline Club	★★	160
Road to Isengard	★★	164

5.7

Route	Stars	Page
Splash	★★	81
Disinclination	★★	160
Lothlorien	★★	164
Doc's Route	★★	198
Night Moves	★	84
Face Off	★	117
Start Me Up	★	154
Sorcerer's Apprentice	★	163
Frictionary	★	225

5.7-

Route	Stars	Page
Depends		203

5.6

Route	Stars	Page
Chouette	★★	81
Don't Get me Started		154
Standard Route		246

GRADED LIST OF BOULDER PROBLEMS

v15

Problem	Page
The Roof Project	258

v14

Problem	Page
Midnight Express	263

v13

Problem	Page
Authentic Battle Damage	256
Free Range	263

v12

Problem	Page
Freak Accident	262
Trainspotting	263

v11

Problem	Page
The Hug	258
Left Graham Arete	259
The Amendment	260
Cage Free	263
Hardboiled	264
Replacement Killers	264

v10/11

Problem	Page
Where the Monkey Sleeps	262

v10

Problem	Page
Headless Horseman	258
The Capps Problem	259
Freedom Direct	260
Surface Tension	263

v9/10

Problem	Page
Right Graham Arete	259
Freedom	260
Caddis	261
Ulysses' Journey	261

v9

Problem	Page
Sleepy Hollow	258
Left Hug	258
Mr Spiffy Direct Start	261
The Barrio Traverse	262

v8

Problem	Page
Davey Jones' Footlocker	256
The Citadel	263

v7/8

Problem	Page
Softboiled	264

v6

Problem	Page
The Fields Problem	259

v5/6

Problem	Page
The Gill Crack	264

v5

Problem	Page
Sloping Arete	261
Standard Bulge	263
Acrobat's Overhang	264

v4

Problem	Page
Warm-Up Corner	259
Nintendo	264

v3

Problem	Page
The South Face	264

v2/3

Problem	Page
North Face Traverse	259

v0

Problem	Page
The North Slab	264

vB

Problem	Page
Southwest Arete	264

GRADED LIST OF TRADITIONAL CLIMBS

5.14

Climb	Stars	Page
☐ Headline (Project)		208

5.14a/b

Climb	Stars	Page
☐ Viceroy	★★★	208

5.14a

Climb	Stars	Page
☐ China Doll	★★★★	245

5.13d

Climb	Stars	Page
☐ Deadline	★★	208

5.13b/c

Climb	Stars	Page
☐ The Throne Crack	★★★	62

5.13b

Climb	Stars	Page
☐ Bed Hog	★★★	107
☐ Alien Sex Toy	★★★	211
☐ Victim of Circumstance	★★	208

5.13a

Climb	Stars	Page
☐ Damaged Goods	★★★	42
☐ Radlands of Infinity	★★★	61
☐ Blues for Allah	★★	42
☐ Tourist Extravagance	★★	213
☐ Holy Ascension	★	54

5.12d

Climb	Stars	Page
☐ Beethoven's Fifth	★★★★	150
☐ Green Panther	★★	44
☐ The Campaigner	★★	208
☐ Hell In A Bucket		166
☐ Nobody's Home		213

5.12c/d

Climb	Stars	Page
☐ Corinthian Vine	★★	211

5.12c

Climb	Stars	Page
☐ Razor Hein Stick	★★	54
☐ The Spins	★★	56

5.12b/c

Climb	Stars	Page
☐ Rude Boys	★★★	42
☐ Mordor	★★★	107
☐ Wallflower	★★	42
☐ Magic Bus	★★	140
☐ Close to the Edge	★★	211
☐ Palm Sunday		54

5.12b

Climb	Stars	Page
☐ Enemy of the People	★★★	74
☐ The Prisoner	★★★	107
☐ The Spoils	★★★	149
☐ Sleeper	★★	40
☐ Dating Game	★★	47
☐ Brainstorm	★★	129
☐ Lovely to See You	★★	169
☐ Rain Shadow	★★	190
☐ Rebellion	★★	208
☐ Dropout Option	★★	208
☐ Obsessive-Compulsive	★	40
☐ Leave it or Lead it	★	48
☐ Nightwind	★	60
☐ Nuclear Winter	★	208
☐ Under the Eagle's Wing		62
☐ Little Man In A Boat		150
☐ Swerve		150

5.12a/b

Climb	Stars	Page
☐ Bearcat Goes to Hollywood	★★★★	61
☐ Tricks Are For Kids	★★★	42
☐ Comfortably Numb	★★★	74
☐ Never a Dull Moment	★★★	211
☐ Astrophysics	★★	62
☐ Limits of Power	★★	64
☐ Downshift	★★	129
☐ Rockin' Horse	★	47
☐ Divine Intervention	★	60
☐ Shock Therapy	★	67
☐ Nightmare Come True	★	236

5.12a

Climb	Stars	Page
☐ The Grand Inquisitor	★★★★	149
☐ Mile High Comic Crack	★★★	67
☐ Arms Bazaar	★★★	150
☐ Thunderdome	★★★	189
☐ The Gill Crack	★★★	211
☐ Frogman	★★	34
☐ Thunder Road	★★	50
☐ Baby Aliens	★★	71
☐ Crocodile Smile	★★	115
☐ Antebellum	★★	145
☐ Coney Island Baby	★★	196
☐ Small Dose	★★	198
☐ The Boot Lead	★★	211
☐ Subterranean Homesick	★★	213
☐ The Jet Stream	★★	248
☐ Electricity	★	54
☐ Rush Hour	★	70
☐ Stingray	★	211
☐ Obscurity Risk	★	216
☐ Mr. Atrophy		33
☐ Eugenics Wars		192
☐ Epiphany Direct		150
☐ Archangel		245

5.11d/12a

Climb	Stars	Page
☐ Jerome Webster Memorial	★★	143

5.11d

Climb	Stars	Page
☐ Manic-Depressive	★★★	40
☐ Conan	★★★	65
☐ Thumb Tack	★★★	86
☐ Inca Stone	★★★	90
☐ Atlas Shrugged	★★★	211
☐ Extreme	★★	65
☐ Case of the Fags	★★	84
☐ Leader of the Pack	★★	104
☐ Smooth Operator	★★	119
☐ Epiphany	★★	150
☐ Cool Operator	★	35
☐ Suite 11	★	166
☐ Rush Of Blood To The Head	★	172
☐ Wagging the Nub	★	190
☐ Psyclone	★	196
☐ Amber	★	225
☐ The Joker and the Thief		38
☐ Seam		42
☐ Pale Horse		47
☐ Split Pea		54
☐ Eur-A-Peon		143

5.11c/d

Climb	Stars	Page
☐ Englishman's Home	★★★	213
☐ Power Line	★★	223
☐ The Reamer	★	62
☐ Black Tiger	★	163

5.11c

Climb	Stars	Page
☐ Country Club Crack	★★★★	213
☐ FM	★★★	32
☐ Peapod	★★★	54
☐ Pass/Fail Option	★★★	208
☐ Ms. Fanny Le Pump	★★	49
☐ Free at Last	★★	83
☐ Spellbound	★★	128
☐ Bloodstone	★★	134
☐ SMERSH	★★	178
☐ After Forever	★★	211
☐ Phantasm	★★	221
☐ Zentropa	★★	245
☐ Steel Blue	★	94
☐ Stickshift	★	128
☐ Blood Donor	★	186
☐ The Sting	★	211
☐ Tree Trimmer	★	214
☐ Phaedra	★	221
☐ Euphoria	★	221
☐ Elephantiasis		30
☐ Pegasus		32
☐ Kangaroof		32
☐ Love or Confusion		40
☐ Racing the Sun		48

Route	Stars	Page
☐ Stalingrad		108
☐ Hubris		114
☐ Automatic Choke		168
☐ Spin Off		213

5.11b/c

Route	Stars	Page
☐ Aging Time	★★★	64
☐ Star Span	★★★	192
☐ Philadelphia Flyer	★★★	216
☐ The Hand is Quicker Than	★★	54
☐ The Titleist	★★	107
☐ Jaguar	★★	163
☐ Imp-Passable Crack	★★	192
☐ Radio Andromeda	★★	213
☐ Whimsey	★★	214
☐ Spiders from Mars	★★	246
☐ Vicious Rumors	★	67
☐ Three Minute Hero	★	150
☐ Greenfield	★	216
☐ IR	★	254
☐ Misdirected		32
☐ Pinnacle of Success		129

5.11b

Route	Stars	Page
☐ Regular Route	★★★★	137
☐ Divine Wind	★★★	60
☐ Momentum Operator Crack	★★★	214
☐ Orion	★★★	253
☐ Schizofrantic	★★	67
☐ Slight of Hand	★★	82
☐ Point Blank	★★	94
☐ Morpheus	★★	99
☐ The Pitts	★★	146
☐ Front Line	★★	151
☐ Front Line Lefthand	★★	151
☐ Frontier	★★	151
☐ Wandervogel	★★	172
☐ White Trash	★★	214
☐ Gimme 3 Steps	★	72
☐ Doctor Patient	★	115
☐ The Throttle	★	123
☐ Ah Ya Punter	★	156
☐ Living on the Edge		37
☐ Ament Crack		42
☐ Avoiding Wounded Knee		61
☐ Cold Snap		169

5.11a/b

Route	Stars	Page
☐ Slow Death	★★	60
☐ Charisma	★★	62
☐ Decade Dance	★★	64
☐ The Resistance	★★	163
☐ Water World	★★	213
☐ Dry Ice	★★	238
☐ Jungle Blues from Jupiter	★★	246
☐ Silent Running	★	61
☐ Fat Tuesday	★	84
☐ Same As It Ever Was	★	123
☐ Cosmic Whimp-Out	★	214
☐ UV	★	254

Route	Stars	Page
☐ Direct		37
☐ My Place In the Universe		154
☐ Barney Rubble Pile		200

5.11a

Route	Stars	Page
☐ Athlete's Feat	★★★★	211
☐ Final Exam	★★★	206
☐ Tongo	★★★	211
☐ Crease	★★	37
☐ Jaguary	★★	54
☐ Last Laugh	★★	70
☐ Teetotaler	★★	71
☐ What's Wrong with Parents	★★	83
☐ The Treadmill	★★	90
☐ Sominex	★★	100
☐ Diving for Kipper Snacks	★★	110
☐ The Threshold	★★	123
☐ Wine & Roses	★★	170
☐ Western Pleasure	★★	210
☐ Crazy Wisdom	★★	243
☐ Blind Date	★	47
☐ Gray Elk's Big Rack	★	67
☐ Eye Opener	★	96
☐ Seamingly Left Out	★	97
☐ Tooth and Nail	★	100
☐ Dachau	★	108
☐ Flight Deck	★	114
☐ Stage Fright	★	177
☐ Don't Panic	★	186
☐ The Escapist	★	186
☐ Beguiled	★	198
☐ Polyester Leisure Suit	★	206
☐ Cadaver Crack	★	208
☐ First Movement	★	213
☐ Apparition	★	221
☐ Phantasmagoria	★	238
☐ Men Are From Mars		74
☐ Nerve Damage		99
☐ Counting Sheep		100
☐ Orange Dihedral		115
☐ Pale and Thin		129
☐ Elder Abuse		203
☐ Transylvania		216

5.11

Route	Stars	Page
☐ Face Route		49
☐ Blitzkrieg		108
☐ Weinachtsfest		108

5.10d/11a

Route	Stars	Page
☐ Loading Zone	★	195

5.10d

Route	Stars	Page
☐ The Umph Slot	★★★	28
☐ Golden Slumber	★★★	99
☐ Super Squeeze	★★	28
☐ What's Up	★★	32
☐ Wait Until Dark	★★	33
☐ Aid Crack	★★	49
☐ Reveille	★★	56
☐ Lichen to Like	★★	62
☐ Long Live Rock	★★	67
☐ Get Smart	★★	73
☐ Platinum Blond	★★	94
☐ The Sheen	★★	94
☐ Direct	★★	107
☐ Iron Curtain	★★	108
☐ The B Boys	★★	119
☐ Filet of Soul	★★	143
☐ Spare Rib	★★	156
☐ Specter	★★	178
☐ Quintet	★★	196
☐ Heart Throb	★★	198
☐ Yosemite Sam	★★	216
☐ The Engine	★★	248
☐ Cozy Overhang	★	29
☐ Groove	★	29
☐ Git 'er Done	★	86
☐ Acrophobia	★	94
☐ Sleep Deprivation	★	100
☐ Elixir	★	129
☐ Parallel Development	★	143
☐ The Horse	★	158
☐ Up Above It	★	221
☐ Entrapment	★	222
☐ Union with Earth	★	248
☐ Direct		28
☐ Familer Face		28
☐ Nothing to Fear		35
☐ Cappuccino		73
☐ Espresso		73
☐ Speak Softly		90
☐ Blue Sheen		94
☐ Himmelbrunch		108
☐ Pri-Moe		196

5.10c/d

Route	Stars	Page
☐ Security Risk	★★★	74
☐ Tempest	★★	61
☐ Sticky Fingers	★★	210
☐ Out to Pasture	★★	214
☐ Wingtip	★	30
☐ Devil's Rain	★	65
☐ Vertical Stall	★	114
☐ Convergence Corner	★	143
☐ Justin Alf Memorial Route	★	143
☐ Just Moo It	★	174
☐ Sue Song	★	214
☐ One Way Out		62
☐ Pigs In Space		143

5.10c

Route	Stars	Page
☐ Left Wing	★★★	32
☐ South Face	★★★	37
☐ Direct Cop Out	★★★	106
☐ Gish	★★★	143
☐ Flake	★★	33
☐ Daydreaming	★★	84
☐ War Horse	★★	162
☐ Blade	★★	162

Climb	Stars	Page
☐ Immaculate Deception	★★	182
☐ Last Tango	★★	220
☐ Evening Stroll	★	28
☐ Black Plague	★	28
☐ Short but Cute	★	35
☐ Corn on the Cob	★	50
☐ Gathering Storm	★	61
☐ Kamikaze	★	61
☐ Blind Trust	★	67
☐ Dirty Love	★	80
☐ Right Crack	★	80
☐ Sweetest Taboo	★	103
☐ Workingman's Blues	★	118
☐ Giggity-Giggity	★	123
☐ Zee Eliminator	★	133
☐ Digital Divide	★	134
☐ Malaise	★	151
☐ Mephistophiles	★	155
☐ Sex Slave	★	156
☐ Safety In Numbers	★	186
☐ Another Roadside Attraction	★	206
☐ Lobo	★	216
☐ Heatwave	★	218
☐ Twisting by the Pool	★	236
☐ Jamie		90
☐ Rama		100
☐ Bloody Monday		139
☐ Deadalus		151
☐ Party On		154
☐ Krakatoa		172

5.10b/c

Climb	Stars	Page
☐ Kama Sutra	★★★	182
☐ Out of Limits	★★	65
☐ Perspective	★★	65
☐ Cold-Rolled Steel	★★	94
☐ Phantom Bridge	★★	252
☐ Mickey Mantel	★	33
☐ The Talon	★	102
☐ Somnambulist	★	114
☐ Birds of Prey	★	248
☐ Azimuth		33
☐ Erickson Crack		62
☐ Left Side		90
☐ Warlock		163
☐ Right Side		179

5.10b

Climb	Stars	Page
☐ Left Side	★★★★	106
☐ Where Eagles Dare	★★★	64
☐ Road Trip	★★★	140
☐ Comeback Crack	★★★	206
☐ Kids Line	★★★	247
☐ Night Vision	★★	49
☐ Sleepwalker	★★	114
☐ Colorado Senior Open	★★	123
☐ Where's Bob?	★★	123
☐ Motorcycle Diaries	★★	140
☐ Gates of Eden	★★	149
☐ Crack Love III	★★	162
☐ Coffin Crack	★★	208
☐ Forbidden Fruit	★★	227
☐ Othello	★	48
☐ Cold Fusion	★	62
☐ Escutcheon	★	104
☐ Prajna	★	111
☐ Liquid Therapy	★	121
☐ Gray Panther	★	131
☐ Hareless in Boulder	★	132
☐ LieBack	★	137
☐ Amrita	★	163
☐ No Preservatives	★	192
☐ Lethal Dose	★	198
☐ Borrowed Time	★	198
☐ Cruisin' For Neo's	★	200
☐ Flying Vee	★	238
☐ Useless One		123
☐ Simba		131
☐ Neutron Star		192
☐ Mike's Short Route		193

5.10a/b

Climb	Stars	Page
☐ East Crack	★★★	49
☐ Right Crack	★★	54
☐ Of Human Bondage	★★	65
☐ Elegant Pleasure	★★	90
☐ Water Hazard	★★	213
☐ South Beach	★★	214
☐ Life on Mars	★★	246
☐ Roc Doc	★★	253
☐ Slimmer	★	62
☐ Get Shorty	★	62
☐ Little Juke	★	64
☐ Nighthawk	★	67
☐ Plotinus		100
☐ Just Another Cow's Climb		174

5.10a

Climb	Stars	Page
☐ Cosmosis	★★★★	149
☐ Dementia	★★★	70
☐ Thrill of the Chase	★★★	70
☐ Bihedral Arete	★★★	86
☐ Fields of Gold	★★★	118
☐ Local Hero	★★★	119
☐ West Crack	★★★	150
☐ West Face	★★★	150
☐ Bong Session	★★★	178
☐ Arcanum	★★★	183
☐ Minnesota Fats	★★★	216
☐ Tough Situation	★★	30
☐ Shallow Jam	★★	42
☐ Hurley Direct	★★	50
☐ A Hike withLudwig Dude	★★	65
☐ Crack Tack R	★★	65
☐ Don't Ask	★★	82
☐ Calling All Trad Climbers	★★	82
☐ Left Side	★★	94
☐ The Slit	★★	104
☐ Right Side	★★	107
☐ The Enemy Within	★★	162
☐ Ghost Ship	★★	162
☐ Ship of Fools	★★	162
☐ Diet of Worms	★★	192
☐ Ebb Tide	★★	198
☐ Frisky	★★	220
☐ Ah Maw	★	32
☐ Belladonna	★	35
☐ Bad Girls Dream	★	60
☐ The S Buttress	★	73
☐ Maximum Security	★	74
☐ Nala	★	76
☐ Arete	★	80
☐ Hound's Tooth	★	83
☐ Venom	★	90
☐ Headstrong	★	94
☐ Mean Streak	★	94
☐ Oversleeping	★	96
☐ Into Temptation	★	114
☐ Cold Plunge	★	114
☐ Storm Warning	★	118
☐ The Ride	★	123
☐ North Face	★	149
☐ Curvilinear	★	159
☐ The Stigmata	★	159
☐ The Dead Zone	★	160
☐ Couch Potato	★	174
☐ Crack of Desperation	★	177
☐ Where's Vaino?	★	180
☐ Crack of Dawn	★	182
☐ The Spell	★	183
☐ Good Vibrations	★	186
☐ Mountain Rose	★	218
☐ Right to Life	★	221
☐ Heart like a Wheel	★	222
☐ After Dark		33
☐ Scorcher		42
☐ Scraping By		74
☐ Something Obscure		99
☐ Diagonal Crack		115
☐ The Route That Dan Missed		149
☐ Five-Ten-Route		151
☐ Center		178
☐ Water Spirit		182
☐ Golden Bull		192

5.10

Climb	Stars	Page
☐ Buried Alive	★	223
☐ The Aid Roof		56

5.9+

Climb	Stars	Page
☐ South Face	★★★	211
☐ Gorilla's Delight	★★	28
☐ Zolar Czakl	★★	33
☐ The Heartland	★★	33
☐ Left Crack	★★	54
☐ Catalyst	★★	58
☐ Devin's Dihedral	★★	81
☐ Bihedral Arete Dihedral Var	★★	86
☐ Join The Party	★★	118
☐ My Way	★★	123

- ☐ The Solution ★★ 163
- ☐ Hypotenuse ★★ 199
- ☐ Boiling Point ★★ 199
- ☐ Skunk Crack ★★ 206
- ☐ Curving Crack ★★ 206
- ☐ By Gully ★★ 208
- ☐ Circadian Rhythms ★★ 210
- ☐ Shiny Toys ★★ 236
- ☐ Body Talk ★ 48
- ☐ Brownies In The Basin ★ 50
- ☐ Hesitation ★ 58
- ☐ Little John's Big Stick ★ 79
- ☐ Helix ★ 110
- ☐ Minutiae Arete ★ 122
- ☐ Quagmire ★ 123
- ☐ If Six Were Nine ★ 130
- ☐ Thin Crack ★ 137
- ☐ Common Denominator ★ 159
- ☐ Prince Charmer ★ 182
- ☐ Night Train ★ 198
- ☐ Black Crack ★ 211
- ☐ Hung Jury ★ 214
- ☐ The Cage ★ 248
- ☐ Skid Row 70
- ☐ The Great Race 71
- ☐ Goin' Down Slow 128
- ☐ Catch You Later 139
- ☐ One Withered Arm 177
- ☐ Beer Belly 185
- ☐ Lost Dentures 202
- ☐ Sponge Bath 203
- ☐ Eulogy 214

5.9

- ☐ Classic Finger Crack ★★★ 30
- ☐ On Ballet ★★★ 62
- ☐ Spirit on the Water ★★★ 121
- ☐ Finger Crack ★★★ 199
- ☐ Buddhist Pest ★★★ 234
- ☐ Mojo Rising ★★ 32
- ☐ The Perfect Route ★★ 37
- ☐ Huston Crack ★★ 49
- ☐ West Cracks ★★ 50
- ☐ Night Stalker ★★ 60
- ☐ Nightcap ★★ 70
- ☐ The Prism ★★ 74
- ☐ Sleepless Child ★★ 98
- ☐ Krishna Orange ★★ 111
- ☐ Clean Sweep ★★ 117
- ☐ Los Pinos ★★ 121
- ☐ Quick Chill ★★ 126
- ☐ Weed Killer ★★ 143
- ☐ Mithril ★★ 153
- ☐ Stellar Drifter ★★ 155
- ☐ Crack Love ★★ 162
- ☐ Mystery Tour ★★ 162
- ☐ Cow Patty Crack ★★ 174
- ☐ Walk on the Wide Side ★★ 182
- ☐ Crack Up ★★ 214
- ☐ Time Traveler ★★ 243
- ☐ Take the Power Back ★★ 246
- ☐ Prelude to King Kong ★ 28
- ☐ Devil's Dream ★ 48
- ☐ Treetop Landing ★ 54
- ☐ Far Left ★ 58
- ☐ Mirage ★ 58
- ☐ Shimmer ★ 62
- ☐ Tipsey ★ 70
- ☐ Cruel Shoes ★ 71
- ☐ Crossfire ★ 73
- ☐ Twisted ★ 83
- ☐ Heterohedral ★ 84
- ☐ Splendor in the Grass ★ 94
- ☐ Closed Open Space ★ 104
- ☐ Cop Out ★ 106
- ☐ Crackdown ★ 118
- ☐ Party Time ★ 122
- ☐ Boulder Slips ★ 123
- ☐ Limited Partnership ★ 129
- ☐ Skin and Bones ★ 131
- ☐ Lion's Den ★ 131
- ☐ Tailspin ★ 140
- ☐ Double Jeopardy ★ 149
- ☐ Tunnel of Love ★ 156
- ☐ Dom Perignon ★ 159
- ☐ Resurrection ★ 162
- ☐ Dragon Direct ★ 163
- ☐ Isis ★ 163
- ☐ Twin Cracks Left ★ 164
- ☐ The Vampire ★ 177
- ☐ East Face ★ 188
- ☐ Next to Imp-Passible ★ 192
- ☐ Left-Angling Crack ★ 198
- ☐ Spread Eagles Dhare ★ 199
- ☐ Constrictor ★ 199
- ☐ Invisible Idiot ★ 206
- ☐ Route 66 ★ 213
- ☐ Undercling ★ 214
- ☐ The Ancient of Days ★ 218
- ☐ War Drums ★ 218
- ☐ Going Down on It ★ 221
- ☐ Ethereal ★ 221
- ☐ Knowoneness ★ 243
- ☐ Weenie Roast ★ 246
- ☐ Killing in the Name ★ 246
- ☐ Jessica's Route ★ 247
- ☐ Gros Vogel 43
- ☐ Rob's Way 55
- ☐ The Big Spit 70
- ☐ Last Call 70
- ☐ Masquerade 90
- ☐ Tumbling Dice 94
- ☐ Corner Pocket 99
- ☐ Pumpkin Corner 122
- ☐ Pinnacle 124
- ☐ Wrinkles 151
- ☐ Harvest Moon 154
- ☐ We Don't Do Crack 170
- ☐ Geritol Generation 170
- ☐ Left Side 178
- ☐ Jungle of Stone 182
- ☐ Proton 192
- ☐ Times Past 206

5.9-

- ☐ Bitty Buttress ★★★★ 55
- ☐ Monster Woman ★★ 32
- ☐ Bihedral ★★ 86
- ☐ Crack Love II ★★ 162
- ☐ Thus Us ★★ 162
- ☐ Jersey Devil ★★ 216
- ☐ Saturday Treat ★ 67
- ☐ Scarecrow ★ 76
- ☐ Electra Glide ★ 139
- ☐ Twin Cracks Right 164
- ☐ Twisted Chopper 193

5.8+

- ☐ Showtime ★★★ 119
- ☐ North Face Left ★★ 49
- ☐ Most of the Time ★ 82
- ☐ Curtain Call ★ 119
- ☐ Crumbs ★ 154
- ☐ Simmer 62
- ☐ Familiar Stranger 169

5.8

- ☐ Northwest Face ★★★ 33
- ☐ Twofers ★★★ 70
- ☐ Grins ★★★ 70
- ☐ Minutiae ★★★ 122
- ☐ Indistinction ★★ 49
- ☐ Northwest Corner ★★ 50
- ☐ West Rib ★★ 50
- ☐ West Dihedral ★★ 50
- ☐ Just Do It ★★ 118
- ☐ Dutch Treat ★★ 119
- ☐ Jam It ★★ 166
- ☐ Salisbury Steak Crack ★★ 174
- ☐ Bailey's Overhang ★★ 206
- ☐ South Crack ★★ 225
- ☐ Dreamscape ★★ 238
- ☐ Long Dong Dihedral ★★ 245
- ☐ Cracks are for Kids ★ 36
- ☐ A's Jax ★ 54
- ☐ South ★ 55
- ☐ Orange Corner ★ 64
- ☐ Left Roof ★ 65
- ☐ The Old Route ★ 65
- ☐ Regular Route ★ 107
- ☐ Eat my Lichen ★ 111
- ☐ Border Crossing ★ 119
- ☐ Mind Shaft Crack Left ★ 127
- ☐ Valor ★ 129
- ☐ Discretion ★ 129
- ☐ Kundalini Express ★ 155
- ☐ Hope and Pray ★ 170
- ☐ Firing Squad ★ 174
- ☐ Wired ★ 179
- ☐ Surprising Slab ★ 199

Route	Stars	Page
☐ North Crack	★	225
☐ Be Here Now	★	243
☐ A Day at the Crags		54
☐ Orange Dihedral		55
☐ It's My Swamp		76
☐ Prayer Wheel		90
☐ The Right Way		154
☐ Dihedral Two		159
☐ Dominatrix		159
☐ Ancient Sight		162
☐ Old Dihedral		168
☐ The Hot Donut		174
☐ Steeping Stone		200
☐ Short but Sweet		218
☐ Five Eight Crack		221

5.8-

Route	Stars	Page
☐ Standard Route	★★★	32
☐ West Face	★★	33
☐ Straight Out of Compton		216

5.7+

Route	Stars	Page
☐ North Face Center	★★★	50
☐ Empor	★★★	50
☐ Fine Fir	★	118
☐ Mind Shaft Crack Middle	★	127
☐ Denver Nugget		216

5.7

Route	Stars	Page
☐ The Owl	★★★	28
☐ Cozyhang	★★★	29
☐ East of the Sun	★★★	29
☐ Cussin' Crack	★★★	208
☐ Left Edge	★★	28
☐ East of East Slab East	★★	29
☐ East Slab Far Right	★★	29
☐ Right Crack	★★	49
☐ I, Robot	★★	70
☐ Au Natural	★★	81
☐ Dihedral One	★★	159
☐ Dan-D-Line	★★	199
☐ Jackson's Wall	★★	210
☐ East Face, Farthest Right	★	29
☐ Are We Not Men	★	70
☐ Malign	★	70
☐ Bent Faith	★	71
☐ Sun Spot	★	84
☐ Creekside Cruise	★	121
☐ Joe Pontiac	★	151
☐ Yoni	★	163
☐ Red Sonja	★	176
☐ Bock	★	198
☐ Hare Balls	★	199
☐ Center Tap Corner	★	234
☐ Lost Ring		36
☐ Hands Off		71
☐ Dancing Hippos		80
☐ Quick Work		86
☐ Truth Serum		90
☐ Mind Shaft Right Crack		127
☐ Tiers		151
☐ Pillar		159
☐ Crack Corner		168
☐ Gull Whackers		169
☐ POS		170
☐ Gomer Pyle		186
☐ Time Lords		218

5.6

Route	Stars	Page
☐ East Slab	★★★★	29
☐ East Slab East	★★	29
☐ Chimney	★★	34
☐ Wayward Puritan	★★	151
☐ Idle Hands	★★	166
☐ Pine Tree Route	★	30
☐ West Ride	★	102
☐ Old and Easy	★	111
☐ Nick Of Time	★	117
☐ West Face	★	206
☐ Approach Pitch	★	252
☐ Flash Dihedral		30
☐ Chimney		30
☐ Cloddy Corner		33
☐ Central Chimney		61
☐ Northwest Ridge		121
☐ Midway		160
☐ Dark Tower		164

5.5

Route	Stars	Page
☐ Great Dihedral	★★	44
☐ To the Sun	★★	44
☐ Right Face	★★	44
☐ Left Side	★★	70
☐ Hummingbird	★★	218
☐ Mons	★	166

5.4

Route	Stars	Page
☐ Ho Hum	★	166
☐ North Face	★	206
☐ Southwest Chimney		33
☐ Fistula		166

5.2

Route	Stars	Page
☐ Mini Moe		104

5.1

Route	Stars	Page
☐ Sleeping Beauty	★	182
☐ Checkpoint Charlie		108

INDEX

A

B

C

D

E

T

U

Photo: Ron Olsen

ABOUT THE AUTHOR

Bob D'Antonio lives in Louisville, Colorado, with his beautiful wife Laurel and their basset hound Daisy. He is the proud father of three wonderful children: Jeremy, Adam and Rachael. He has on occasion climbed rocks, mountain biked, run trails, and fly fished. He has made hundreds of first ascents in Boulder Canyon and throughout the US.